Advanced Diving

Technology and Techniques

National Association of Underwater Instructors

Published in the United States of America by
NAUI.

4650 Arrow Highway, Suite F-1
Montclair, California 91763-1150

ISBN #0-916974-39-1

First Edition January, 1989
Second Edition January, 1991

Item #097

ACKNOWLEDGMENTS

Editor: Dennis Graver

Contributing Authors:
Susan Bangasser - Women in Diving
Steven Barsky - Dry Suits, Commercial Diving
Ted Boehler - Night Diving
Jeff Bozanic - Cave Diving, Drift Diving
Dennis Graver - Diving Physics, Diving
    Physiology, Diving Equipment,
    Diving Environment, Navigation, Leadership
Leonard Greenstone - Search and Light Salvage
Tom Griffiths, E.D. - Psychological Fitness
Eric Hanauer - Boat Diving
Paul Heinmiller - Decompression
Ken Heist - Wreck Diving
Dick Jacoby - Photo and Video
John Kessler - Boating & Seamanship
Marcel Lachenmann - Ice Diving
Peter Lynch - Marine Life Injuries
Ella Jean Morgan - Safe Diving Techniques
Yancy Mebane - Diving Physiology
Milledge Murphey, Ph.D. - Altitude Diving,
    Limited Visibility Diving
Erin O'Neill - Safe Diving Techniques
Dan Orr - Research Diving
Ron Pavelka - Underwater Hunting
John Reseck - Diving Environment
Bob Rutledge, M.D. - Recompression Chambers
Pat Scharr - Deep Diving
Lee Somers - Portions of various chapters
George Swan - River Diving
Bob Weathers - Diving Fitness

Reviewers:
Fred Bove
Robert Brandeberry
Don Frueh
Otto Gasser
Bill High
John Reseck
Dick Rutkowski
Keith Sliman
Larry Taylor

Illustrations:
Betsy Franks
Jim Mitchell

Design and Layout:
Derrick Story
Lisa Ambrose

Proofreading:
Jim Arkison
Dorothy Winkel

Facilities and Support:
Transportation to Belize for photography
    courtesy of TACA Airlines
Accommodations in Belize for photography
    courtesy of Ramon's Reef Resort
Diving services in Belize for photography
    courtesy of Reef Diver, Ltd.
Boat trip for photography courtesy of Norine
    Rouse
Equipment loan courtesy of Scubapro and Blue
    Cheer Dive Store

Photography:
Cover Photographs by Dennis Graver
(Chamber photo by Dick Rutkowski and ice
diving photo by John Kessler)
Text photographs by authors or by Dennis Graver
unless otherwise noted

Principal Photo Models:
Jamie Barrows
Ronnie Damico
Barbara Graver
John Kessler

Printed in the USA by:
Precision Litho
Santa Ana, California

Note: Some chapters contain information from the
U.S. Navy Diving Manual.

CONTRIBUTORS

Steven M. Barsky, M.A. (Human Factors/ Ergonomics), Diving consultant, underwater photographer, and author. Marine Marketing and Consulting, Santa Barbara, California.

Jeffrey E. Bozanic, M.A. (Education), M.B.A., B.S. (Geology), Executive Director, Island Caves Research Center. Chairman, Board of Directors, National Speleological Society Cave Diving Section. NAUI Board of Directors. Huntington Beach, California.

Dennis K. Graver, Director of Education, National Association of Underwater Instructors, Montclair, California.

Tom Griffiths, Ed.D., Director of Aquatics, McCoy Natatorium, Pennsylvania State University, University Park, Pennsylvania.

Eric Hanauer, Associate Professor of Physical Education, Diving Safety Officer, California State University, Fullerton. Freelance writer and photographer. Author of *The Egyptian Red Sea: A Diver's Guide.*

Paul A. Heinmiller, M.S. (Ocean Engineering), Director of Engineering, Orca Industries, Inc. NAUI Instructor since 1978, ITC Director 1980-1987. NAUI North Atlantic Branch Manager 1985-1987. Toughkenemon, New Jersey.

R. Kenneth Heist, M.S. Electrical Engineering. NAUI #1036L; Mid-Atlantic Branch Manager 1978-1986; Board of Directors President 1988-1989. Photographer and lecturer for North Atlantic wrecks since 1967.

Richard K. Jacoby, M.S.J., B.A., Educator and consultant for underwater photography and videography, John G. Shedd Aquarium, Chicago, Illinois; College of DuPage, Glen Ellyn Illinois.

Capt. John R. Kessler, Master's License, NAUI Instructor Trainer, Former NAUI Western Regional Business Consultant.

Marcel Lachenmann, B.S. (Zoology/Cemistry), M.S. (Science Ed. and Marine Biology), Sc.D. (Clinical Physiology); Faculty, Marquette University; Owner, Sea Trips/Sea Techs Ltd.; Milwaukee, Wisconsin.

Milledge Murphy, Ph.D., C.R.C., N.C.C. Graduate research faculty member and director, Academic Diving Program, Dept. of Exercise and Sport Sceinces, College of Health and Human Performance, University of Florida, Gainesville, Florida.

Dan Orr, B.S., M.S., Coordinator of Instruction, Associate Diving Officer, Academic Diving Program, Florida State University, Tallahassee, Florida. NAUI Midwest Branch Manager 1987-1988.

Ronald G. Pavelka, Northwest District Sales Representative, DACOR. Previously Scuba Products Manager, Sherwood; Owner of JBL Spearguns. Author of numerous articles.

Bob Rutledge, M.D., Board Certified Anesthesiologist; NOAA Hyperbaric and Diving Medicine Training graduate; Miami, Florida.

George A. Swan, B.A., Fishery Research Biologist, Unit Diving Supervisor, NOAA Diving Program, Inland Diving Operations, Northwest Fisheries Center, National Marine Fisheries Service, Seattle, Washington.

Robert D. Weathers, Ed.D., School of Physical Education and Athletics, Seattle Pacific University, Seattle, Washington.

TABLE OF CONTENTS

SECTION ONE

	Introduction	1
1	Diving Physics	5
2	Diving Physiology	25
3	Diving Equipment	75
4	Diving Environment	105
5	Decompression & Recompression	131

SECTION TWO

	Introduction to Diving Techniques	157
6	Safe Diving	159
7	Navigation	173
8	Limited Visibilty Diving	183
9	Night Diving	187
10	Search & Light Salvage	191
11	Deep Diving	197
12	Diver Rescue	203
13	Boat Diving	209
14	Boating & Seamanship	215

SECTION THREE

	Introduction to Diving Specialties	225
15	River Diving	227
16	Dry Suit Diving	233
17	Ice Diving	237
18	Cave & Cavern Diving	243
19	Wreck Diving	247
20	Drift Diving	253
21	Cameras & Video Equipment	257
22	Underwater Hunting	267
23	Research Diving	273
24	Commercial Diving	279
25	Diving Leadership	285
	Looking Back Toward the Future	287

GLOSSARY	289
INDEX TO TABLES	296
INDEX	297

INTRODUCTION

Congratulations on your decision to increase your knowledge and skills as a diver! The NAUI Advanced Scuba Diver course will enable you to take advantage of more diving opportunities. The knowledge you acquire will help make those experiences safe and enjoyable.

Thus far in your diving education you have learned the fundamentals of diving. You know what you should and should not do and you understand some basic theory. You are qualified to dive only under conditions similar to those in which you have received training. The purpose of this book, when used as part of a course of instruction, is to increase your understanding of why certain things are done or are not done in diving and to expand your skills and qualifications. Upon successful completion of this course you will be qualified to handle new diving circumstances and engage in additional diving activities.

About the NAUI Advanced Course

The NAUI Advanced Scuba Diver course is an intensive program consisting of 16 hours of academics plus the application of the knowledge acquired via a schedule of at least eight open water dives. A maximum of three dives per day may be credited toward the certification requirements. Open water training activities may include:
- Skin diving
- Basic skills review
- Dive rescue techniques
- Environmental study or survey
- Underwater navigation*
- Limited visibility or night diving*
- Search and recovery*
- Light salvage*
- Deep/simulated decompression diving*
- Boat diving
- Hunting and collecting

* Required activities for the NAUI Advanced course.

The information presented in the academic sessions of your course will increase your knowledge to near the instructor level for the topic areas of physics, physiology, equipment, environment and decompression.

The skills you develop during the open water training dives in this course will increase your abilities as a diver. The dives are also orientations to different special interest areas of diving. They will help you decide which specialty subject is of the greatest interest to you. In addition, the training dives will introduce you to new diving locations and opportunities.

Prerequisites for the NAUI Advanced course include a minimum age of 15 and either NAUI Openwater II certification or equivalent training or experience. You are usually expected to provide your own equipment for the course. This includes full open water scuba gear with instrumentation, an alternate air source, and two dive lights—a primary light and a backup light.

To qualify for certification, you will need to attend all academic sessions, demonstrate the ability to safely participate in all open water training activities and demonstrate comprehension and retention of the material presented by scoring at least 75% on a comprehensive written examination.

Responsibilities

Both you and your instructor have certain responsibilities during the Advanced Scuba Diver course.

Your instructor must determine that you have the necessary background and experience to safely participate in the activities of the course, provide an academic session plus an on-site briefing for each activity, ensure that you are properly equipped for the training dives, and oversee your diving activities.

You are already certified to dive with a buddy. You will be responsible for your own safety and for the safety of your assigned dive buddy. It is not the responsibility of your NAUI instructor to accompany you during the dives, although he or she must be present at the dive site, in control of the activities, and ready to lend assistance if needed. You will be instructed what to do, how to do it, and how to avoid potential hazards. It will then be your responsibility to follow the instructions given. You will learn by doing controlled activities at sites selected to safely introduce you to each interest area.

About This Book

This *Advanced Diving Technology and Techniques Manual* is divided into three primary sections.

The first section is Advanced Diving Theory, and consists of chapters designed to increase your knowledge of the technical aspects of scuba diving. Specific learning objectives are stated at the beginning of each chapter. Review these carefully before and after studying each chapter to make sure you meet the educational goals.

The second section is Advanced Diving Techniques, which is designed to preview the possible skill areas that may be introduced during the course.

The third section introduces various specialty diving activities. The "Specialty Diving Activities" section provides an overview of many underwater pursuits to help you decide if you would like to learn more about them by taking a NAUI specialty course.

Your instructor may schedule the course in any sequence desired as long as the curriculum requirements are met. The chapters in this book should be read in the order assigned by your instructor, not necessarily sequential. You may not be assigned to read some sections at all, but you are encouraged to read the entire book at your leisure in order to learn as much as you can about the varied aspects of diving.

THIS BOOK IS NOT INTENDED TO TEACH YOU ADVANCED DIVING ACTIVITIES WITHOUT THE GUIDANCE AND SUPERVISION OF A QUALIFIED NAUI INSTRUCTOR. Local knowledge, techniques and regulations for all areas cannot possibly be incorporated into this text. This publication provides only part of your education for advanced diving. The bulk of what you will learn will be provided by the instructor. Do not attempt to participate in any of the activities described in this book without the supervision of a qualified instructor.

Getting the Most From the Course

To learn as much as possible and to become the best diver you can become, the following actions are recommended:

1. Read and study each assigned section prior to the academic session on the subject matter.

2. Keep the learning objectives in mind as you study the chapters, then review them after completing the chapter to be sure you have acquired the knowledge.

3. As you study the chapters, keep notes on areas that are unclear to you so you can obtain clarification from the instructor during the academic sessions.

4. Become familiar with the terms identified in CAPITAL LETTERS. When a term is presented a second time in lower case letters, refresh your memory of its meaning if it is unclear to you. The terms are defined in the glossary if you are unable to locate them quickly in one of the sections.

5. Obtain a notebook and take it with you to every session, including the open water dives. Take notes on all presentations. Save the notebook for future reference. You will be glad you did.

6. Log your dives in detail.

We commend you on your decision to become a NAUI Advanced Scuba Diver. You must do more to acquire this rating than to obtain an Advanced Diver rating with other diver training organizations, but we feel you will agree that it is worth it! A NAUI Advanced Diver is knowledgeable, skilled and respected. You will know more, be able to do more, and feel more comfortable and confident as a diver when you have successfully completed this program. You will have met one of the highest standards of diver education.

Best wishes with your training.

DIVING
PHYSICS

Physics is the study of natural physical laws. We perceive the world around us through our various senses. Because we have lived submerged in the earth's atmosphere all our lives, we see the world through a set of laws which apply to the atmosphere. When we enter the underwater environment, all the laws by which we have lived are magnified. At times these changes can be dangerous and drastic. An understanding of physics is, therefore, important because the effects of pressure and other phenomenon can very quickly become threats to health and even to life.

Where do we start? Most physics books are two inches thick and weigh more than five pounds. How much of this information do you need to understand to be safe and enjoy the underwater world? This chapter is devoted to only that part of physics which concerns diving. Your goal is to understand the forces which can threaten your safety as a diver. To accomplish this, you need to increase your knowledge of physics—the science of matter and energy and their interactions.

LEARNING OBJECTIVES

By the end of this course, you need to be able to:

1. Correctly define the physics terms presented in CAPITAL LETTERS in this chapter.

2. Correctly solve diving physics problems similar to the ones presented in this chapter.

3. State how each of the principles of diving physics presented in this chapter applies to diving situations.

THE PHYSICAL WORLD

MATTER is the substance of which the universe is composed, and the forces which work within that substance are termed ENERGY. The various properties and inter-relationships of matter and energy form the foundation of the study of diving physics. Of particular importance is a knowledge of the behavior of gases, the principles of buoyancy and the properties of heat, light and sound underwater.

Matter

An element is the simplest form of matter that exhibits distinct physical and chemical properties, and which cannot be broken up into other, more

basic forms by chemical means. Elements are comprised of atoms, which are so infinitely small that it would take more than a million of them, laid side-by-side, to match the thickness of this page. Atoms can be broken down into smaller particles—electrons, neutrons and protons—but the atom is the smallest particle of matter which carries the properties of an element. The various elements combine to form the approximately four million substances known to man.

As atoms group together, they form molecules, which usually exhibit different properties than any of the contributing atoms. For example, when two hydrogen atoms combine with one oxygen atom, water—a radically new substance—is formed.

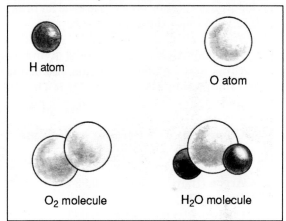

Figure 1.1 Atoms combine to form molecules.

Some atoms are active and try to combine with almost anything they encounter. Other atoms are INERT, and do not naturally combine with other substances. The presence of inert elements in breathing mixtures is of particular importance in diving.

The Three States of Matter

Any element or substance produced by the joining of atoms can exist in one of three natural forms—a SOLID, LIQUID or GAS.

A SOLID has definite shape, weight and volume. LIQUIDS have definite volume and weight, but they take the shape of whatever is containing them. GASES have definite weight and occupy space, but lack definite volume or shape. A gas will expand indefinitely to fill a container of any size, a room or, if completely unconfined, will spread continuously throughout the atmosphere. Gases and liquids are collectively referred to as FLUIDS.

Whether a particular substance exists as a solid, liquid or gas depends principally upon temperature and partially upon pressure.

Figure 1.2 Solid, Liquid, Gas

GASES IN DIVING

Gases are the most elusive and intangible of substances, but a knowledge of the properties and behavior of gases—especially those used for breathing—is of vital importance to a diver.

Compressed air is the gas used for recreational diving. In certain types of commercial diving, special mixtures may be blended, using one or more gases in combination with oxygen. Air is a mixture of gases and vapors with the following composition:

Component	Percent by Volume
Nitrogen (N_2)	78.084
Argon (Inert)	0.934
Oxygen (O_2)	20.946
Carbon Dioxide (CO_2)	0.033
Rare Gases	0.003
	100.000

The components of air are commonly simplified as 80% Nitrogen and 20% Oxygen. This simplification will be used within this chapter.

Oxygen (O_2)

Oxygen is the most important of all gases and is one of the most abundant of all elements on earth. It is colorless, odorless, and tasteless. It is an active gas that combines readily with other elements. Oxygen is the only life-supporting gas used by humans. All other gases serve only to transport or dilute the oxygen. This gas is dangerous when excessive amounts are breathed under pressure; this harmful effect is called OXYGEN TOXICITY and explains why scuba tanks may not be filled with pure oxygen.

Nitrogen (N_2)

Chemically inert (does not combine with other elements) and incapable of supporting life, nitrogen is also colorless, odorless and tasteless. It is a component of all living organisms. Nitrogen is essentially a carrier for oxygen in air. When breathed at higher pressures, nitrogen has a distinct anesthetic effect, producing NITROGEN NARCOSIS, a condition characterized by loss of judgment and disorientation. This is one of the reasons compressed air diving is limited to a depth of 130 feet.

Carbon Dioxide (CO_2)

CO_2 is colorless, odorless and tasteless when found in small percentages in the air. In greater concentrations, however, it has an acid taste and odor. It is a chemically active gas which is commonly observed as bubbles in soda water. It is widely used as an extinguishing agent in fire extinguishers.

Carbon dioxide is a natural by product of the respiration of animals and humans (among other sources) formed by the oxidation of carbon in the body to produce energy. For divers, the major concern with CO_2 is the elimination of it during breathing.

In high concentrations, carbon dioxide can be extremely toxic and can cause unconsciousness and convulsions. A person should not breathe air containing more than 10% by volume CO_2.

Carbon Monoxide (CO)

Carbon monoxide is a poisonous gas. It is colorless, odorless, tasteless and difficult to detect. This gas is chemically highly active and seriously interferes with the ability of the blood to carry oxygen. CO is produced by incomplete combustion of hydrocarbons such as occurs in the exhaust systems of internal combustion engines. The gas may also be produced in overheated oil-lubricated air compressors. A level of 20 parts per million (ppm) should not be exceeded in a pressurized breathing system. Great care should be taken when scuba cylinders are being filled, since a possible source of CO contamination may be the exhaust system of the air compressor itself.

Water Vapor

Like other gases, water vapor behaves in accordance with the gas laws. However, unlike other gases encountered in diving, water vapor condenses to its liquid state at temperatures normally encountered by man.

UNITS OF MEASUREMENT

The science of physics relies heavily upon standards of comparison of one state of matter or energy to another. Understanding and applying the principles of physics requires that you be able to employ a variety of units of measurement.

Two systems of measurement of force, length and time are used in the world—English and metric. The English system, based upon the pound, foot and second, is commonly used in the United States, but is replaced throughout the rest of the world with the metric system. The metric system employs the kilogram, meter and second as fundamental units of measure.

The metric system is so widely used, particularly in scientific work, that a diver sooner or later will come into contact with it. The metric system has an advantage in that all its units are so related that it is not necessary to use calculations when changing from one metric unit to another. This system is based on decimals, as in the American system of money. A sum of money may be expressed either in dollars or in cents by simply moving the decimal point. Similarly, the metric system changes one of its units of measurement to another by moving the decimal point, rather than by the lengthy calculations necessary in the English system.

Length: The principal metric unit of length is the METER (39.37 inches). For measuring smaller lengths, MILLIMETERS (mm) or CENTIMETERS (cm) are used.

1 meter (m)	= 100 centimeters (cm)
	= 1,000 millimeters (mm)
	= 3.281 feet or 1.09 yards
	(exactly .3048 m per foot)
1 millimeter	= 0.10 (1/10) centimeter
	= 0.001 (1/1000) meter
1 centimeter	= 0.3937 inches
	(exactly 2.54 cm per inch)

For longer distances, the metric system uses the KILOMETER (about six-tenths of a mile):

1 kilometer	= 1,000 meters
	= 0.621 statute miles
	(1.609 km per mile)
1 meter	= 0.001 kilometers

Problems:
1. *How many meters does 45 feet equal?*

Solution: 45/3.281 = 13.7 meters
OR .3048 x 45 = 13.7 meters.

2. *How many yards are 25 meters?*
Solution: 1.09 x 25 meters = 27.25 yards.

Area: The metric system uses its units of length squared to measure area, as does the English system. As in converting from one metric unit of length to another, converting units of area is merely a matter of moving the decimal point. In this case, the decimal point is moved twice as many places as in measures of length:

1 meter = 100 cm
1 square meter = 10,000 square centimeters

Compare this operation with that of multiplying by 144 to convert from square feet to square inches!

Volume or capacity: Volumes are expressed as units of length cubed. Conversion of volumes from one metric unit to another requires only moving the decimal point three times as many places as in converting units of length. For example, 1,662 cubic millimeters equals 1.662 cubic centimeters. To convert cubic inches to cubic feet, you would have to divide by 1,728 (12 x 12 x 12). In addition to cubic feet, the English system also uses other units of volume or capacity. No simple relationship exists between these units of volume and the cubic measurements, and consequently calculations involve the uses of numerous conversion factors. The metric system uses the liter (about the same as a quart) for similar purposes, but a liter equals 1,000 cubic centimeters or 0.001 cubic meter and conversion is greatly simplified.

1 liter (l)	= 1,000 cubic centimeters (cc)
	= 1.057 quarts
	= 0.035 cubic feet
	= 61.02 cubic inches
	= 0.001 cubic meters (m³)
1 cubic centimeter (cc)	= 0.061 cubic inches
	(16.39 cc per cubic inch)

Problems:
1. *How many liters of air are in a full 71.2 cubic feet cylinder?*
Solution: 71.2/.035 = 2,034 liters

2. *The internal volume of a 71.2 cubic feet tank is .420 cubic feet. What is the internal volume of the tank in liters?*
Solution: .420/.035 = 12 liters

Weight: The kilogram (kg) is the standard metric unit of mass or weight. One kilogram is approximately the mass of one liter of water or about 2.2 pounds at 4 degrees C. For smaller masses the gram (g) and milligram (mg) are used.

1 kilogram	= 1,000 grams
	= 1,000,000 milligrams
	= 2.205 pounds
	(0.454 kg per pound)

| **1 gram** | = 0.001 kilogram |
| | = 1,000 milligrams |

| **1 milligram** | = 0.001 gram |

Pressure: The force acting on a unit area is termed PRESSURE. Expressed mathematically:

$$\text{Pressure} = \frac{\text{Force}}{\text{Area}} \text{ or } P = \frac{F}{A}$$

The standard metric unit of pressure is the Newton per square meter (N/m^2). However, the most commonly used metric unit of pressure is kilograms per square centimeter (Kg/cm^2). Another commonly encountered metric pressure unit is millimeters of mercury (mmHg). This unit of measurement is based upon the pressure exerted by a column of mercury one millimeter high. The following table shows the relationships between various barometric pressure units.

Temperature: The temperature of a body is a measure of the intensity of its heat and is produced by the average kinetic energy or speed of its molecules. Temperature is measured by a thermometer

and is expressed in degrees centigrade (C) or Fahrenheit (F). Countries using the English system of weights and measures generally employ the Fahrenheit temperature scale. Countries that use the metric system, and most scientific laboratories, use the Centigrade scale, which is also known as the "Celsius" scale. This scale is based upon the temperature of melting ice (32 degrees F) as 0 degrees C and the temperature of boiling water (212 degrees F) as 100 degrees C.

Temperatures measured in Centigrade may be converted to Fahrenheit using either of the following formulas:

F = (1.8 x degrees C) + 32 *or* F=9/5 + 32

Temperatures measured in Fahrenheit may be converted to Centigrade (Celsius) using the following formula:

$$C = \frac{\text{degrees F - 32}}{1.8} \text{ or } C=5/9 \text{ (f-32)}$$

Temperature values must be converted to absolute values for use with the Gas Laws. The absolute temperature scales are based upon absolute zero—the lowest temperature that could possibly be reached—at which all molecular motion would cease. On the Fahrenheit scale this is -459.72 degrees F; in Centigrade it is -273.13 degrees C. These numbers are normally rounded off to -460 degrees F and -273 degrees C. Conversion to the Kelvin and Rankine scales is done by adding 273 units to the temperature in Centigrade or 460 units to the temperature in Fahrenheit.

| **Rankine (R)** | = degrees F plus 460 |
| **Kelvin (K)** | = degrees C plus 273 |

Conversion Table for Barometric Pressure Units									
	Atm	**N/M²**	**bars**	**mb**	**kg/cm²**	**gm/cm²**	**mm Hg**	**In Hg**	**lb/in²**
1 Atmosphere	1	1.013×10^5	1.013	1013	1.033	1033	760	29.92	14.70
1 Newton/M²	$.9869 \times 10^{-5}$	1	10^{-5}	.01	1.02×10^{-5}	.0102	.0075	$.2953 \times 10^{-3}$	$.1451 \times 10^{-3}$
1 bar	.9869	10^5	1	.1000	1.02	1020	750.1	29.53	14.51
1 millibar	$.9869 \times 10^{-3}$	100	.001	1	.00102	1.02	.7501	.02953	.01451
1 kg/cm²	.9681	$.9807 \times 10^5$	.9807	980.7	1	1000	735	28.94	14.22
1 gm/cm²	968.1	98.07	$.9807 \times 10^{-3}$	.9807	.001	1	.735	.02894	.01422
1 mm Hg	.001316	133.3	.001333	1.333	.00136	1.36	1	.03937	.01934
1 In Hg	.0334	3386	.03386	33.86	.03453	34.53	25.4	1	.4910
1 lb/in²	.06804	6895	.06895	68.95	.0703	70.3	51.70	2.035	1

Table 1.1 Conversion for Barometric Pressure Units

Problems:

1. Convert 17 degrees Celsius (Centigrade) to Fahrenheit.

Solution: 1.8 x 17 + 32 = 63 degrees F.

2. Convert 84 degrees Fahrenheit to Celsius.

Solution: 84 - 32/1.8 = 29 degrees C.

3. Convert 120 degrees Fahrenheit to absolute temperature.

Solution: 120 + 460 = 580 degrees Rankine

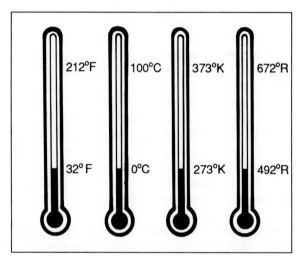

Figure 1.3 Equal temperature measured by four different methods.

HUMIDITY

The amount of water vapor in a gaseous atmosphere is referred to as HUMIDITY. In proper concentrations, water vapor aids a person by mois-

Figure 1.4 The amount of water air can contain is affected by temperature. As air cools, water droplets condense.

tening body tissues. As a condensing liquid, however, water vapor can turn to a liquid at normal atmospheric temperatures and can cause the freezing and blockage of air passageways in your hoses and equipment, can fog your faceplate, and can corrode your equipment. Consequently, a knowledge of humidity under changing conditions of pressure, temperature and volume is essential.

The amount of water vapor that a given quantity of gas can retain is governed almost entirely by one factor—temperature. The higher the temperature of a gas, the more water vapor the gas can retain.

When air containing a normal amount of moisture is compressed, the air temperature increases. Although the compression produces an increased amount of water vapor in a smaller space, the water remains as vapor due to the increased temperature. However, as the compressed air is cooled back to normal temperature, the partial pressure of the water vapor will exceed the DEW POINT (saturation temperature), and water will condense out of the air until the maximum partial pressure without condensation is reached. This means that moisture is removed from compressed air during compressor operation.

Advantages and disadvantages stem from the dehydrated air of scuba compressors. There is a benefit for scuba equipment because the formation of condensation is prevented. A disadvantage is that too little moisture in the breathing mixture causes dryness and dehydration in your mouth, throat, nasal cavities and sinus passages. You increase the humidity of your inspired gas to 100% by providing moisture from your respiratory organs. You should, therefore, drink plenty of fluids before and after dives to compensate for your respiratory moisture losses.

Expired air contains more moisture than is found in normal air. This is why you can see your breath on a cold day. The water vapor in exhaled air condenses into tiny droplets when your breath is cooled. The same effect can cause freezing in a regulator second stage in very cold weather. To prevent second stage freezing and the resultant free-flowing of air, do not breathe from your regulator until it is underwater, where the second stage will be kept at a temperature above freezing.

When water condenses on a surface, the water tends to bead up because of contractive forces at the surface of the liquid. This force is known as SURFACE TENSION. Fogging of your face mask is due to warm, humid air inside being cooled by the colder water on the outside. Defogging involves the use of some wetting agent applied to the interior of the mask lens to reduce the surface tension of the water, which runs off in a thin film, rather than beading into tiny droplets.

Moisture-laden warm air trapped inside camera or video housings or other equipment will produce condensation when the equipment is cooled in water. When moisture and oxygen are in contact with metal, rusting or oxidation take place. Salt speeds the process. It may seem strange to discuss the effects of humidity for an aquatic activity, but unless the principles are known and procedures related to controlling the effects of humidity are applied, many undesirable events will occur.

ENERGY

The concepts of work and energy are closely interrelated and constitute the second major factor in the physical world. WORK is defined as the application of a force through a distance. It is a force measured in pounds or kilograms which lifts, pulls or pushes an object over a specific distance, such as feet or meters. Work may be applied in numerous ways. The rate at which work is performed is referred to as power.

ENERGY is the capacity to do work. Energy can neither be created nor destroyed. It can however, be changed, from one form to another. Six basic forms of energy exist—mechanical, heat, light, chemical, electrical and nuclear. Four types of energy—mechanical, heat, electrical and chemical—are commonly encountered in a wide variety of forms while diving. From these forms come the numerous energy phenomenon noted in everyday life, such as weather, tides, sound, cold and heat.

Light

Sight is possible due to images created by the reflection of light from various surfaces. Under water, light is affected by factors not usually encountered at the surface, and these factors directly affect what you see. Among these factors are DIFFUSION—the scattering of light, TURBIDITY—the blockage of light, ABSORPTION—changes in color and intensity or light, and REFRACTION—bending of light rays.

The light that does penetrate water decreases in intensity with depth, as light rays are diffused and absorbed. In clear water, enough light remains to permit vision to about 300 feet (100 m). If the water is very turbid—filled with particles—the light is absorbed much sooner. If the level of turbidity is high, vision is impaired by particles even though light may be present.

Just as the intensity of light is altered with depth, so is the color quality of light. Light is comprised of different wavelengths, which appear as different colors. Water progressively absorbs and filters wavelengths of the visible spectrum of light. Red is absorbed first, then orange and yellow. As depth increases, most objects take on a bluish hue and red objects appear black.

Light rays in water are diffused—scattered and deflected in all directions. This diffusion contributes to a reduction in total illumination, but at the same time aids vision by spreading the light evenly through the water at a given depth. Shadows are softened and often eliminated.

Divers are familiar with the effects of refraction, or the bending of light rays as they pass from one

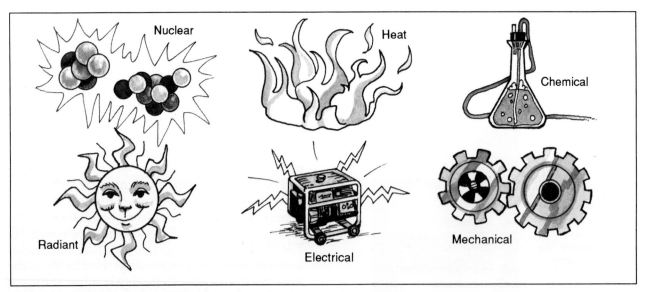

Figure 1.5 Different Types of Energy

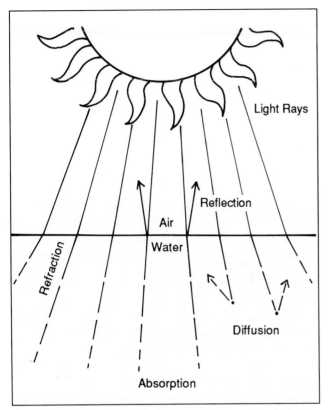

Figure 1.6 Light in water—reflection, refraction, diffusion and absorbtion all affect light in water.

medium to another. This phenomenon causes magnification and results in objects appearing larger and closer than they actually are. Light rays travel faster in air than in water—at a ratio of about four to three. A fish 20 feet (6.5 m) away from you will seem to be about 15 feet (5 m) away.

Sound

The differences in sound underwater are in many ways similar to the differences in light. Sound, like light, is made up of waves which seem to behave in an alien fashion in water; however, with sound the waves are waves of pressure, rather than of radiation.

Sound is produced by the vibration of an object which sets up a pattern of waves of moving molecules in air, water or some other medium. These waves in turn cause corresponding vibrations in a detector, such as an eardrum or the diaphragm of a microphone.

Sound travels best in a dense medium, since the more closely packed molecules more efficiently transmit waves. Sound will not travel at all in a vacuum because there are no molecules.

Water, which is fairly dense, is an excellent sound conductor and will transmit at a rate of 3,240

mph (1,500 m/sec). This is approximately four times the speed of sound in air. The efficiency of sound waves in water is so great that the sound of an underwater bell can be detected at 15 miles (24 km).

In contrast, however, since sound travels so fast underwater, human ears cannot detect the difference in time of arrival of a sound between each ear. Consequently, your ability to locate the direction of a sound source is severely impaired.

Talking underwater as one would talk at the surface is impossible. Man's vocal chords are designed to operate in an environment of air, and sound cannot be coupled from air to water, or from water to air, to any major extent.

Noises of a given intensity are heard more clearly and rapidly underwater than the equivalent noise at the same distance in the air.

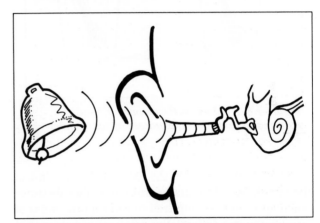

Figure 1.7 Hearing occurs when vibrations from a sound source cause corresponding vibrations in the ear drum. The movement of the ear drum is conveyed to the brain via connecting bones, the hearing organ and the auditory nerve.

Heat

Heat, or the absence of it, is crucial to man's environmental balance. The human body functions only within a very narrow range of internal temperature and contains delicate mechanisms to control that temperature. These aspects are presented in the chapter on Physiology. The following examines the external factors which influence body temperature.

Heat is a form of energy associated with and proportional to the molecular motion of a substance. It is closely related to temperature, but must be distinguished from it because different substances do not necessarily contain the same heat energy even though their temperatures may be the same. Temperature is measured in degrees, while heat is measured in British Thermal Units (BTUs), calories or kilogram-calories. One BTU is the amount of heat required to raise the temperature of one pound of pure water one degree Farenheit. A calorie is the amount of heat required to raise the temperature of one gram of water one degree Celsius. 1 BTU=252 calories. One K calorie or Calorie is the amount of heat needed to raise the temperature of one kilogram of water one degree C. 1C=1,000c.

Figure 1.8 A calorie is the amount of heat required to raise the temperature of 1cc of water 1°C.

SPECIFIC HEAT is the ratio of the amount of heat transferred to raise a unit mass of a substance one degree to that required to raise a unit mass of pure water one degree. Specific heat is a ratio that uses water as the base with a value of 1.0. The specific heat of air is 0.24, which means that .24 calories will raise the temperature of a gram of air by one degree Celsius. If one converts air from a weight to a volume basis and compared to water, it will be found that a volume of water will absorb 3,600 times as much heat as a volume of air for the same rise in temperature.

Heat is generated in many ways. Heat is transmitted from one place to another in three ways: conduction, convection and radiation. Conduction and convection are of the greatest concern to divers. Radiation is the transmission of heat by electromagnetic waves of energy such as heat waves from the sun or an electric heater.

CONDUCTION is the transmission of heat by direct material contact. A typical example of conduction is the heating of a cooking pot handle. Water is a much better conductor of heat than air, and an unprotected diver can lose a great deal of body heat to the surrounding water by conduction.

CONVECTION is the transmission of heat by the movement of heated fluids. This is the principle behind the operation of most home heating systems which set up a flow of air currents based on the natural tendency of warm air to rise and cool air to fall toward the ground.

If you were seated on the bottom in a tank of cold water, you would lose heat not only by direct conduction to the water, but also by convection currents in the water. The warmed water next to you would rise and be replaced by the colder water in the tank.

Conduction is of much greater significance to divers than convection. The rate at which heat is transferred by conduction depends on two basic factors—the difference in temperature between the warmer and cooler material, and the conductivity of the materials. Some substances are excellent conductors of heat—metals and water are examples. Some, like air, are very poor conductors. A poor conductor, if placed between a source of heat and another substance, insulates the substance and appreciably slows the transfer of heat. Most of the materials used for insulation of the human body—such as wool or foam—are effective because they contain thousands of pockets of trapped air, each too small to be subject to convective currents, but each blocking conductive transfer of heat.

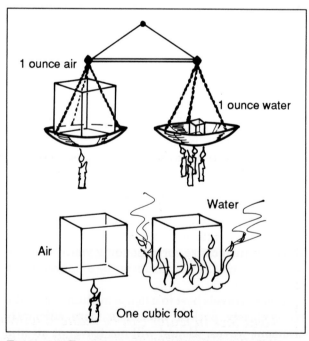

Figure 1.9 Four times as much heat is required to heat water equal in weight to a quantity of air, but 3,600 times as much heat for an equal volume of water.

Several factors contribute to the problem of maintaining body temperature including suit compression, increased gas density and respiratory heat loss.

A cellular neoprene wet suit loses much of its insulating capability as depth increases and the material is compressed.

The heat transmission characteristics of a gas are directly proportional to its density. Therefore, heat loss through respiratory heat loss to the surroundings increases with depth.

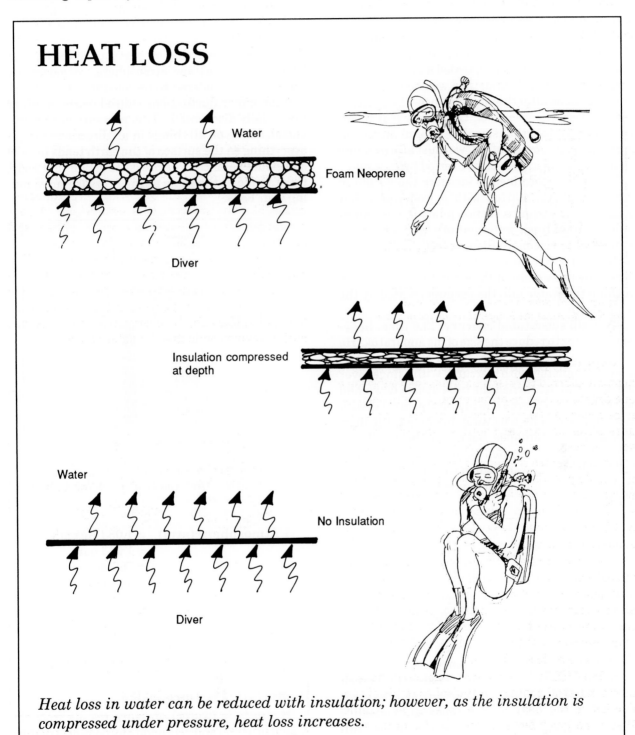

HEAT LOSS

Water

Foam Neoprene

Diver

Insulation compressed at depth

Water

No Insulation

Diver

Heat loss in water can be reduced with insulation; however, as the insulation is compressed under pressure, heat loss increases.

Figure 1.10

PRESSURE

Underwater pressure is the result of two factors: the weight of the water surrounding the diver—and the weight of the atmosphere above the water.

Atmospheric Pressure

Galileo, a 17th Century scientist, discovered that air has weight. He took a sealed container filled with nothing but trapped air and balanced it on a scale against a pile of sand. He then pumped more air into the container, sealed it again, and put it back on the scale. The air then weighed more than the sand. Soon after this, an Italian mathematician named Toricelli heard of Galileo's experiment. Toricelli surmised that since "we live submerged at the bottom of an ocean of air", we must also be living under some constant weight exerted by that air."

Toricelli, determined to measure the weight of the atmosphere, started with a well-known but puzzling fact—using a suction pump it was impossible to pump fresh water out of a well where the water had to rise more than 34 feet (10.4 meters). He theorized that the rise of the water was actually caused by the weight of the air in the atmosphere, pushing the water into the vacuum created by the removed air.

Toricelli substituted mercury (13.6 times heavier) for water to reduce the size of his apparatus. He took a four-foot glass tube, sealed at one end, and filled it completely with mercury. With a finger over the open end, he turned the tube upside down and submerged the covered end in a bowl also filled with mercury. When he took away his finger, the mercury in the tube dropped, but not all the way down. The falling stopped when about 30 inches of mercury (760 mmHg) were still in the tube. Above the mercury a vacuum was now created by the falling liquid.

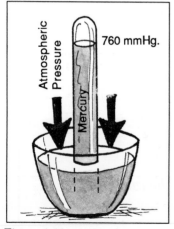

Figure 1.11
Toricelli's Barometer

Toricelli was thereby able to state that the weight of air pressing on the mercury in the bowl was sufficient to offset the weight of the 30-inch column of mercury.

Later the French scientist, Pascal, repeated Toricelli's experiment in full scale using glass tubes. He demonstrated that the weight of a column of air reaching miles above the earth would balance and was therefore, equal to the weight of a column of fresh water 34 feet high (or a column of sea water, which is heavier, 33 feet high). This would hold true if the air and water columns were one inch square in cross section, or even one mile square—as long as the same area measurement was applied to the columns.

The pressure acting on one square inch at sea level is known as one atmosphere. Atmospheric pressure is considered to be constant at sea level, and the minor fluctuations caused by the weather are usually discounted. This pressure is also universal, acting on all things in all directions so that everything on the surface of the earth tends to be in a pressure balance. The pressure inside your body, for example, is the same as the pressure surrounding your body.

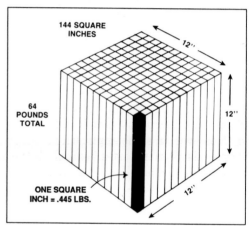

Figure 1.12 One cubic foot of salt water (64 pounds) exerts .445 pounds per square inch (64/144=.445). This pressure multiplied by 33 feet of salt water equals 1 ATM. of pressure (14.7 psi).

1 Atmosphere (atm) = 1.033 Kg/cm^2
= 1.013 bars
= 760 mm of Mercury (mm Hg)
= 29.92 inches of Mercury (Hg)
= 760 Torr
= 14.7 pounds per square inch (psi)

Hydrostatic Pressure

Hydrostatic (water) pressure results from the weight of a fluid and acts upon any body or structure immersed in the fluid. Like atmospheric pressure, it is equal in all directions at a specific depth. This effect is known as PASCAL'S PRINCIPLE, which states that, "in a fluid, pressure is transmitted uniformly in all directions."

1 atm = 10 meters of salt water
= 10.3 meters of fresh water
= 33 feet of salt water
= 34 feet of fresh water

Water pressure at 1 meter (3.3 feet) in salt water = 0.1 atm.

Water pressure at 1 meter (3.3 feet) in fresh water = 0.097 atm

Water pressure at 1 foot (0.303 m) in salt water = 0.445 psi

Water pressure at 1 foot (0.303 m) in fresh water = 0.432 psi

Units of Pressure

Since atmospheric pressure is universally applied, it does not, for example, register on the pressure gauge of a compressed air cylinder. The air in the cylinder, the cylinder itself, and the gauge itself are already under a base pressure of 1 atm (14.7 psi or 1 Kg/cm²). The gauge measures the pressure difference between the atmosphere and the air in the tank. This reading is called GAUGE PRESSURE and, for most purposes, this is the pressure specified. However, in some applications—especially in diving—it is often important to include the already-existing "one atmosphere" in a computation. This total pressure is called ABSOLUTE PRESSURE and is normally expressed in units of "atmospheres". Since the distinction is important, pressure must be identified as either gauge or absolute. When the type of pressure is not identified, it refers to gauge pressure; absolute pressure is identified as "ata" or "psia".

In water, pressure is the direct result of the weight of the water itself, and this pressure from weight is cumulative. The water on the surface pushes down on the water below, and so on down to the bottom. This force, due to the weight of the water column, is referred to as HYDROSTATIC PRESSURE.

Recalling the findings of Toricelli and Pascal, it is obvious that the pressure of sea water at a depth of 33 feet (ten meters) will be equal to one atmosphere. The absolute pressure, which is a combination of atmospheric and water pressure for that depth, will be two atmospheres. For every additional 33 feet (10 meters) of depth, another atmosphere of pressure (14.7 psi) will be encountered. Thus, at 99 feet (30 m), the pressure will be equal to four atmospheres absolute.

Surface	1 atm
First 33 feet (10 m) (gauge)	+1 atm
Second 33 feet (10 m) (gauge)	+1 atm
Third 33 feet (10 m) (gauge)	+1 atm
Absolute Pressure at 99 feet (30 m) =	4 atm

Gauge pressure is converted to absolute pressure by adding 14.7 if a gauge reads in psi or 1.03 if the gauge reads in kg/cm². Pressure must be converted to absolute values for use with the Gas Laws.

A special definition of pressure used in diving is AMBIENT PRESSURE which is defined as the pressure of the fluid surrounding an object. Ambient pressure is always absolute pressure.

Another formula that is useful for calculating absolute or ambient pressure is:

$$\text{Pressure} = \frac{\text{Depth} + 33}{33}$$

Use these numbers for sea water and "34" for fresh water.

Problems:

1. What is the gauge pressure at a depth of 57 feet (17.4 meters) in fresh water?
Solution: .432 psi/ft. x 57 feet = 24.6 psi (.097 atm/m x 17.4 meters = 1.69 atm)

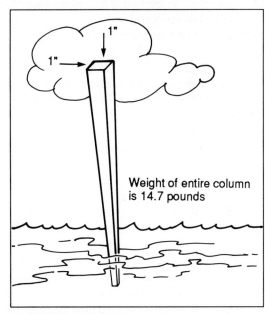

Weight of entire column is 14.7 pounds

Figure 1.13 Water pressure alone is called Gauge Pressure, but the weight of the atmosphere must also be considered. When combined, atmospheric and water pressure are called Absolute Pressure.

2. What is the absolute pressure at a depth of 61 feet (18.6 meters) in sea water?
Solution: .445 psi/ft. x 61 feet + 14.7 psi = 41.8 psia (.1 atm/m x 18.6 meters + 1 atm = 2.9 ata)

3. What is the ambient pressure at a depth of 66 feet (20 m) in sea water?
Solution: 14.7 psi x 2 + 14.7 psi = 44.1 psia (.1 atm/m x 20 m + 1 atm = 3.0 ata)

Partial Pressure

The pressure exerted by each individual gas within a mixture of gases is known as PARTIAL PRESSURE. In a typical air mixture of 20% oxygen and 80% nitrogen at sea level, the partial pressure of each gas is:

Pp (Partial pressure) O_2 (oxygen)=.2 atm (2.94 psi)
Pp N_2 (nitrogen) =.8 atm (11.76 psi)

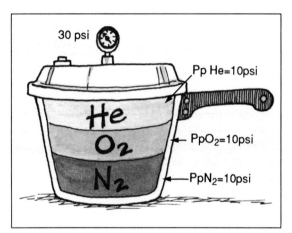

Figure 1.14 In a gas mixture comprised of equal parts of helium, oxygen and nitrogen, one third of the total pressure is exerted by each of the three gases. Thus, the partial pressure (Pp) of each gas is ten psi.

DALTON'S LAW: named for the English scientist who discovered the principle of partial pressure—states, "The total pressure exerted by a mixture of gases is equal to the sum of the pressures that would be exerted by each of the gases if it alone were present and occupied the volume." In other words, the whole is equal to the sum of the parts. The pressure contributed by any gas in the mixture is proportional to the number of molecules of that gas in the total volume.

This law of physics pertains to divers because the effects of pressure on divers are those that come about due to changes in the partial pressure of an inspired gas, as well as those that are direct and mechanical.

Problem:

What are the partial pressures of oxygen and nitrogen in air at five atmospheres?
Solution: 5 atm = 73.5 psia Pp 02 = .2 x 73.5 = 14.7 psia = 1 atm.
Pp N_2 = .8 x 73.5 = 58.8 psia = 4 atm

Note that the partial pressure of oxygen at this pressure is equivalent to atmospheric pressure at sea level. Because nitrogen is inert and not used by the body, breathing air at an ambient pressure of five atm is the same as breathing 100% oxygen at sea level. You would inspire five times as many oxygen molecules at five atm as you would breathing normal air at the surface.

If air in a scuba tank contained two percent carbon dioxide (CO)—a level which could be tolerated by a normal body at one ata—the partial pressure of the carbon dioxide at 5 atm would be extremely dangerous. This effect is commonly referred to as SURFACE EQUIVALENT (SE) for gas.

$$SE = \frac{Pp \text{ at depth (atms)}}{1 \text{ atm}} \times 100\%$$

This term implies that the concentration and physiological effect of a gas at a given partial pressure at depth is the same as would be experienced at X% breathed at 1 atm.

Problem:

Breathing two percent carbon dioxide (CO_2) at a depth of 99 feet (30 meters) is equivalent to breathing what percent of carbon dioxide at sea level?
Solution: The pressure at 99 feet (30 meters) is 4 ata Pp CO_2 = .02 x 4 = .08 ata
SE = .08 atm/1 atm = .08 x 100 = 8%

DENSITY

Atmospheric Density

The weight and volume of a given object can be expressed as its DENSITY, or weight per unit volume. (The term "weight" is assumed to be the absolute measurement of mass in the science of physics.) The average density of the atmosphere at sea level is approximately 1.3 ounces or 0.08 pounds per cubic foot (1.21 grams per liter). This means that the air in a full 80 cubic foot (2,286 L) scuba tank would weigh about 6.4 pounds (2.8 Kg).

The density of the atmosphere is not constant. Air density decreases as altitude increases. The rate of change is not constant. An elevation change from sea level to 1,000 feet (3,280 m) results in a greater change in pressure than an elevation change from 10,000 feet (32,808 m) to 11,000 feet (36,089 m). Decreased atmospheric pressure at altitude can seriously affect anyone diving at higher elevations.

The density of a gas varies in accordance with its pressure and increased density affects the flow of air. Maximum breathing capacity is reduced by 50% at 100 feet (30 meters) due to increased air density, while air consumption is greatly increased due to the large number of molecules of air consumed with each breath.

Hydrostatic Density

Liquids are, for all practical purposes, incompressible. The density of a liquid remains constant, regardless of depth, as far as scuba diving depths are concerned. The density of seawater is 64.0 pounds per cubic foot (1.025 Kg per liter). Slight variations can occur due to changes in temperature or salinity, but these variations will not be considered for the purposes of this book. The density of fresh water is 62.4 pounds per cubic foot (1.0 Kg per liter).

Buoyancy

SPECIFIC GRAVITY is the density of a substance compared with pure water. Some substances, such as lead, are much denser than water, so they tend to sink when placed in water; other substances, such as wood or cork, are less dense than water, and tend to float when placed in the fluid.

The human body has a specific gravity of approximately 1.0. This varies slightly from one person to the next—the average man will float in water; a fat person will readily float, and a person with a thin, lean body may experience difficulty trying to float.

The force that allows objects to float—whether they are pieces of cork or steel-hulled ships—is known as BUOYANCY. It was first defined by the Greek mathematician, Archimedes, who stated, "any object wholly or partly immersed in a fluid is buoyed up by a force equal to the weight of the fluid displaced by the object". This is known as ARCHIMEDES' PRINCIPLE, and it applies to all objects in all fluids.

The buoyant force of the fluid depends upon its density. Salt water has a slightly greater buoyant force than fresh water. This is why a fresh water diver requires additional weights to dive in salt water when the same equipment is used.

The two factors which decide an object's state of buoyancy are its DENSITY (weight per unit volume) and its volume. An object's weight will exert a downward force, while the object's volume will displace the same volume of liquid. The weight of this displaced volume of fluid exerts an upward force or thrust on the object. It is the difference between these two forces that determines whether the object will float (positive buoyancy) sink (negative buoyancy) or be neutrally buoyant. Using Archimedes' Principle to determine the buoyant force, the buoyancy of an immersed body can be established by subtracting the weight of the object from the weight of the displaced fluid.

Buoyancy = Displaced Weight - Dry Weight

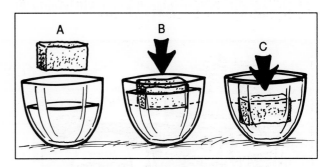

Figure 1.15 Buoyancy—Water is displaced by the weight of an object (B). More water is displaced when a buoyant object is submerged (C).

Problem:

An anchor in the sea with a dry weight of 100 pounds (45.3 Kg) has a volume of .22 cubic feet (6.3). How much does it weigh in the water?

Solution:

Displaced weight = .22 cubic feet x 64 lbs./Cu.Ft. = 14 Pounds. (6.3 L x 1.025 Kg/L = 6.3 Kg). Net weight equals displaced weight (14) less dry weight (100), or 86 pounds. Or, net weight equals displaced weight (6.5 Kg) less dry weight (45.3 Kg), or 38.8 Kg.

If the total displacement, that is the weight of the displaced liquid, is greater than the weight of the submerged body, the buoyancy will be positive and the body will float or be buoyed upward. If the weight of the body is equal to that of the displaced liquid, the buoyancy will be neutral and the body will remain suspended in the liquid. If the weight of the submerged body is greater than that of the displaced liquid, the buoyancy will be negative and the body will sink.

Problem:

A diver and his equipment weigh 224 pounds (101.6 Kg) when he is properly weighted for diving in the ocean. How much weight will the diver need to add or remove in order to be neutrally buoyant in fresh water when using the same equipment?

English Solution:

The diver displaces 3.5 cubic feet of water (224/64 = 3.5). He will displace the same volume of fresh water, but the weight of the displaced water will be only 218.4 pounds (62.4 x 3.5). For weight to equal displacement, the diver must remove 5.6 pounds of weight to achieve neutral buoyancy.

Metric Solution:

The diver displaces 99 liters (101.6 Kg/1.025 Kg/L). He will displace the same volume of fresh water, but the weight of the displaced water will be only 99 Kg (1.0 Kg. x 99 L). For weight to equal displacement, the diver must remove 2.6 Kg of weight to achieve neutral buoyancy.

Eventually you will be faced with the problem of lifting an object underwater by means of a lifting device. This device is an air-filled container that is attached to a submerged object for the purpose of lifting that object. There are hazards associated with the use of lift devices. The proper procedures for use of the devices will be covered elsewhere in this book. Buoyancy calculations for lifts will be presented here, however.

Lifting Buoyancy = Buoyancy - Lift Device Weight

Problem:

How many 50 pound (22,.68 Kg) lift bags, weighing two pounds (0.9 Kg) each, will it take to lift an object with a volume of 3.1 cubic feet (87.8 L) and a dry weight of 292 pounds (132.4 Kg) when the object is submerged in the ocean?

English Solution:

Buoyancy = displaced weight (3.1 x 64 pounds = 198 pounds) less dry weight (292 pounds) = -94 pounds. Two lift bags provide 100 pounds of lift less their own weight (two at two pounds each = four pounds) for a lifting buoyancy of 96 pounds. Therefore, two lift bags will accomplish the task.

Metric Solution:

Buoyancy = displaced weight (87.8 L x 1.025 Kg/L = 90 Kg.) less dry weight (132.4 Kg.) = 42.4 Kg. Two lift bags provide 45.4 Kg of lift less their own weight (2 at 0.9 Kg each = 1.8 Kg) for a lifting buoyancy of 43.6 Kg. Therefore, two lift bags will accomplish the task.

GAS FLOW (VISCOSITY)

Flow processes are complicated, involving the effects of many kinds of forces caused by gravity, viscosity, compressibility, pressure, shear (resistance caused by molecules rubbing against each other and the container walls), and friction. The two most significant aspects of gas flow for divers are the density and velocity of the air being breathed.

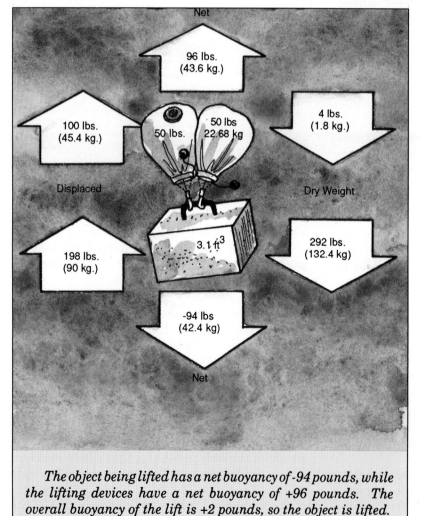

The object being lifted has a net buoyancy of -94 pounds, while the lifting devices have a net buoyancy of +96 pounds. The overall buoyancy of the lift is +2 pounds, so the object is lifted.

Figure 1.16

As air becomes more dense, it is more difficult for it to move through hoses and orifices. Imagine the exit for a theater. The more people trying to pass through the exit at once, the greater the resistance for an individual trying to get through. The deeper you dive, the greater your breathing resistance becomes.

Breathing resistance also increases as you increase the rate and depth of breathing, which increase the velocity of the air being breathed. As velocity increases, the resistance to the flow of air increases directly.

DRAG, PROPULSION AND TRIM

DRAG is the force of resistance to your movement through the water. Drag acts in a direction opposite to that of the direction of your path through the water. TRIM is the control of your assumed position, or body attitude (head up, level, head down).

Several forces are at work when you swim through the water. There is a buoyant force (B), a weight force (W), a lift force (L), a thrust force (T) and a drag force (D) as noted in the illustration.

The buoyant force is always upward, and the weight force is always downward. The lift force will be upward when buoyancy is positive and downward when buoyancy is negative. The lift force decreases as the ANGLE OF ATTACK decreases and is zero when the body is level. An angle of attack is the angle between your longitudinal axis and your trim. The drag force is always opposite the direction line regardless of body attitude. The thrust force is

usually forward, aligned with your longitudinal axis and comprised of two components—a horizontal one (along the direction line) and a vertical one. The illustrations show the thrust components for both negative and positive angles of attack.

PROPULSION is the act of driving forward, like swimming with fins, and is measured as thrust force. As you swim, part of your thrust force provides propulsion and part of it acts in the direction of either the buoyant force or the weight force, unless you are neutrally buoyant. When you are neutrally buoyant, your direction line will be parallel to your thrust force and all of your thrust will be used for propulsion.

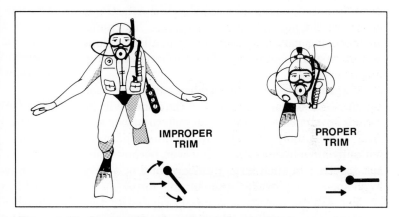

Figure 1.17 Increased cross sectional area equals increased resistance equals increased energy requirement.

Drag force is proportional to your frontal area. The greater your angle of attack while swimming, the greater your frontal area and the greater the resistance to your movement through the water. A second factor related to drag force is your speed.

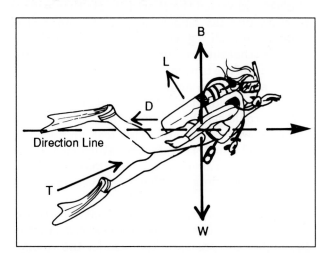

Figure 1.18 A positive angle of attack. Ideally the diver should be level.

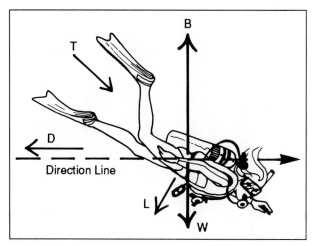

Figure 1.19 A negative angle of attack which is also undesirable.

Drag is proportional to the square of your speed. This means that doubling your speed increases resistance to movement by a factor of four. It also means that four times as much effort is required when your speed is doubled.

Since the greatest portion of your thrust is used to overcome drag, and since drag is greatly affected by the angle of attack, the need for neutral buoyancy to achieve level trim is obvious. Also obvious is that attempting to swim rapidly is inefficient.

KINETIC THEORY OF GASES

The basic explanation for the behavior of gases under all variations of temperature and pressure is known as the KINETIC THEORY OF GASES. The term "kinetic" means "of motion", which effectively describes the normal condition of a gas. The molecules are in constant motion, flying in all directions at high speed, rebounding off each other and changing directions.

If a gas is confined at atmospheric pressure, each square inch on each side of the container will be struck by about two quadrillion molecules per second. These molecules are infinitesimal and individually have little impact. However, because they act together in such large numbers, and at a very high speed, they produce measurable force.

The kinetic energy of a gas is related to two factors: the speed at which the molecules are moving (which is a function of the temperature), and the weight of each gas molecule (which is a function of the type of gas). At a given temperature, molecules of heavier gases move at slower speed than those of lighter gases, but their combination of weight and speed results in the same kinetic energy level and impact force. The measured impact force, or pressure, is representative of the kinetic energy of the gas.

Figure 1.20 Gas contained in a liquid bubbles out as the liquid is heated.

The kinetic theory of gases, therefore, states, "The kinetic energy of any gas at a given temperature is the same as the kinetic energy of any other gas at the same temperature." Consequently, the measurable pressures of all gases resulting from kinetic activity are affected by the same factors.

For any given gas, if the number or force of the "impacts" in a container is changed, the pressure will change. If the temperature is increased, for example, the increased speed of the molecules will cause impacts of higher force and greater frequency.

The pressure will also change if the volume of a gas is changed. By squeezing a given quantity of gas molecules into a smaller volume, the number of impacts per square area of container wall will increase and so will the pressure. The same thing happens if more molecules of a gas are pumped into a given volume—more molecules causes more impacts, which results in higher pressure.

Gas Laws

The behavior of all gases is affected by three factors: the temperature, pressure and volume of the gas. The relationships between these three factors have been defined in what are termed the GAS LAWS, which include Dalton's Law, Boyle's Law, Charles' Law, Henry's Law and the General Gas Law. Each of these laws is of special importance to divers.

Boyle's Law

In 1660 Robert Boyle, having heard of the discoveries of Toricelli and Pascal, set out to determine what would happen to a given quantity of confined air if the pressure changed. He took a J-shaped tube of glass and sealed the short leg. He then poured mercury into the longer leg until the amount of mercury in each leg was equal. At that point he reasoned that the pressure of the air trapped in the closed end of the tube must be equal to the pressure of the atmosphere acting on the mercury in the longer, open end. Boyle then added more mercury until he could see the volume of air trapped in the short leg was cut in half. This took an added 30 inches (760 mmHg) of mercury, which meant that he had added an amount equal to atmospheric pressure and had thus doubled the pressure on the trapped gas.

Boyle's demonstration showed that the pressure and volume of a gas are inversely related—that is, the higher the pressure, the smaller the volume, and vice versa. Boyle's Law states, "For any gas at a constant temperature, the volume will vary in-

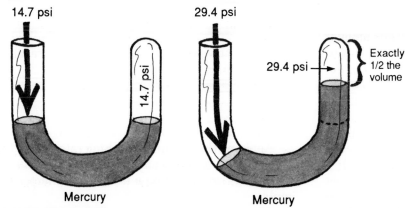

Figure 1.21 Boyle's
U-shaped glass tube experiment

versely with the absolute pressure while the density will vary directly with the absolute pressure". Expressed as a working formula for a constant temperature, Boyle's Law is:

P1V1 = P2V2
P1 = Initial absolute pressure
P2 = Final absolute pressure
V1 = Initial volume
V2 = Final volume

To illustrate Boyle's Law, imagine a buoyancy compensator containing six quarts (6.3 l) of air and forced to a depth of 49 feet (15 m) in fresh water. The final volume can be determined by rearranging the previous formula and solving for V2 as follows:

$$V2 = \frac{P1V1}{P2}$$

Solution (English): P1 = 14.7 psia.
P2 = 49 ft. x .432 psi/Ft. + 14.7 psi = 35.9 psia.
V1 = 6 qts. V2 = (14.7 x 6)/35.9 = 2.45 qts.
Solution: (Metric): P1 = 1 ata
P2 = 15 x .1 atm/m + 1 atm = 2.5 ata.
V1 = 6.3 l. V2 = (1 x 6.3)/2.5 = 2.52 l.

For a diver, Boyle's Law has extremely important applications. Squeezes, pulmonary injuries, air consumption and buoyancy control are some of the considerations.

Air Consumption

You should already be familiar with the basics of air consumption and should be able to calculate your Surface Air Consumption Rate (SCR) using a formula or a NAUI Sac-Rate Calculator (which greatly simplifies the process). You should also be aware of the many factors affecting air consumption, which include depth, activity, body temperature, breathing patterns, air losses, etc. This section on the subject will review the basic calculations and help you apply them to practical advanced diving situations.

Your Depth Consumption Rate (DCR) is determined with the following formula:

$$DCR = \frac{Air\ used}{Time}$$

Where rate of air used = the amount of air used in a given time at a constant depth and time = the given length of time. For example, if you used 500 psi (34 atm) of air in ten minutes, your DCR would be 50 psi per minute (3.4 atm per minute) for the size tank being used.

The ambient pressure in atmospheres for any depth in sea water may be determined using the following formula:

$$P = \frac{D + 33'\ (10\ meters)}{33'\ (or\ 10\ meters)}$$

where P = Pressure (ambient) and D = Depth.

Figure 1.22 Air consumption calculations are easy to figure using a NAUI SAC-Rate Calculator.

Air consumption calculations must always be based on Surface Air Consumption Rates (Sac-rates). This rate can be easily obtained by dividing your DCR by the ambient pressure fraction. For example, a DCR of 75 psi/min. (5.10 atm/min.) at a depth of 66 feet (20 meters), results in an SCR of 25 psi/min. (1.7 atm/min.).

$$SCR = 75/P \text{ where } P = \frac{66' + 33'\ (20m + 10m)}{33'\ (10m)} = 3$$

SCR = 75/3 = 25 psi/min. (1.7 atm/min.)

The next task is to determine DCR for a new depth based on the same tank capacity and amount of activity. This is obtained by multiplying your SCR by the new ambient pressure fraction. For example, the DCR at a depth of 99 feet (30 meters) is 100 (6.8 atm/min.) for an SCR of 25 psi/min. (1.7 atm/min.)

$$DCR = SCR \times P, \text{ where } P = \frac{99' + 33' \ (30m + 10m)}{33' \ (10m)} = 4$$

DCR = 25 x 4 = 100 psi/min. (6.8 atms/min.)

Breathing rate is usually expressed in psi per minute or atmospheres per minute because it is easy to calculate using those units. Volume/time units, such as cubic feet per minute (Ft.³/min.) or liters per minute (l/min.) are the only true measure of breathing rate, however, because tanks of different sizes do not allow a rate to be expressed in just psi/min. or atm/min. Rates measured with one set of units with one size tank do not accurately transfer to another tank of a different size unless psi/min. (atms/min.) is converted to volume per minute rate.

Conversion of psi/min. to Ft.³/min. (or atm/min. to l/min.) is accomplished by multiplying the SCR by the "tank factor", which is a ratio of tank volume to tank pressure. The following example applies to an SCR of 25 psi/min. (1.7 atm/min.) and an 80 Ft.³ (2,265 liter), 3,000 psi (204 atm) cylinder.

Figure 1.23 Pressure used per minute must be converted to volume per minute when a tank of a different size is used.

English: $\quad Ft.^3/min. = \dfrac{psi}{min.} \times \dfrac{Tank \ Ft.^3}{Tank \ psi}$

Notice how the terms psi cancel and result in cubic foot per minute.

$$Ft.^3/min. = \frac{25 \ psi}{1} \times \frac{80 \ Ft.^3}{3,000 \ psi}$$

Ft.³/min. = 25 x .02666 = .666 Ft.³/min.

Metric: $\quad l/min. = \dfrac{atm}{min.} \times \dfrac{Tank \ liters}{Tank \ atms}$

Notice how the terms atms cancel and result in liters per minute.

$$l/min. = \frac{1.7}{1} \times \frac{2265}{204}$$

l/min. = 1.7 x 11.1 - 18.9 l/min.

Applying this volume breathing rate to a 50 Ft.³ tank (1,416 l), you can determine the psi/min. (atm/min.) rate by using a similar tank factor formula:

English: $\quad Psi/min. = \dfrac{Ft.^3}{min.} \times \dfrac{Tank \ psi}{Tank \ Ft.^3}$

Notice how the terms "Ft.³" cancel and result in psi per minute.

$$Psi/min. = \frac{.666}{1} \times \frac{3,000}{50}$$

Psi/min. = .666 x 60 - 40 psi/min.

Metric: $\quad atm/min. = \dfrac{liters}{min.} \times \dfrac{Tank \ atms}{Tank \ liters}$

Notice how the terms liters cancel and result in atmospheres per minute.

$$atm/min. = \frac{18.9}{1} \times \frac{204}{1,416}$$

atm/min. = 18.9 x .144 - 2.7 Atm/min.

Note that 40 psi/min. (2.7 atm/min.) with a 50 cubic foot (1,416 l) tank is equivalent to the volume of air of 25 psi/min. (1.7 atm/min.) with an 80 cubic foot (2265 l) tank.

Using these formulas, you should be able to determine DCR and SCR for a given time at any depth in both psi/min. and Ft.³/min. (atm/min. and l/min.) and should also be able to convert the breathing rates so they can be applied to cylinders of different capacities.

Charles' Law

Temperature significantly affects the pressure and volume of a gas, therefore, it is essential to have a method of calculating this effect.

Charles' Law (also referred to as Gay-Lussac's Law) states: "For any gas at a constant pressure, the volume of the gas will vary directly with the absolute temperature". A related law, AMONTON'S LAW, states: "For any gas at a constant volume, the pressure of the gas will vary directly with the absolute temperature".

Stated mathematically:

$\dfrac{P1}{T1} = \dfrac{P2}{T2}$ (Amonton's Law for constant volume)

$\dfrac{V1}{T1} = \dfrac{V2}{T2}$ (Charles' Law for constant pressure)

P1 = initial pressure (absolute)
P2 = final pressure (absolute)
T1 = initial temperature (absolute)
T2 = final temperature (absolute)
V1 = initial volume   (Absolute Temperatures
V2 = final volume   and pressures must used.)

The following example illustrates Amonton's Law in action.

If a scuba cylinder contains 80 cubic feet (2,286 l) of air at 3,000 psi (204 atm) at a temperature of 70 degrees Fahrenheit, what will the cylinder pressure be if the temperature of the air inside reaches 110 degrees Fahrenheit?

Solution (English): Amonton's Law is used since the volume is constant. The formula is arranged mathematically to:

$P2 = \dfrac{P1 T2}{T1}$ = 3,014.7x (110 + 460 = 570 degrees R)

= 1,710,000 divided by (70 + 460 = 530 degrees R)
= 3,242psi.

Solution (Metric):
205 x (110 + 460 = 570 degrees R)
= 116,280 divided by (70 + 460 = 530 degrees R)
= 220.5 atm

The General Gas Law

Boyle and Charles demonstrated that with a gas—any gas—the factors of temperature, volume and pressure are so interrelated that a change in any of these factors must be balanced by a corresponding change in one or both of the others. Boyle's Law illustrates pressure/volume relationships, and Charles' Law basically describes the effect of temperature changes on pressure and/or volume. The GENERAL GAS LAW is a convenient combination of these two laws in predicting the behavior of a given quantity of gas when changes may be expected in any or all of the variables. The formula for the General Gas Law is:

$\dfrac{P1 V1}{T1} = \dfrac{P2 V2}{T2}$

P1 = initial pressure (absolute)
V1 = initial volume
T1 = initial temperature (absolute)
P2 = final pressure (absolute)
V2 = final volume
T2 = final temperature (absolute)

The following rules must be applied when using the formula:
1. There can be only one unknown.
2. If it is known that a value remains unchanged, or that the change in one of the variables will be of little consequence, the value may be cancelled out of both sides of the equation to simplify the computations.

The following example illustrates use of the General Gas Law. A portable compressor has the capacity to pump five cubic feet (142 l) per minute at a temperature of 25 degrees C at sea level. How long will it take the compressor to fill a 50 cubic foot (1,416 l) lifting device at a depth of 99 feet (four atm) when the temperature at the depth is 12 degrees C?

Solution (English): The unknown is the final volume, so the General Gas formula must be rearranged to solve for V2 as follows:

$$V2 = \dfrac{P1 V1 T2}{P2 T1}$$

Temperatures are converted to Kelvin and values substituted:

$$V2 = \dfrac{1\ ata \times 5\ cfm \times 285}{4\ ata \times 298} = \dfrac{1,425}{1,192} = 1.2\ cfm$$

At a rate of 1.2 cfm, it would take 42 minutes (50/1.2) to fill the lifting device.

Solution (Metric):

$$V2 = \dfrac{1\ ata \times 142\ L \times 285}{4\ ata \times 298} = \dfrac{40,470}{1,192} = 34\ l/min.$$

At a rate of 34 l/min., it will take 42 minutes (1,416/34) to fill the lifting device.

VAN DER WAAL'S EQUATION is a more correct representation of the behavior of ordinary gases than the General Gas Law, but the latter is simpler to use and sufficient for the purposes of this book.

GAS DIFFUSION

A physical effect of partial pressures and kinetic activity is that of gas DIFFUSION, which is the process of intermingling or mixing of gas molecules. The movement of gas molecules is totally random; given sufficient time they will eventually occupy the whole space which confines them. This movement of gas molecules is referred to as diffusion. If two different gases are placed on either side of a perforated partition, they will diffuse and intermingle. The rate of diffusion depends on the molecular weight of the gas. The heavier the molecule, the slower it travels.

The amount of an individual gas which will move through a permeable membrane (a solid which permits molecular transmission) depends upon the partial pressure of the gas on both sides of the membrane. If the partial pressure is higher on one side than on the other, the gas molecules will diffuse through the membrane to the lower partial pressure side until the partial pressure is equalized (EQUILIBRIUM). Molecules are actually passing through the membrane at all times in both directions due to kinetic activity, but more move from the side of higher concentration.

Gases in Liquids

Whenever a gas is in contact with a liquid, a portion of the gas molecules will diffuse (or more commonly, dissolve) into the liquid. This factor of solubility is of vital importance, since significant amounts of gases are dissolved in body tissues at the pressures encountered while diving.

Some gases are more soluble than others, and some liquids are better solvents than other liquids. For example, nitrogen is five times more soluble (on a weight-for-weight basis) in fat than it is in water.

Apart from the individual characteristics of the various gases and liquids, there are two physical conditions which have a great effect upon the quantity of gas which will be absorbed: temperature and pressure.

The amount of gas dissolving into a liquid (INGASSING) is best expressed by HENRY'S LAW, which states, "the amount of gas that will dissolve in a liquid at a given temperature is almost directly proportional to the partial pressure of that gas". If one unit of gas is dissolved at one atm, then two units will be dissolved at two atm, three units at three atm, etc.

When a gas-free liquid is first exposed to a gas, quantities of gas molecules will rush to enter into solution, pushed along by the partial pressure of the gas. As the molecules enter the liquid, they add to a state of GAS TENSION, which is a way of identifying the partial pressure of the gas in the liquid. The difference between the gas tension and the partial pressure of the gas outside the liquid is called the PRESSURE GRADIENT, which gives an indication of the rate at which the gas will tend to enter or leave the solution. When the gradient is high—with low tension and high partial pressure—the rate of absorption into the liquid is high. As the number of molecules of gas in the liquid increases, the tension increases until it reaches a value equal

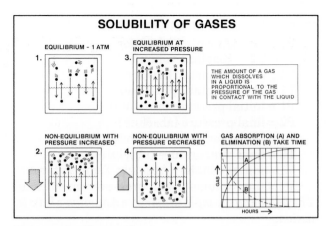

Figure 1.24 Henry's Law

to the partial pressure and at that point, the liquid is SATURATED with the gas and the pressure gradient is zero. Unless there is some change in temperature or pressure, the only molecules of the gas to enter or leave the liquid are those which may, in random fashion, change places without altering the balance.

The solubility of gases is affected by temperature—the lower the temperature, the higher the solubility. If the temperature of an existing solution is increased, some of the already dissolved gases will leave solution. The bubbles which rise in a pan of water being heated (long before it boils) are bubbles of dissolved gas coming out of solution.

The gases you breathe as a diver are dissolved in your body in proportion to the partial pressure of each gas in the mixture. Because of the varied solubility of gases, the quantity of a particular gas which becomes dissolved will also be governed by the length of time you breathe the gas at the increased pressure. If you breathe a gas long enough, your body will become saturated, but this occurs slowly. Depending on the gas, it would take anywhere from eight to 24 hours.

Whatever the quantity of gas which has been dissolved in your body, at whatever depth and pressure, it will remain in solution as long as the pressure is maintained. However, as you start to ascend, the dissolved gas will come out of solution (OUTGASSING). If your rate of ascent is slow, the dissolved gas will be carried by the blood to the lungs, passed into the lungs by diffusion, and exhaled before it accumulates sufficiently to form bubbles in the blood and tissues. If, on the other hand, you rise suddenly and reduce the pressure at a rate greater than the body can accommodate, bubbles will form and decompression sickness may result.

DIVING PHYSICS

DIVING
PHYSIOLOGY

2

Physiology is the branch of biology that deals with the processes, activities and phenomena of life and living organisms; the study of the functions of the organs during life. As a diver you need to understand the effects that diving has and can have upon your body processes and organs. Increasing that understanding is the purpose of this section.

LEARNING OBJECTIVES

By the end of this course, you should be able to:

1. Correctly define the terms presented in CAPITAL LETTERS in this chapter.

2. Explain generally and diagram roughly the processes of human respiration and circulation and give examples of how these processes are affected by diving.

3. State the causes, signs and symptoms, effects and general first aid for:
   • Respiratory distress
   • Circulatory distress
   • Nitrogen narcosis
   • Decompression sickness
   • Barotrauma
   • Thermal stress
   • Seasickness
   • Disorientation
   • Dehydration
   • Infections

4. Explain the physical fitness requirements for diving and list at least five ways to achieve and maintain fitness for diving.

5. Explain the cause, signs, symptoms, remedies and prevention of diver stress.

6. Explain the effects of diving on women and state proper recommendations regarding pregnancy and other female considerations.

RESPIRATION AND CIRCULATION

The body is comprised of millions of separate cells, each of which fulfills a particular function and each of which needs a steady supply of food and oxygen to carry out a variety of delicate reactions. The total process of life is called metabolism, which is represented by the following equation:

FOOD + OXYGEN = ENERGY + WATER + CARBON DIOXIDE

Respiration is the process whereby oxygen (O_2) is transported from the atmosphere to the cells for use in metabolism, and carbon dioxide (CO_2) is removed from the cells and transported to the atmosphere.

Included in respiration are breathing, the uptake of O_2 by the blood at the lungs, the transport of O_2 to the cells by circulatory system, the uptake of O_2 by the cells from the blood, and the reverse process involving carbon dioxide. The act of breathing is frequently termed "external respiration" while the other aspects are identified as "internal respiration".

External Respiration

Air is drawn through the nose or mouth down to a junction of two tubes—the esophagus (food pipe) and the trachea. The EPIGLOTTIS prevents food from passing into the trachea. The trachea passes into the chest where it divides into two tubes called BRONCHI (one tube is called a bronchus). The bronchi continue to divide into smaller tubes called BRONCHIOLES, which continue to divide into

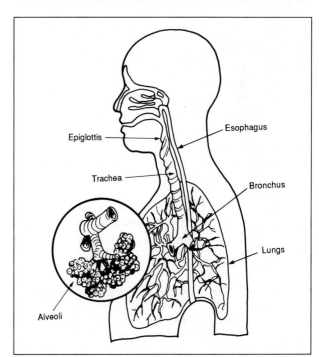

Figure 2.1 Respiratory Anatomy

smaller tubes until they terminate into microscopic (alveoli) air sacs. One air sac is known as an ALVEOLUS. These sacs are extremely small and number some 300 million in an average person. Each alveolus is surrounded by a network of very fine capillaries or blood vessels which act as the transfer site for the exchange of gases.

The lungs are surrounded by two layers of very thin membrane called the PLEURA. One layer covers the lungs and the other lines the chest wall. The closed space between the two layers (pleural cavity) contains only a thin layer of lubricant to facilitate movement. Damage to the pleura may result in air entering the pleural cavity. If this occurs, the lungs may collapse.

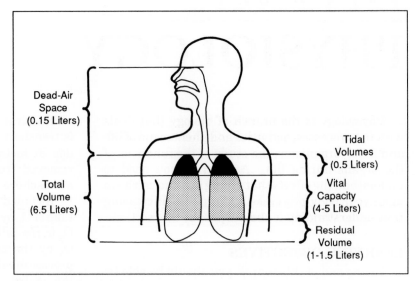

Figure 2.3 Lung Capacities

Ventilation of the lungs is achieved by changing pressure within the lungs. During inhalation, the diaphragm muscle contracts and flattens while the rib cage muscles lift the ribs up and out. This action enlarges the volume of the lungs, creating a negative pressure within the lungs in relation to the atmosphere. Air flows into the lungs until a pressure equilibrium is achieved. Exhalation occurs when the diaphragm and the muscles around the

rib cage relax and return to their resting position. The air pressure within the lungs rises in relation to the atmosphere due to the elastic recoil of the lungs. The greater pressure within the lungs at this point causes the air to escape to again equalize the pressure in the lungs to atmospheric pressure.

The degree of ventilation of the lungs is controlled by the muscular action of the diaphragm and the chest wall under the control of the nervous system, which itself is responding to changes in blood oxygen and carbon dioxide levels. The normal respiratory rate at rest is about 12-16 times per minute. During and after heavy exertion, the rate may be several times the resting rate.

Following a normal expiration, the lungs contain about two and one-half quarts (liters) of air. Even when one forcefully expels all the air possible, about one and one-half quarts remain (liters) and are called RESIDUAL VOLUME. The volume of air that is inspired and expired during rest is called TIDAL VOLUME, which averages about one half-quart (liters) per cycle. The additional air that can be breathed in after a normal inspiration—the INSPIRATORY RESERVE—varies greatly from person to person, but averages about four and one-half quarts (liters). The total volume of breathable air, called the VITAL CAPACITY, depends upon the size, development and physical condition of the individual. Residual volume is usually about 25% of the total lung volume, the sum of vital capacity plus residual volume. The term "respiratory minute volume" (RMV) represents the amount of air breathed in one minute. The average is about 25 to 30 quarts (liters) per minute of moderate work.

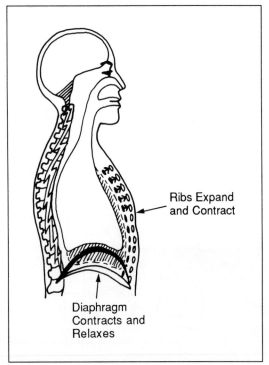

Figure 2.2 Mechanics of Breathing

Internal Respiration

Oxygen drawn into the alveoli is absorbed into the blood by the process of osmosis (diffusion through a membrane separating two solutions and tending to equalize concentrations). Blood can carry greater quantities of oxygen and carbon dioxide than can a simple solution. HEMOGLOBIN, a constituent in red blood cells that makes blood red, has the chemical property of combining with oxygen, carbon dioxide and carbon monoxide. The oxygen-carrying capability of blood is increased nearly 50 times by virtue of its hemoglobin content.

The exchange of oxygen and CO_2 between the blood and body cells occurs in opposite directions. Oxygen, being used continuously in the tissues, exists there at a lower partial pressure than in the blood. Since carbon dioxide is produced in the cells, its concentration is high relative to that of the blood reaching the tissues. Therefore, blood gives up oxygen and receives carbon dioxide during its transit through the tissue capillaries (smallest blood vessels).

When tissues are more active, the need for oxygen is greater. The additional oxygen required is supplied not from an increase in the oxygen content of the blood, but by a larger volume of blood flow through the tissues and by more complete extraction of oxygen from a given volume of blood. There can be a ninefold increase in the rate of oxygen supplied to active tissues.

The body has a respiratory control center that responds to oxygen and carbon dioxide levels in the blood. The control center of the brain is sensitive to the level of carbon dioxide and acid in the blood. This center controls rate and volume of respiration. Peripheral CHEMORECEPTORS monitor the level of oxygen and CO_2 in the blood leaving the lungs. These sensors respond primarily to HYPOXIA (low oxygen level). A high CO_2 level in the blood provides the greatest stimulus to breathe, while hypoxia is a relatively minor stimulus. The regulatory system of breathing is very complex because the respiratory rate is not only affected by high levels of carbon dioxide, but by oxygen partial pressure, increased gas density, and emotional states (such as anxiety or stress). The respiratory cycle is completed when CO_2-laden blood arrives at the lungs and gives up the carbon dioxide to the atmosphere through the processes of osmosis and

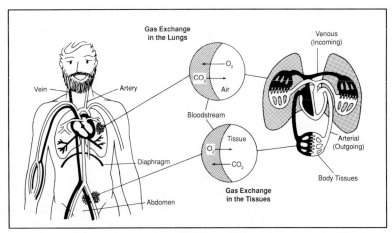

Figure 2.4 Circulation and respiration. Gas exchange in the blood occurs between the lungs and the blood stream and between the blood stream and body tissues.

diffusion. The taking up of oxygen at that time actually favors the unloading of carbon dioxide, whereas the absorption of CO_2 into the blood in the tissues favors the release of oxygen there.

Immersion Effects on Respiration and Circulation

Breathing in a vertical position in water requires more effort than breathing on land. The range of movement of the diaphragm is shortened by the increased AMBIENT (surrounding) pressure, so lung volume is slightly less than normal because the lungs cannot be fully expanded.

Any time you are in a head-up position in the water, your body collects blood in the chest area. This occurs because the ambient pressure is greater on the lower parts of the body, compared to a higher head which pushes the blood upward. The column of blood bearing down on the legs, when upright in air, causes blood to collect in the lower body. In water, the pressure of the blood column is exceeded by the pressure of the water column and blood shift from the legs to the chest.

The pooling of blood in the chest area causes the right side of your heart to fill with a larger volume of blood than it normally would. When the volume of blood being pumped increases, the amount of energy required to discharge the blood also increases. This can result in as much as a 30% increase in discharge volume and a proportionally increased energy requirement for the same pulse rate.

Because more blood than usual is being pumped from the heart into the lungs, the volume of air in the lungs is reduced slightly by this effect as well.

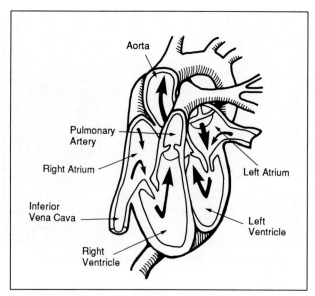

Figure 2.5 The heart works harder under water.

These physiological changes in your body emphasize the importance of good physical conditioning for diving. The overall efficiency of the respiratory system is not affected by immersion changes in normal, healthy divers, but the changes do pose an increased risk for those with heart and respiratory problems. Good health is essential for safe diving.

Respiratory Distress

ASPHYXIA is the existence of both HYPOXIA (oxygen shortage) and carbon dioxide excess in the body. Asphyxia results if breathing ceases for any reason. SUFFOCATION is a term indicating stoppage of breathing for any cause and the resulting asphyxia.

STRANGULATION means stoppage of breathing due to obstruction of the airway, such as crushing of the windpipe, lodging of a foreign body in the windpipe, spasm or swelling of the larynx, or the inhalation of water or vomitus. A victim will struggle violently and try to breathe in spite of the obstruction before losing consciousness from asphyxia. Artificial respiration produces little movement of air unless the obstruction is removed.

Breathing Resistance

In the human body, air flow in large airways is turbulent and is inversely proportional to the square root of gas density. If the gas density increases fourfold, breathing resistance is doubled and flow is approximately one-half normal. However, most individuals use only 50 to 60 percent of their maximum ventilation capabilities at sea level;

so at a pressure of four atm absolute, there should be no ventilation-imposed limitation for divers. Some regulators however. can impose a formidable workload on the respiratory system. A few regulators have unsatisfactory flow characteristics at depths in excess of 100 feet (30 meters) during periods of increased ventilatory requirements.

Carbon Dioxide Excess

The CO_2 tension in the human body increases with the rate of production due to physical exertion and inadequate ventilation of the lungs. The normal concentration of CO_2 in atmospheric air is about .04 percent. As carbon dioxide build up occurs, a progression of effects will be noted. The initial response to excess CO_2 is an increased rate of respiration; higher concentrations produce distracting respiratory discomfort; a very high concentration of CO_2 causes dizziness, stupor and unconsciousness.

Inadequate ventilation of the lungs (HYPOVENTILATION) produces insufficient elimination of carbon dioxide, and this results in excessive levels of CO_2 in the blood (HYPERCAPNIA). The term "Carbon Dioxide Excess" applies to forms of hypoventilation and hypercapnia in which a diver is capable of eliminating CO_2 in a normal manner but, for some reason fails to do so. The usual cause of such a situation for a scuba diver is an alteration of the breathing pattern due to anxiety or apprehension.

The amount of CO_2 retained in the body during exertion varies from person to person. Some individuals retain more than others and are more prone to carbon dioxide excess. Loss of consciousness from carbon dioxide excess is not supposed to present a problem with scuba equipment, but inadequate respiratory response to exertion, combined with a tendency to retain CO_2, can cause unconsciousness. Shallow, rapid breathing during exertion must be avoided. The situation will occur even more rapidly when poorly maintained breathing equipment with high breathing resistance is used.

The proper CO_2 level in the body is maintained by breathing a sufficient amount of air to dilute and exhale the carbon dioxide produced in the body and carried to the lungs. This is easily accomplished while scuba diving if severe exertion is avoided and a proper breathing pattern is maintained.

Deliberate reduction of breathing (SKIP BREATHING) causes CO_2 excess. Skip breathing is practiced by scuba divers who wish to extend bottom time. Each breath is held for a number of seconds. This practice is extremely dangerous because CO_2 excess gives little or no warning, because the diver's breath-hold ability is very limited in the event of an air supply loss, and the habit of breath holding could lead to a lung expansion injury during an ascent. Skip breathing should be avoided and considered hazardous.

A diver unconscious from CO_2 excess revives quickly when the lungs are ventilated with fresh air. After-effects include headache, nausea, dizziness and sore chest muscles.

Overexertion

It is possible to exceed your respiratory capabilities before realizing the impending difficulties. There is a delay between exertion and increased respiratory demands to meet the oxygen requirements imposed by the demands. On land this poses no problem, but under water it can create a sensation of suffocation and anxiety. The resulting labored breathing demands air at a higher rate than your regulator can provide, producing a tendency to panic. Prevention is the best solution. Pace your efforts to avoid overexertion. At the onset of a feeling of air starvation and labored breathing, stop all activity, rest, and allow breathing to gradually return to normal. Factors contributing to overexertion, besides prolonged heavy exertion, include poorly designed and/or maintained regulators, wasted effort and excessive cold.

Carbon Monoxide Toxicity

Carbon monoxide (CO) is a serious breathing media contaminant. CO readily combines with blood hemoglobin, forming carboxyhemoglobin and rendering the hemoglobin incapable of transporting sufficient oxygen to the body tissues. Hemoglobin combines with CO about 200 times as readily as with oxygen. Due to the decreased oxygen-carrying capability of the blood when CO is present, hypoxia develops even though the supply of oxygen to the lungs is adequate. However, at depth a diver may tolerate a degree of CO toxicity because some of the oxygen transport requirements are met by oxygen dissolved in the blood plasma. The reconversion of carboxyhemoglobin to oxyhemoglobin takes hours, however, so an affected diver is likely to develop symptoms of CO toxicity during ascent. Consequently, contamination of scuba air with even small amounts of CO is very dangerous.

The wide spectrum of symptoms associated with CO toxicity include headache, dizziness, nausea, weakness and confusion. Signs include failure to

Figure 2.6 Diver resting on bottom (recovering).

respond, clumsiness, and bad judgment. Frequently, no signs or symptoms are evident; a diver may lose consciousness without warning, and breathing may cease. In general, the symptoms parallel those of other forms of anoxia with one exception—the victim's coloration is red instead of blue. This is because carbon monoxide combined with hemoglobin is bright red. A victim who becomes anoxic from CO toxicity may exhibit unnatural redness of lips, nail beds and sometimes skin.

First aid for CO toxicity includes fresh air. Oxygen should be administered as soon as possible. Artificial respiration is required if breathing has stopped. A CO victim requires medical care. The treatment of CO toxicity with oxygen in a recompression chamber is a standard method of treatment.

Carbon monoxide contamination can arise from the fumes of an internal combustion engine being drawn into the air intake of a compressor or from the partial combustion of lubricating oil within a compressor that is not properly operated or maintained.

Purity standards for breathing air allow for a maximum of 0.001 percent carbon monoxide. You must be certain that your air supply meets recommended purity standards. Air must be obtained from reliable sources where periodic air analyses are obtained.

Oxygen Toxicity

Oxygen becomes toxic when a partial pressure greater than one atmosphere is breathed for a period of time. The U.S. Navy depth limit for diving with 100% O_2 is 25 feet. The higher the partial

Figure 2.7 A high-pressure, low-volume compressor for scuba air.

pressure of the oxygen, the shorter the time before symptoms develop. Susceptibility is further increased by exercise. Oxygen toxicity affects the brain and leads to convulsions. Tolerance to high partial pressures of O_2 varies with individual divers and may also vary within individuals from day to day. The U.S. Navy has established an "oxygen tolerance test" to identify divers with unusual susceptibility.

Warning symptoms of O_2 toxicity, in order, are: muscular twitching, nausea, abnormal vision and hearing, breathing difficulty, anxiety and confusion, fatigue, uncoordination and convulsions. The symptoms are reversible. Convulsions are self-terminating, but are dangerous underwater because they can lead to air embolism and drowning.

Recreational divers should never experience problems with oxygen toxicity because they breathe compressed air which has a partial pressure of oxygen of only about 21%. Attempts by recreational divers to use rebreathers, cryogenic scuba units, gas mixtures or oxygen-filled scuba tanks can, however, result in oxygen toxicity. Scuba tanks should be filled only with pure, dry compressed air.

Hyperventilation and Shallow-Water Blackout

Rapid, unusually deep breathing in excess of the necessary rate for the level of activity is HYPERVENTILATION, a form of manual interference with the normal operation of respiratory control mechanisms. Hyperventilation lowers the CO_2 level in the body below normal, producing a condition known as HYPOCAPNIA, which normally results in a feeling of lightheadedness. When hy-

perventilation is extended, weakness, faintness and blurring of vision can result. Excessive hyperventilation can prevent the respiratory control mechanism from responding until the oxygen level in the body has fallen below the level necessary to maintain consciousness.

Extended breath holding following hyperventilation is hazardous. During long breath-hold periods, your oxygen level can fall to a low value before you realize you must return to the surface and resume breathing. The oxygen level is lowered because exertion not only causes O_2 to be used faster, but decreases the sensitivity of the CO_2 breakpoint mechanism. This allows the O_2 level to go even lower than it would otherwise. When you ascend, the drop in the O_2 partial pressure in the lungs may be sufficient to stop further uptake of oxygen completely. Simultaneously, the partial pressure of CO_2 in the lungs drops also, giving the false impression that you do not need to breathe.

Involuntary hyperventilation may be initiated by anxiety or physical stress and may result in unconsciousness or muscle spasms. You may not be aware of the impending problem. Some individuals are more susceptible to hypocapnia than others, but anyone will lose consciousness with sufficiently prolonged hyperventilation.

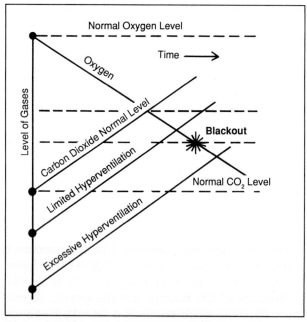

Figure 2.8 Hyperventilation and shallow-water Blackout. Blackout results from prolonged breath holding following excessive hyperventilation.

Be aware of the hazards associated with hyperventilation. If you notice you are involuntarily hyperventilating, take immediate steps to slow your breathing rate. Avoid excessive hyperventilation prior to prolonged breath holding.

NEAR DROWNING

NEAR DROWNING is the term for a clinical condition that follows suffocation by submersion in liquid after which there is at least 24 hours of survival. The term DROWNING indicates death due to asphyxia (lack of oxygen) which occurs within 24 hours of suffocation by submersion.

In severe cases, signs of near drowning include unconsciousness, CYANOSIS (blue skin), cessation of breathing and froth in the mouth. However, in mild cases, early signs may consist only of labored breathing and confusion.

Brain tissues suffer permanent damage after four to five minutes of hypoxia, but the time may be lengthened for extremely cold conditions. Additionally, the degree of hypoxia initially suffered by a near drown victim is difficult to determine. Near drown victims have recovered after up to 40 minutes of immersion in cold water. Attempts should be made to revive victims in all cases.

Near drownings have been categorized as "wet" or "dry." The dry type results from asphyxiation due to SPASM of the larynx caused by water striking it. (Like "choking" on a bit of food "going the wrong way.") This occurs in all cases where the victim is conscious enough to have reflexes. The wet type can occur initially or result from the dry drowning victim taking a breath as consciousness is lost. In the wet type some volume of the immersion liquid enters the lungs. When this happens, various physiological events occur depending upon the volume of fluid aspirated and the nature of the fluid. Neither sea water nor fresh water have the same concentration of salts as the human body. As a result, both sea water, which is HYPERTONIC (saltier than blood) and fresh water, which is HYPOTONIC (less salty than blood), cause damage to alveolar tissue. Because of the damage done, body fluids from the blood stream can weep into the alveolar spaces in a process termed SECONDARY DROWNING. As alveolar spaces fill with these secondary fluids, hypoxia becomes worse and froth formed by the fluids and proteins washed out of the lungs may be seen in the mouth and nose. Secondary drowning can occur hours after the initial incident. Continued medical observation of apparently stable near drown victims is necessary.

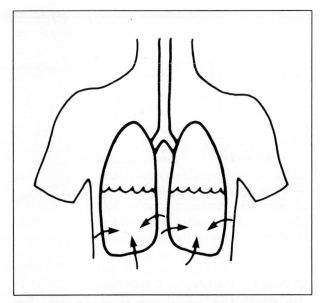

Figure 2.9 Body fluids from the blood stream can weep into the alveolar spaces in a process termed Secondary Drowning.

If a near drown victim is unconscious and not breathing, immediate artificial respiration is imperative. Care should be taken to not inflate the stomach as aspiration of vomit causes further lung injury. Oxygen should be administered as soon as possible and should be continued even if the victim begins to breathe. The pulse on a cold unconscious diver is difficult to detect, so check very carefully before beginning chest compressions. Because near drowning can progress from mild to very severe distress, all near drown victims should be administered oxygen and transported immediately to a medical facility for observation and care; even those that are conscious, breathing and apparently fine.

Hospital treatment can include chest X-rays, sampling of arterial blood gases, blood tests and electrocardiograms. Intravenous fluids and drugs may be given. Prolonged mechanical ventilation with supplemental oxygen may be required. The lungs are the prime target of injury and of treatment in near drowning. But associated hypoxia affects sensitive organs like kidneys, heart and brain. Recovery may not be complete.

NITROGEN NARCOSIS

Although nitrogen is physiologically inert under normal conditions, it can induce signs and symptoms of narcosis or anaesthesia at sufficiently raised partial pressures.

The exact cause of inert gas narcosis is not known, but it is clear that basically it is due to interaction of the gas with nerve cells.

Narcosis becomes evident at depths approaching 100 feet. The signs and symptoms are similar to those of the early stages of hypoxia. There is a wide variation in individual susceptibility, which also varies from day to day. Symptoms become more severe with increased time and depth and include impairment of thought, judgment, reasoning, memory, and the ability to perform mental or motor skills. Some divers feel EUPHORIA (elation and well-being), some feel apprehension and anxiety, and others may feel they are unaffected. Everyone is affected, no matter how they may feel. Narcosis is a significant hazard because it increases the risk of an accident and diminishes the ability to cope with an emergency.

The onset of narcosis is rapid, but recovery is equally as rapid and is accomplished by ascending to a shallower depth so the narcotic effect of the inert gas is reduced. Amnesia for events occurring at depth may result.

Carbon dioxide excess increases the severity of narcosis. A diver doing work or exercising experiences narcosis more rapidly than a resting diver. Other factors that increase susceptibility include alcohol, hangovers, fatigue, anxiety, cold and the effects of medications. Novices tend to be affected more readily than experienced divers.

The hazards of narcosis are one reason why recreational diving depths are limited to a maximum of 130 feet.

DECOMPRESSION SICKNESS

Nitrogen Absorption and Elimination

Upon exposure to altitude or diving depths, the partial pressure of nitrogen in the air in the lungs changes, so body tissues either lose or gain nitrogen to reach a new equilibrium with the nitrogen pressure in the lungs. The taking up of nitrogen in tissues is called ABSORPTION or INGASSING, while the release of nitrogen is termed ELIMINATION or OUTGASSING.

Absorption consists of several phases, including transfer of inert gas from the lungs to the blood and

Figure 2.10 Nitrogen narcosis can make even simple tasks extremely difficult.

then from the blood to the various tissues through which it flows. The GRADIENT (driving force) for gas transfer is the partial pressure difference of the gas between the lungs and the blood and the blood and the tissues. The volume of blood flowing through tissues is usually small compared to the mass of the tissue, but over a period of time the gas delivered to the tissue will cause it to become equilibrated with that carried in solution in the blood. This state is called SATURATION. Some tissues, such as bone marrow, take much longer to reach a state of saturation, while others, such as brain tissue, saturate very quickly.

For the purposes of developing mathematical models of gas solubility in tissues, a series of tissue compartments has been postulated. Each tissue compartment represents a time in minutes equal to the time needed for the tissue to become 50% saturated. The range of half times for modern models is from five minutes to over 500 minutes. The five minute tissue is considered 50% saturated in five minutes. The unsaturated portion becomes 50% saturated in an additional five minutes, making the tissue 75% saturated. The tissue becomes 99% saturated during a period of six half times (30 minutes). A 120 minute tissue attains 50% saturation in two hours, and 99% saturation in 12 hours.

The process of elimination is the reverse of absorption. During ascent and after surfacing, the tissues lose excess inert gas to the circulating blood by DIFFUSION, which is the movement of molecules from an area of greater concentration to an area of lesser concentration. In your body, the diffusion gradient is the difference between the inert gas partial pressure in each tissue and that in the blood vessels after the blood has equilibrated to the gas in the lungs. The amount of inert gas that can be taken into the blood is limited, so the tissue inert gas tension falls gradually. As in absorption, the rate of blood flow, the difference in the partial pressures, and the amount of inert gas dissolved in the tissues and blood determine the rate of elimination.

During outgassing, the blood and tissues can theoretically hold gas in SUPERSATURATED SOLUTION without bubbles being formed. A supersaturated solution is one holding more gas than is possible at equilibrium for a particular temperature and pressure. Because of the ability of the blood and tissues to become supersaturated for short periods of time, a diver can ascend at least part of the way regardless of the depth and duration of a dive. An outgassing gradient is established and inert gas is eliminated from body tissues. This permits the diver to ascend further after some period of time. The process is continued until the diver reaches the surface safely. The diver's body will still contain inert gas in some tissues, but this is normally safe if kept within decompression limits and if further pressure reduction from altitude does not occur.

Decompression Sickness

If the elimination of gas is inadequate to parallel the rate of reduction of external pressure, the amount of supersaturation of gas in the tissues may permit the gas to come out of solution in the form of bubbles. The English physiologist, Haldane, theorized that bubbling occurred when the tissue pressure was twice that of the external pressure. His work formed the basis for a model developed by the U.S. Navy which established different pressure surfacing ratios for different tissues and led to the development of the U.S. Navy Dive Tables.

The formation of bubbles causes a condition known as DECOMPRESSION SICKNESS or "THE BENDS", which refers to the condition caused by rapid reduction in pressure from a higher to a lower level of pressure. The primary constituent of bends bubbles is nitrogen.

Depth in Feet	Narcotic Effects
30-100	Mild impairment of performance on unpracticed tasks. Mild euphoria.
100	Reasoning and immediate memory affected more than motor coordination and choice reactions. Delayed response to visual and auditory stimuli.
100-165	Laughter and loquacity may be overcome by self control. Idea fixation and overconfidence. Calculation errors.
165	Sleepiness, hallucinations, impaired judgment.
165-230	Convivial group atmosphere. May be terror reaction in some. Talkative. Dizziness reported occasionally. Uncontrolled laughter approaching hysteria in some.
230	Severe impairment of intellectual performance. Manual dexterity less affected.
230-300	Gross delay in response to stimuli. Diminished concentration. Mental confusion. Increased auditory sensitivity, *i.e.*, sounds seem louder.
300	Stupefaction. Severe impairment of practical activity and judgment. Mental abnormalities and memory defects. Deterioration in handwriting, euphoria, hyperexcitability. Almost total loss of intellectual and perceptive faculties.
300	Hallucinations (similar to those caused by hallucinogenic drugs rather than alcohol).

Table 2.1 Narcotic Effects of Compressed Air Diving

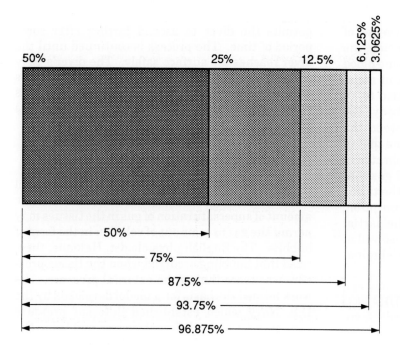

50%   25%   12.5%   6.125% 3.0625%

←——— 50% ———→
←———— 75% ————→
←———— 87.5% ————→
←———— 93.75% ————→
←———— 96.875% ————→

Figure 2.11 The box represents the way nitrogen fills a compartment. During a time interval of one half time, one half of the remaining unfilled spaced is filled with nitrogen. After 5 half times, the compartment is 96.875% filled to its capacity.

If bubbles are formed in the bloodstream, they block circulation; bubbles in tissues distort the tissues as the bubbles expand. Symptoms depend on the location of the bubbles, whether in joints, muscles, bones or nerves. The degree of severity, in order, is: skin bends, limb bends, central nervous system bends, and chokes, where bubbles actually block the circulation to the lung.

Types of Bends

With skin bends, the skin itches, burns and is mottled. It is a rash that disappears spontaneously over a period of time from a few hours to a few days. In some cases when skin mottling occurs more severe bends may develop in the central nervous system.

Limb bends are the most common form of decompression sickness. Shoulder and elbow joints are the most frequent sites. The pain is usually steady, but occasionally may be throbbing. It reaches a peak in minutes to hours and often subsides spontaneously several hours later. The limb usually looks completely normal, although there is tenderness. Treatment by recompression helps relieve the pain and may decrease subsequent tissue damage.

Central nervous system bends—those in the spinal cord or brain—are an especially serious type of decompression sickness because they can cause permanent nerve damage, such as paralysis. It is important to recognize the early manifestations of this type of bends because immediate treatment in a recompression chamber may result in recovery, whereas delay significantly decreases the chances of a good outcome. Soon after surfacing the first symptom may be transient back pain radiating pain to the abdomen, which may manifest as attributed to lifting or a pulled muscle. Therefore, the first symptom to catch the diver's attention is PARESTHESIA AND HYPESTHESIA, or a feeling of "pins and needles" in the legs. Next the legs become weak and the walk unsteady; urination becomes difficult or impossible, although the bladder may be distended. Finally, paralysis below the waist or neck may ensue. The condition is similar to that of a broken back with spinal cord injury; however, a diver is more fortunate because with prompt treatment recovery is likely.

Injury to the central nervous system is often associated with an unusually rapid rate of ascent in an emergency situation. Symptoms may appear immediately and progress to paralysis within minutes or hours.

Rarer forms of bends include brain damage, inner ear bends and the "chokes". Symptoms of brain damage include visual disturbances or weak-

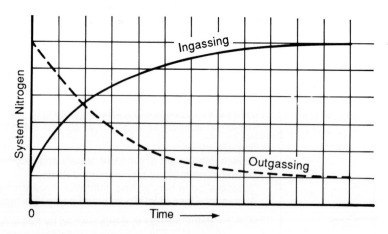

Figure 2.12 Ingassing and Outgassing

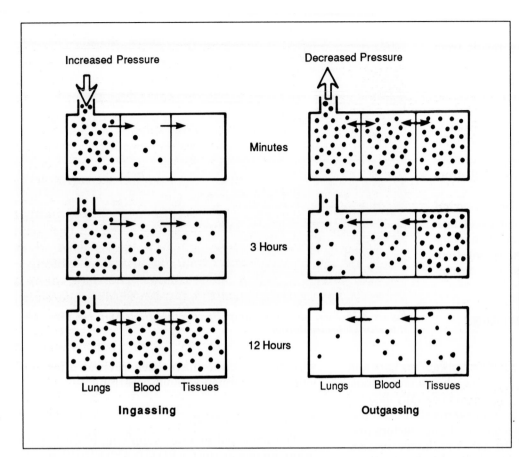

Minutes

3 Hours

12 Hours

Lungs Blood Tissues

Ingassing

Lungs Blood Tissues

Outgassing

Figure 2.13 It takes time for gas to move from the lungs to the blood to the tissues and for the reverse to occur.

Figure 2.14 Microscopic bubble formation

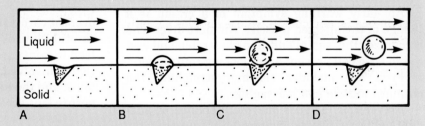

Liquid

Solid

A   B   C   D

According to Haldane, bubbles will not form in a supersaturated solution unless the pressure is halved. Modern studies, however, using ultrasonic doppler detectors have identified the presence of asymptomatic intravascular bubbles even though the no-decompression limits have not been exceeded. These intravascular bubbles have been termed "silent bubbles". Silent bubbles are microscopic in size and are believed to originate from tiny gas pockets in the walls of tissues. Excess nitrogen during decompression dissolves into the microscopic pockets, causing them to enlarge and extend into the circulatory path until they finally break free and become tiny bubbles, which by themselves cause no harm. These bubbles can join together, however, to form larger bubbles that can produce symptoms of decompression sickness.

The theory of microscopic gas separation within tissues helps explain why bubbles are formed in the body when they are not formed in a pure liquid subjected to the same changes in pressures. If your body contained a pure liquid, you could dive to a depth of over six miles and then ascend directly to the surface with no bubble formation!

During an ascent, the volume of a microscopic bubble increases due to Boyle's Law. This lowers the gas pressure inside the bubble, which attracts more gas into the bubble. Therefore, bubbles grow not only because of the laws of physics, but also because of the inward diffusion of gas. Recompression, on the other hand, compresses bubbles and increases their internal pressure. Gas then diffuses out of the bubbles.

ness on one side of the body. VER-TIGO (dizziness) may result from damage to the inner ear. This condition is sometimes called "the staggers". The "chokes" is a severe, although rare form of the disease characterized by shortness of breath, chest pain, and a cough. Without recompression therapy, circulatory collapse and death may result from the chokes.

Treatment of recompression sickness consists of recompressing a diver to a depth sufficient to cause the bubbles to return to solution. The victim is then slowly decompressed.

Figure 2.15 First aid for a cramp. Stretch the affected muscle, then rub it to stimulate circulation.

CIRCULATORY DISTRESS

Cramps

A CRAMP is a muscle spasm producing pain and temporary disability. It occurs when a muscle outworks its supply of blood. Cramps usually develop in untrained muscles or from overuse (for example, swimming with oversized fins). Other factors predisposing to cramps include circulatory restrictions, cold, sudden exertion, dehydration and sweating, fatigue, poor nutrition and poor health. Although the most common sites are the calf of the leg and the sole of the foot, other muscles can cramp.

An early warning symptom of a cramp is a twinge of the affected muscle. An alert diver who recognizes this signal and stops to stretch and rest the muscle can prevent a full locking contraction.

First aid includes slowing, stretching the cramped muscle and massaging.

Prevention includes the maintenance of adequate physical fitness, regular diving, properly fitting equipment, good nutrition and health and adequate thermal protection.

The Diving Reflex

Cold water in contact with your face causes a slight slowing of the heart rate, called BRADYCARDIA. This effect is known as the DIVING REFLEX, which is very pronounced in marine mammals, but may not be particularly good for you. Associated with the bradycardia are cardiac irregularities which probably pose no threat to a healthy person, but which may contribute to otherwise inexplicable deaths of people who are not in good health. The diving reflex has some protective value in the drowning situation, however, and helps explain why some victims have been revived after prolonged submersion without breathing.

Carotid Sinus Reflex

The principal arteries supplying blood to your brain, known as the CAROTID ARTERIES, have a sinus (small bulge) at a bifurcation (fork) of the artery in the neck. The purpose of the carotid sinus is to control your heart rate according to your blood pressure. A tight hood or neck seal applies pressure over the carotid bifurcation. Pressure applied to the carotid sinuses produces bradycardia which can lead to fainting or dizziness, especially when exertion is involved. Be aware of the reflex, its symptoms; and the hazards it poses, then select your exposure suit accordingly.

Sudden Death Syndrome

Diving is often blamed for fatalities which actually result from heart attacks or cardiac irregularities. These problems do not always stem from cardiac disease.

Diving increases the workload of the heart. Overall blood volume is reduced, blood chemistry is changed, the heart rate is increased, blood pressure is increased, and signals to the heart are changed. The heart's ability to receive or supply an adequate supply of blood is altered, so fatal problems can result for an individual with a marginal or unknown heart condition. A good, sound heart and physical fitness are very important for diving fitness.

Heart Attack and Arrest

You should be able to recognize the signs and symptoms of a heart attack, which are:

1. Chest pain under the breastbone which may radiate to one or both shoulders or arms, or to the neck.
2. Shortness of breath, exhaustion
3. Bluish discoloration of the lips and skin
4. Shock
5. Indigestion, nausea and vomiting

First aid involves placing the victim in a comfortable, sitting position, administering oxygen, summoning help, and waiting for medical assistance prior to transporting the victim.

Signs and symptoms of cardiac arrest (heart stops) include unconsciousness, no respiration, no pulse, cyanosis, and dilated (expanded) pupils.

First aid for a heart attack includes CPR and the urgent summoning of medical aid.

BAROTRAUMA

Your body contains several rigid or semi-rigid air spaces that are subject to mechanical damage when a pressure differential exists between the air space and the ambient pressure. The pressure

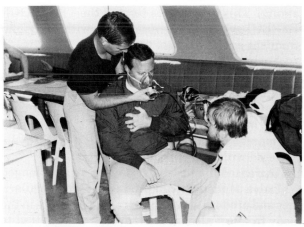

Figure 2.17 First aid for a heart attack patient does not include laying the person down.

differential usually occurs because restricted openings to the air spaces prevent equalization. The structures involved include the middle ear spaces, the paranasal sinuses, the lungs and airways, and the gastrointestinal tract. With the exception of these spaces, the entire body consists of fluids and solids, which for all practical purposes are incompressible.

The middle ear and sinuses are lined with membranes containing tiny blood vessels called CAPILLARIES. When ambient pressure is increased without a corresponding increase in pressure within an air space, the external pressure is transmitted through the body to the blood vessels in the membranes lining these air spaces. Unless equalization of pressure is prompt, EDEMA (tissue swelling) and and tissue damage will occur. Physical damage to the body as a direct result of pressure changes is known as BAROTRAUMA.

Ear Barotrauma

You should be familiar with the anatomy of the ear, which is depicted in the Figure 2.19, and with the basics of middle ear squeezes. The "Valsalva Maneuver" for ear clearing should also be well known to you. This section addresses more advanced aspects of potential middle ear problems and how they can be avoided.

The middle ear is connected to the throat by the EUSTACHIAN TUBE, which serves to drain and ventilate the middle ear. The throat-end of this tube is normally closed and located in very soft tissue. A delay in ear clearing during descent results in the ambient pressure sealing the Eustachian Tube opening closed and preventing equali-

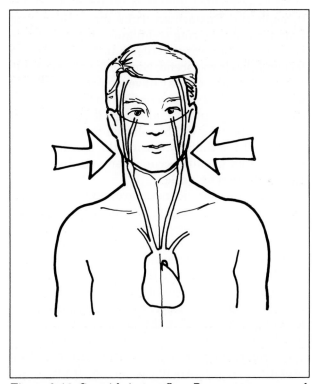

Figure 2.16 Cartoid sinus reflex. Pressure on your neck can slow your heart rate and lead to unconsciousness.

zation. This condition is termed the TRAPDOOR EFFECT which can be prevented with early and frequent equalization of pressures.

Some divers attempt to overcome a trapdoor effect incorrectly by means of a forceful Valsalva Maneuver. This action is ineffective, however, because the increased pressure in the throat caused by the maneuver only serves to seal the tube opening more tightly. There are also several hazards associated with this practice.

Increased lung pressure caused by a prolonged Valsalva Maneuver can produce heart irregularities and produce fainting. Increased pressure in the body from a Valsalva Maneuver is transmitted to the inner ear. With a closed Eustachian Tube and the middle ear at reduced pressure, the pressure differentials can damage or rupture the ROUND WINDOW of the inner ear. If this occurs, fluid from the inner ear will leak into the middle ear, resulting in hearing loss, TINNITUS (ear ringing) and VERTIGO (dizziness). This condition is serious, can result in permanent hearing loss, and must be prevented. Also, too vigorous a Valsalva Maneuver can cause inner ear damage by shearing forces from too rapid a pressure change. Forceful, prolonged attempts to clear your ears must be avoided. Descend slowly, feet first and equalize gently and frequently. Ascend to relieve any discomfort, clear your ears, and continue your descent.

You should be aware of ear clearing techniques which are alternatives for the Valsalva Maneuver and develop the ability to use them. The FRENZEL MANEUVER involves sealing the nose and mouth, contracting various muscles in the mouth to open the Eustachian Tubes and using the tongue as a piston to push air up the tubes. The TOYNBEE MANEUVER involves swallowing with the mouth and nose closed. Jaw movements, tilting the head to the side, and yawning with the mouth closed may also be helpful, as may a combination of various maneuvers.

Failure to equalize pressure in the middle ear creates a pressure differential across the TYPMANIC MEMBRANE (ear drum), which can cause it to rupture with a pressure difference of as little as three psi. If this occurs underwater, cold water rushing into the middle ear can produce vertigo because of thermal effects on the inner ear and semicircular canals, which control your equilibrium. The dizziness can be hazardous, must be avoided, and will subside when the water within the ear has warmed to body temperature. Holding onto a secure object or hugging yourself may help combat dizziness until you can regain equilibrium.

Ted Boehler photo

Figure 2.18 All divers should be able to perform cardiopulmonary resuscitation.

A painful REVERSE BLOCK or REVERSE EAR SQUEEZE occurs when pressure builds in the middle ear during ascent because air cannot escape through the Eustachian Tube for some reason. Standard ear clearing techniques only worsen the situation. The correct action is to descend several feet and slowly re-ascend. Since you will eventually have to ascend, you may have to surface and tolerate the pain until you can receive medical care. The ear drum may rupture, although it is more likely that the pressure will be relieved through the Eustachian Tube than by tearing the ear drum. Reverse blocks usually occur when you dive with a sinus infection or a cold.

Decompression sickness involving the inner ear can also produce vertigo and hearing loss. Ear bends are rare, however, and tend to result from rapid ascents when no-decompression limits have been reached or exceeded. Recreational divers should never experience this malady.

Signs and symptoms of middle ear barotrauma include ear pain, vertigo, hearing loss, ear ringing, a feeling of "fullness" in the ear, and the spitting of blood which may drain into the throat through the Eustachian Tube. Diving should be terminated and prompt treatment should be sought from an ear, nose and throat doctor who understands diving injuries.

DIVING PHYSIOLOGY

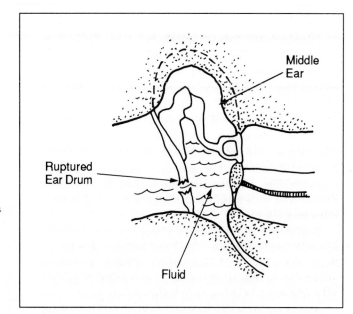

Figure 2.20 The rupture of an
ear drum is a serious and
avoidable injury.

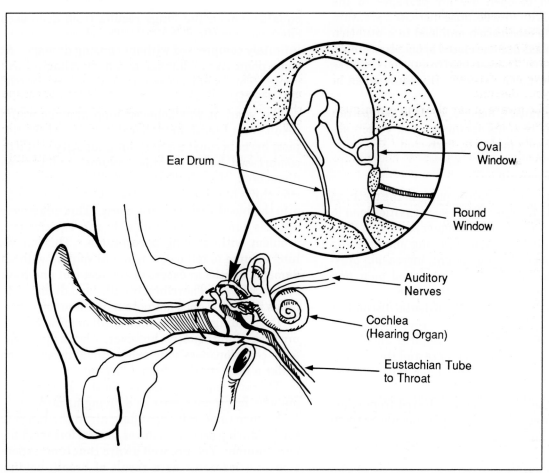

Figure 2.19 Anatomy of the ear.

Sinus Barotrauma

Blockage of the air passages to a paranasal sinus results in a sinus squeeze with painful EDEMA (tissue swelling) and HEMORRHAGE (bleeding) within the sinus cavity. These cavities are located within the skull and are lined with mucous membrane. When ambient pressure exceeds that within the sinus, pressure is transmitted to the sinus membrane lining via the blood, and a vacuum effect is created within the cavity. Without prompt equalization, the capillaries within the mucous membrane will swell and rupture causing severe pain and injury.

Signs and symptoms of sinus squeeze include intense localized pain, blood and mucous discharge from the nose, and headache. Diving activities should be terminated; medical attention is generally required. Aspirin will help relieve pain.

Sinus squeeze can be avoided by refraining from diving when there is nasal congestion as a result of allergy, cold, or infection. Some divers attempt to dive with these conditions by using various medications designed to open the air passages to the sinuses. This is unwise because increased pressure may nullify the medication and lead to a situation where the sinuses become closed spaces containing high pressure air. This can lead to a serious reverse block condition during ascent. Dive only when in good health.

Nasal deformities, masses, cysts or polyps can cause blockage to sinus openings. Many such abnormalities can be medically corrected.

Dental Barotrauma

Tooth decay can create air spaces in the teeth, as can incomplete fillings. When such cavities lead to pressure differentials, a tooth squeeze results. This produces pain due to tissue swelling and bleeding into the air space. During ascent, increasing pressure in the tooth will cause increased pain and bleeding and may even break the tooth.

Diving should be terminated if dental discomfort is experienced. Regular visits to your dentist can prevent dental barotrauma. Aspirin should be given to victims of a tooth squeeze and the patient should be referred to a dentist for repair of the affected tooth.

Pain in a tooth can also be referred from sinus barotrauma because the roots of some upper teeth extend into sinus cavities.

Lung Barotrauma

During breath-hold dives the lungs become compressed with increasing depth. Pressure

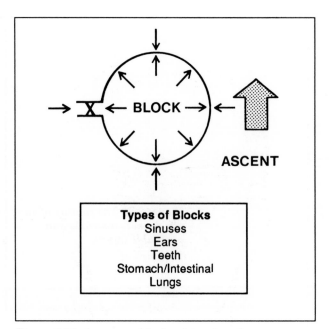

Figure 2.21 A reverse block exists when the pressure within an air space is greater than the surrounding pressure.

equalization in the lungs results from decreased chest volume (Boyle's Law). The chest cannot be infinitely compressed without causing damage. At some point tissue damage and hemorrhaging will occur. This condition is known as a THORACIC SQUEEZE.

For years it was believed lung damage would result from breath-hold dives in excess of five atmospheres because a diver's lung capacity would be compressed below residual volume. It has been discovered, though, that during descent compression shifts blood from the extremities and abdomen into the blood vessels of the chest. This effectively reduces lung volume and aids the equalization problem without lung barotrauma. This allows lung volume to fall below residual volume without damage; depths in excess of 200 feet can and have been achieved. Therefore, breath-hold diving with lungs full of air does not pose a problem for you.

Descending with less than a full inspiration can produce a lung squeeze, however. Also, a diver who loses consciousness may exhale involuntarily and suffer a lung squeeze from a descent.

Thoracic squeeze can be fatal. It is a rare malady, but it does exist as a diving hazard.

Failure to permit expanding air in the lungs to escape during ascent produces several forms of lung barotrauma. You are well aware that lung expansion injuries occur as a result of breath-holding ascents involving compressed air. This section will address the potential injuries in detail.

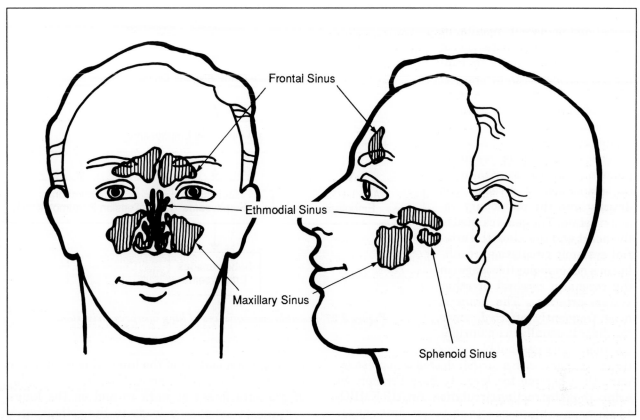

Figure 2.22 Paranasal Sinuses

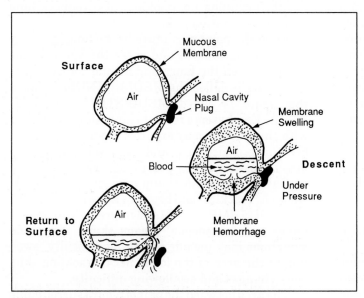

Figure 2.23 Sinus block. Blocked sinuses lead to swelling, bleeding, pain and injury. Diving requires healthy sinuses.

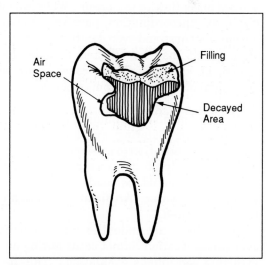

Figure 2.24 Tooth barotrauma. High pressure air beneath an improperly filled tooth can cause pain and discomfort.

Failure to exhale during a scuba diving ascent results in lung overexpansion, distension of the alveoli, and finally in ruptures of the alveoli. Depending on where the rupture occurs, several forms of pulmonary barotrauma may occur, either separately or in combination.

The most serious result of pulmonary overpressurization is the dispersion of alveolar gas directly into the pulmonary venous system. The gas is carried to the heart and then into the arterial systemic circulation, resulting in a gas embolus (blockage) in the coronary, cerebral or other system arteries. The brain is most frequently affected, since the diver is usually in an upright position. The gas bubbles continue to expand with a further decrease in pressure until they become too large to pass through an artery thus obstructing circulation. An AIR EMBOLISM means a blockage of the bloodstream by an air bubble. This injury can result with a pressure change as small as 0.1 ATA (four feet or slightly over one meter).

The signs and symptoms of an air embolism, which are dramatic, sudden and usually occur within seconds of surfacing, are determined by the location of the blockage. Circulation to the heart can be cut off, producing symptoms similar to a heart attack. Frequently, however, the blockage arrests blood flow to the brain. When this occurs, dizziness, uncoordination, paralysis, convulsions, unconsciousness and even death may result. Other organs that may be affected include the liver, spleen, or kidneys. Many cases occur with no development of any symptoms prior to unconsciousness.

First aid involves inclining the victim in a prone position, administering oxygen, and arranging immediate evacuation to a recompression chamber, which is the only effective treatment for the disease. No attempt should be made to recompress the victim in the water. Artificial respiration or CPR may be required.

Many divers are under the impression that lung over-pressurization cannot occur during an ascent involving continuous exhalation. This has been proven an incorrect theory. Lung ailments, deformities, contaminants, etc., can cause airway

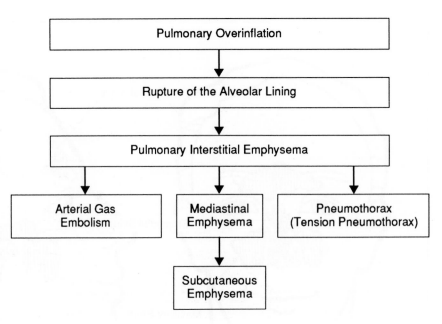

Figure 2.25 Possible consequences of lung overpressurization.

blockage in a portion of the lung; this is sufficient to rupture alveoli in the area. Also, due to a number of pressure forces at work in and on the lungs, continuous exhalation leads to the collapsing of small airways in the lungs. Air in alveoli beyond the collapsed airways will expand as ambient pressure decreases and can lead to ruptures. The recommended breathing cycle for an ascent is a continuous breathing cycle. If no air is available for inhalation, attempted inhalation is sufficient to reopen any airways which may have collapsed. Good health, including no smoking, also reduces lung over-pressurization risks.

From the point of rupture in the lung, gas may dissect along bronchi and enter the space in the chest between the lungs and behind the sternum. This space is called the MEDIASTINUM. Gas in this space is called MEDIASTINAL EMPHYSEMA. Emphysema refers to air in tissues. A diver with this malady may experience substernal pain, breathing difficulties, and even collapse due to direct pressure on the heart and great vessels.

Gas in the mediastinum may rise to the neck, where it "crackles" and becomes known as SUBCUTANEOUS EMPHYSEMA. The prefix "sub" means under and "cutaneous" means skin. Signs and symptoms may include breathing difficulty, swelling in the area of the lower neck, crackling skin, voice changes and swallowing difficulty.

The area between the pair of pleura surrounding each lung is called the pleural cavity. Normally there is no space between the pleura, which simply

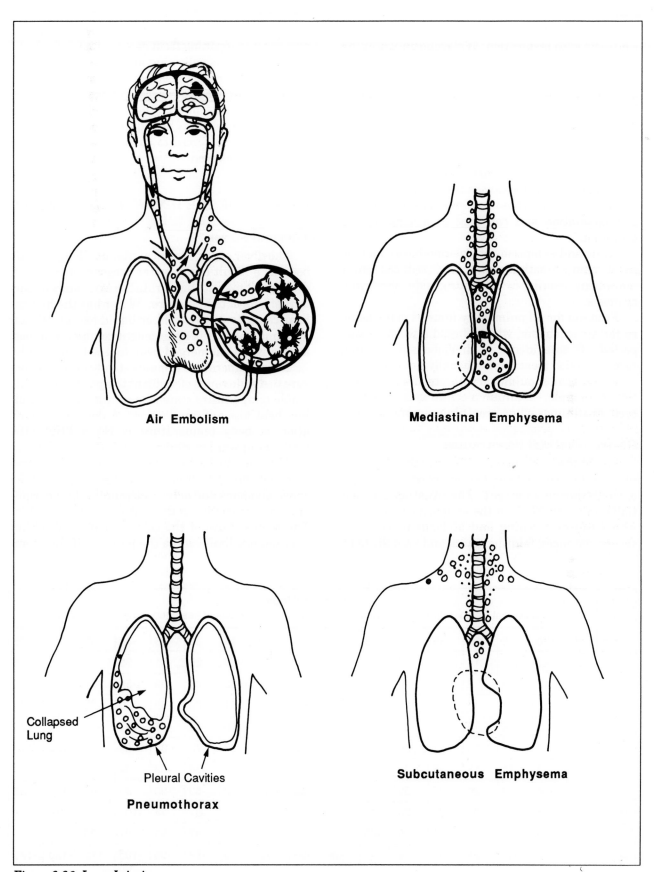

Air Embolism

Mediastinal Emphysema

Collapsed
Lung

Pleural Cavities

Pneumothorax

Subcutaneous Emphysema

Figure 2.26 Lung Injuries

slide against each other as the lung expands and contracts with respiration. If alveoli rupture at the pleura, a tear in the lining may occur. Air can escape into the pleural space and result in the partial or total collapse of the lung. This condition is known as PNEUMOTHORAX, which means air in the chest. "Pneumo" pertains to air, and "thorax" refers to the chest. This malady is an infrequent but serious complication.

If a pneumothorax occurs during ascent, further reduction in pressure causes the air in the pleural space to expand. This interferes with respiration and circulation and can lead to a very serious condition.

Signs and symptoms of pneumothorax include chest pain, breathing difficulty, reduced chest movement, leaning to the injured side, shock and cyanosis.

First aid for all pulmonary injuries is the same as for air emoblism, which should always be suspected. If no evidence of air embolism is found, recompression treatment is usually not needed.

Prevention of pulmonary barotrauma is essential and simple. Maintain a continuous breathing cycle at all times when breathing compressed air.

Gastrointestinal Barotrauma

Foods that produce gas during the digestive process can lead to diver discomfort when such gas expands during an ascent. The situation is essentially a reverse block in the stomach or intestines which causes belching and abdominal pain. In severe instances, fainting, shock and even the tearing of tissues may result. This condition can be avoided by refraining from gas-producing food and drink and from swallowing air while diving.

If you experience gastrointestinal barotrauma during ascent, stop your ascent or descend again to relieve any discomfort, then slowly re-ascend. Medical attention may be required for severe cases where a diver is forced to surface before the pressure can be relieved.

EFFECTS OF THE DIVING ENVIRONMENT

Thermal Stress

The diver expects to encounter challenges to his body as a result of the water pressure involved in diving, but may not be alert to the extremely important effects of temperature. Water has the highest heat capacity of any solid or liquid except lithium and ammonia. It is an excellent conductor of heat and causes a submerged body to lose heat rapidly.

Body temperature remains steady despite exposure to a wide range of ambient temperatures. This stable temperature state is maintained by controlling heat loss and production. A downward variation of body temperature is HYPOTHERMIA while an upward variation is HYPERTHERMIA.

The body can be considered to consist of a central core containing the brain, spinal cord, organs of the chest, abdomen and pelvis, surrounded by a peripheral shell consisting of the limbs, muscles and skin. The temperature of the core is controlled within very narrow limits while the peripheral shell tem-

Wind mph	Wind-Chill Index (Equivalent Temperature)—Equivalent in cooling power on exposed flesh under calm conditions																
Calm	35	30	25	20	15	10	5	0	-5	-10	-15	-20	-25	-30	-35	-40	-45
5	33	27	21	16	12	7	1	-6	-11	-15	-20	-26	-31	-35	-41	-47	-54
10	21	16	9	2	-2	-9	-15	-22	-27	-31	-38	-45	-52	-58	-64	-70	-77
15	16	11	1	-6	-11	-18	-25	-33	-40	-45	-51	-60	-65	-70	-78	-85	-90
20	12	3	-4	-9	-17	-24	-32	-40	-46	-52	-60	-68	-76	-81	-88	-96	-103
25	7	0	-7	-15	-22	-29	-37	-45	-52	-58	-67	-75	-83	-89	-96	-104	-112
30	5	-2	-11	-18	-26	-33	-41	-49	-56	-63	-70	-78	-87	-94	-101	-109	-117
35	3	-4	-13	-20	-27	-35	-43	-52	-60	-67	-72	-83	-90	-98	-105	-113	-123
40	1	-4	-15	-22	-29	-36	-45	-54	-62	-69	-76	-87	-94	-101	-107	-116	-128
45	1	-6	-17	-24	-31	-38	-46	-54	-63	-70	-78	-87	-94	-101	-108	-118	-128
50	0	-7	-17	-24	-31	-38	-47	-56	-63	-70	-79	-88	-96	-103	-110	-120	-128

Table 2.2 Wind-chill index. Wind speeds greater than 40 mph have little additional chilling effect.

DIVING PHYSIOLOGY

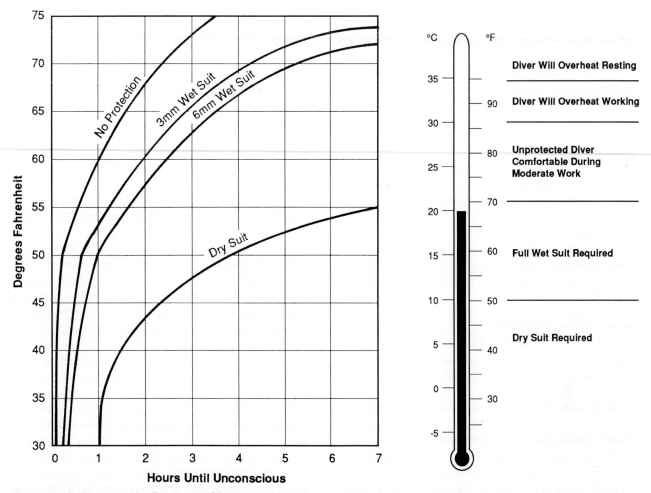

Figure 2.27 Temperature Protection Charts

perature is subject to variation. Normally, the core is warmer than the periphery. The heat which the body uses to maintain the core temperature results from basal metabolism plus the heat produced by exercise. Heat production can increase only as a result of muscular activity or shivering. Unfortunately, in some circumstances this activity may lead to increased heat loss.

Heat transfer occurs by physical means whenever there is a temperature gradient and always moves from the system with the higher temperature to the system with the lower temperature.

Hypothermia

Exposure to cold results in body chilling at a rate dependent on many factors. The rate of heat loss will depend on the initial amount of stored heat and the body shape. The head, groin and chest wall beneath the arm pits are the areas of the greatest heat loss. The rate of loss also depends on whether the individual is wet or dry, protected or unprotected.

Features of Hypothermia

An individual suddenly exposed to very cold water with no thermal protection will experience immediate disabling effects. As immersion occurs, there is a sudden involuntary inspiration or gasping response which may lead to inhalation of water. This response continues for one to two minutes with an extremely rapid breathing rate which the victim cannot control. As time progresses, there is decrease in muscle strength, accompanied by pain and mental disorganization, with fear and panic reaction developing.

If the individual has some thermal protection, upon exposure to cold water the immediate effects will not be as severe. However, heat loss will occur. Exercise or shivering will increase heat production, but the agitation of water by the activity increases heat loss; the result is a loss of body heat and drop in core temperature. Exercise increases the heat loss much more at low than high water temperatures and always increases the rate of body heat loss. It is futile to attempt to stay warm by exercise.

Therefore, caution should be observed in attempts at self-rescue by swimming, as heat loss will be accelerated.

As hypothermia progresses and the core temperature falls, the individual will show predictable effects which loosely correspond to the core temperature.

Mild Hypothermia

95-98.6 degrees Fahrenheit: sensation of cold, shivering, increased heart rate, urge to urinate, slight uncoordination in hand movements.

Moderate Hypothermia

90-95 degrees Fahrenheit: increasing muscular uncoordination, stumbling gait, shivering slows or stops, weakness, apathy, drowsiness, confusion, slurred speech.

Severe Hypothermia

85-90 degrees Fahrenheit: shivering stops, inability to walk or follow commands, paradoxical undressing, complaints of loss of vision, and confusion progressing to coma.

85 degrees Fahrenheit or lower: muscle rigidity, decreased blood pressure, heart rate, and respirations, dilated pupils, appearance of death.

65 degrees Fahrenheit: man begins to take on the temperature of the environment.

Hypothermia can also occur in relatively warm or even tropical waters. Scientific divers have experienced fatigue with impaired awareness and judgment as a result of slow body cooling while preoccupied with the task at hand. Very little is known about the effects of long, slow body cooling and the development of undetected hypothermia. This may occur in individuals with no protection in 82-91 degrees Fahrenheit water or wearing a wet suit in cooler water. The skin temperature remains near the comfort zone at 91 degrees Fahrenheit and the insidious heat drain from the body by the cooler water is scarcely noticed until core temperature drops enough to induce shivering. In some cases, shivering does not occur. The diver may not recognize the problem, but it is usually expressed as a reluctance to dive. Recreational divers may encounter this phenomenon during repeated vacation dives with no thermal protection in warm water and suddenly find themselves very tired with no desire to continue their vacation diving plans.

Management of Hypothermia

Suspecting the existence of hypothermia is the first step in management. Hypothermia may be mild with little risk to the individual or severe with death a possibility. The mildly hypothermic individual will be awake, complaining of cold, possibly shivering, and able to converse intelligently. The moderately hypothermic individual will be awake, but may be confused, apathetic or uncooperative, and may have difficulty with speech. If severely hypothermic, the victim may be unconscious with slow heart rate and respiration or may even appear dead with no detectable heart beat. The victim who is moderately or severely hypothermic may be made worse or placed in cardiac arrest by careless attempts at re-warming. Hypothermia is an emergency in slow motion and may not be harmful to the individual unless the heart stops. The cold heart is especially sensitive, and victims alive when found may develop cardiac arrest if handled roughly during the initial evaluation and transportation. The rescuer has the responsibility to transport and re-warm without precipitating cardiac arrest.

Re-warming is of extreme importance, of course, but should not be attempted unless it can be done properly. However, it sometimes becomes necessary to re-warm a hypothermic victim in an area far from medical care. The first attempts should use passive methods, including protection against further heat loss by removing wet clothing and covering in layers. Do not forget to provide layers between the victim and the ground or deck and to cover the head which is a major source of heat loss. The fully alert and cooperative victim may be given warm liquids to drink; this will deliver negligible amounts of heat, but will help to correct the dehydration. Coffee, tea, caffeine drinks and alcohol should be strictly avoided. Oral fluids may include balanced electrolyte solutions such as Gatorade, Gastriolyte or Infalyte, which are available in powder form. If the victim is awake, he/she should not be exercised; muscular activity will bring cold blood from the periphery to the core. The mildly or moderately hypothermic victim will soon return to a near normal temperature.

Immersion of the victim in a hot bath was thought to be risky unless limited to the trunk only with the extremities left out. Similarly, body-to-body contact has been limited to bare skin in the trunk area only. Current research indicates that the victim will not have increased cooling of the heart on immersion, limbs and all, in a hot bath.

The severely hypothermic victim may be unconscious or appear dead. Look very carefully for signs of life such as breathing, movement or a pulse at the groin or in the neck over the carotid artery. If breathing or movement is present, the heart is beat-

beating and CPR is not needed. If the breathing rate is six or less per minute, then very gentle mouth-to-mouth breathing at a slow rate may be started while being extremely careful to avoid rough handling of the victim.

If there are no signs of life, CPR and arrangements for emergency transport to the nearest medical facility should be started. Re-warming of the severely hypothermic victim cannot be accomplished in the field! CPR should be continued, if possible, until emergency assistance is obtained. There have been successful resuscitations after prolonged CPR, in part because of the protective effect of hypothermia.

The prevention of hypothermia requires training, judgment and experience. The diver must understand the use of external insulation to conserve body heat and must be able to control heat loss. Recreational divers sometimes encounter very cold conditions in ice diving or winter diving in deep quarries and lakes. All ocean dives are in water below body temperature. Wet suits provide some degree of thermal protection depending on the style, material, and thickness, but they become compressed with increasing depth and lose much of their insulating properties. The "wooly bear" or open cell undergarment worn under a dry suit is

effective, but also compresses and loses some insulation value. If wet, the "wooly bear" loses practically all of its insulating value.

Prevention of hypothermia also includes a preparation for unexpected immersion. Divers traveling by boat to the dive site should have a flotation device available other than their diving equipment. The personal flotation device (PFD) should be designed to keep the wearer afloat with no effort on his/her part, must keep the head out of water, and be self-righting. The diver should practice using the PFD ahead of time to become familiar with its use. Seat cushions or flotation devices which require the victim to hold on are not satisfactory in cold water, as hypothermia will cause the loss of muscle power, and the victim will lose his/her grip. The diver should be prepared for actions to be taken once in the water. These include efforts to minimize heat loss, such as remaining still and assuming the H.E.L.P. position (heat escape lessening position). This position is assumed by drawing the knees up to the chest and holding with crossed arms. The position is unstable and not easy to achieve without practice as one tends to roll forward or backward. Consequently, it is well to practice the position from time to time. The huddle position with other persons is surprisingly effective in con-

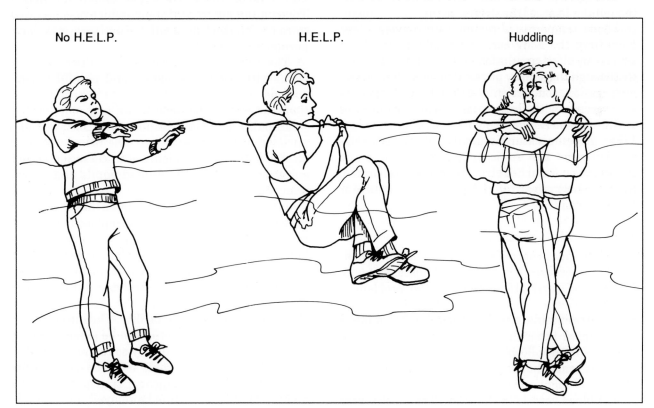

Figure 2.28 H.E.L.P. Position. Cover the high heat loss areas to preserve body heat.

serving heat. Everyone wraps arms around one another and pulls into a tight circle, remaining as still as possible.

The psychological preparedness of knowing what to expect if suddenly immersed in cold water, how to use flotation, and how to stay put and wait for rescue will significantly increase the chances for survival.

Hyperthermia

High environmental temperatures are capable of producing illness in otherwise healthy persons. The diver is not very likely to develop a problem as a result of high environmental temperatures while diving. However, conditions at the dive site may produce a heat-related illness. A diver working at a high energy output while in water near or above body temperature is at risk. There have been injuries and deaths in recompression chambers when divers were subjected to high temperatures due to inadequate environmental control.

The body produces heat as a result of metabolism; if the heat is transferred to the environment, the body temperature remains unchanged. The heat from the body core is brought to the body surface by blood circulation and eliminated primarily through the skin by physical means—radiation, evaporation, conduction or convection. If there is interference with this process, heat accumulates within the body and the core temperature rises. When air temperature is equal or above body temperature and the air is humid with little or no breeze, the normal heat transfer process is blocked. Such conditions lead to a rising body temperature or hyperthermia.

Features of Hyperthermia

As the heat control mechanisms fail and heat overload increases, a spectrum of illnesses appears. During the early stages most of the problem is related to water loss because the body has attempted to eliminate heat by sweating. The mildest heat-related illness is heat cramp as a result of muscle spasm following exercise. A more severe illness is heat exhaustion which may be a mild form of shock brought on by dehydration and the dilatation of blood vessels in the skin. The most severe problem is heatstroke (sometimes called sunstroke)

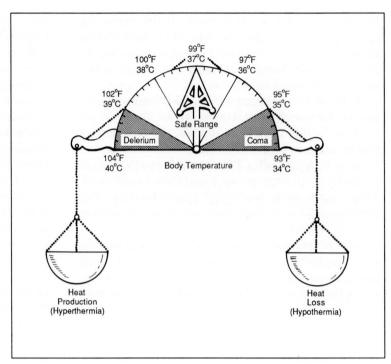

Figure 2.29 Body temperature must be maintained within a narrow range.

which develops as the temperature regulating mechanisms fail completely and body temperature may rise to 105 degrees Fahrenheit or higher. There is damage to vital organs which may progress to coma followed by death. Survivors may have permanent brain damage.

The symptoms of heat-related illness usually begin with profuse sweating and painful muscle spasms. As the problem increases to heat exhaustion, the victim becomes weak and pale, with a weak pulse and rapid respiration. Dizziness and unconsciousness may occur. The next level, heat stroke, may occur suddenly with cessation of perspiration, hot dry skin, dilated pupils and unconsciousness.

Emergency care for heat-related illness requires protection from further injury, replacement of the water loss, and reduction of body temperature. The individual with mild symptoms can be removed to a cool place and his water deficit corrected by drinking water or a balanced electrolyte solution. When symptoms are more severe, the victim should be transported to a medical facility. During transportation, the conscious victim can be given fluids by mouth and kept flat or nearly so to prevent shock. The victim who has become semi-conscious or unconscious is a true emergency; transportation to a medical facility should not be delayed. Measures to reduce body temperature should be started immediately at the scene. The victim should have his clothing removed. He may then be wrapped in a sheet, soaked with cold water and fanned vigorously to reduce body temperature. Ice can be applied to the groin, armpits and neck. Do not give a semi-conscious or unconscious person anything by mouth. Protect the airway at all times.

Prevention of Hyperthermia

Heat-related illness can be avoided by proper attention to water intake and protection from environmental heat. Sweat contains salt; however, the major threat is the loss of water. A normal individual will obtain enough salt in their diet so a salt supplement is rarely necessary. If heat exposure is to occur for many hours, commercial electrolyte solutions provide adequate salt. Salt tablets are too concentrated and may irritate the stomach, causing vomiting. The normal kidney is very efficient in conserving salt; the risk of salt depletion in heat-related illness has been overstated. The body can tolerate extreme temperatures when provided with adequate water. Great quantities of fluid are needed to replace that lost through the sweating mechanism. Water intake should be about six to ten fluid ounces every 20 minutes during heavy exertion under excessively warm conditions. The very young, very old or those impaired by alcohol or recreational drug usage, are at increased risk. Repeated exposure to heat causes a gradual adjustment, resulting in the ability to tolerate heat stress much better than when first exposed. The physically fit person tolerates heat exposure better than one in poor physical condition.

Hypothermia beyond the level of feeling cold should not be experienced. Excessive heat loss can be prevented with an appropriate exposure suit for diving, proper nutrition to meet heat production needs, the avoidance of alcohol, and the avoidance of currents.

The prefix "hypo" means less than normal, while hyper means more than normal. Just as hypothermia is dangerous, so is HYPERTHERMIA, or body heat greater than normal. Divers insulate their bodies to minimize heat loss. This can lead to the retention of body heat unless the diver is wet or immersed.

Prolonged wearing of an exposure suit out of the water on a hot day can lead to HEAT EXHAUSTION, a response characterized by fatigue, weakness and collapse due to inadequate fluid intake to compensate for loss of fluids through perspiration. Symptoms include pale and clammy skin, profuse sweating, fatigue and weakness, headache, nausea,

Figure 2.30 Overheated Diver

and fainting. First aid involves lying the victim down, cooling them and administering fluids.

MOTION SICKNESS

Sea sickness can ruin diving trips, vacations, and travel. It prevents many divers from even attempting adventures involving travel by boat. Unfortunately, susceptibility to motion sickness is universal, although the amount of motion required to produce the problem varies among individuals. No one is immune. Motion sickness can be induced in anyone by sufficient angular acceleration. Fortunately, there are ways of avoiding motion sickness by controlling the factors which produce it.

Motion sickness is primarily nausea, which is a result of the brain's inability to resolve conflicting signals that it is receiving from the ears, eyes, and the body. The balance organs of the ears are stimulated by the repeated angular acceleration of the vessel while the signal from the eyes is that of no motion if there has been loss of visual contact with the outside horizon. The sensors of body position are sending still another signal and the brain is unable to resolve the conflict. Anxiety, confusion and dismay result leading to the first symptoms of yawning, pallor and headache, followed by nausea and vomiting, a fear response and palpitations.

The prevention of motion sickness is more successful than treatment after the onset of symptoms. Position in the vessel is very important. The susceptible individual should remain on deck at the point of least motion (usually the center) and maintain visual contact with the horizon. A position near the bow will allow a person to remain oriented with the motion of the vessel relative to the water and the fixed horizon, but the motion will be greater than near the center. Do not sit on the bow with feet hanging over the edge because of the danger of falling. If visual contact is not possible, then the eyes should be kept closed. It is important to move away from other individuals experiencing motion sickness. Psychological support from companions is helpful for the individual and the group.

A diver may develop motion sickness during a dive because of interference with spatial orientation. A common cause is the motion from surge encountered during an entry from shore into the ocean accompanied by loss of visual clues in the poor visibility usually found in such conditions. Neutral buoyancy distorts the clues provided by gravity and the brain is unable to reconcile the abnormal sensory input. Motion sickness develops and may

Figure 2.31 Seasickness may be prevented by getting fresh air, sitting near the middle of the vessel, watching the horizon or closing the eyes, or with wrist pressure bands.

result in the necessity of vomiting through a regulator. The safety of the diver under these conditions is seriously impaired. A panic reaction could easily occur. The experienced diver will recognize clues which provide spatial orientation. Entering and exiting along a line is important if visibility is poor and the bottom cannot be seen. Exhaust bubbles move toward the surface and weight belts drag toward the bottom in response to gravity. Likewise, the chest will rise and the feet sink if the diver is not swimming. The inadequately trained diver will not be aware of these clues and may ignore them during a panic situation.

Prevention of motion sickness requires adequate rest before a trip, avoiding dietary and alcohol excesses, and following the guidelines discussed here.

DISORIENTATION AND VERTIGO

On land you have several means to maintain equilibrium. These include visual reference, pressure differences on joints and the center of balance in the inner ear. Your ability to remain oriented to your surroundings is much more limited when you are weightless underwater, especially when visibility is restricted by turbidity or low light levels. Your principal means of orientation while diving is the reference provided by a series of semi-circular canals in your inner ear. This is called your VESTIBULAR SYSTEM.

Your semi-circular ear canals are oriented along different planes. They contain fluid and sensors to sense the orientation of the fluid. The relationship of the fluid to the sensors provides information that your brain uses as points of reference for equilibrium.

Signals of equilibrium to your brain can be distorted by body positioning, visual contradictions, lack of reference, pressure changes and caloric stimulation. The effect of each of these is a feeling of vertigo or dizziness, which results in disorientation. You literally do not know which way is up. Obviously, this hazard must be prevented. The following information explains how equilibrium can be affected by diving and how the risk of disorientation can be minimized.

Vertigo can result from unequal stimulations of your ears. These stimulations can be differences in temperature or pressure. If cold water enters one ear and not the other, as may be the case if a hood is worn or there is an accumulation of ear wax in one ear canal, vertigo may result. This condition is intensified if the diver is in a head-down position, so feet-first descents are advised.

If one ear equalizes with ambient pressure and the other ear does not, the unequal stimulation can produce vertigo. This is more pronounced if the pressure change is sudden. When there is a pressure build up in an ear during ascent (reverse block), the sudden release of pressure can produce dizziness. This condition is known as ALTERNO-BARIC VERTIGO.

Excessive force used for ear clearing can cause vestibular damage and produce vertigo. Failure to equalize middle ear spaces can result in perforation of the ear drum, allowing cold water rush into the middle ear and stimulate the vestibular system, producing sudden and intense vertigo.

Diving when deprived of a reference at night or in very turbid water can result in disorientation, as can remaining in the swirling waters of a halocline. These situations are compounded in the presence of surge.

Should vertigo be experienced while diving, stop, grasp a stationary object for reference, and wait for the dizziness to pass. If the problem persists, terminate diving and seek medical assistance. If vertigo occurs in mid-water where there is nothing to grasp, hugging yourself may provide some assistance. The value of a nearby buddy in such instances is apparent.

DEHYDRATION

Water comprises the greater part of the blood. Abnormal loss of fluid from the body is termed DEHYDRATION, which occurs when you take in less fluid than you lose in urine, exhaled moisture, and perspiration. Dehydration problems compounded by diving can predispose divers to other diving ailments, especially decompression sickness.

Overheating during diving preparations can cause profuse sweating and loss of fluids. This should be avoided by working in shaded areas and by wetting down to remain cool.

The effects of cold on the body, combined with the effort required to suck air from a regulator (negative pressure breathing), stimulate divers to urinate more frequently than normal. This response is called DIURESIS. Substances that increase the output of urine by the kidneys are DIURETICS and include coffee, tea, etc. Divers should avoid diuretics before and during diving and should drink fluids before and between dives to offset the diuretic effects of diving.

Scuba air is dehydrated. You increase the humidity of inspired air to 100%, and this moisture is drawn from your body. This is another reason why the replacement of body fluids during diving activities is required.

INFECTIONS

Infections from injuries, aspirated water or water in body cavities can occur. Illnesses can and should be prevented with immunizations and preventive measures. Innoculations for water-borne diseases, such as typhoid, should be kept current.

Figure 2.33 Proper descent techniques help minimize disorientation.

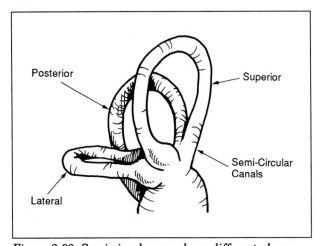

Figure 2.32 Semi-circular canals on different planes provide reference for equalibrium.

Table 2.3
Definitions of Diving Medical Terms

1.	Alveolus	A small membranous sac which is the end portion of the respiratory system in the lung wherein the gaseous exchange takes place.
2.	Anoxia	Absence of oxygen.
3.	Apnea	The cessation of breathing for short intervals of time.
4.	Asphyxia	The existence of both hypoxia and hypercapnia in the body.
5.	Barodontalgia	Pain in teeth associated with changes in barometric pressure.
6.	Barotrauma	Physical damage to the body as a direct result of pressure changes.
7.	Bradycardia	Slowness of the heartbeat.
8.	Bronchi	Fibromuscular tubes connecting the trachea to the smaller portions of the respiratory tract.
9.	Carotid Sinus	A small dilatation in the carotid artery just below its bifurcation that is surrounded by an extensive nerve network, and which is sensitive to pressure changes within the carotid artery, ensuring that arterial pressure is maintained at a suitable level.
10.	Chemoreceptor	Carotid and aortic bodies sensitive to changes in the partial pressures of oxygen and carbon dioxide in the blood which play an important part in the regulation of respiration.
11.	Cyanosis	A bluish discoloration of the skin from insufficient oxygenation of the blood.
12.	Dysbarism	A general term applied to any clinical condition caused by a difference between the surrounding atmospheric pressure and the total gas pressure in the various tissues, fluids, and body cavities.
13.	Diuresis	Excessive excretion of urine.
14.	Dyspnea	Difficulty in breathing.
15.	Edema	Swelling caused by excessive amounts of fluid in tissues.
16.	Embolus	A plug brought by the blood from one vessel and forced into a smaller one so as to obstruct the circulation.
17.	Emphysema	A swelling or inflation caused by the presence of air or other gas in body tissues.
18.	Eustachian Tube	The canal, partly bony and partly cartilaginous, connecting the throat (pharynx) with the middle ear (tympanic cavity), serving as an air channel by which air pressure within the middle ear is equalized with that outside.
19.	Exhalation	Expelling air from the lungs.
20.	Expiratory Reserve	The amount of air that can be exhaled from the lungs after normal expiration.
21.	External Ear	That portion of the ear from the outermost portion to the tympanic membrane, encompassing the external canal.
22.	Hemoglobin	A component of red blood cells that combines with oxygen, carbon dioxide or carbon monoxide.
23.	Hemorrhage	The loss of blood from the vascular system.
24.	Hypercapnia	Undue amount of carbon dioxide in the blood, causing over-activity in the respiratory center.
25.	Hyperventilation	Breathing excessively fast.
26.	Hypothermia	The lowering of the body's core temperature below normal.
27.	Hypoventilation	Inadequate ventilation of the lungs.
28.	Hypoxia	Failure of the tissues to receive enough oxygen.

29. **Inner Ear**	That portion of the ear located within the bony confines of the temporal bone, containing the organs of equilibrium and hearing.
30. **Inhalation**	Drawing air into the lungs.
31. **Inspiratory Reserve**	The maximum amount of air that can be breathed in after normal inspiration.
32. **Mediastinum**	That portion of the chest cavity located between the right and left lungs, containing the heart, the major vessels and some of the major nerves traversing from the neck to the abdomen.
33. **Middle Ear**	That portion of the ear between the tympanic membrane and the bony enclosure of the semi-circular canals. This portion contains the three bony ossicles for the transmission of the movement of the tympanic membrane and also contains the opening of the Eustachian canal.
34. **Normoxic**	A breathing gas mixture that supplies the diver with a "normal" partial pressure of oxygen, about 0.21 ATA, at any specific depth.
35. **pH**	A symbol representing hydrogen ion concentration in a fluid, thus indicating acidity or alkalinity. A pH of 7 is neutral. Less than 7 is acidic, and more than 7 is basic or alkaline.
36. **Pleura**	Two layers of thin membrane surrounding the lungs.
37. **Pneumothorax**	The presence of air or gas in the pleural cavity resulting from a rupture of an alveolus, which allows the pleural space to come into equilibrium with the external pressure.
38. **Residual Volume**	The amount of air left in the lungs after a maximal expiratory effort.
39. **Sinuses**	Cavities within the bones of the skull lined by epithelium and connected by small openings to the nasal passageways.
40. **Tachycardia**	Excessive rapidity of heart beat.
41. **Thrombus**	A plug or clot in a blood vessel or in one of the cavities of the heart.
42. **Tidal Volume**	The amount of air breathed in and out of the lungs during normal respiration.
43. **Tinnitus**	Ringing in the ear.
44. **Trachea**	That portion of the breathing apparatus that extends from the posterior oropharynx or the posterior portion of the mouth to the chest cavity.
45. **Tympanic Membrane**	A thin membranous partition (eardrum) separating the external ear from the middle ear.
46. **Vital Capacity**	Maximum volume of air which can be expired after maximal inhalation.

Tetanus prevention should be considered if wounded. Infections of the external ear canal (swimmer's ear) should be prevented by irrigating the ear with an appropriate solution after diving.

PHYSICAL FITNESS FOR SCUBA DIVING—By R. Weathers

Physical fitness can be defined as the ability to perform physical activity. Diving fitness is the ability to perform diving-related tasks. Physical fitness has many interrelated components such as medical and nutritional status, strength, endurance, flexibility, and skill. A high level of physical fitness reduces your vulnerability to the potential hazards of diving, and it allows you to safely and effortlessly enjoy a variety of diving experiences.

The purpose of this chapter is to consider some of the factors which can significantly affect ability to meet the physical demands commonly imposed by scuba diving. We will identify medical conditions which make diving unsafe, we will discuss the effects of drugs and foods, and we will present guidelines for improving selected components of physical fitness.

Health Requirements for Diving

Physical contraindications to diving are physical characteristics which make it impossible or unwise to engage in the sport. Conditions are generally considered absolute contraindications if they risk the loss of consciousness, significantly restrict physical exertion, or prevent the lungs, middle ears, or sinuses from equalizing pressure. Most authorities also place pregnancy in the category of conditions which absolutely rule out diving.

Determination of medical fitness for diving typically begins with examination of a diver's medical history form. For young, apparently healthy candidates for instruction, this review is usually performed by a diving instructor. Complete medical exams and physician approval are required for all applicants with questionable histories. The medical exam is desirable for all prospective divers— particularly males over 35 years of age and those with family histories of conditions of concern in diving safety. Common tests include resting and exercise electrocardiograms (ECGs) to screen for cardiovascular disease and exercise tolerance, chest x-rays and pulmonary function tests to determine lung health, blood and urine tests for infec-

Figure 2.34 A medical exam is recommended at least every other year.

tious and metabolic disorders, and examination of the eyes, ears, nose, and throat.

Cardiovascular Disorders

In spite of encouraging improvements in the past few years, more than half of all deaths in the United States are the result of heart and blood vessel diseases. There are many disorders in this category—some are congenital (you are born with them) and some are acquired over a period of time. The two most common causes of death are acquired cardiovascular diseases, heart attack and stroke. Both of these typically result from the process of arterosclerosis which gradually narrows the arteries to the point that blood flow is stopped. When this occurs in the coronary arteries serving the heart muscle, it is called coronary artery disease (CAD) or coronary heart disease (CHD) and the result is a heart attack. When blood flow to the brain is stopped by plugging of the cerebral arteries, the condition is called cerebrovascular disease (CVD) and a stroke occurs.

Both of these conditions are rare in individuals below 40 years of age, but they have become of increasing concern as the diving population has aged. Family history, age, and gender seem to play significant roles in determining risk for arterosclerosis; you obviously have no choice in these matters. However, there are many other significant risk factors over which you do have control. The three major ones are high blood cholesterol, high blood pressure (hypertension), and smoking.

The arterosclerotic process typically begins in childhood and must be very significantly advanced to show symptoms. For about half of the people who have CAD, the first known symptom is a heart attack; sudden death is the result in about half of these cases. Screening for latent (asymptomatic) heart disease is obviously of great importance in determining the medical fitness of males in the coronary prone years—over 40. Resting ECGs are of some value in this regard, but they often fail to reveal abnormalities which will show up on an exercise stress test. An annual stress test is recommended if you have several known risk factors.

If you have suffered a heart attack and have undergone corrective procedures, it may be possible to initiate or resume diving activities. As in most cases, there is not unanimous agreement among physicians. However, some feel that diving is perfectly safe if you can perform at a moderately high level on a stress test without pain, contrary ECG, or irregular blood pressure response.

Similarly, there are several types of heart murmurs and ECG abnormalities which show up in routine medical exams but do not rule out diving. A history of rheumatic fever is of some concern, but resulting cardiovascular effects may not prevent diving. Your physician will make the judgment on the basis of whether or not there is risk of dangerous heart rhythm or limitation of exercise tolerance.

Pulmonary Disorders

With the exception of cancer and emphysema, disorders of the lungs are not particularly common causes of death in the normal population. However, diving creates concern over any condition which temporarily or permanently blocks the escape of air from the lungs. Chest x-rays, pulmonary function tests and listening to the chest with a stethoscope all shed light on the condition of your lungs. These tests can determine lung status only at the time of the exam. There is debate in the medical community regarding the frequency with which these tests should be administered to divers.

Some people are born with, but are never aware of, lung abnormalities which are incompatible with scuba diving. Many other people acquire disorders as a result of infection, environmental pollution, smoking, and other circumstances. These disorders prohibit diving only if they prevent normal ventilation of the lungs or limit exercise tolerance. Asthma, chronic bronchitis, emphysema, and other obstructive lung diseases are among the most common contraindications. The effects of childhood

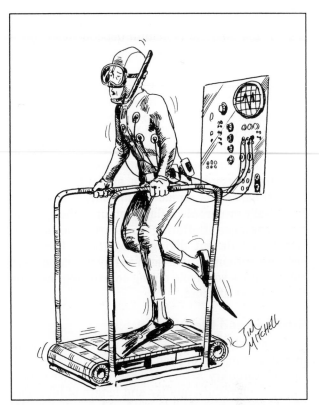

Figure 2.35 A stress test is a good idea for those over 40 who would like to dive.

asthma are frequently outgrown—so adults with a history of asthma may sometimes receive medical clearance to dive.

Temporary conditions such as bronchitis, colds, and flu may not be present at the time of a diving medical exam. However, they may restrict the airways enough to prevent expanding air from being vented during a scuba diving ascent. Even though you breathe normally, ascend slowly, and have normally healthy lungs, these conditions could result in fatal lung overexpansion injuries.

Nervous System Disorders

There are many abnormal conditions of the nervous system which may show up on a diver's medical history or examination. Several of these are of potential danger in diving, but epilepsy is the most common disorder of major concern. Epileptic seizures are an obvious threat to diving safety and are cause for exclusion from diving.

Metabolic Disorders

Many diseases of the kidneys, liver, and endocrine glands may temporarily or permanently prevent you from diving. However, diabetes mellitus is a relatively common disorder which is generally considered an absolute contraindication for diving—if the diabetic is insulin-dependent or has a history of hypoglycemic episodes.

Ear and Sinus Disorders

Some individuals are born with abnormal passages to the middle ears and/or sinuses. These may make it difficult or impossible to equalize pressure on descent, and attempting to dive may result in severe pain, damage to related tissue, complications from secondary infection, and/or hearing loss. Similar hazards occur more commonly as a result of temporary or chronic inflammation of the ear and sinus passages. Suffering from chronic inflammation may rule out diving altogether. However, seasonal inflammations such as hay fever and head colds require you avoid diving only during the time that you are affected.

Smoking and the Diver

It is well established that cigarette smoking increases the risk of bronchitis, emphysema, lung cancer, coronary artery disease, and other conditions which reduce quality and length of life. The effects of pressure changes and cold exposure make these diseases much more hazardous for divers than for the population in general.

Years of heavy cigarette smoking are usually required for the above-mentioned disorders to develop, but there are also immediate, temporary negative effects of smoking which should be of special concern to divers. Smoking a single cigarette typically irritates the airways—leading to excess mucous secretion, airway spasm, and increased resistance to airflow. This could result in possible trapping of air and lung over-expansion injuries. Smoking is also likely to elevate blood carbon monoxide levels to the point of limiting oxygen delivery and exercise tolerance. When combined with the coronary-artery-narrowing and heart-beat-increasing effects of nicotine, this also increases the risk of heart attack. The risk is particularly real under conditions of cold exposure so common to diving.

If you don't smoke, don't start. If you do smoke, consider cutting back or stopping. At the least, refrain from smoking for several hours before diving!

Drugs and the Diver

Divers take a variety of drugs for a variety of reasons. Any drug which should not be used when driving a motor vehicle or operating machinery should not be used when diving. The added effects of cold and pressure often make diving even more dangerous after taking drugs. Alterations in heart and nerve cell membranes may cause a drug to have a dangerously different effect on a diver.

Alcohol—You already know that alcohol impairs alertness, coordination, and judgment and is associated with increased risk of a variety of accidents. The effects of cold, nitrogen narcosis, and other diving factors magnify the negative effects of alcohol on judgment and performance. Alcohol also causes constriction of arteries serving the heart and dilation of vessels to the skin. The results are potential heart problems and excessive heat loss—increasing the risk of hypothermia. These facts make it obvious that drinking before diving is unwise, but it is also potentially hazardous following a dive. If you drink heavily after diving, you may be unaware of decompression sickness or other symptoms which sometimes develop during the after-dive hours.

Amphetamines—Speed and other stimulant drugs are dangerous enough on land and have been

Contaminant	Maximum Allowance for Surface Air	Maximum Allowance for Compressed Air for Diving	Cigarette Smoke
Carbon Monoxide	100 ppm	10 ppm	42,000 ppm
Saturated Hydrocarbon	500 ppm	50 ppm	87,000 ppm
Unsaturated Hydrocarbon	5,000 ppm	50 ppm	31,000 ppm
Acetone	200 ppm	No Detectable Trace	1,100 ppm
Formaldehyde	5 ppm	No Detectable Trace	30 ppm

Figure 2.36 The hazards of smoking are great, especially for divers.

Figure 2.37 No drugs or alcohol for divers

found to reduce coordination, judgment, and problem-solving ability under hyperbaric conditions. They also can dangerously alter heart rhythm and mask symptoms of fatigue.

Antihistamines—A variety of antihistamines is found in commonly used medications. Because of their negative effects on alertness and performance, they carry warnings against use before or during demanding activities. Blurred vision and excessively dry mouth have also been reported as effects of antihistamines during diving.

Caffeine—Coffee, tea, and several soft drinks contain this stimulant. It increases alertness but also may cause anxiousness, trembling, heartburn, irregular heart rhythm, and slight elevation of blood pressure and heart rate. Like alcohol, caffeine is a diuretic—it causes fluid loss by increasing urination. For this reason, there have been some warnings of increased risk of decompression sickness with caffeine use.

Cocaine—This currently popular social drug would be dangerous enough for divers if it just caused the characteristic alternations in mental function. However, it also is known to elevate blood pressure and heart rate, increase the sensitivity of the brain and heart, and accelerate the development of arterosclerosis. There are medical reports of heart attacks suffered by individuals in their 20s and 30s following use of cocaine.

Marijuana—Marijuana has many of the combined effects of alcohol and tobacco smoking, and some of these effects seem to be more pronounced with increased diving depth.

Medicinal Drugs—Divers suffer from most of the ailments common to people in general, and they sometimes desire relief from their symptoms in order to dive. The first thing you should consider in this situation is whether or not you should be diving in your present condition. Diving under the influence of medication may make a bad situation even worse. There are a host of medicines which may be used to deal with diarrhea, ear/sinus congestion, seasickness and other maladies. Some are clearly dangerous to use when diving, and others are relatively safe for most individuals. Consult your diving physician about side effects or interactions, which might range from drowsiness to increased sensitivity to the sun. Remember, sport diving should be engaged in only when your personal condition is appropriate to the probable demands of the planned dive! Ask yourself if you should really be diving when you feel like you need medication.

Nutrition and the Diver

Some divers are particularly sensitive to spicy and gas-forming foods and beverages such as pizza, beans, and carbonated drinks. If you are in this category, you would be wise to avoid them before diving. Failure to do so may mean that you will suffer discomfort or significant pain during ascents—because of expanding abdominal gases. Eating a lot of anything immediately before diving may also cause discomfort and may be genuinely dangerous if it leads to vomiting while submerged.

Other nutritional advice to divers is similar to that offered for good health and reduction of risk for degenerative disorders such as coronary artery disease, cancer, diabetes, hypertension, and obesity. A prudent diet is high in complex carbohydrates (cereals and cereal products, fruits, and vegetables) and has limited amounts of alcohol, caffeine, salt, saturated fats (primarily animal fats), and sugar.

Developing and Maintaining Fitness for Diving

Since diving fitness is the ability to perform diving-related activities, and since there are a great variety of activities related to diving, diving fitness is a very complex matter. It is clear that you may be in great shape for one task while totally unable to perform another. This specificity in fitness is sometimes very obvious. Consider the demands of mounting a regulator on your tank; compare them with the demands of walking a quarter of a mile in soft sand with that tank on your back. These two diving-related activities have quite different energy and neuromuscular requirements. You may be fit for one and not the other. The differences between fitness requirements for casual underwater swimming and making a scuba rescue are not quite as obvious, but they are just as real.

Diving opportunities are limited, in part, by the number of diving tasks you can perform. Increasing your ability to perform these activities will broaden your comfort zone. You will be able to execute each task with less sense of stress—making the experience more enjoyable. Dives which are made easy by good planning and conditioning are also less likely to lead to exhaustion, panic, errors in judgment, and the accidents which sometimes follow. You need to possess the ability to meet all the demands normally imposed by your type of diving—plus you need to be reasonably prepared to meet unusual demands when the unexpected does occur, and you can be sure it will. We will limit our considerations to aerobic fitness and muscular strength and endurance although there are many other important components of physical fitness.

The basic principle of conditioning is the "Law of Use and Disuse". The principle here is that (within certain limits) the more you use your body in a particular way, the better it gets at meeting the demands of that activity. If your body is not required to meet those particular demands often enough, it will lose its ability to meet them. Imposing demands on your body is known as overload and may be accomplished by increasing Frequency, Intensity, or Time of exercise—the so-called FIT principle.

Aerobic Fitness

Aerobic fitness is determined by the ability of your heart and lungs to deliver oxygen and the ability of your muscles to utilize oxygen. This type of fitness is required for cycling, jogging, rowing, and swimming—and for long fin-swims or hikes along the beach to the dive site. Since roughly the same muscles will be used in about the same way as during a hike down the beach, jogging might be just as effective as any other activity to improve aerobic fitness for this type of diving-related activity. However, none of the above activities does a very good job of approximating the demand on the muscles involved in swimming with fins. It appears that the best way to condition yourself for performance in the water is with regular fin swimming—combined with common tasks such as entries, surface dives, and gear handling (to keep your skills sharp as well). Although significant aerobic demands may not occur most frequently in the water,

they are probably most critical there—the consequences of exhaustion are much greater.

There are a variety of aerobic training guidelines recommended by different individuals and organizations. In general, it is suggested that you exercise at about 70-85% of your maximum heart rate, at least three times per week; for at least 20-30 minutes a session. This is appropriate if you have nearly average resting and maximum heart rates for your age. Maximum heart rate (in beats per minute) is estimated by subtracting your age from 220, but this is subject to considerable individual variability—as is resting heart rate. You should use exercise heart rate as a general guide while being very attentive to how you feel. Train, don't strain—in a range of exertion from moderately hard to hard. The effort should not be extremely hard or exhausting. Be patient. Run the risk of doing too little, rather than too much, as you begin an exercise program.

These guidelines are based primarily on research with people exercising on land. The recommended exercise heart rates are chosen because they occur at the desired percent of maximal aerobic power (oxygen consumption). Research has shown maximal work with fins to result in oxygen consumption values which are generally 15-25 percent lower than those found during land-based exercises. Maximum heart rates are typically five to ten percent lower. Heart rates and ratings of perceived exertion may also be lower at submaximal workloads. Some authorities have recommended that exercise heart rates be lowered about ten beats per minute when establishing appropriate intensity of training in the water.

A lack of aerobic fitness is not one of the three major risk factors, but good aerobic fitness reduces the risk of coronary heart disease by reducing blood cholesterol and hypertension and in a variety of other ways. A good aerobic exercise program is one of the best things you can do to improve your diving safety and enjoyment.

Muscular Strength and Endurance

Diving equipment is heavy, and you should be able to handle your own gear. That takes strength and muscle endurance. These qualities are best developed by repeatedly contracting muscles against some resistance such as weights. For maximum benefit, the muscles should be exercised by mimicking the movements involved in diving-related tasks, but you should take care to exercise all major muscle groups for general well-being. For a good balance of strength and muscle endurance, resis-

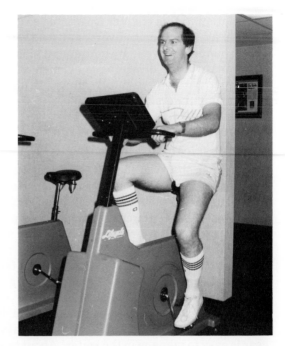

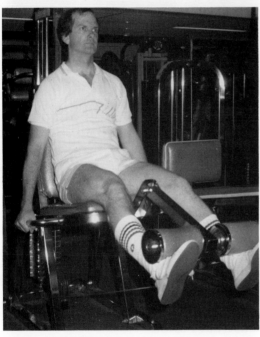

Figure 2.38 Build stamina with exercises that approximate diving activities. Building strength also helps.

tance should be such that each exercise can be repeated a maximum of about 10-20 times without rest. That is called one set. You should do about three sets of 10-20 repetitions maximum, three days each week with a day off between exercise days.

WOMEN AND DIVING—By S. Bangasser

Scuba diving began as a sport for young, daring, and male adventure seekers who somehow managed to survive homemade gear and lack of information with true grit. Since those early days, diving has evolved into a recreational sport suitable for almost anyone with a love for the water and a quest to explore. Along with the new diver came the de-

velopment of equipment to fit all sizes and sexes and to help assure safer and more pleasurable diving. One of the changes in the diving industry was the increasing number of female divers. Most certification agencies report that at least 25% of entry-level certifications are earned by women. As this population of divers grew, questions evolved that had never been asked by the male, macho divers from the prehistoric era. And so, data and information began to grow regarding women and diving.

Many topics discussed in this chapter are questions you may have had but were reluctant to ask in your class. Some topics will probably touch on subjects that you may not yet have questioned. The information in this chapter is suitable reading not just for all the women divers, but for their male diving buddies as well. By addressing many of the questions women divers have, women and their diving partners will, hopefully, dive with more confidence and understanding.

Men and Women—
Some Physical Differences

You have observed some of the obvious physical differences, such as an increase in muscle mass, when comparing men and women in good physical condition. This difference happens because the male hormone testosterone, present in only minute levels in women, is needed to produce large muscle mass. Nevertheless, all divers, male and female, will benefit from an exercise program designed to build strength and aerobic capacity.

A difference in strength does not make a difference in ability to dive. Fortunately, even heavy dive gear is easy to manage in the water. About the only time a woman may feel she is struggling is when carrying gear around out of the water. (Many men share this complaint.) While waiting for scuba tanks that weigh only five pounds and for wet suits that do not require weight belt usage, you can continue to apply the common sense that you surely have developed by now when it comes to diving. Equipment can be carried in more than one load. Also, wearing the tank is easier than carrying it a long distance. And now, devices are being brought into the scuba market that allow the diver to pull the equipment, rather than carry it.

An anatomical difference between men and women that is not so obvious is in the cardiovascular system (heart, lungs, and circulation). Since a woman's heart and lungs are smaller than a man's, the woman diver tends to breathe more shallowly, but just as efficiently. So, women take less air into their lungs with each breath. One nice consequence is that a woman's tank of air may last longer than her male buddy's.

Another facet in the cardiovascular system is the heart rate. A woman's pulse tends to be slightly more rapid than a man's. During strenuous activity, a woman's respiration rate and pulse are both higher than a male's, participating in the same activity. Since women will be closer to their maximum exertion level, they will want to prevent pushing themselves to the extreme limit. Two suggestions are the following: 1) Stay in as good a physical condition as possible. Since in general, a woman has less upper body strength, be sure to include

Figure 2.39 Equipment innovations and improved diving facilities are attracting more women to diving.

some upper body builders in the exercise program, as well as aerobics and kick strengthening exercises. 2) Pace yourself when diving to avoid the need for maximum exertion.

The Menstrual Period

A common question asked by women divers is, "Can I dive during my period?" As with many questions in diving, if you feel well, then go ahead and dive. If, on the other hand, you feel ill the first day or two of your period, you may want to postpone diving for a couple of days. As long as you feel fine, go ahead and enjoy your dives.

If you dive during your period, you may wonder, "Will I attract sharks?" This is not a question usually addressed in scuba classes, yet is a concern for many ocean diving women. According to Australian research, there is no evidence that sharks are attracted to menstruating females. Also, based on questionnaires and surveys, sharks have posed no problems to the female respondents diving during their period. So relax, concentrate on your dive, not the sharks (real or imagined), and enjoy the dive.

DIVING PHYSIOLOGY

A physiological change takes place during the menstrual period in many women that results in fluid retention a couple of days prior to and during the first days of the period. This may affect how you plan your dives. Since anything that impairs a diver's circulation is considered a possible factor in susceptibility to decompression sickness, fluid retention and the resulting impaired circulation can theoretically increase your susceptibility to decompression sickness. The good news is that this has not been documented with actual cases of bends. However, if you experience swelling and other symptoms of fluid retention, you should dive safely and avoid pushing the tables to their limits. As usual, common sense and good dive planning are the two most important ingredients for a fun dive.

Birth Control and Diving

Birth control techniques are hardly something you would think of when planning your dives. Most thoughts on this subject would be to just remember to bring the pills on that dive vacation. But your method of birth control may affect how you feel on that dive vacation and, may therefore influence the number of dives you make. For example, many women using the IUD experience heavy and uncomfortable periods. If you have this discomfort, you will not feel much like diving. If, on the other hand, you use birth control pills, you probably experience lighter and more comfortable periods. Consequently, you are more willing to dive during your period. Diving is not the only consideration you use when selecting a method of birth control. You should discuss the best methods for you with your doctor.

Another method of birth control is use of the diaphragm, which seems fairly benign as far as affecting your diving. It is not recommended to use the diaphragm to replace tampons when diving during your period. Leaving the diaphragm in place during diving has been done, but some women have complained of pain when diving with a diaphragm still in place. So removal before a dive makes good sense.

In the past, there was speculation that since early forms of birth control pills impaired some women's circulation, these pills might pose a risk to divers. This theory has never been shown to be valid. Also, birth control pills used now have much lower hormone levels than those held in suspicion. So the common consensus is that women using birth control pills do not have any increase in susceptibility to decompression sickness.

Figure 2.40 There are several good alternatives to carrying equipment for diving.

Figure 2.41 Diving during menstruation is acceptable if you feel physically well. Tampons may be used.

Diving in Thermal Comfort

The pleasure of diving can quickly end when a diver becomes too cold to function safely or just too uncomfortable to enjoy the dive. You may wonder why you sometimes are shivering while your male diving buddy appears comfortably warm. There are physiological reasons why some people get cold more quickly than others.

There are several factors involved when measuring sensitivity to cold. Subcutaneous fat, that layer of fat just under the skin, is higher in women than in men. This fat does act as a good insulator. However, there are other significant factors in thermal sensitivity. A large ratio of surface area to body mass will allow that person to cool more quickly. Most women and smaller men have a larger surface area compared to body mass, and therefore, fall into this category which results in a more rapid chilling. Another factor enters the picture. A large muscle mass generates more heat through exercise or shivering than a smaller muscle mass. So a woman or a smaller male may feel the effects of cold sooner than a diver with a larger muscle mass.

Fortunately, exposure suits are made to compensate for the cold water. Be sure to wear a suit that fits properly and that satisfies your needs. For example, your dive buddy may be comfortable in just a swim suit in the Caribbean, but you may be more comfortable in a one-eighth inch wet suit. Or perhaps, everyone you know does not use a hood in the summer when wearing their one-quarter inch wet suit. But if you are cold, wear that hood. Around 20% of body heat can be lost through the head. If a wet suit does not keep you warm in the waters in which you dive, then you may want to invest in a dry suit. It is hard to have fun diving if you are miserably cold.

Try to stay warm between dives as well. Some divers prefer to remove the jacket of a wet suit during a long surface interval, dry off and don a jacket. As the water in the wet suit evaporates, the diver cools down. Try to stay out of the wind, as this will cut down on rapid evaporation. You can have a warm, non-alcoholic drink between dives to help counter the cold.

Diving on a warm, sunny day can be a pleasurable experience, for now you can thaw out between dives. But, how do you feel getting ready for that dive? You have carried gear, checked out the conditions, and expended a lot of energy before even getting wet. In these pleasant conditions, you may encounter a different problem—building up too

Figure 2.42 Women tend to chill more rapidly than men. Wear appropriate insulation.

much body heat. Women have fewer sweat glands and do not begin to perspire until their temperature is two to three degrees higher than a man's. Since sweating is the method the body uses to cool itself, you may be building up an unsafe body temperature. Of course, your male buddy may be sweating profusely and getting close to dehydration. So, both of you need to use your heads, cool off in the water before continuing with your plans to dive, and drink enough liquid to replace fluids lost in getting ready for and during the dive.

Decompression Sickness in Women

The Navy Dive Tables were designed and tested using healthy, young males as models. So, if a diver does not fit into these categories, is she or he more likely to get decompression sickness, or the bends? As the number of sport divers has grown, more and more divers began to fit into groups other than those used to test the dive tables. As a woman diver, you may wonder if the tables apply to you.

Women seem more likely to be susceptible to decompression sickness than male diver's for several reasons. First, women have a higher percentage of adipose tissue (fat) than men, and fat has a high affinity for nitrogen, the culprit gas that bubbles in decompression sickness. Second, during a woman's menstrual period, any resulting edema, or fluid retention, seemed likely to increase the chances of suffering from the bends. And third, would birth control pills be likely to impair circulation and lead to a higher chance of getting the bends? These were the concerns, so some researchers began looking for answers.

The questions were first approached by Dr. Bruce Bassett using data gathered by the U.S. Air Force altitude flight training program during 1968-1977. In altitude training, the subjects are saturated at one atmosphere, and then are brought to decreased pressures (altitude). The results of the study showed a four-fold greater incidence of altitude decompression sickness in women than in men undergoing flight training. These results may not be directly applicable to sport divers since we are not saturation diving.

In another study, female and male scuba diving instructors were surveyed on diving habits and incidence of decompression sickness. Once again, the female group had a three-point-three fold greater incidence of the bends. This result is questioned because the data was based on the response of the participants, which may not have been accurate.

Recently, a more controlled analysis was done on Navy divers attending the Naval Diving and Salvage Training Center. During the training period, 29 of the 6,000 divers trained were female. The data gathered on this group shows that women are *not* at greater risk of sustaining decompression sickness than males at similar exposures for short duration dives. These types of dives are comparable to those sport divers make when the bottom time is less than one hour.

Observations made by recompression chambers support this information, since the operators have not reported a proportionally larger number of female divers being treated.

So, for female sport divers, the guidelines are the same as for male divers; stay within the Navy Dive Tables. Since there are several conditions that predispose an individual to the bends, such as being overweight, middle aged, or fatigued, please do not push the tables; *i.e.*, stay as long as tables indicate for a particular depth. Give yourself a safety margin. Following a deep dive, take a three minute safety stop at ten feet. By planning a safe dive and following that plan, you can have freedom to enjoy the dive.

Pregnancy and Diving

Diving during pregnancy is not a topic most divers think about—until the time comes. There you are with the airline tickets to a dream destination and you learn you are pregnant. Or, on returning from a wonderful dive vacation during which you dived many times, you learn you were pregnant during the trip. Should you spend the next months worrying about the health of your child?

The Undersea Medical Society and the major diving organizations currently say, "Do not scuba dive during pregnancy." This, however, is not necessarily based on the facts known, but rather on what is not known about the issue. The statement is also a legal necessity. So lack of information has led to this absolute rule.

The following information relates to what is known about the physiological effects of diving

Figure 2.43 Women are not at greater risk of sustaining decompression sickness than men.

during pregnancy. This information should help allay fears. Many women have contemplated an abortion because of lack of information on diving during pregnancy. This is a hasty solution. For the avid diver who becomes pregnant and would like to contiue diving, the information presented may help you make an informed decision.

During your entry-level scuba class, you learned about many potential physiological problems. These medical issues and their effects on the fetus will be discussed here.

Squeeze

One of the first diving problems you learned about was squeeze, which was defined as the pain and damage that occur to an air space on a diver. The fetus is completely enclosed in amniotic fluid and has no air spaces. So the fetus will not experience any pressure or squeeze.

Air Embolism

Air embolism is a serious problem that occurs when a diver breathes compressed air and swims directly to the surface, while holding her breath. This results in ruptured alveoli, and air bubbles enter the arterial system. Since the fetus does not have functional lungs and does not breathe air, an air embolism cannot harm the fetus.

Should an air embolism occur in the mother, the fetus's life would be in jeopardy simply because the mother's life was threatened. A diver suffering from an air embolism (or decompression sickness) is treated in a recompression chamber. This high pressure oxygen treatment may theoretically pose a problem for the fetus (see next section). The pregnant diver, just like any other diver, needs to dive with knowledge, experience, and care, to avoid air embolism.

Gas Toxicity

At depth divers absorb increased amounts of oxygen and nitrogen, the two major gases that comprise the air we breathe. One of the potential problems you have learned about is nitrogen narcosis. This occurs on deep or sometimes moderately deep dives when the nitrogen absorbed affects the diver's mental and physical abilities. This places any diver in a potentially dangerous situation and should be avoided by all divers, not just pregnant ones. Absorption of nitrogen which results in decompression sickness will be discussed in the next section.

Increased absorption of oxygen also happens while scuba diving. Can this be harmful to the

Figure 2.44 Diving activities should be suspended during pregnancy.

developing fetus? Divers may suffer from too much oxygen (hyperoxia) if diving to depths of 132 feet or more. Will the fetus experience an increase in oxygen and will smaller increases be a problem to the fetus? These and other diving related questions were studied using pregnant sheep in recompression chambers. Studies showed that the fetuses of pregnant sheep did not experience a significant increase in oxygen content even when the mothers were given a pressure equivalent to 297 feet (two atmospheres of oxygen). An increase in fetal oxygen content occurred at three atmospheres. Since recreational divers are limited to a diving depth of 130 feet, an increase in oxygen to the fetus should not be a problem.

If a diver suffers from air embolism or decompression sickness, the routine treatment is to be subjected to high pressures in a recompression chamber. Usually, two atmospheres of oxygen are used for short durations to treat the injured diver. Because years ago premature infants treated with oxygen sometimes developed a serious eye condition (retrolental fibroplasia), some researchers speculated that a female diver treated in a recompression chamber late in pregnancy may cause this disorder in the fetus. This has not been demonstrated to happen. Actually, chamber operators who treat medical (not diving related) problems with recompression chambers have by necessity, treated pregnant women late in gestation. This complication did not occur. Nevertheless, all divers should dive safely so the need for chamber treatment is avoided.

Insufficient oxygen (hypoxia) seldom is a problem to a scuba diver. If this problem did happen to a pregnant diver for whatever reason, the fetus would not suffer until the mother had severe hypoxia (for example, she stopped breathing). The placenta regulates the oxygen for the fetus and there are physiological mechanisms that provide it with an adequate oxygen supply.

Decompression Sickness

Decompression sickness, or the bends, is the formation of nitrogen bubbles from supersaturated tissues. If the mother suffers from decompression sickness, is this a problem for the fetus? Can the fetus develop bubbles? These and other questions make the issue of decompression sickness the most complicated issue concerning diving during pregnancy. To simplify this topic, three questions will be discussed.

1. If a pregnant diver gets decompression sickness, will the fetus be harmed? Studies have been done on pregnant sheep which were exposed late in gestation to pressures considered high, but not high enough to result in decompression sickness. These sheep delivered normal lambs. If, however, the sheep did suffer from decompression sickness and were not treated in a chamber, the lambs were stillborn. The sheep suffering from the bends that were treated in a chamber delivered normal lambs. Clearly, decompression sickness should be prevented by pregnant divers; if it develops, it should be treated.

A pregnant woman who develops decompression sickness early in her pregnancy, is treated and has no apparent lasting effects, is still another problem. Unfortunately, there is not sufficient scientific evidence to answer this question. Hyperbaric chamber operators treating pregnant women with medical problems may have an opinion based on their observations. In the meantime, the pregnant diver should avoid dives that may result in decompression sickness.

2. Are bubbles likely to form in the fetus at the same rate as in the mother? A concern for the pregnant diver is the possibility of bubbles forming in the fetus, even though the diver made a safe no-decompression dive. Is the fetus more likely to have bubble formation? Resistance to bubble formation by the fetus was seen in early experiments. More recent experiments with pregnant sheep have presented conflicting results. For example: sheep, taken to the equivalent depth of 165 feet, resulted in bubbles in the mothers but not the fetuses. In a similar experiment with sheep and goats, bubbles were detected in both the mothers and fetuses, but the lambs and kids were normal at birth. Because of this data, many researchers feel that bubbles are less likely to form in the fetus than in the mother.

3. Will bubbles cause birth defects? Nitrogen bubbles formed during a scuba dive are sometimes termed "silent bubbles" and apparently do no harm. They get trapped in the divers' lungs and never reach the arterial side of the circulatory system. Bubbles formed in a pregnant diver would also get trapped in the placenta, and never reach the fetus.

However, if bubbles form in the fetus, are these a problem? You have just read that it is believed that the fetus has some resistance to bubble formation. But, even one bubble may be enough to cause harm to the developing fetus. Two surveys of pregnant divers have been done to see the extent, if any, of birth defects and other problems to the baby. In one survey, a group diving to 100 feet or more had a higher rate of birth defects than the non-diving control group. However, this incident rate did not vary much from the normal range of all birth defects. In the other survey, no increased incidence of birth defects was found.

Although animal studies have been done, no conclusive evidence has been given demonstrating birth defects from bubble formation. The evidence from one experiment is encouraging. Pregnant sheep were exposed to very high pressures early in gestation, at the time of peak embryonic development. When the fetuses were studied later, no abnormalities were found.

Since many women dive deep before they know they are pregnant, this last study and the results of the surveys are comforting. If you found out you were pregnant after making deep dives, do not spend the rest of your pregnancy worrying. Discuss your concerns with your obstetrician and continue your pregnancy with medical care and the common sense guidelines recommended for a healthy baby.

Recommendations to the Pregnant Diver

Before the question of diving during pregnancy was ever formulated, many prominent women divers such as Dr. Eugenie Clark did dive during pregnancy. Now, however, the recommendation most often given is, "Do not dive during pregnancy." This is a safe suggestion and is based more on lack of sure proof that diving to any depth is unquestionably safe.

Women who dive during pregnancy fall into two general categories. The first group is those who dived before they knew they were pregnant. If you are in this category, read through the information presented here and talk to your doctor. I have met and talked to many women who made deep dives early in their pregnancy and spent the remainder of their term agonizing over the possible outcome. One woman even had plans for a special education program for her sure-to-be retarded baby. Fortunately, the outcomes were happy and healthy.

The second group of women, is those who are pregnant, read the information available, and make a decision to dive during pregnancy. If you fall into this category, I would still recommend shallow (30 feet) diving. I (the author) dived through term with two children, but did limit the depth to 30 feet. Many women in this category dive only on a vacation to warm, beautiful destinations. Others dive at home, but discontinue around the fourth month when the wet suit no longer fits.

For those women planning a family now, you can limit the depth of your dives or postpone the dives during the time of month when you feel you could be pregnant. Be sure to check with your doctor about other health questions, such as the medicine you can take. Remember, motion sickness medication, commonly taken for boat trips, should not be taken by pregnant women. After the birth of your child, doctors usually recommend that you do not dive for six weeks. So check with your doctor before resuming your diving activities.

PSYCHOLOGICAL FITNESS—By T. Griffiths

Scuba diving involves not only your brains and muscles but also your attitudes, expectations and personality. You must understand that athletic ability does not predict success as a scuba diver but rather your attitude does. This chapter should give you an understanding of why some divers become nervous while diving, how excessive anxiety effects underwater performance and illustrates the causes, symptoms, treatment and prevention of excessive diver stress.

Additionally, good breath control and relaxation are the keys to safe and enjoyable diving. Too often, scuba divers are unable to relax sufficiently to control their breathing. Any changes involving tension, anxiety or stress results in breathing pattern and rate changes. Therefore, this section will also focus on the role of breath control and relaxation in scuba diving.

Definitions

Stress and anxiety are two very ambiguous and difficult terms. Although they have extremely similar meanings, there are subtle but important differences between them that you should understand.

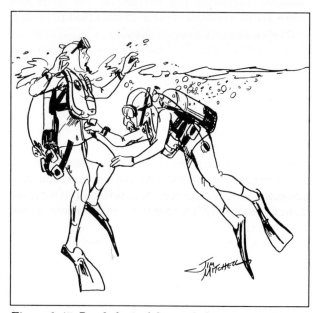

Figure 2.45 Psychological fitness helps prevent panic.

Stress—is a state that evokes effort on the part of the individual to maintain or restore equilibrium. The agents producing such a state are called *stressors* and may be physical or psychological. The response to stress may include many physiological and psychological reactions which attempt to restore the organism to a balanced state. This response is often referred to as the "fight or flight" reaction because the individual responds by either attacking or retreating from the stressor.

Anxiety—refers to fear or apprehension which you experience in the face of real or imagined danger. Some sports psychologists make a further distinction by describing that state of fear or apprehension experienced by an individual just prior to engaging in a risky or threatening activity as state anxiety.

Most scuba diving literature uses the term *stress* when discussing the psychological aspects of the sport. The term *anxiety* is often associated only with personality traits, and anxiety is thought by many to be a phobic response; thus the term usually carries a negative connotation.

It is important to note that stress reactivity is perfectly normal and healthy. However, if the stress becomes extreme and continues unchecked, it may lead to panic, which can be dangerous. Panic is an emotional and volatile human reaction which occurs in the presence of a real or imagined danger; it is characterized by a total loss of logic and mental control. Panic is the leading cause for both diver death and dropout.

Stress and Underwater Performance

Different individuals respond to identical stressors in different ways. Some enter rapidly into a stress state, others show increased alertness and apparently improved performance, and still others appear to be immune to the stress-producing qualities of the environmental conditions.

While vulnerability to stress varies from individual to individual, so does the cause of diver stress. As a diver, you may be stressed because of physical risks, social risks or both. Too often, divers are motivated by the fear of looking foolish rather than the fear of being harmed. In other words, you may be tempted to do a dive you're not capable of doing safely rather than look foolish to your peers.

Human performance underwater is influenced by varying levels of psychological stress. Stress prior to a dive can make the diver more aware of the problems and procedures of the dive, while overwhelming stress during a dive can disable the diver. A diver in the panic state becomes all action and movement but is not capable of thinking clearly. Panicked divers are almost impossible to assist and are incapable of helping themselves.

Excessive stress, which can lead to loss of control underwater, usually begins well before the diver enters the water. By being able to detect the telltale signs of extreme apprehension, divers may be able to help themselves avoid panic and other divers may be able to help them, either before the dive begins or in the water.

Psychological Responses

Psychological stress is accompanied by several physiological responses, including increased heart rate, respiration, muscle tension and perspiration. These increased energy expenditures lead to additional stress problems of hypoxia, hyperventilation, fatigue, and exhaustion, which in turn, pave the road to panic. Changes of voice and shaking hands also indicate heightened stress levels.

Since a stressed diver breathes more often and exhales more forcefully while underwater, the frequency and intensity of the exhaled air bubbles can alert other divers to a problem. Another symptom of high stress levels that is easy to detect underwater is the "wide-eyed look." When divers are overly stressed underwater, they will often open their eyes extremely wide and stare at a person or object. Because underwater communication requires good eye contact, this sign of stress is easily recognizable.

In general, moderate amounts of stress may actually enhance performance. Optimum performance for complex tasks usually occurs when stress is neither extremely high nor extremely low. In some situations, high states of arousal enhance performance, but in others, the same levels of stress can be detrimental.

Relaxation techniques, particularly slow, rhythmic breathing exercises, can be effective in significantly reducing stress levels and thus improving performance. It is important to note that stress must be controlled, but not necessarily completely eliminated, in order to promote safe diving.

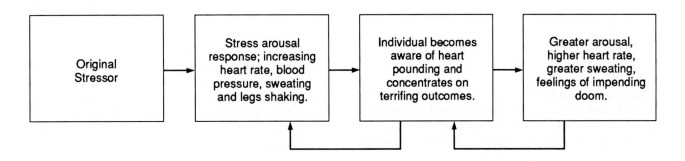

Figure 2.46 Stress Feedback Loop

CAUSES OF STRESS

Physical Stressors

The physical stressors present in the diving environment include cold water, limited visibility, strong currents, and rough waves. The physical state of the diver may also present stressors, including fatigue, cramps, rapid respiration, overloading (performing too many tasks at one time), and time pressure (racing against the clock). Lack of physical fitness and poor swimming ability are major contributors to these forms of stress. Additionally, the equipment used in scuba diving is generally cumbersome and, therefore, causes the following stressors: confinement or restriction of movement, overweight, fatigue and discomfort.

Any one of these physical stressors may increase the stress level of the diver. When several physical stressors occur simultaneously, the diver may feel threatened, resulting in dangerously high levels of psychological stress.

Psychological Stressors

Peer pressure—the pressure placed by peers on fellow divers, keeps stress levels relatively high. Humans are very social beings, and peer approval is extremely important to most individuals. *Pride* and respect of others is a goal most people attempt to achieve. This self-imposed peer pressure can be significant, and when colleagues make statements like, "If I can do it, so can you," additional pressure is created. Failure in the face of peers is a definite ego threat. Any possibility of failure in the face of peers is also an ego threat. A damaging blow to your pride may be inflicted if you fail at a task or refuse to attempt or complete a task. The combination of peer pressure and ego threat increases stress levels among scuba divers. Research findings at the University of Maryland have consistently shown that peer pressure, ego threat, concern about receiving a good grade and concern about receiving the certification card, in short, pride, are the most significant stressors for college students in dive courses.

The possibility of underwater dangers is also a cause of stress, although it takes a back seat to peer pressure. Humans know they are not fish, but they adapt very well to the underwater world with the aid of sophisticated equipment. Subconsciously, some divers fear drowning because they are entirely immersed in the water for an extended period of time. They realize that if equipment problems arise, they do not possess the ability to breathe in the water without a mechanical device.

Psychological stress produces a stress reaction in the body which, in itself, is often the cause of additional stress. The stress reaction is part of a feedback loop perpetuating and augmenting the stress response.

The physiological symptoms of panic are similar to those of excessive stress. These symptoms include involuntary hyperventilation, the wide-eyed look, dilated pupils, excessive muscle tension, and increased heart rate and respiration. These responses lead to breathing difficulties, fatigue, exhaustion, and muscle cramps, which add to the existing panic state and can easily cause drowning. Scuba experts refer to this progression as the panic syndrome, and it is the most significant threat to the diver in the water.

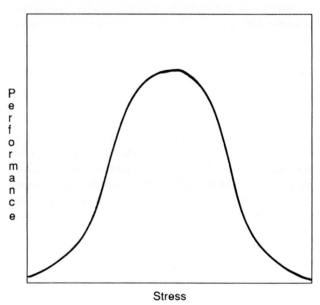

Figure 2.47 Stress actually improves performance up to a certain point.

A Special Note on Breathing

Breath control and relaxation go hand in hand when it comes to diving safety. Breathing, which is perhaps the most critical stressor in diving, is also a major *sign* of stress. Breathing also serves as a major *source* of stress. Overbreathing underwater clearly signals that you are being stressed. When you *realize* your breathing rate and/or pattern has changed, this will cause increased stress, thus producing a deteriorating breath control cycle. In order to control excessive diver stress and panic, good breath control is required at all times.

You should make a habit of spending three to five minutes of "quiet time" prior to each dive working on slow, deep rhythmic breathing with eyes closed. This will not only relax you but may even increase your bottom time.

Behavioral Responses

Many dive masters and instructors rely on certain behavioral cues to detect nervous divers. You should learn to spot these signs of stress in yourself and dive buddy.

Before the Dive

Most of the behavioral patterns seen before the dive are forms of procrastination, which are defense mechanisms used by divers to delay entering an uncertain or threatening situation. Subconsciously, these nervous divers are seeking help. Examples of these behavioral patterns follow. You should know these signs of pre-dive stress.

Introversion

The diver who withdraws from the rest of the group and remains continually quiet throughout the day might be dwelling on the possible negative aspects of the dive.

Tardiness

Some divers will continually be late for several meetings convened the day of the dive. A diver who misses a ride to the dive site or the dive orientation meeting, who is late picking up equipment, or who is the last one to suit up, might be procrastinating because of fear.

Mental Errors

Divers who are excessively nervous will often make simple mistakes prior to entering the water. Placing the regulator on the tank backward, putting the fins on upside down, and getting hair under the mask are just a few of the many mistakes that can occur. Some of these mistakes are made innocently enough, but some divers may subconsciously make these mistakes to delay the dive.

Forgetfulness

There is much to be remembered for a scuba dive, and it is, therefore, easy to overlook something. But when divers forget several items (bathing suit, mask, wet suit, money), this may indicate another type of defense mechanism used by the nervous diver.

Extreme Cockiness

Many very competent divers are ashamed and embarrassed when they experience excessive apprehension prior to the dive. To mask the fear, they will often brag about how easy the dive will be or make a big joke about the entire experience. These people probably possess more anxiety than they would like to admit. Many a macho-diver, whether male or female, actually does not possess supreme self-confidence but is really a nervous diver. The true macho-diver is also a problem in that he/she often fails to follow safe diving practices.

Irritability

Some scuba students display a loss of patience and a quick temper on the day of the open water dive. Any slight change in plans or a delay propels these divers into a mild tantrum. This sudden irritability is quite possibly a manifestation of the stress built up in them which they cannot mentally accommodate and must, therefore, impose on others.

During the Dive

Once in the water, a stressed diver may display other behavioral patterns.

Inefficient Swimming

Rather than moving through the water smoothly and slowly to conserve air and energy, a highly stressed diver will swim erratically in the water. Usually the arms and legs will move wildly underwater as the diver becomes overly dependent on the muscles and fins to make progress. Inefficient swimming manifests itself in many ways. While on the surface, the highly stressed diver may tread water extremely high out of the water without the aid of buoyancy compensation. If an anchor line or trail line is being used, the diver becoming panicky can often be found "clinging and clambering" on it. A diver in this state is simply too nervous to swim smoothly through the water. Swimming inefficiently leads to excessive fatigue which often leads to panic.

Equipment Rejection

Divers who are highly stressed tend to lose faith in the scuba equipment. While on the surface, the diver may quickly and abruptly remove the mask and/or regulator. Underwater, the diver may continually readjust one piece of equipment, like the weight belt, or frequently fuss with just about every item of equipment being used.

Fixation

Some highly stressed divers will not be attentive to or aware of what is going on around them, but instead may concentrate or stare at one person or object. Also, a diver who appears listless or apathetic underwater may be a victim of excessive stress. Some experts refer to this concept as "narrowing", which may be either mental or perceptual.

Human Errors

When making procedural mistakes and errors in judgment while underwater, the diver may become overly stressed and unable to function properly. A key contributing factor to panic is a mistake, either mental or physical, made by the diver while attempting to correct a small problem. Typically, after divers become overly stressed they make mistakes which ultimately lead to a total loss of control. For example, the mistake a diver might make in dealing with the problem of too much lead is either not removing lead from the weight belt or not using the B.C. Failure to compensate for the excessive lead might lead to fatigue, cramps, and, ultimately, panic.

Perhaps the most critical factor in the panic progression after stress increases is whether or not a problem arises. If a problem does occur, it is usually accompanied by another increase in stress levels. Problems include being overweighted, losing one's buddy, or running out of air, among others. Fortunately, quite often no problems occur even though the diver is highly stressed. If a problem does not arise, no threat is posed to the diver. If a problem does develop, it must be confronted by the diver regardless of how insignificant it appears to be.

It must be emphasized that you need not be a psychologist or a counselor to treat and prevent diver stress. The techniques described here have been used and tested by scuba instructors and sports psychologists. Don't be afraid to give them a try!

Treatment of Stress

Excessive stress displayed by divers is a problem largely because the stress reaction distracts them from concentrating on the specifics of the dive.

If a diver displays the physiological and/or behavioral symptoms described before the dive begins, the dive should be delayed or canceled. The stressed diver should be counseled with the aim of decreasing stress and increasing concentration on the task at hand. Several methods may be used to help a highly stressed diver.

Talk

Taking the time to explain all the dive procedures in detail is perhaps the easiest and most efficient way to help the diver. While doing this, however, attention should not be drawn to the diver's nervousness. Talk to the diver should be friendly, informative and full of encouragement.

Accentuate the Positive

Highly stressed divers find themselves in a poor mental state for the dive because they dwell on the negative aspects of the dive. In order to combat this, focus verbally on all aspects of the dive (for example, the good weather, the unusually good visibility, and the warm water temperature) while de-emphasizing the negative aspects.

Fight Distraction with Distractions

Excessive stress distracts the diver from functioning properly underwater. One way to eliminate this distraction is to give the divers something to do while diving which will keep them occupied and distracted from their nervousness. Some examples are helping to collect samples, identifying certain forms of marine life, and keeping track of depth and time. The diver must not, however, be overburdened with too many tasks.

Buddy-Up Weak with Strong

Every attempt should be made to pair up the stressed diver with a strong, confident diver, preferably a talkative and responsible person who will go out of the way to be helpful. However, as diver training continues, the weaker diver must be given progressively more responsibility to prevent him or her from becoming a dependent diver and, therefore, a liability.

Use a Buddy Line

Even in clear water, a buddy line can help to reduce stress by increasing contact and communication with the dive partner. Actually holding the hand of the nervous diver might also be beneficial.

Offer Praise and Encouragement

The extremely stressed diver may be helped by continually offering praise and encouragement, even when the diver makes mistakes.

Practice the Calming Response

A deep-breathing exercise has been recently developed which promotes relaxation and enhances respiratory efficiency in a matter of minutes. It is easy to learn and practice and may be used on land prior to the dive or underwater. The technique, called the "Calming Response", is an adaptation of the "Quieting Response" developed by Dr. Charles Strobel. The Calming Response combines yogic breathing (diaphragmatic or stomach breathing) with autogenic phrases. As the diver inhales deeply, the stomach (not the chest) is pushed out and then drawn in during exhalation. During the slow, deep inhalation, the diver mentally says, "I feel calm." During the slow, deep exhalation, the diver mentally says, "I feel warm."

It should be remembered that you should have a friendly and encouraging manner while attempting to help an extremely nervous diver. Above all, if unable to help a diver cope with excessive stress prior to the dive, you must have enough courage to tell the diver *not* to dive.

Perhaps the most efficient way to combat excessive stress while the diver is in the water is to remove the victim slowly and carefully from the situation. Another method of treating a stressful diver underwater is to have the diver stop, breathe

deeply, and then think about the situation (the diver can do this even if he/she is alone). Gaining control during a stressful situation is extremely important. In order to stop the chain of events which may lead to panic, the following progression is recommended:

Stop ➡ Breathe ➡ Think ➡ Breathe ➡ React

Conscious breath control should permeate each of the three states.

Once on the surface, the victim should be made positively buoyant as discreetly as possible, in order to avoid additional stress, by dropping the weight belt and/or inflating the B.C. vest. At this time, the victim may be treated for stress in the same fashion as during the pre-dive state. Verbal reassurance, encouragement, and accentuating the positive while minimizing the negative aspects of the dive will all aid in reducing stress.

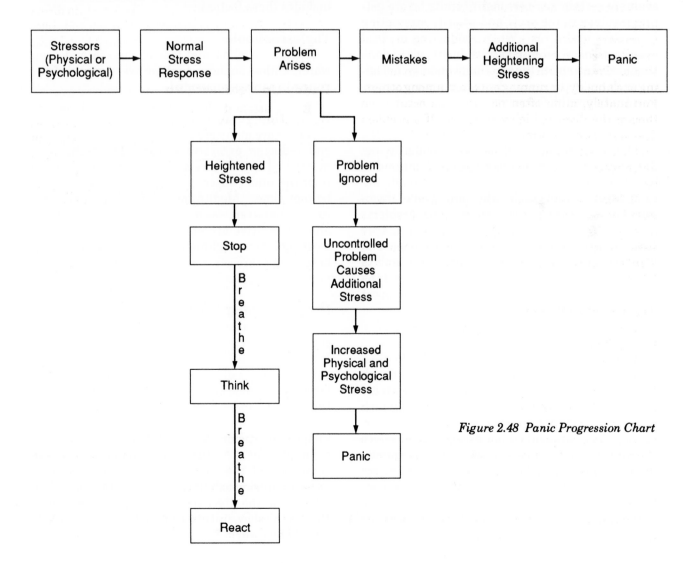

Figure 2.48 Panic Progression Chart

Stress Reduction Methods

Because stress is caused by environmental, social, mental, and physical factors and occurs in many different and varying situations, no single technique can be recommended to prevent, reduce and control excessive stress. Divers faced with high levels of stress must develop a program of various techniques to learn to relax, control stress and ultimately improve diving performance. Once again, scuba divers should not attempt to eliminate all stress, but can actually enhance the dive by making it more exciting, challenging and safer. This is true because a moderately stressed diver tends to focus more on particular aspects of a dive than the totally relaxed diver. Conversely, excessive stress will impair performance, thus making the dive more dangerous.

Psychological Evaluation

It is essential that every scuba diving candidate evaluate certain key personality traits before getting involved in the sport and prior to attempting more advanced dives. When conducting medical examinations of potential scuba divers, physicians should also attend to the emotional and psychological wellness of the diver. Some of the more important traits are the following:

Positive Self-Esteem

This is a prerequisite of successful scuba diving. The ability to see oneself in a positive light and to feel good about oneself is a must for scuba diving candidates. Individuals who downgrade themselves or who are experiencing emotional problems should refrain from scuba diving. While it is true that scuba diving can and does build confidence in divers, students with emotional problems tend to focus on the negative aspects of their lives, and the physical and psychological demands of the sport only add to their problems.

Confidence

This is closely associated with positive self-esteem and means believing in oneself to get the job done. Students who lack confidence repeatedly underrate themselves during scuba training, which erodes their ability to perform scuba skills correctly. These students often program themselves for failure. Poor self-expectation leads repeatedly to poor performance. All scuba certification courses require a simple prerequisite swim test. Scuba candidates should realize that anyone passing the initial swim test possesses enough skill to pass the course.

Anxious Reactive Personality

A few divers may be described as having anxious reactive personalities. Anxious reactive individuals exaggerate the existing stress and actually perpetuate it after the stress is gone. People prone to this reaction can become mentally and physically incapacitated in the face of the mildest stressor. Needless to say, anxious reactive personalities probably should not engage in scuba diving. The anxiety feedback loop, which anxious reactive personalities often experience 'narrowed spaces'. The diving mask eliminates peripheral vision, the wet suits constrains and confines, and often dives occur in closed quarters. Therefore, those who cannot deal with their claustrophobia should not dive.

Agoraphobia

This abnormal fear of crossing large expanses of land or water and fear of open spaces is also contraindicated to diving because much of dive travel includes these factors.

Thalassophobia

This is an abnormal fear of the sea and deep water. Unless an individual can overcome this fear, diving is not recommended.

Relaxation Techniques

There are many effective methods of preventing and reducing excessive stress. The techniques mentioned not only relax divers but also help to improve underwater performance and increase bottom time. Meditation, biofeedback and neuromuscular exercises have worked to benefit divers and competitive athletes alike. Perhaps the two most effective techniques for divers are deep breathing exercises, namely the calming response and mental rehearsal.

Deep-breathing Exercises

Proper breathing is the key to achieving relaxation just as it is the key to safe scuba diving. Practicing breathing techniques strengthens and conditions the pulmonary system, enhances circulation of the blood and promotes oxygenation, calms the nerves, and ultimately promotes relaxation. The Calming Response combines yogic breathing (diaphragmatic or stomach breathing) with autogenic phrases. As the diver inhales deeply, the stomach (not the chest) is pushed out and then drawn in during exhalation. During the slow, deep inhalation, the diver mentally says, "I feel calm." During the slow, full exhalation, the diver mentally says, "I feel warm."

Mental Rehearsal

One method of reducing stress in diving is by rehearsing the key diving skills mentally before entering the water. Experts believe that mental practice is just as important as physical practice and that basic diving skills and emergency techniques should be mentally practiced on a regular basis. The mental scenes created by the diver should be as vivid as possible, and the diver should perform the skill perfectly in his/her mind. In this way the physical skills become ingrained in the mind and stress is reduced because the diver has mentally rehearsed the proper procedure to follow in a given situation.

One popular form of mental rehearsal is called "psychocybernetics." Maxwell Maltz popularized this mental practice program in the 1960s and many people, especially athletes, have since used this technique to reduce stress and enhance performance. Psychocybernetics incorporates several psychological strategies in order to improve performance. A positive self-concept, mental practice through imagery, and relaxation are all essential to the Maltz technique. When divers practice this program they must first work diligently on improving the self-concept and learn to approach everything, including diving, with confidence. Second, all skills to be performed in real life should be rehearsed mentally beforehand. The key to this mental practice is the performance of each skill perfectly in the mind without errors or mistakes. Last, improving the self-concept and mentally rehearsing skills must be done while in a relaxed state; they cannot be forced or pressured into being. The works of Maxwell Maltz are inspiring and are recommended to all divers who lack confidence or suffer from excessive stress.

Author's Note: I am greatly indebted to Arthur Bachrach, whose pioneering work in diver stress contributed greatly to this section. For more information, consult "Stress and Performance in Scuba Diving" by Bachrach and Egstrom.

3

DIVING
EQUIPMENT

You are familiar with the equipment used for diving. As an advanced diver you need to know more about the equipment you use and you should also know about equipment such as dry suits and dive computers. The purpose of this chapter is to increase your knowledge about diving equipment.

Learning Objectives

By the end of this course, you need to be able to:

1. Correctly define the equipment terms presented in CAPITAL LETTERS in this chapter.

2. Briefly describe the basic types, theories of operation, care and maintenance of the various items of equipment discussed in this chapter.

3. Briefly describe the theory of operation of a breathing air compressor; contrast high-pressure, low-volume compressors and low-pressure high-volume compressors; and explain how compressors are rated.

4. List the primary components of an air station.

Types of Scuba Equipment

There are three categories of Self-Contained Underwater Breathing Apparatus (SCUBA): Open-circuit demand, semi-closed-circuit and closed-circuit. Only open-circuit demand scuba is used by recreational divers. A scuba system where the breathing gas is inhaled upon demand from the breathing apparatus and exhaled directly into the water is called OPEN-CIRCUIT DEMAND SCUBA. CLOSED-CIRCUIT SCUBA units, often referred to as "rebreathers" are complex types that remove CO_2 from exhaled breathing gas and add oxygen as needed. A very small amount of gas escapes into the water. SEMI-CLOSED SCUBA recycles part of each exhaled breath while allowing some gas to escape into the water. The use of semi-closed or closed-circuit scuba equipment is reserved for specially trained military and scientific divers and should not be used by recreational divers.

SCUBA CYLINDERS

You know that there are steel and aluminum tanks, but you should also know that there are different metal alloys for each type. This results in different physical dimensions, wall thicknesses and capacities. The following chart lists the specifications for the most popular sizes.

Note on the chart that the rated capacity of steel tanks is achieved only when the cylinder is filled to 10% over its rated service pressure. For example, a 71.2 cubic foot steel tank contains only 65 cubic feet at 2,250 psi. An increase in pressure of 225 psi to a

ALLOY	ADVERTISED VOLUME	CAPACITY RATED	(CU. FT.) @ 10% O.F.	SERVICE PRESSURE	OVERFILL PRESSURE	CUBIC INCHES	LENGTH (INCHES)	DIAMETER (INCHES)	EMPTY WT. (LBS.)	BUOYANCY (SEA WATER) EMPTY	FULL
Steel	15	14.24	15.65	3000	3300	120	13.80	4.00	07.5	-1.300	-2.5
Alum.	14	14.06	-	2015	-	176	16.60	4.40	05.4	3.20	2.1
Alum.	50	50.43	-	3000	-	425	19.00	6.90	21.5	2.25	-1.8
Steel	45	40.99	45.05	2015	2216	513	19.10	6.80	20.0	1.40	-2.2
Steel	38	37.86	-	1000	-	530	19.10	6.80	20.0	1.40	-1.6
Steel	42	38.00	41.77	1800	1980	532	19.10	6.80	20.1	1.40	-1.9
Steel	52.2	47.43	52.14	2250	2475	532	19.37	6.90	22.0	neutral	-4.2
Steel	53	47.43	52.14	2250	2475	532	19.10	6.80	20.5	1.40	-2.8
Alum.	63 or 50	63.13	-	3000	-	532	18.70	7.25	25.1	0.80	-3.04
Steel	71.4	65.15	71.39	3000	3300	549	20.47	6.84	28.6	-4.600	-10.3
Alum.	72	72.39	-	3000	-	610	26.00	6.90	28.5	3.60	-1.8
Steel	55	44.79	49.23	1800	1980	627	22.50	6.80	20.8	2.40	1.4
Alum,	80	79.87	-	3000	-	673	26.40	7.25	33.3	4.00	-1.9
Alum.	80	80.70	-	3000	-	680	27.00	7.25	34.5	4.10	-1.9
Steel	71.2	65.08	71.55	2250	2475	730	25.00	6.80	29.5	3.50	- 2
Alum.	71.2	71.55	-	2475	-	730	28.80	6.90	30.6	10.600	5.2
Steel	75.8	69.39	76.29	2400	2640	730	26.18	6.76	29.3	1.50	-4.6
Steel	94.6 or 96	86.63	95.25	3000	3300	730	25.00	7.00	39.0	-6.000	-13.3
Steel	95.1	85.98	95.62	2400	2640	915	23.82	8.02	37.2	1.50	-6.2
Steel	103.5 or 104	96.01	105.550	2400	2640	1010	26.50	7.80	44.0	neutral	-8.2

Table 3.1 Scuba Cylinder Specifications

total of 2,475 results in a capacity of 71.55 cubic feet. The 10% overfill pressure was introduced during World War II due to economics and has been in effect ever since. For a cylinder to safely be charged 10% beyond its service pressure, the tank must pass a special elastic expansion test which is different and more complex than the standard permanent expansion test of HYDROSTATIC (non-moving water) pressure testing of cylinders.

Scuba cylinders that may be safely overfilled by 10% have a "+" sign stamped on the cylinder following the last test date. Since overfill retesting is not commonly done, you will need to request it when having your tank tested. If a cylinder does not qualify for overfilling, it may still pass the permanent expansion test and can continue to be used at its rated working pressure. The elimination of overfilling ratings and replacement with a higher working pressure is being considered by the regulating agency.

In addition to the optional "+" sign, there are several codes which must be stamped onto scuba cylinders. These codes provide valuable information to those who use and service them.

DOT stands for the Department of Transporta-tion, which specifies the regulations for all high pressure vessels. CTC is the Canadian Transport Commission, the Canadian equivalent of the DOT. Some older tanks may have the code "ICC"—the Interstate Commerce Commission—which regulated cylinders prior to 1970.

Following the regulating agency code is the metal alloy code. "3AA" or "3A" stands for steel alloys, while "3AL" stands for aluminum alloy. Some tanks may have "SP6498", which means special permit alloy. Others may have "E6498", which stands for exemption.

Following the metal code number is an important four digit number that is the working pressure of the cylinder. Common pressures are 1,800 psi, 2,250 psi and 3,000 psi. A few cylinders are rated at over 4,000 psi.

On the line beneath the agency code, metal code and working pressure is the serial number for the cylinder. You should record this in your training record so you will have the information in case your tank is ever stolen or lost. The tank manufacturer's name or code may be next to or below the serial number. The name is required on cylinders made after 1982.

Perhaps the most important code is the test date code, which must contain the month, a special hydro facility mark and the year of the test.

Another advanced aspect of scuba cylinders is buoyancy. Refer to the tank capacities chart and note the change in buoyancy between full and empty tanks of various sizes. Air weighs approximately .08 pounds per cubic foot. The weight of the varying amount of air (usually four to six pounds), combined with external tank volume and tank weight, result in the buoyancy specifications. The less the change in tank buoyancy, the better.

Care of Scuba Cylinders

Beyond preventing physical damage to your cylinder from dropping, banging or overheating it, the most important consideration is keeping moisture out. There are sev-

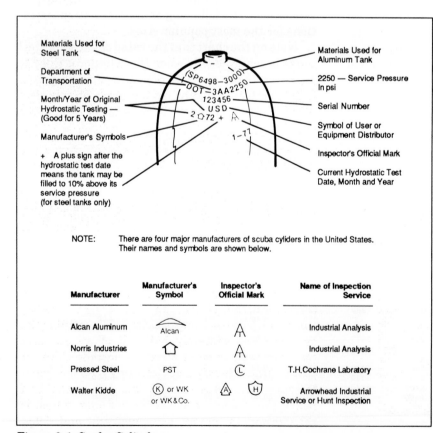

Figure 3.1 Scuba Cylinders

Figure 3.2 At least once a year a visual cylinder inspection should be performed by a qualified professional.

eral ways in which moisture can enter a tank. Being aware of the ways can help you prevent the accumulation of moisture or water, which will cause corrosion by working with the high pressure oxygen inside the cylinder.

Water may enter a scuba cylinder from:

1. An improperly operated air compressor.

2. Droplets in the tank valve or filler attachment during filling.

3. Back flow through the regulator when the tank is empty.

4. Changes in temperature when the tank is empty and the valve is left open.

5. Bleeding tank air rapidly.

A serious problem in, addition to corrosion, can result from the prolonged storage of air in a tank containing water. The oxidation process will, over time, consume the oxygen in the air, leaving only nitrogen. An unsuspecting user would then lose consciousness without warning. This is one of the reasons tanks should be stored with only a small amount of air in them.

Prevent moisture accumulation. Always maintain a small amount (300 psi) of air in your tank. If whitish mist is detected when the valve is opened, if sloshing can be heard when the tank is tipped back and forth, or if the air has a damp, metallic odor, have the tank inspected as soon as possible.

All scuba cylinders must be inspected internally by a qualified professional at least once a year. This testing requires special training, procedures and equipment. NAUI sanctions a special Visual Cylinder Inspection (VCI) program and authorizes the issuance of Evidence of Inspection (EOI) stickers by qualified tank inspectors.

William High photo

Figure 3.4 A device for tumbling tanks.

If internal inspection reveals corrosion in a scuba tank, the cylinder may have to be cleaned by tumbling. The tumbling process involves filling the cylinder approximately half full of an abrasive material such as palet abrasive, carbide chips, or aluminum oxide chips, and rotating it for a number of hours. The abrasive materials remove rust and polish the inside surface of the cylinder, which is then rinsed to remove loose material and dehydrated internally to remove all traces of moisture.

Figure 3.3 Tank Inspection Decal

Figure 3.5 A scuba cylinder being lowered into water jacket for hydrostatic testing.

At least once every five years in the United States, and even more frequently in some countries, scuba cylinders must be pressure tested. There are several methods of HYDROSTATIC TESTING, including direct expansion, pressure recession, and the water jacket method, which involves filling the cylinder with water, placing it in a water-filled pressure chamber, raising the pressure inside the cylinder with a hydraulic pump, and measuring the amount of cylinder expansion in terms of water column displacement. The pressure is increased to five-thirds the rated pressure of the cylinder. A permanent expansion of 10% or more of the total expansion indicates the cylinder is unsafe and must be condemned. The cylinder will not be rated for a lower working pressure.

Cylinder Care Rules:

1. Do not exceed the maximum allowable pressure.

2. Do handle tanks carefully.

3. Do prevent moisture from entering the cylinder.

4. Do not drain a tank completely of air except for internal inspections, then have the tank drained slowly.

5. Rinse the outside of the cylinder thoroughly with clean, fresh water after diving.

6. Do store cylinders in a cool, dry place with a small amount of pressure in them.

7. Do have cylinders visually inspected annually or more frequently if tank damage is suspected.

8. Do not use a dented, welded or deeply scarred cylinder.

9. Do remove cylinder boot periodically and inspect for corrosion.

10. Do not heat tanks to high temperatures (baking, welding, etc.).

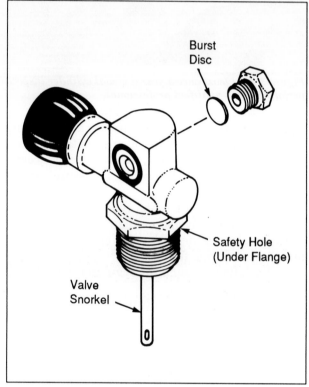

Figure 3.6 Cylinder Valve Safety Features

Cylinder Valve Assemblies and Manifolds

A scuba cylinder valve is a simple, manually operated on-off valve that controls the flow of high-pressure gas. Features of all scuba valves include a valve snorkel and a burst disc. The purpose of the VALVE SNORKEL or "dip tube" is to prevent foreign matter from entering into and perhaps blocking the valve when the tank is inverted. The BURST DISC is a safety feature to prevent cylinder pressure from reaching dangerously high levels during filling or under conditions of extreme heat (such as a fire).

Some scuba valves have a safety hole located near the top of the valve threads. The purpose of the hole is to indicate there is pressure in a tank if

DIVING EQUIPMENT

Figure 3.7 Two different types of tank valves. On the left is a "K" valve and on the right is a "J" valve.

someone tries to remove the valve when the tank is not empty. Air hisses from the valve and warns the worker.

A cylinder valve assembly houses a high-pressure blowout disc as a safety feature. Burst discs are rated at a maximum of five-thirds the working pressure of a cylinder. The rated bursting pressure range of burst discs for 2,250 psi tanks is from 3,375 to 3,750 psig and for 3,000 psi tanks the bursting pressure range is from 4,500 to 5,000 psig. The thin, metal burst discs are usually both color coded and stamped with their maximum pressure rating.

When a burst disc ruptures, which can occur under normal circumstances from time to time, loud noise and hissing result, but the only danger is to your hearing. The escape of air cannot be stopped, and the burst disc must be replaced by a qualified professional before the cylinder may be used again.

The standard, on-off cylinder valve is known as the "K-valve". A cylinder valve that incorporates a low-air warning/reserve air mechanism is known as a "J-valve". The J-valve is a spring-loaded check valve that begins to close as cylinder pressure approaches a predetermined pressure (usually 300 or 500 psi). The J-valve permits unrestricted flow of air to the regulator throughout a dive until the valve closing pressure is approached. At the predetermined closing pressure, a spring forces a flow check against the air passage and restricts air flow, causing increased breathing resistance. This is followed by total obstruction of air flow unless the spring-loaded check valve is manually overridden by turning the external lever. When the reserve lever is manually depressed, a plunger pin forces the flow check valve away from the air passage and the remaining 300-500 psi becomes available for use.

K-valves tend to be more popular with experienced divers than J-valves. The following are some of the reasons why:

1. The reserve pressure of a J-valve may be either 300 psi gauge pressure or 300 psi above gauge pressure. If the reserve is not depth compensated, available reserve air is decreased as depth is increased.

2. The J-valve reserve lever must be fully up in order for the reserve mechanism to function. A diver may forget to put the lever up prior to diving, it may be turned down by another diver, or the lever may be accidently depressed by diving activities. Any of these actions allow the reserve air to be exhausted without warning.

3. The J-valve reserve lever must be depressed when the cylinder is being filled. Failure to do this may damage the reserve mechanism and will prevent correct fill.

4. J-valves cost more initially than K-valves and also are more expensive to have serviced.

5. A J-valve mechanism retains a reserve air supply in only one cylinder of a multiple set of cylinders. When the reserve is activated, the reserve air distributes itself equally among all cylinders and the reserve pressure is reduced by a ratio equal to the number of cylinders. The reserve pressure can be set to a higher pressure to compensate for multiple tanks.

Galvanic corrosion or electrolysis occurs when dissimilar metals are in contact and moisture is present. This can occur between aluminum tanks and brass scuba valves. Ions will flow from the aluminum and deposit themselves on the brass. Fortunately, the chrome plating of brass scuba valves and the scuba tank coating, combined with a periodic coating of a dielectric compound, negate electrolysis in most instances. If the valve plating is worn away however, galvanic corrosion can be a problem and will appear as pits or missing threads in the tank adjacent to the valve. If this problem develops, it should be corrected by a qualified professional. The valve should also be serviced any time there is air leakage or when the handle becomes difficult to turn.

Excessive force should not be used when turning a scuba valve on or off. Valve seat discs, gaskets and seals will be damaged. Open valves slowly and gently. Open the valve fully, then close the valve one-quarter turn (but no more) to relieve pressure on the stem seal. Some divers open a tank valve only slightly to measure tank pressure, then forget to open the valve fully before diving. This produces a restricted opening that limits air flow and causes you to think that you have had an air supply failure. Always open a valve fully.

Tank valves can seize to the threads of a scuba cylinder, especially in aluminum tanks. This is a result of galvanic corrosion. Having your tank valves serviced annually as recommended will prevent valve seizure.

Special Valves and Manifolds

Special scuba valves are available for specialty applications and multiple tank configurations. The activities requiring the use of such valves are considered advanced specialties requiring special training.

A dual valve for a single tank, known as a Slingshot valve, is available. This allows a diver to mount two regulator systems on a single tank. This configuration is useful for deep dives or enclosure dives made with a single tank. A high pressure connection between two or more cylinders is called a MANIFOLD. This device allows multiple tanks to

be ganged together for specialty activities which mandate a large reserve of air for safety.

SCUBA REGULATORS

Your scuba regulator reduces the pressure of air in your scuba tank to ambient pressure and delivers the air on demand, using the pressure differential created by the respiratory action of your lungs to regulate air flow. Scuba regulators automatically adjust to changes in depth and in your respiration rate.

High pressure air from your scuba tank is reduced in STAGES (pressure-reduction stops) to ambient pressure. Nearly all scuba regulators are two-stage devices. The FIRST STAGE reduces tank pressure to an INTERMEDIATE PRESSURE (or LOW PRESSURE) of 90-130 psi. The SECOND STAGE reduces the low pressure air to ambient (surrounding) pressure.

To understand the operational theory of a regulator, you need to be familiar with the types of

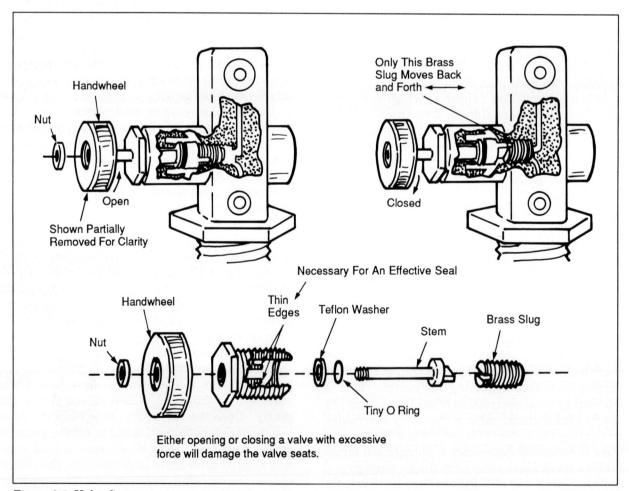

Figure 3.8 Valve Seats

DIVING EQUIPMENT

internal regulating valves used. The fundamental types are downstream and upstream valves. An UPSTREAM VALVE is one which is forced closed by high-pressure air, and a DOWNSTREAM VALVE is one that is forced open by high-pressure air. Upstream valves are rare in modern regulators. As cylinder pressure decreases, less ambient pressure is required to open an upstream valve. The downstream valve is configured with springs that can keep the valved closed at the maximum cylinder pressure and is, therefore, more resistant to opening as cylinder pressure decreases.

Types of Regulators

There are three basic types of regulators: Two-hose, single hose and integrated. The original scuba consisted of a TWO-HOSE REGULATOR in which both stages were combined into one mechanical assembly that mounted onto a scuba tank valve. Two flexible, low-pressure hoses led from either side of the regulator to a mouthpiece containing both inhalation and exhalation non-return valves. The hose that leads over the right shoulder carried fresh air to the diver, while the hose over the left shoulder carried exhaled air back to the regulator assembly on the tank where the used air was exhausted into the water. Regulator design evolved to SINGLE-HOSE REGULATORS, which are the standard type in use today because of their reliability, simplicity and ease of maintenance.

Although many hoses may be attached to a single hose regulator, only a single hose is involved in the operation of the regulator itself. With a single-hose regulator, the first pressure reduction stage is attached to the scuba tank, while the second reduction stage and the exhaust port are included in the mouthpiece portion that is attached to the first stage via a low pressure hose.

INTEGRATED REGULATORS are those which are incorporated into other items of equipment such as a buoyancy compensator low pressure inflator or a small contingency scuba unit.

First-Stage Valves

The internal valves of scuba regulator first stages are available in two types, diaphragm and piston. Both valves are produced in an unbalanced or a balanced configuration. A BALANCED VALVE is one in which air pressure does not affect the force needed to operate the valve. In other words, the valve operates the same regardless of tank pressure. The operation of an UNBALANCED VALVE is affected by tank pressure.

Figure 3.9 Manifold and Slingshot Valves.

The DIAPHRAGM FIRST-STAGE VALVE is an unbalanced upstream valve. A spring opposes the force of cylinder pressure and acts against a flexible diaphragm. The forces exerted by the spring, ambient pressure and high-pressure air, combine to activate the valve. During descent, the increasing water pressure in the spring chamber (which is free flooding) causes the diaphragm to bulge, which displaces the diaphragm and opens the valve until pressure equilibrium is restored. When you inhale, the reduced pressure in the INTERMEDIATE PRESSURE CHAMBER allows the spring to push in on the diaphragm and open the valve until equilibrium is restored.

The BALANCED DIAPHRAGM FIRST-STAGE VALVE is designed so the stem of the upstream valve extends completely through the high-pressure chamber, so the operation of the valve is not affected by tank pressure.

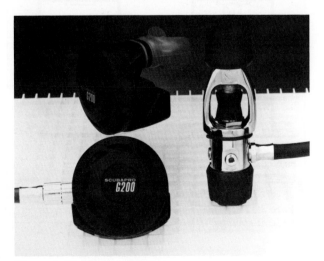

Figure 3.10 Modern Regulator

DIVING EQUIPMENT

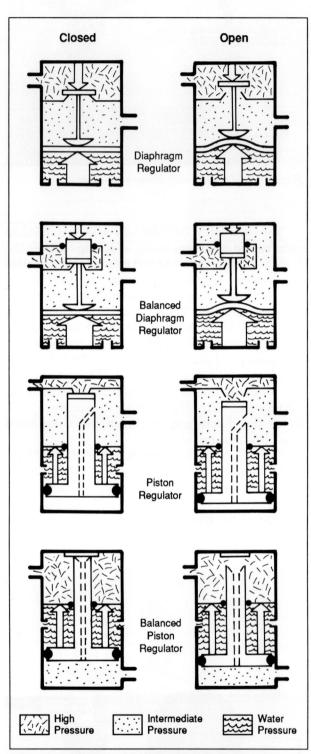

Closed   **Open**

Diaphragm Regulator

Balanced Diaphragm Regulator

Piston Regulator

Balanced Piston Regulator

High Pressure   Intermediate Pressure   Water Pressure

Figure 3.11 Typical regulator first stages. Arrows represent springs. Black dots represent O rings.

For both types of diaphragm first-stage valves, a failure of the diaphragm—although very rare—will cause the valve to close.

The UNBALANCED PISTON FIRST-STAGE VALVE is a downstream valve. A bias spring in the free-flooding spring chamber controls the intermediate pressure. A hole in the shaft of the piston allows the dry side of the piston to equalize at the intermediate pressure. During descent, increasing water pressure in the spring chamber displaces the piston and opens the valve until equilibrium is restored. When you inhale, the reduced pressure in the intermediate pressure chamber displaces the piston, opening the valve until equilibrium is restored. The balanced piston first-stage valve is designed so the piston movement is isolated from the high-pressure chamber by an O-ring; the operation of the valve is, therefore, independent of the tank pressure.

For both types of piston first-stage valves, a failure of the piston seal tends to cause the valve to fail in the open or FREE FLOW position.

Second-Stage Valves

Located in the mouthpiece of your regulator, the DOWNSTREAM SECOND-STAGE VALVE is connected to the first stage by a low pressure hose. A reduction in pressure in the second stage chamber causes the second stage diaphragm to bulge inward and depress a lever, which opens the valve and admits air into the mouthpiece at ambient pressure. As long as you continue to inhale, air will continue to flow. When inhalation ceases, the diaphragm returns to a flat position, releasing pressure on the lever, which closes the valve with spring pressure. Upon exhalation, pressure in the second stage chamber unseats the non-return exhaust valve, allowing used air to be exhausted into the water. With a downstream second-stage valve, any build up of pressure in the first stage of the regulator will simply push past the second-stage valve.

An UPSTREAM SECOND-STAGE VALVE, although rarely encountered, should be understood due to its potential hazards and inefficiency. A dangerous feature of this regulator is that if there is a build up of pressure in the first stage, the valve will be held tightly against its seat and shut off the flow of air. The low pressure hose will rupture if its burst pressure is exceeded. Regulators with upstream second-stage valves must be equipped with a pressure relief valve in the intermediate pressure chamber of the first stage to relieve any excess pressure,

DIVING EQUIPMENT

or an extra second stage with a downstream valve must be attached to the first stage.

An upstream second-stage valve operates in a manner similar to a downstream second-stage valve, but the diaphragm pushes against a stem instead of a lever. The stem is attached to the valve seat, and the valve is tilted or partially unseated when the stem is depressed by the diaphragm.

Tha main valve of a PILOT-VALVE REGULATOR is opened and closed using air pressure rather than mechanical leverage. The valve opening pressure is generated by air flow through a diaphragm-activated downstream pilot valve. A simple mechanical linkage is used between the diaphragm mechanism and the pilot valve. Because the pilot valve is tiny, only a small spring tension is required to counterbalance the pressure, and, therefore, less force is required to open or close it. The pilot valve opens only slightly and operates the air supply valve by passing a small amount of air into a control chamber.

Because there is a piston opposite the valve opening that exactly counteracts the opening force pressure, the supply valve is balanced and unaffected by variations in the intermediate pressure. The system can be described as a pneumatically amplified second stage—the small pilot valve pneumatically moves the larger air supply valve.

A pilot valve requires only one-fourth the inhalation effort required for other types of second stages. The operation of the second stage is initiated when the diaphragm is depressed. The linkage opens the pilot valve. Air flows through the pilot valve faster than it can flow through the hole in the flexible main valve, so a pressure difference occurs in the chamber, causing the main valve to open. This allows air to flow into the second stage until the pilot valve is closed and a build-up of pressure in the air chamber closes the main valve. The pilot valve acts as a safety relief valve in the event of a pressure build up in the first stage.

Regulator Attachments

Although single-hose regulators are used today, they can have many hoses attached to them. The following are required, recommended and optional regulator attachments:

1. Submersible pressure gauge—required.
2. BC low pressure inflator hose—strongly recommended.
3. Extra second stage (octopus)—strongly recommended.
4. Dry suit inflator hose—optional.

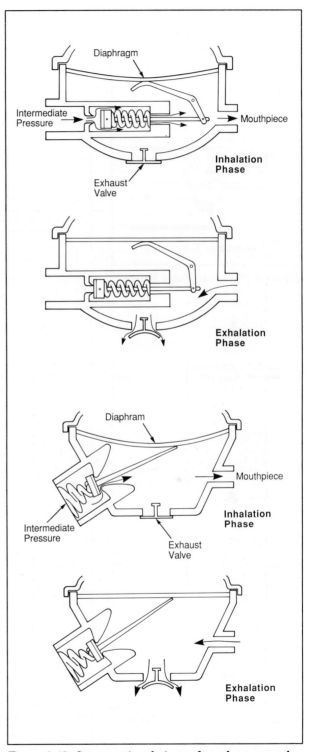

Figure 3.12 Cross-sectional views of regulator second stages.

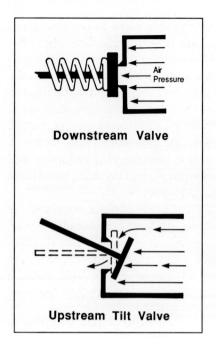

Figure 3.13 Second Stage Valves

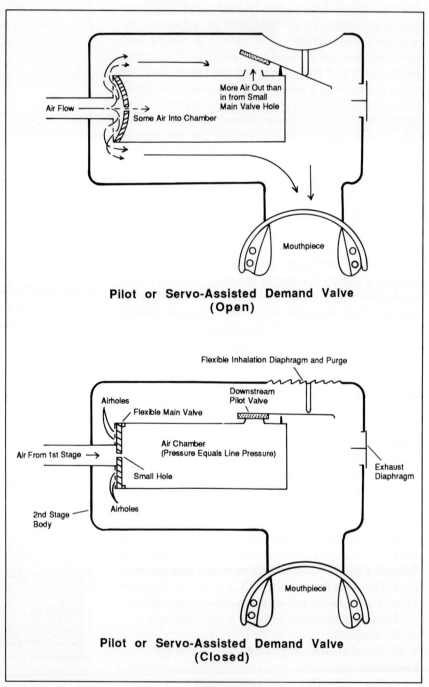

Figure 3.14 Pilot Valve Regulator Second Stage

DIVING EQUIPMENT

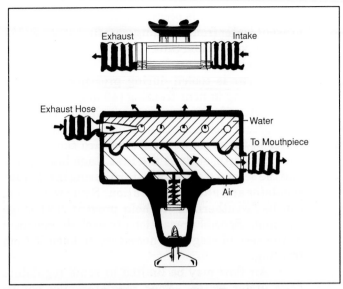

Figure 3.15 Single Stage Double Hose Regulator

A number of regulators have several low pressure ports in the first stage. If your regulator will not accommodate all of the items you would like to attach to it, multiple port adaptors are available at dive stores.

Regulator Care and Maintenance

You know your regulator should be rinsed after each use, that the purge button should not be depressed when there is water in the second stage, and that your regulator should be professionally serviced annually. You also know that the first stage dust cover should be in place any time the regulator is not in use. There are some other aspects of care that you should know at the advanced level.

1. It is better to soak your regulator in warm water and then rinse it, than it is to just rinse it. Be sure the first stage dust cover is well secured.

2. Do NOT lubricate your regulator. Especially avoid the use of silicon spray which ruins regulator parts and can allow the second stage diaphragm to be sucked out.

3. Your regulator should be functionally tested every six months. This test, which is quick and inexpensive, involves only a simple manometer.

4. An extra second stage attached to a regulator should also be functionally tested semi-annually and serviced annually.

5. Regulators used frequently in swimming pools require more frequent service than normal because the chlorine used to purify the pool dispels the lubricant used on internal seals.

6. Coloration of the filter on the first stage of your regulator may provide clues about the condition of the scuba cylinder you are using. A greenish filter indicates corrosion from moisture inside a tank or dripped onto the filter, a reddish filter indicates rust from a steel tank, and a blackish filter indicates carbon dust in your tank from a compressor filter. None of these problems is good for your regulator and any such indicator should prompt you to have the problem corrected.

7. Leaks from parts of your regulator, or tiny bubbles oozing from hoses under water, require prompt repair by a professional before the leakage becomes more serious. It is O.K. to finish a dive with a minor air leak, but the problem should be corrected before the next outing.

8. Have strain reliefs installed on every hose on your regulator. These sleeves relieve strain on the hoses and prolong their life.

9. Secure all regulator attachments while diving. This helps prevent damage to the attachments and to the diving environment. Dangling and dragging pressure gauges and extra second stages snag easily.

Regulator Concerns

There are several aspects of scuba regulators that may be of concern to you from time to time. As an advanced diver, you should be aware of the following:

1. Water can flow through a regulator if your tank is empty. Although you are not supposed to use all of the air in your tank, you may inadver-

Figure 3.16 Integrated Regulator

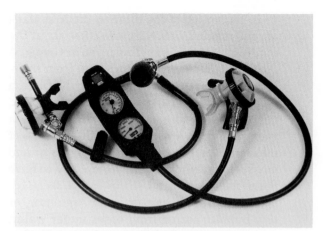

Figure 3.17 A modern scuba regulator with a combination low-pressure inflator, extra second stage and a console with memory depth gauge, submersible pressure gauge and digital timer.

Figure 3.18 First stage low pressure ports for accessories and an adaptor to increase the number of outlets.

Figure 3.19 First stage filters. Standard, flat type is on the right and newer, cone-shaped is on the left.

tently do so. If this occurs, close the tank valve to prevent water from reaching your first stage and/or entering your scuba tank.

2. Regulators can freeze with ice in very cold water. Air is cooled during pressure reduction. When diving in near-freezing (40 degrees Fahrenheit) water, the air flowing through your regulator can further decrease the temperature and cause water in the regulator to freeze. Ice can jam mechanical parts, such as the first stage bias spring and the second stage lever return spring inside your regulator and affect its operation. Some regulators can be "weatherized" to help prevent first stage freezing. Special precautions to exclude moisture in the second stage are necessary to keep it from freezing.

3. Air flow may be limited in some regulators deep under water. Your regulator may not be capable of delivering high flow rates at low tank pressures when two divers are breathing from it at the same time. Keep this in mind when selecting a regulator and choose one that can meet high demands at low pressures at depth.

DIVING INSTRUMENTS

Hopefully you use several gauges for diving—a submersible pressure gauge, a depth gauge, etc. You are about to find out how your gauges function and how to care for them.

Bourdon Movement

The quantity most often measured is pressure, and the BOURDON MOVEMENT GAUGE is used for such measurement. A Bourdon movement is a flattened helical tube that is sealed at one end. The

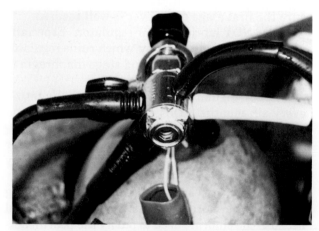

Figure 3.20 Strain relief sleeves greatly extend hose life.

DIVING EQUIPMENT

tube tends to uncurl when pressurized due to pressure differences between the inner arc of the tube and the outer arc. One end of the tube is attached to a linkage that moves an indicator needle.

If both ends of a Bourdon tube are sealed, the tube may be used to measure external pressure, which tends to curl the tube inward when a pressure greater than the internal pressure of the tube is surrounding the tube.

Another form of Bourdon Movement is a spiral, consisting of numerous coils with the closed end connected directly to the indicator needle. As pressure uncoils the spiral tubing, the needle moves. This design is commonly used for submersible pressure gauges.

Figure 3.21 Bourdon Tubes

Analog versus Digital

An ANALOG instrument has hands which move on a dial, while DIGITAL instruments provide a numeric information display. Mechanical instruments give analog data, and electronic instruments give digital information. Analog gauges are reasonably accurate and reliable. Digital gauges are very accurate, but are more subject to failure and are more expensive than mechanical instruments.

Cylinder Pressure Gauges

There are two types of pressure gauges for determining the amount of air in a scuba tank. A SURFACE CYLINDER PRESSURE GAUGE is used to check the amount of air in a tank above water. It attaches to the tank valve in the same manner as a regulator to provide a one-time check of tank pressure. A bleed valve relieves trapped pressure so the gauge can be removed when the tank valve has been closed.

A SUBMERSIBLE PRESSURE GAUGE (SPG) is the one attached to the first stage of your regulator. It provides a continual readout of the air in your tank. Some units have a CONSOLE to incorporate other gauges. SPG gauge movements are designed with an accuracy range of ±35 to 100 psi at a reading of about 500 psi. At full scale the accuracy is about ±5%.

An SPG is attached to the high pressure port of your regulator. There is some important information you need to know about this attachment point.

1. The high pressure regulator port is larger than the low pressure ports on modern regulators. This prevents attachments with low pressure hoses from being installed in the high pressure port, which is obviously dangerous. Older regulators still in use have the ports of equal size for both high and

Figure 3.22 Cylinder pressure gauge (left) compared to submersible pressure gauge.

Figure 3.23 Submersible Pressure Gauge

low pressure, so care is required when making first stage attachments. Adaptors are available for connecting old-style attachments to newer regulators.

2. Regulator high pressure ports have a restricted ORIFICE (opening) to limit the flow of air in case of a rupture of the SPG or its hose. The tiny hole (0.005 inches in diameter) prevents rapid depletion of the air supply. A high pressure leak does not constitute an emergency situation. Should one occur, simply make a normal ascent and close the tank valve.

Figure 3.24 First stage high pressure port. Note tiny hole. Also shown are the high pressure plug and a high pressure port adaptor to adapt old style smaller diameter high pressure hoses to newer regulator.

Cylinder pressure gauge types include spiral Bourdon movements or digital instrumentation. A digital gauge uses a pressure-sensitive transducer, a battery, some electronic circuitry and a liquid crystal display to provide information.

Should a leak develop in the Bourdon movement, high pressure air will flow into the gauge housing. This is why you are instructed not to look at your gauge when opening your tank valve. To prevent injury from an explosion of the housing in this instance, a safety plug is incorporated into the housing of most cylinder pressure gauges. Avoid obstructing the area over the plug so the plug will be free to blow out and release pressure if necessary.

If water is visible inside a cylinder pressure gauge, the gauge should not be used until repaired and tested. Pressure gauges require professional service and repair.

Cylinder pressure gauges should not be subjected to shock and abuse and should be inspected and verified for accuracy annually.

Depth Gauges

There are several types of depth gauges: Capillary, Bourdon tube, diaphragm and electronic.

The simplest and cheapest of all gauges is the CAPILLARY GAUGE. Air is compressed according to Boyle's Law in a length of clear tubing that is sealed at one end. Water enters the open end when

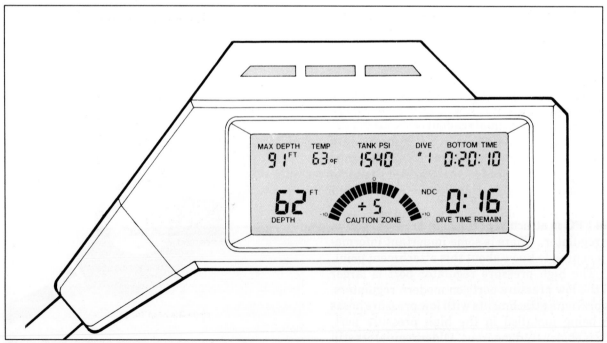

Figure 3.25 A digital submersible pressure gauge incorporated into a dive computer.

DIVING EQUIPMENT

the tube is submerged and compresses the column of air in proportion to the depth. The scale is non-linear, so the graduations on the scale become difficult to read in deeper water. A well-constructed capillary gauge can be extremely accurate, however, in shallow water and is also of value for altitude diving because it automatically provides equivalent depth readings at higher elevations.

Problems associated with capillary gauges include clogging of the tube, air bubbles in the tube, and difficulty in reading at low light levels. For these reasons, a capillary gauge should not be used as your primary depth gauge.

OPEN BOURDON TUBE depth gauges are the cheapest form of Bourdon movement depth gauge. The tube is mounted inside a case with the open end exposed to the water, which enters the tube. This type of gauge is subject to corrosion, silting and blockage by salt crystals, is no longer readily available, and is unpopular due to maintenance problems.

The SEALED BOURDON TUBE depth gauge was developed to overcome the problems associated with the open tube design. This gauge is fundamentally the same as the open Bourdon tube, except the tube is fluid-filled and the end is sealed with a rubber diaphragm. Water pressure is transmitted through the diaphragm to the oil, which exerts pressure on the tube.

The OIL-FILLED BOURDON TUBE gauge consists of a Bourdon movement sealed at both ends and enclosed in an oil-filled case. Either a pliable case or a diaphragm transmit pressure through the case and the oil to the Bourdon movement.

The DIAPHRAGM DEPTH GAUGE is the only mechanical gauge that does not use a Bourdon movement. They are expensive but accurate. A thin, metal diaphragm is mounted in a case which is rigid and hermetically sealed. Most of the air is removed from the case to form a partial vacuum. Water pressure on the diaphragm moves mechanical linkage attached to the indicator needle. Some diaphragm gauges are adjustable for use at altitude.

An electronic depth gauge is frequently called a DIGITAL DEPTH GAUGE. This gauge operates in the same way an electronic cylinder pressure gauge does, but at lower pressures. Digital depth gauges can be sensitive to temperature variations and they require batteries for operation. A digital depth gauge can also be difficult to read in low light levels unless the instrument has a backlit screen feature. These gauges are, however, extremely accurate and

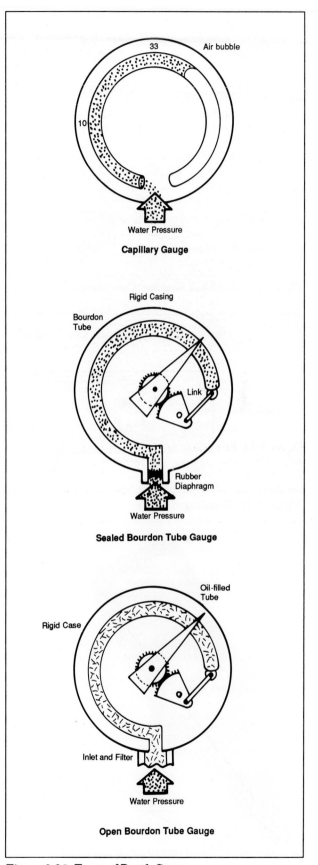

Figure 3.26 Types of Depth Gauges

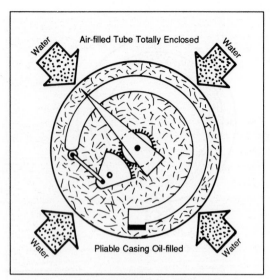

Figure 3.27 Enclosed Bourdon Tube Gauge

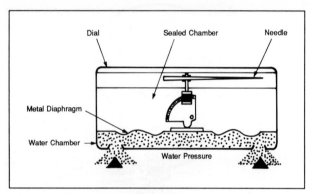

Figure 3.28 Diaphragm Gauge

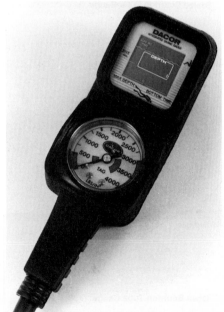

Figure 3.29 A digital diving gauge combined with a tank pressure gauge in a console.

easy to read without error. Other features, such as a maximum depth indicator or an ascent rate indicator, may be easily incorporated.

Depth gauges measure pressure. The dials are calibrated in fsw. 33 fsw may equal 34 fsw, but the pressure is the same. Gauges may be subject to damage if exposed to reduced pressures when flying and should be transported inside pressure-tight containers or inside a pressurized cabin.

A desirable feature of a depth gauge is a MAXIMUM DEPTH INDICATOR, which retains the maximum depth reached during a dive. The indicator can be mechanical on analog gauges or electronic on digital gauges. The maximum depth indicator resets automatically on digital gauges, but you must remember to manually reset the indicator on mechanical gauges.

Accuracy for mechanical gauges is typically ± 1% of the full scale for the first half of the depth scale and ± 2% of the full scale for the second half of the scale. This accuracy is further affected by age, abuse and reduced ambient pressure exposures. The accuracy of electronic depth gauges is ±1 foot (30 cm). All depth gauges should be calibrated annually, either by means of a marked line for comparison or with the use of a "pressure pot" at your local dive store. Interim checks can be performed by comparing your depth gauge to a capillary gauge at shallow depths.

Depth gauges should be treated with care. Prevent shock and low pressure damage. Avoid leaving gauges—especially oil-filled gauges—in the sun because heat will expand the oil and can produce leakage.

Underwater Timers

Both analog and digital dive watches are available, and some watches feature both types of displays. An analog dive watch usually has a rotating outer bezel to indicate elapsed time. A bezel that rotates anti-clockwise only is preferred so the indicated elapsed time can only err on the side of safety.

BOTTOM TIMERS are pressure-activated instruments that automatically record the time spent below a depth of about three feet (one meter). Both digital and analog types are available. A distinct advantage of a bottom timer over an underwater timer is the automatic operation since you may forget to set a watch.

Dive watches and bottom timers should be rinsed with fresh water after diving, and should be cleaned and inspected annually. Avoid wearing your dive watch in a jacuzzi, hot tub or in the

90

shower. The combination of high temperature and soap can result in damage.

Dive Computers

A DIVE COMPUTER (DC) is an instrument that provides a digital display of several or all of the following items of information:
1. Current depth
2. Maximum depth
3. Elapsed bottom time
4. Surface interval
5. Temperature
6. No-decompression time remaining
7. Dive time remaining based on air supply and consumption
8. Repetitive group designation
9. Ascent rate
10. Dive number
11. Dive profile
12. When flying is safe
13. SCROLLING (Displaying in sequence the no-decom limits for various depths for repetitive dives.
14. CEILING (decompression stop depth).

A dive computer (DC) has the capability of becoming the "ultimate instrument" for diving activities. Some DCs merely combine information that would usually require several instruments and present the information in a single digital display. Other DCs are decompression computers that continuously calculate nitrogen pressure in various tissue models and allow longer bottom times because they compensate for time spent at varying depths throughout a dive compared to square wave dive profiles required by use of the U.S. Navy tables.

You may be encouraged to use an DC only as a back-up for dives planned according to the U.S. Navy dive tables. This is inconsistent with the purpose of a diving computer, which provides information based on MULTI-LEVEL DIVING (dives at more than one depth level) computations, not on the "total time at the maximum depth" calculations of the dive tables. Limiting a dive to the Navy time limits defeats the purpose of the computer. The use of Navy table rules may specify that decompression

Figure 3.30 Maximum Depth Indicators

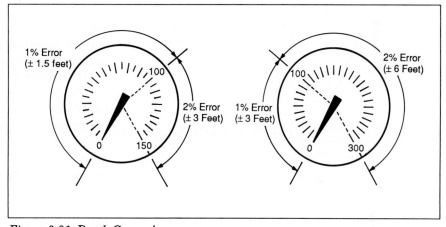

Figure 3.31 Depth Gauge Accuracy

Figure 3.32 Dive Watches

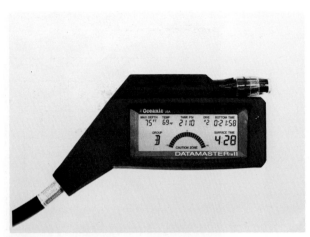

Figure 3.33 Typical Dive Computer Display

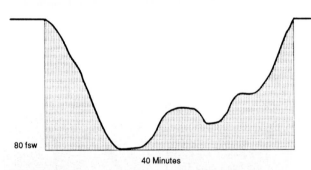

80 fsw

40 Minutes

Figure 3.34 Square wave vs. Actual Dive Profile. Shaded region indicates times during the dive where less inert gas is absorbed than what the tables assume.

D. Story photo

Figure 3.35 Decompression Computers

is required, while a DC indicates otherwise due to multi-level calculations.

Because DC dive limits are derived differently than those of the Navy tables, it is not credible practice for a diver to revert to the tables during a day of diving following dives in which an DC has been used unless the "maximum time at maximum depth" rule is applied. In short, it is not feasible to dive according to the Navy tables when using a DC. Divers using computers must, therefore, understand the devices and use them properly.

The basic design of a decompression computer electronic dive monitor (DC) is presented in figure 3.36.

A pressure transducer in the decompression computer DC produces a signal which is changed from analog to digital by the Analog-to-Digital (A/D) converter. A microprocessor reads the digital transducer signal, makes calculations and controls the display. The Read Only Memory (ROM) contains the program for the microprocessor, which the Random Access Memory (RAM) stores the information resulting from computations. A clock synchronizes the operations and serves as a timer. A battery supplies power for the operation of the circuitry, and a housing protects all of the components from the environment.

There are two basic types of DCs: TISSUE-BASED and TABLE-BASED. A tissue-based computer calculates nitrogen absorption in a number of theoretical body tissues and displays a warning or ceiling if the nitrogen level in any tissue approaches or exceeds programmed limits. A table-based dive computer compares time and depth data to the mathematical model of established dive tables. Warnings are displayed when the no-decompression limits of the tables programmed into the computer are approached or exceeded. A table-based computer does more than simply store a set of dive tables electronically. The computer compares time and depth input against the tables continuously to credit the diver for multi-level dives. This provides longer dive times than can be obtained using conventional dive tables. A table-based computer can also provide a repetitive group designation following a dive so the user can revert to use of standard dive tables even following multi-level dives.

A DC does not take all factors into consideration, so it must be used accordingly. It makes the same computations in cold water and in warm water, for older divers and younger divers, for those who are feeling well and for those who are not, for those who are exerting and for those who are not. You must,

DIVING EQUIPMENT

therefore, adjust and limit your dive profiles based on such factors.

As with any electronic device, there is always the possibility of operational failure. You should carry a back-up depth gauge and underwater timer in case of a failure of your DC. The possibility of a DC failure is quite low, but not all together impossible. If your DC should fail while diving, you are to ascend immediately and perform, as a safety precaution, a decompression stop of at least five minutes.

Failure of a DC or the accidental switching off of one of these instruments when it contains information from current diving activities poses a problem which can be handled only by delaying further diving for the number of hours required for the particular make and model of instrument to outgas completely. This time is not necessarily 12 hours, and is specified by the manufacturer of the device.

DCs are to be used for no-decompression diving only. The devices are to be used in such a way that any ceiling is avoided at any time during a dive.

Dive buddies may not share a single DC. Each diver relying on a computer for dive planning and no-decompression status must be equipped with a DC.

The care of an electronic dive monitor should be appropriate for an expensive submersible computer. Prevent shock, extreme heat, close proximity of magnetic fields, etc. DCs are not damaged by reduced pressure at higher elevations. In fact, some computers adjust for reduced atmospheric pressure and function correctly for altitude diving. Rinse your DC well after every use. Carefully follow battery replacement procedures. Your DC will provide ample warning when replacement of batteries is needed.

A DC can make diving easier and allow you to spend more time underwater than conventional dive tables. You must, however use your dive computer wisely and properly.

Diving Compasses

A freely suspended magnet tends to align itself with the magnetic field created by the earth, which acts as a large magnet. This principle is the basis for a valuable reference device called a compass. Special compasses designed to withstand the environment are available for diving and are extremely useful reference instruments.

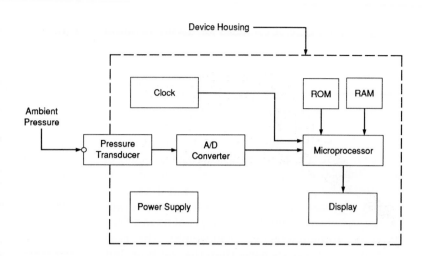

Figure 3.36 Decompression Computer Block Diagram

Figure 3.37 A dive computer provides useful information, which should not be misconstrued as instructions.

Diving compasses are either dry or liquidfilled. The preferred type of compass for diving is liquid filled. This type consists of a magnetic disc called a COMPASS CARD that rests upon a bearing. Incorporated into the card is a float that minimizes the weight of the card on the bearing. Well-constructed wet compasses can correctly indicate direction even when tilted considerably from a level position. The liquid also serves to dampen the movement of the compass card, which makes the instrument easy to use. Since the instrument is full of liquid, it is unaffected by pressures encountered at depth.

Dry compass construction is similar to the wet compass, but the compass card does not have a float assembly and must be lighter in weight. This type of compass is less expensive than the wet type, but a dry compass is less accurate; the card tends to oscillate (swing back and forth) and is subject to the effects of pressure.

Use of diving compasses is described in the Navigation chapter in the Diving Techniques section of this book.

Your compass merits the same treatment that should be accorded all diving instruments. Rinse it well after use, giving particular care to the BEZEL (rotating collar). Prevent shock and prolonged exposure to sunlight and high temperatures. Heat will cause the liquid in a wet compass to expand and can cause leakage. Recalibration of compasses is not required.

BUOYANCY COMPENSATORS

As an advanced diver you need to know more about the engineering and maintenance of a buoyancy compensator (BC). There are many types, designs and features of BCs, all of which contain some essential components with which you are about to become more familiar.

All BCs are equipped with a pressure relief valve which prevents overpressurization of the bladder. The valve is held closed by a spring with a tension of about two psi (0.1406 kg/cm$_2$). When the internal pressure of the BC exceeds this amount, the spring pressure is overcome and any excess pressure is vented.

Some buoyancy compensators are equipped with a DUMP VALVE to allow rapid manual deflation of the bladder. A lanyard from a point high on the bladder extends to a location that enables easy operation by the user. The functions of the pressure relief valve and a dump valve are combined by some manufacturers.

BCs may be equipped with a carbon dioxide (CO_2) inflator. The intent of this device is to enable

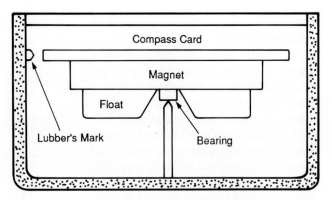

Figure 3.38 Parts of a typical diving compass.

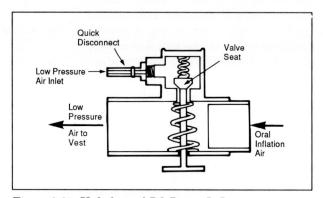

Figure 3.39 Unbalanced BC Power Inflator

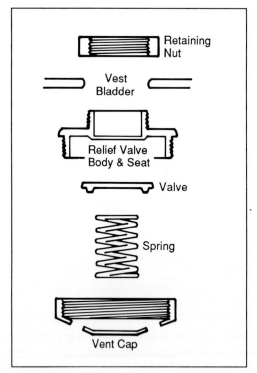

Figure 3.40 BC Over Pressure Relief Valve

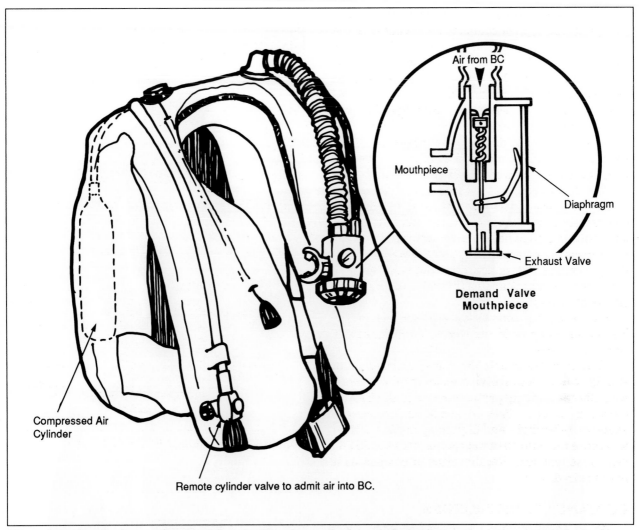

Figure 3.41 *A scuba buoyancy control device with a demand valve mouthpiece*

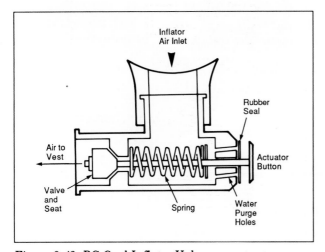

Figure 3.42 *BC Oral Inflator Valve*

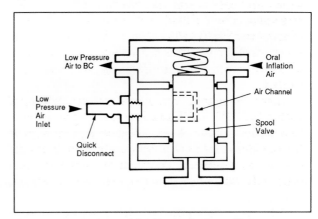

Figure 3.43 *Balanced BC Power Inflator Valve*

Figure 3.44 BC and a typical CO_2 inflator assembly shown disassembled.

DIVING EQUIPMENT

rapid inflation of the BC at the surface. Alternative inflation by means of a low-pressure inflator, which is a recommended component for a BC, combined with a high degree of care and maintenance required to ensure reliable operation of a CO_2 inflator, have resulted in unpopularity of CO_2 devices. As a result, some manufacturers offer CO_2 inflators as an option.

If a CO_2 inflator is desired or used, its care is important. Following every dive the mechanism must be carefully rinsed and dried. The cartridge must then be removed and the threads cleaned and lubricated prior to replacement. Expended cartridges must be promptly replaced or rust particles will form, which can cause damage to the mechanism and to your BC.

A recommended alternative to a CO_2 inflator is a LOW PRESSURE INFLATOR, which uses low pressure air from your regulator to inflate your BC. The inflators are available with either balanced or unbalanced valves. A balanced valve is recommended because its operation is easier, since it is unaffected by low pressure air.

A type of BC that is available in Europe and in Canada includes a small air tank for emergency inflation of the bladder independent from the primary scuba unit. The unit also has a demand mouthpiece that allows air in the bladder to be inhaled, while the exhausted breath passes into the water just as it does in a scuba regulator. Depressing the manual inflator valve allows rebreathing of exhaled air to prolong the air supply. The use of a BC as a breathing bag is a skill that requires training and which must be reserved for emergency use only. Such a technique may be appropriate for highly specialized diving in enclosed areas, but is inappropriate for typical recreational diving. Serious injury can result if the high concentration of carbon dioxide from a CO_2 cartridge is breathed accidently from a BC.

BCs merit more than casual care. Internal rinsing is critical, especially for ocean diving. Prevent water from entering the bladder by orienting the mouthpiece of the deflation valve downward when the valve is open. The BC can still be deflated by raising the deflator valve above the BC, but the inverted mouthpiece will act as an air trap to exclude water. Your buoyancy compensator should be inflated for storage. The storage area should be temperature regulated and free from smog and ozone. Many divers store their expensive diving equipment in a garage, which is not a good environment for the materials used in the equipment.

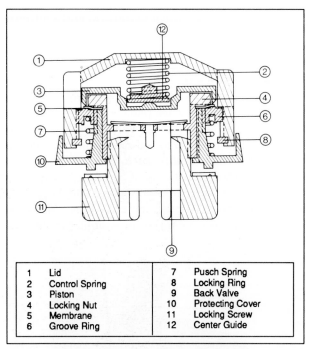

1	Lid	7	Pusch Spring
2	Control Spring	8	Locking Ring
3	Piston	9	Back Valve
4	Locking Nut	10	Protecting Cover
5	Membrane	11	Locking Screw
6	Groove Ring	12	Center Guide

Figure 3.45 Dry suit exhaust valve that vents automatically.

DRY SUITS

Dry suits are the most efficient way for a scuba diver to remain comfortable in cold water. The most popular dry suits on the market today are made from a variety of waterproof materials, including vulcanized rubber, waterproofed nylons, and compressed neoprene. The suits seal at the neck and wrists and are equipped with waterproof zippers for entry. Low pressure inflator mechanisms prevent suit squeeze and suit exhaust valves allow air to escape upon ascent. The theory behind these suits is that they form a waterproof barrier but offer little or no insulation value themselves. To be warm, you must wear some type of thermal insulation beneath the suit. These suits also have no inherent buoyancy.

Compressed neoprene suits possess the ability to stretch, which allows the suit to be tailored well to the diver's body. The seams of these suits are glued and stitched. On site repairs to this material, when punctured, can be difficult.

Waterproof laminated nylons have almost no stretch. Suits made from these materials must be cut quite loosely to allow you to dress into them without difficulty. This creates some added volume in the suit which may increase your weight requirements. You can do some minor repairs to these types of suits yourself but major repairs must be handled by the manufacturer.

Vulcanized rubber dry suits should be manufactured from a combination of natural and synthetic materials to resist ozone. This material has very good stretch. Repairs to this material are similar to patching an inner tube or inflatable boat and can be done at the dive site.

All dry suits should be equipped with attached hard sole boots and knee pads.

Automatic suit exhaust valves which vent air upon ascent without manual operation by the diver, are another important feature. Exhaust valves are usually located on a sleeve of the suit.

Better dry suit inflator valves and hoses are designed with restricted orifices. This helps prevent accidental over-inflation should the inflator

Figure 3.46 In water colder than 55° F, a polypropylene liner, worn beneath dry suit underwear, will provide added insulation and wick sweat away from your body.

valve stick. Valves with large orifices or high flows may freeze during ice diving. The exhaust valve on the suit should vent the suit faster than the inflator valve can supply air. Inflator valves are normally located on the chest of the suit.

Inflator hoses for dry suits should only be connected to a low pressure port on your regulator's first stage. The hose should reach the inflator valve

without strain. Some inflator valves can be rotated to provide you with a choice of how to route the inflator hose (i.e., under the arm, over the shoulder, etc.).

Not all inflator hoses are compatible with all dry suit inflator valves.

The quality of waterproof zippers varies greatly among manufacturers. A careful comparison will assure you of reliable operation. Generally speaking, the larger waterproof zippers are the strongest.

There are many options available on today's dry suits and one of the most important is a dry hood. More than 50% of your body heat is lost through your head. A dry hood with an insulating liner will help keep you warm under the coldest conditions. If a dry hood is used, you must remember to equalize the air space in the hood during descent by exhaling through your nose into your mask and forcing a small amount of air into the hood. Scuba mask purge valves can be mounted in dry hoods to allow excess air to escape during ascent. Ordinary wet suit hoods can also be worn with dry suits. Other dry suit options include pockets, relief zippers (for men only), and dry gloves.

Dry gloves are recommended for diving in water colder than 50 degrees Fahrenheit. A complete dry

Figure 3.47 Most dry suits come equipped with latex seals at the wrist and neck.

DIVING EQUIPMENT

glove system is composed of a set of insulating liners. The inner rings are designed to fit inside the sleeve of the dry suit at the cuff. The outer rings fit over the sleeve and snap into position when properly aligned with the inner rings. The dry gloves or mittens stretch over the outer rings and are held in place by a compression fit.

Figure 3.48 Your weight belt should be trimmed to the correct length while wearing your dry suit and the maximum amount of insulation you will use during cold water diving.

Dry suits generally fit quite a bit looser than wet suits. Unless you have an unusual shape, custom suits are not usually necessary. The most critical part of a dry suit's fit is the length. The suit should be long enough that you can bend and squat comfortably, without being too long. If the suit is too short, you will not be able to swim effectively or climb a ladder comfortably.

Once you have purchased a dry suit, be sure to take the time to adjust the neck seal to your neck size. Neck seals are cone shaped and must be trimmed with sharp scissors. As a rule of thumb, the circumference of the neck seal opening should be approximately 10%-15% less than the circumference of your neck.

Dry suits must be carefully maintained. Latex wrist and neck seals should be periodically washed with mild soap and water to remove body oils which attack the rubber. When dry, dust the latex seals of your suit with pure, unscented talc.

Clean your dry suit zipper periodically using a small nylon brush and soapy water on the teeth.

Dry suit zippers should be lubricated with paraffin wax on the outside only. Silicone spray should never be used on dry suits or dry suit zippers. Silicone on your suit will make it impossible to create a strong bond when patches are applied during repairs.

Rinse the outside of your suit after each diving day, paying particular attention to the valves. If the suit has been flooded in salt water, or if you sweat heavily while wearing the suit, rinse the inside, too. Be sure to allow both the outside and the inside of the suit to dry before storage. Many people make the mistake of only feeling inside the upper torso of the suit to check if it is dry at the end of the diving day. However, sweat accumulates in the lower portions of the suit, creating mold if the interior of the suit is not allowed to dry before storage. Turn the suit inside out and be sure it dries thoroughly before you put it away. Your dry suit should always be stored rolled up in a bag.

Figure 3.49 Dry gloves and a dry hood provide maximum warmth in the coldest water.

Waterproof zippers are especially vulnerable to mishandling. More zippers are broken through improper storage and handling than through actual use. Zippers have a reasonable bend radius when open but less than 50% of the same bend radius when closed. If your suit is stored with the zipper closed and a weight belt is dropped on the zipper, it may possibly break. Always store your suit with the zipper open!

Effective dry suit underwear is critical to the optimum performance of your dry suit in cold water. The function of dry suit underwear is to trap a layer of air inside the suit. The number of layers and type of underwear you will require is contingent upon the water temperature, your individual body type and physiology. There are several different types of underwear materials commonly used for diving including open cell foam, Thinsulate, radiant insulating material, "wooly bears" and polypropylene liners.

Dry suit underwear must not drastically compress when pressure is applied or it will not work efficiently at depth. Open cell foam, Thinsulate, and radiant insulating material are all examples of dry suit underwear which maintain most of their original thickness in use. Conversely, "wooly bears" lose much of their insulating capacity during a dive.

You may not realize it while you are diving, but frequently you will sweat while wearing your dry suit. For this reason, you will want to launder your dry suit underwear occasionally. Open cell foam and "wooly bears" may be laundered with mild detergents. Radiant insulating material may only be laundered with non-phosphate detergents. Thinsulate can only be laundered with bleach. Improper laundering of Thinsulate garments will destroy their insulating abilities.

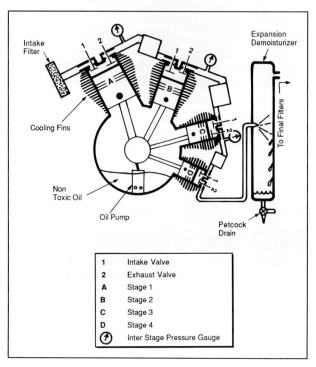

Figure 3.51 Typical Four Stage Compressor

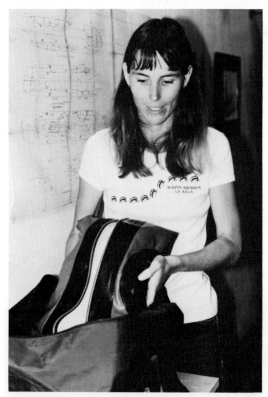

Figure 3.50 Dry suits should always be stored in a bag, with the zipper open, in a cool, dry place.

Be especially cautious of undergarments which produce lint. "Wooly bears", in particular, will create lint and clog your dry suit exhaust valve. Lint can cause the valve to jam, either open or closed. If the valve jams open, it will leak and you will get wet. If the valve jams closed, you will not be able to vent air from the suit and you could experience an uncontrolled ascent.

Thinsulate and radiant insulating material are both efficient insulators, even when wet. Open cell foam maintains good efficiency when damp but will not keep you warm if your suit floods. "Wooly bears" rapidly lose their heat trapping capabilities when damp.

The dry suit and insulation combination worn will determine the amount of weight you will need for diving. The more insulation worn, the more air will be trapped in the suit. In general, most dry suit underwear combinations require some additional weight beyond what you might wear with a full one-quarter inch thick wet suit. Open cell foam underwear and radiant insulating undergarments require the least amount of additional weight. "Wooly bears" and Thinsulate require the greatest amount of additional weight.

Polypropylene liners are worn next to your skin, beneath the dry suit undergarments. The purpose of the liner is to wick moisture (sweat) away from your body to keep you feeling dry. The liner also serves as an extra bit of insulation in colder waters.

Other equipment adaptations must also be made when using a dry suit. Extra large fins are a necessity with most dry suit boots. Back mounted buoyancy systems work better with most dry suit valve configurations. Low pressure swivel "Ts" may be needed on some regulators to accommodate the addition of the dry suit inflator hose. Ankle weights may be used to help distribute additional weight.

Careful selection of the components of your dry suit system will give you the greatest comfort, safety and productivity for cold water diving.

AIR COMPRESSORS

Advanced divers should be familiar with the basics of breathing air compressors, filtration systems and storage systems. There are two main types of compressors: high-pressure, low volume, used to fill scuba tanks; and low-pressure, high volume, used for surface-supplied diving.

High-pressure, low volume compressors are similar to other types used for industrial purposes except that non-toxic oil must be used for lubrication, and special attention is required to prevent contamination of the air.

A compressor operates on the principle of Boyle's Law—pressure is increased by reducing volume. The air is compressed in stages. The volume of each successive stage in a compressor is smaller in order to achieve an increase in pressure at that particular stage. Air is prevented from returning to a previous stage by the use of one-way check valves located between each stage. Each stage is equipped with an overpressure relief valve to protect the machine from damage.

Compressors may be powered by either internal combustion or electric motors. Fewer toxins are produced by an electric motor.

Air compressors are rated according to how many cubic feet per minute (CFM) they can pump on the average. If an empty 80 cubic foot cylinder were pumped to 3,000 psi in ten minutes, the rating of the compressor would be eight CFM.

Air is heated when it is compressed, and the compressed air contains moisture, which is undesirable in scuba cylinders. Air from the final stage of a compressor is usually directed into an expansion chamber, where the expansion reduces the temperature and causes the condensation of most of the moisture. Water collects at the bottom of this "moisture trap", which requires periodic draining.

Air from a compressor usually passes through two or more filters in series. These filters remove odors and further reduce the humidity of the air, but will not remove carbon monoxide. Some filtration systems incorporate a catalytic converter, which converts carbon monoxide to carbon dioxide, which can be removed. The air then passes through a manifold system into large storage cylinders, each equipped with a separate shut-off valve. A storage system, sometimes called an "air bank", allows high pressure air pumped over a relatively long period of time to be used to fill scuba tanks in a comparatively short period of time. The storage cylinders are charged during periods of low demand, and air from both the storage cylinders and the compressors is used during periods of high demand.

One or more filler hoses with tank connectors, on-off valves and bleed valves is connected to the storage cylinder bank.

Small, portable compressors are available for filling scuba cylinders at remote locations. Portable compressors are usually rated at about three to five CFM and are similar to larger, fixed position com-

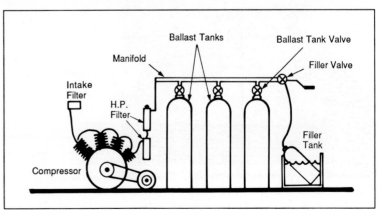

Figure 3.52 A typical scuba air station.

Figure 3.53 Hookah Compressor

Figure 3.54 A portable compressor. The air intake at the end of the hose must be located well away from the exhaust.

pressors with the exception that storage cylinder banks are usually not used. Tanks are filled directly from the compressor. Positioning of the air intake and faithful maintenance are extremely important for safety when portable compressors are being used. Follow manufacturers instructions carefully.

Low-pressure, high-volume compressors are available for surface-supplied diving, often referred to as HOOKAH DIVING. A standard regulator second stage is attached to a harness that is attached to an air hose leading to the compressor on the surface. Such a compressor should have a volume tank on its output to provide a limited emergency supply of air in case the compressor should stop. A backup air supply in the form of scuba cylinders on the surface or a bailout bottle—a small scuba cylinder carried by the diver—should also be used for surface-supplied diving operations. Divers should be trained for diving with an umbilical hose prior to engaging in surface-supplied diving.

DIVE LIGHTS

A dive light is essential for diving at night and useful for daytime diving. The two basic types of lights are those that are rechargeable and those that are not. Rechargeable lights are more expensive initially, but do not require batteries to be purchased, so may be less expensive over a long period of time if the light is used frequently. The manufacturers instructions should be followed for the recharging of dive lights. Overcharging is discouraged.

Two lights are recommended for diving at night—a high-powered, primary light and a small backup light. High-powered dive lights should not be switched on above water because heat generated inside the lights may damage them. Use of the small backup light or a regular flashlight for above-water activities is recommended.

Attach a lanyard to the dive light and use the lanyard to prevent loss while diving. Rinse the

DIVING EQUIPMENT

dive light after use, open it for drying, and clean and lubricate the sealing O-rings prior to reassembly of the light. Do not store a dive light with disposable batteries inside. Avoid mixing brands of batteries and avoid using new batteries with older ones.

Closing Thoughts

The more you learn about diving, the more you will learn about diving equipment. NAUI specialty courses on equipment are available. If you have further interest in this area, consider taking the Equipment Specialty course.

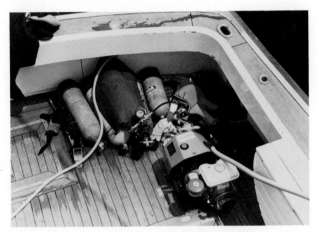

Figure 3.55 A portable compressor in operation. The air intake is out of sight to the right upwind from the compressor.

Figure 3.56 Various Dive Lights and Chargers.

THE DIVING ENVIRONMENT

4

The diving environment is all the external conditions and influences affecting the life and development of the organisms contained in the water in which we dive. It takes into account the life forms that live there and its effects upon us as visitors. The purpose of this section is to increase your knowledge and understanding of both the physical and biological aspects of diving environments that can affect or engage you. As a diver you need to know how to move in and under the water in such a way that you can protect both yourself and the life forms you encounter in the waters.

LEARNING OBJECTIVES:

By the end of this course, you need to be able to:

1. Identify and explain the cause, possible effects upon divers, and ways to cope with certain effects of:

Tides, seiches, waves, surge surf, currents, thermoclines, haloclines, bottom composition, weather conditions, water conditions, man-made structures, plankton, algae, hazardous aquatic animals, and pollution.

2. Correctly define the environmental terms presented in CAPITAL LETTERS in this chapter.

3. State at least three actions a diver can take to preserve the underwater environment.

4. Explain the need and value of diving orientations and how to obtain them.

PHYSICAL ASPECTS

Waves

WAVES are a series of undulating energy forms moving through water while the water remains in the same place. Waves are generally propagated on the water's surface by wind and move in the same direction as the wind. They are secondarily caused by geological disturbances and by the gravitational influences of the sun and moon.

Waves are measured in terms of their height, length and period. The height of a wave is the vertical distance from its CREST (highest point) to its TROUGH (lowest point). A WAVELENGTH is the horizontal distance between successive crests (or troughs), and the PERIOD is the time required for two successive crests to pass a given point.

The volume of water transported by a passing wave is negligible and can be disregarded for all practical purposes unless the wave breaks. The water particles within a wave move in an orbital motion as the wave form moves forward, returning to nearly their original position as the wave passes. The surface particles move in a circular orbit which equals the wave height. Beneath the surface, the orbits become smaller and smaller, finally diminishing to nothing at a depth equal to approximately one-half the distance between waves. If waves have a wavelength of 50 feet, the influence of those waves will be greatly diminished at a depth of 25 feet or more.

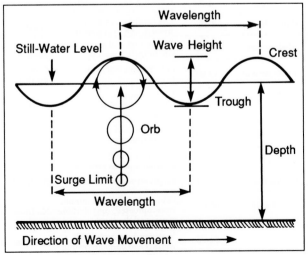

Figure 4.1 Wave Terminology

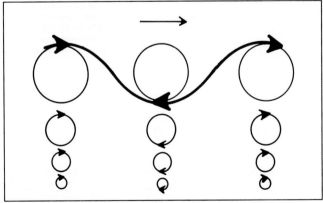

Figure 4.2 Orbital Movement of Water–as a wave passes, water particles (represented by the circles) do not move with the wave; rather, they complete their orbit by returning to their starting point.

Water waves develop under the influence of newly formed winds. The air pressure changes on the surface of the water and the frictional drag of the moving air develops ripples on the surface which evolve into waves whose dimensions increase with the wind velocity, duration and fetch. FETCH is the distance over which the wind blows. Energy is transferred directly from the air to the water. Waves pushed by the wind continue to grow until the wind subsides or until their steepness increases and they break to form whitecaps. In a steady wind, waves of various dimensions develop with progressively increasing heights and periods until a steady state is reached in which the surface is fully developed for the prevailing wind speed. This steady state, known as SEA, is maintained as long as the wind remains constant.

When the wind velocity decreases or the waves leave the fetch area, their height decreases, their crests round, their wavelength shortens, and they are called SWELLS—waves which are fairly regular in height, period and direction. In this form, waves can travel thousands of miles while retaining much of their energy.

Extremely large, destructive waves can be generated by earthquakes beneath the seas. These rare

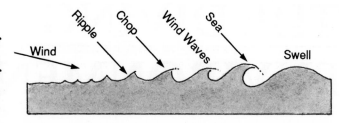

Wave Development

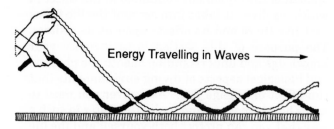

Figure 4.3 Wave Development and Movement—Wave movement is a flow of energy similar to that caused by vertically shaking one end of a rope.

occurrances generate waves, once called tidal waves or "Tsunamis". In reality, they have nothing to do with the tides, and are now properly called SEISMIC WAVES. These great waves travel at tremendous speed and build to great heights as they approach land. For this reason, diving must be

BEAUFORT WIND SCALE

Beaufort International Number	Wind	Nautical Miles per Hours (knots)	Feet per Second	Indications at Sea	Wind	Statute mph recorded at 33ft above ground level	Indications on Land	Diving Outlook
	AS USED AT SEA				**AS USED ON LAND**			
0	Calm	<1	< 2	Sea mirror smooth	Calm	<1	Smoke rises vertically.	Excellent
1	Lt. air	1-3	2-5	Sm. scale wavelets, no foam crests.	Lt. air	1-3	Direction shown by smoke but not by wind vanes.	Excellent
2	Lt. breeze	4-6	6-11	Waves short and more pronounced; crests begin to break; foam has glassy look.	Lt. breeze	4-7	Wind felt on face; ordinary vanes move; leaves rustle	Very good
3	Gentle breeze	7-10	12-18		Gentle breeze	8-12	Leaves & sm. twigs in motion; wind extends flag.	Good
4	Mod. breeze	11-16	19-27	Waves are longer, many white horses.	Mod. breeze	13-18	Raises dust and waste paper; sm. branches moved.	Care needed
5	Fresh breeze	17-21	28-36	Waves pronounced & long, white foam crests	Fresh breeze	19-24	Sm. trees in leaf begin to sway.	Great care needed
6	Strong breeze	22-27	37-46	Larger waves; white foam crests more extensive.	Strong breeze	25-31	Lg. branches in motion; whistling heard in telephone wires.	No Dive!
7	Strong wind	28-33	47-56	Sea heaps up; wind blows foam in streaks.	Mod. gale	32-38	Whole trees in motion; difficult to walk against wind.	No Dive!
8	Fresh gale	34-40	57-68	Height of waves & crests increases visibly; foam blown in denser streaks.	Fresh gale	39-46	Breaks twigs off trees; greatly impedes progress.	No Dive!
9	Strong gale	41-47	69-80		Strong gale	47-54	Slight structural damage.	No Dive!
10	Whole gale	48-55	81-93	High waves with long overhanging crests; great foam crests.	Whole gale	55-63	Seldom experienced inland; trees uprooted; considerable structural damage.	No Dive!
11	Storm	56-65	94-110	Waves that hide ships within the troughs; sea covered with streaky foam; spray fills air.	Storm	64-75	Very rarely experienced; widespread damage results.	No Dive!
12	Hurricane	>65	>110		Hurricane	>75		No Dive!

Table 4.1

avoided following major geological disturbances. Seismic wave predictions are announced on radio and television.

Waves in Shallow Water

As a train of waves moves into water shallower than half a wavelength, the bottom begins to interfere with the orbital motion of the water moving within the waves. The orbits flatten into ellipses, and the net movement of the water becomes a back-and-forth motion known as SURGE. The shallower the water, the higher the waves, the longer the wavelength, the greater the surge.

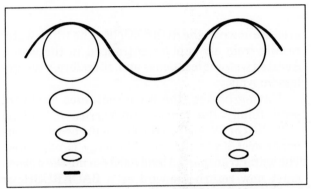

Figure 4.4 Surge (simple wave)—In shallow water there is not sufficient depth for the water particles to complete their circular orbits. The orbits are therefore compressed into oval shapes and, at the very bottom,to horizontal back and forth movements.

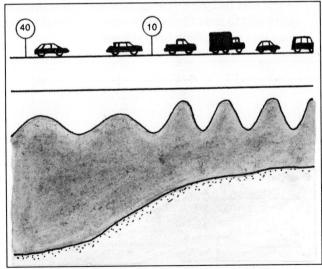

Figure 4.5 When waves move in shallow water they slow down and crowd together. This shortens their wave lengths and is analogous to automobiles crowding together when they go from a fast speed zone to a slow one. When waves crowd together their wave heights increase.

The effect of surge on your diving activities is to sweep you to and fro as the waves pass overhead. Diving in strong surge can be hazardous and should be avoided. It is better to drift back and forth with moderate surge than it is to waste energy fighting it. In light surge, it is possible to secure yourself by holding onto a structure while the surge passes. The movement of water toward shore is greater than the movement of the water away from shore, so it is possible to use this tendency to assist you in shallow water when returning to shore. Simply hang on or dig in while the motion is offshore and move with the motion when it is toward shore.

As wave forms approach shore and move across shallow bottoms, they are reflected, diffracted (bent) and refracted. When a wave encounters a vertical wall, such as a seawall or a steep cliff rising from deep water, the wave is reflected back upon itself with little loss of energy. The surface chop resulting from such reflected waves can produce uncomfortable situations for divers, who should avoid being at the surface in areas of reflected waves.

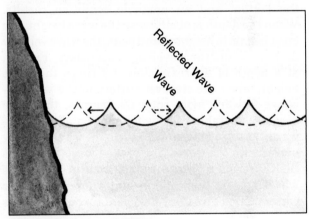

Figure 4.6 Reflected Waves

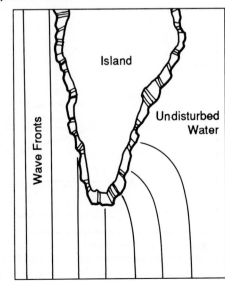

Figure 4.7 Wave Diffraction

When waves encounter an obstruction, their motion is diffracted around it. As the waves pass the obstruction, some of their energy is propagated sideways due to friction with the obstruction and the waves bend around into areas that would otherwise be sheltered.

When a wave front approaches a shoreline at an angle, successive portions of the wave front are slowed as the waves encounter resistance with the bottom. Since different segments of the waves are moving in water of varying depths, the crests bend and the direction of the waves bend until the wave front nearly parallels the contours of the bottom. Thus, waves become parallel to a straight shoreline, concentrated on points of land, and dispersed in coves or bays. Entries and exits on rugged outcroppings of land are usually unwise when wave action is significant.

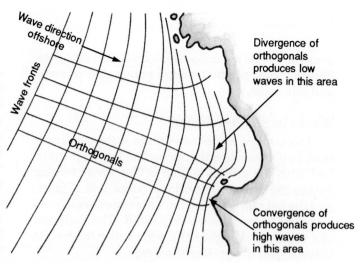

Figure 4.8 Wave Refraction

Surf

As the lower portion of a wave is slowed in shallow water, the top portion moves faster than the bottom and an unstable condition results. When the depth is about twice the wave height, the crest begins to heighten and peak, the wave velocity decreases, and the wavelength decreases. Finally, at a depth of approximately 1.3 times the wave height, when the steepest surface of the wave inclines forward more than 60 degrees, the wave becomes unstable and the top portion plunges forward. At this point, water within the wave actually moves with the wave. The broken wave, known as SURF, forms a "white water" area in which the waves give up their energy and where systematic water motion gives way to violent turbulence. This area is known as the SURF ZONE. The white water results from air bubbles entrapped in the water. Aerated water is less dense and, therefore, provides less buoyancy.

Having broken, the wave continues landward until finally the momentum carries it into an UPRUSH or SWASH on the face of the beach. At the uppermost limit, the wave's energy is expended. The water transported landward during the uprush must now return seaward as a BACKRUSH, or counter current flowing back to the water. This offshore movement of water is usually not evident beyond a depth of three feet, and is **not** to be considered an undertow. An undertow–a current that flows seaward and pulls swimmers under–is a myth that does not exist. The backrush on a steep beach can be quite strong, however, and may require you to crawl out of the water to avoid having your feet swept from beneath you.

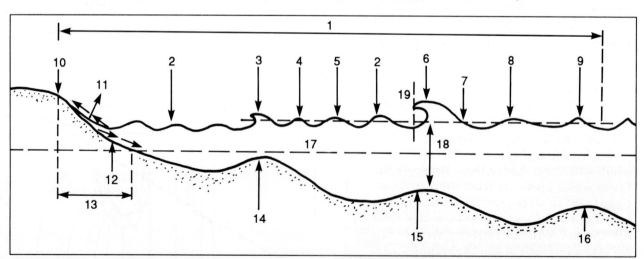

Figure 4.9 Surf zone and Surf—1. Surf zone; 2. Translatory waves; 3. Inner line of breakers; 4. Peaked-up wave; 5. Reformed oscillatory wave; 6. Outerline of breakers; 7. Still-water level; 8. Waves flatten again; 9. Waves break-up, but do not break on this bar at high tide; 10. Limit of uprush; 11. Uprush; 12. Backrush; 13. Beach face; 14. Inner bar; 15. Outer bar (inner bar at low tide); 16. Deep bar; 17. Mean lower low water; 18. Breaker depth; 19. Plunge point.

THE DIVING ENVIRONMENT

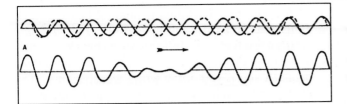

Figure 4.10 Wave Sets and Surf Beat—Two waves of equal height and nearly equal length traveling in the same direction shown with resulting wave pattern.

If the water deepens again after a wave has broken–such as water does where sand bars or reefs are adjacent to shore–the wave may reform into systematic orbital motion. The new wave will be smaller than the original one. It will proceed into water equal to 1.3 times its height and break again. You may use the presence of waves breaking offshore as an indicator for the location of formations.

A frequent characteristic of breaking waves is the variability in their height. They generally approach in SETS of smaller waves followed by another group of larger waves, each of which is usually higher than its predecessor. These sets of waves result from the arrival of two trains of swells from two different sources. When the crests of two sets of swells coincide, they reinforce each other and produce waves higher than those of either of the swell trains individually. When the crests of one set coincide with the troughs in the other set, a cancellation effect produces smaller waves. A definite cycle or pattern of the sets often results. By studying breaking waves, you can determine the SURF BEAT, or frequency of the sets, and time your entry or exit to coincide with the lull period of minimum wave height.

Types of Surf

The width of the surf zone and the violence of breaking waves are influenced significantly by the slope of the beach. On a gradually sloping beach, a moderately large swell will form SPILLING BREAKERS. These waves break far from shore and continue to break all the way to the beach. The long surf zone allows waves to release their energy gradually. The water is usually turbid in the surf zone due to the sediment that is disturbed over a wide area.

PLUNGING BREAKERS release their energy quickly. This type of surf forms from large swells over a moderately steep bottom. As the swell moves toward shore, the waves steepen quickly and break suddenly. These waves break with tremendous force, and they are the most hazardous type of wave because large ones (over three feet) can easily knock over a standing diver. The crest of a plunging breaker curls over, forming a "tube" or large air pocket. A spectacular crash of water results and foam is thrown into the air as the air pocket expands after being compressed by the weight of the wave. Visibility is usually good beyond plunging breakers because these waves expend their energy in a very narrow area.

COLLAPSING BREAKERS form from swells of medium height over a very steep bottom. As the

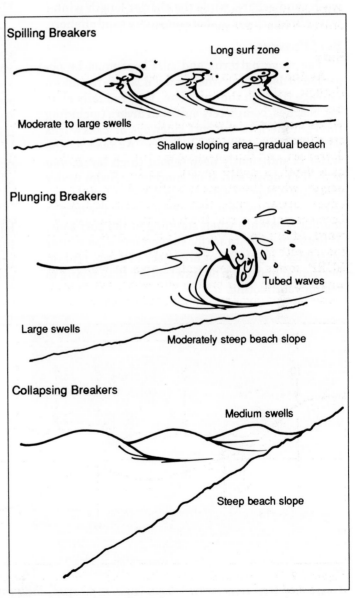

Figure 4.11 Spilling Breakers

waves break over their lower half, very little splash or foaming occurs. Thus, the wave breaks rather uneventfully.

Small swells approaching a very steep bottom produce SURGING BREAKERS. These waves slide up and down the steep incline with little or no foam production.

Effects of Surf on Beaches

During the winter, waves break closer together than they do during the summer months. The winter wave action carries sand to offshore bars and exposes rocks on the beach and in the surf zone. During the summer, the waves push the sand back onto the beach, covering the rocks again. The longer period waves of the summer break well offshore and wash sand ashore, while the shorter length winter waves break closer to shore and carry sand offshore.

Surf Passages

The wave patterns and surf beat must be observed to determine when and if it is safe to make a passage through the surf zone. On gradually sloping beaches, completely outfitted divers (including fins) shuffle into the surf sideways or backwards while watching incoming waves. As soon as the water is sufficiently deep (about thigh level), you should lie down and start snorkling. Swim under incoming waves. If a float is used, it should be towed through the surf zone. Your knees should be bent to maintain balance when standing in the surf zone. Maintain a wide stance for support and a low center of gravity. If you fall or are knocked down, remain horizontal and swim or crawl rather than trying to regain your footing.

A high surf on a steeply sloping beach can be dangerous for a fully equipped diver. The surf zone is only a few feet wide, but the waves break violently directly on the beach. Your feet may be swept from beneath you if you enter while wearing fins. The waves can then break directly on top of you. When conditions are severe, it is best to seek a safer alternate location. If conditions are reasonable, the following procedures are suggested:

1. Have your BC partially inflated for *slight* positive buoyancy.

2. Be fully equipped, except for your fins, which should be carried.

3. Get as close to the water's edge as possible after timing the sets and lulls to coincide your entry with the smallest waves.

4. Enter the water as quickly as possible immediately after a wave breaks and get beyond the surf zone quickly before the next wave breaks. If you cannot wade through this area quickly enough, rapidly don one fin after entering the water and use it to propel yourself beyond the surf zone, then don your other fin. This is an advanced skill, however.

It is obvious that you will need to be proficient at donning your fins in water too deep to stand and at swimming with one fin before this type of entry is attempted.

Surf entries over shallow rocks or coral are hazardous and require special training to prevent injuries. Such entries should be avoided until the proper procedures are developed under the supervision of a trained and experienced instructor.

When exiting through surf, stop outside the surf

Figure 4.12 Surf Entries–Training is required for surf entries and exits, and the training applies only to the beach where trained. Different techniques must be learned for different conditions.

THE DIVING ENVIRONMENT

zone and evaluate the surf conditions. Your exit should be timed so you ride the back of the last large wave of a set. Hold your mask continuously while in the surf zone. To exit through spilling breakers, swim toward shore to waist-deep water, stand, turn your back toward the beach, watch the oncoming waves, lean forward with your knees bent, and shuffle to shore. You should duck beneath any oncoming waves that are higher than chest level.

To exit through plunging breakers, again time the surf beat and ride the back of a wave to the beach. Beware of being sucked into the wave and "over the falls". Swim hard to pass quickly through the surf zone before the next wave breaks. Remain horizontal and literally crawl clear of the water before standing.

Keep all equipment in place until clear of the water when exiting through surf. During surf exits, avoid having a float between yourself and oncoming waves or the float could be pushed into and over you.

Tides

Tides are the predictable, periodic rising and falling of waters primarily due to the gravitational attraction of the moon and secondarily of the sun upon the earth. The moon, being closer to the earth, influences the tides about twice as much as the sun. On seacoasts, tides are regular and rhythmic and are essentially long-period waves with a wave length equal to half the circumference of the earth.

The gravitational attraction between the earth and the moon results in a tide-producing force on the earth's hemisphere nearest the moon. On the hemisphere opposite the moon, the tide-producing

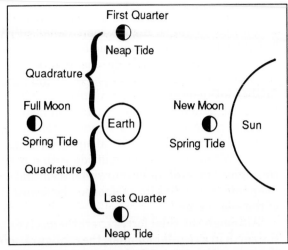

Figure 4.14 Tide Cycle–The relationship of the sun and the moon affect the tides.

force is the direction of the centrifugal force of the celestial bodies (away from the moon). The resulting effect is two bulges of water on opposite sides of the earth. Visualize the bulges remaining relatively stationary as the earth rotates on its axis. Ideally, most points on the earth should experience semi-diurnal (twice daily) tides, but the position of the moon relative to the equator results in an inequality of tidal patterns in many locations.

The sun acts similarly upon the waters, but with lesser effect. The total tide-producing force is the result of both the sun and the moon. Sun tides increase or reduce lunar tides. The two most important situations are when the earth, sun and moon are aligned (in phase) and when the three are at right angles to each other (out of phase). When in

Figure 4.13 Standing is permissible for some surf exits, but crawling is required for others.

phase, the solar tide reinforces and amplifies the lunar tide to cause higher than usual SPRING TIDES, which occur at new and full moons. NEAP TIDES–lower than usual tidal changes–occur when the sun and moon are out of phase. Tidal range is further influenced by the proximity of the moon to the earth. When the moon is in its orbit nearest the earth (at perigee), tides are higher; when the moon is farthest from the earth (at apogee), tides are lower. When spring tides coincide with a perigee, the highest tides of the year are produced, and when neap tides coincide with an apogee, the lowest tides of the year occur.

Although the tidal forces exert themselves over the earth in a regular manner, the configurations of the ocean basins and the interference of land masses prevent the tides from assuming a simple, regular pattern. Friction, as water flows over land, creates drag and slows water movement. Water is funnelled between and around land masses. All of this results in tidal variances around our planet. The variations are usually documented, however, and tables are available to assist with dive planning.

A body of water has a natural period of oscillation (back and forth movement like water sloshing in a basin) that depends on its dimensions. The waters of the earth comprise numerous oscillating basins rather than a single oscillating body. The response of a basin of water to tide-producing forces determines the type of tide produced in the basin.

Tides are classified in three types:

1. Diurnal (daily) - One high and one low tide occurring every 24 hours and 50 minutes (time required for the moon to pass a fixed point on the earth twice).

2. Semi-diurnal (twice daily)–Two high and two low tides of approximately equal height every 24 hours and 50 minutes. A tidal change occurs approximately every six hours.

3. Mixed–A combination of diurnal and semi-diurnal; the heights are unequal.

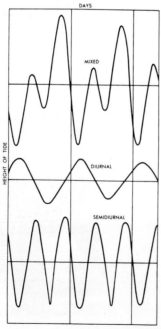

Figure 4.15 Types of Tide Curves

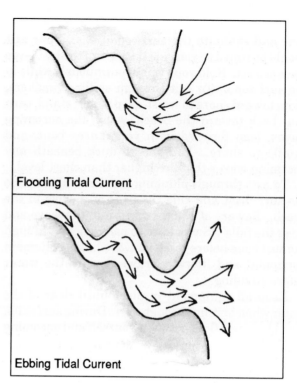

Flooding Tidal Current

Ebbing Tidal Current

Figure 4.16 Flood and Ebb–Tides have significant effect in narrow waterways on the coast.

The height of tides varies considerably with shoreline configuration, time of month and year, wind conditions and other factors. Tidal amplitude on an open shore is usually two to five feet, but the tidal range in harbors and estuaries can be very great (40 feet or more), resulting in extremely strong currents. Further, the height of tides may vary over 30 feet between two locations only a few hundred miles apart.

A TIDAL CURRENT is the periodic horizontal water movement associated with the tides, reversing the direction of flow as the tide changes. Water flowing toward shore or upstream with a rising tide is called a FLOOD TIDE, and water flowing offshore or downstream with a falling tide is called an EBB TIDE. Tidal currents can be very strong, especially through narrow areas. A narrow channel connected to a large body of water concentrates and amplifies tidal currents. On an open coast, where the direction of flow is not restricted, tidal currents flow continuously, with the direction changing according to the tidal period.

At each reversal of current, a short period of little or no current exists, called SLACK WATER. During flow in each direction, the speed will vary from zero at the time of slack water to maximum strength about midway between the slack periods.

Divers are encouraged to refer to local tide tables and make personal evaluations of water movement in order to determine slack water times which often present more favorable diving conditions. Tide tables and specific information are contained in various forms in many navigational publications and in newspapers. Tidal current tables, issued annually, list daily predictions of tides.

In some channels or straits, you will be limited to 15-20 minutes of easy diving time during slack water. Precautions are essential when diving in such areas. You should not attempt to swim against a strong current. If caught in a current, inflate your buoyancy compensator and swim perpendicular to the current toward shore, or signal and wait to be picked up by a boat.

Seiches

When the surface of a large, partially enclosed body of water, such as one of the Great Lakes or a bay, is disturbed, long waves may be established

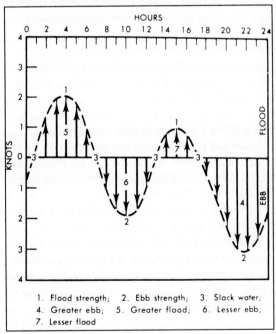

1. Flood strength; 2. Ebb strength; 3. Slack water;
4. Greater ebb; 5. Greater flood; 6. Lesser ebb;
7. Lesser flood

Figure 4.17 Tidal Current Terms

which rhythmically oscillate as they reflect from opposite ends of the basin. These waves, called SEICHES (pronounced "say-chez"), have a period that depends on the size and depth of the basin. Many people are unaware of seiches due to their very low wave height and extremely long wavelength.

In large lakes, seiches result primarily from differential barometric pressure changes, but more frequently are caused by winds. For example, a strong wind blowing for several hours along the axis of a large lake will drive the surface water toward the leeward (downwind) end of the lake, raising the water surface there as much as ten feet, while lowering the level at the windward end of the lake. This oscillation, which diminishes rapidly in amplitude, has a period that may exceed 12-14 hours.

In bays that are open to the ocean, seiching nearly always results from a long-period wave train. When the water in the bay is sent in motion by the initial wave, seiching continues at the natural period of oscillation for that harbor or bay.

Seiches can affect diving by reducing visibility and by rapidly changing the water level at entry and exit points.

CURRENTS

In addition to tidal currents, there are several other types with which you need to be familiar.

Longshore Current

Waves approaching shore at an angle cause a current system that flows parallel to near the shore. These currents, which can achieve a velocity too

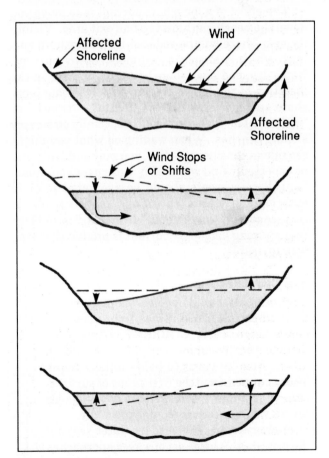

Figure 4.18 Seiching

great to swim against when the surf is large, are known as LONGSHORE CURRENTS. The speed of the current is usually less than one knot, but the speed increases with wave height, increased angle of waves to the shore and the steepness of the beach. The intensity of a longshore current is greatest inside the surf zone, diminishing as you move away from shore.

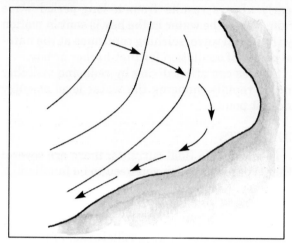

Figure 4.19 Longshore Current

The effect of a longshore current is to move you down the beach, perhaps to a bad exit area. Visibility near shore will be reduced by a longshore current which transports sediment down current. Items dropped near shore will tend to move in the direction of the longshore current. A strong longshore current tends to form a "cut", "trench" or "inshore hole" in the surf zone, especially on steeply sloping beaches. When wading on what you might consider a continous incline, you may suddenly and unexpectedly find yourself in water over your head. Longshore currents should be evaluated prior to entering the water, so actions can be taken to compensate for any effects. If the surf is so large that a strong longshore current is produced, diving is inadvisable.

Rip Currents

When water piled upon a shore by waves runs off in one place rather than along the entire shore, a RIP CURRENT results. The distance a rip current may flow varies in length from 20 yards to half a mile or more. These currents are the first cause of surf rescues of swimmers and can pose problems for divers when encountered unexpectedly.

A rip current is formed by water seeking its own level. A large set of waves approaches the beach; the surge of the water builds the water level on the incline of the beach. This water, being higher than the average water level, seeks to return to that level. The return occurs through a deeper section of the offshore bottom.

The intensity of a rip is greatest during the lull in a set of waves. There is a direct relationship between the size of the surf and the intensity of a rip current -- larger surf equates stronger current.

There are four types of rip currents:

1. Permanent–Formed by a rock channel or subsurface topography which changes very little. Permanent structures, such as piers, jetties, pipelines or outcroppings can also create rips.

2. Fixed–A fixed rip is second in longevity of location only to a permanent rip current. A hole or gully in the offshore bottom can create a rip current that can last from several hours up to several months.

3. Flash–Temporary in nature for any given location. Caused by a large surf buildup during a short period of time. They appear suddenly and without warning and are relatively shortlived.

4. Traveling–A traveling rip current is propelled along a shore frontage by a strong longshore current. This type of rip may travel over large segments of beach before dissipating itself.

There are three basic parts of a rip current:

1. Mouth–This is the shoremost part known as a FEEDER ZONE. It can be fed by longshore current and by the buildup of water on the incline of a beach.

2. Neck–This is the midpoint of a rip where the offshore motion has its greatest velocity.

3. Head–The area where the rip current dissipates its energy and ceases to flow offshore.

Rip currents may be recognized by a fan-shaped buildup of water on a beach, a stream of dirty water extending outward from the shore, foam on the

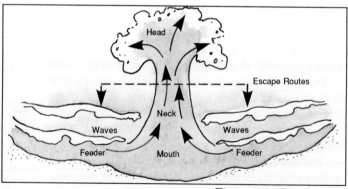

Figure 4.20 Rip Current

THE DIVING ENVIRONMENT

Figure 4.21
A Rip
Current

1. Water depth–The speed of a wind-driven current decreases rapidly with depth.

2. Bottom formations–The bottom acts to resist water movement. A current is weakest at the bottom.

3. Water temperature - water becomes colder with depth. As the temperature decreases, the density or weight of the water increases. Heavier water impedes wind-driven currents.

If unexpectedly caught downstream from your exit point, your preferred order of options is:

1. Return upstream on the bottom if air is available. Pulling hand over hand is best.

2. Swim perpendicular to the current to try to get clear of it.

3. Obtain positive buoyancy, signal for assistance, and wait to be rescued. Useful devices to signal rescuers include a whistle and your mask faceplate used as a reflector.

surface extending beyond the surf zone, and a distinct lack of surf where the current flows outward. Detection of a rip is most difficult on windy days when the surf is choppy.

Modest rip currents may be used to aid offshore movement. If you realize you are in a rip and wish to escape, do so by swimming perpendicular to the current, which is seldom more than 100 feet wide. The velocity of a rip current is often greater than one knot, and should not be fought. You may choose to ride the current to its head; swim parallel to shore in the direction of any longshore current for 30 to 50 yards and then swim toward shore.

Wind Currents

Offshore currents in large bodies of water are caused by the wind. They are essentially streams of water moving within a larger body of water. Temperature differences create convection currents in the oceans, although the convection currents have very low velocities.

The stress of wind blowing across water causes the surface layer of water to move. This motion is transmitted to succeeding layers of water beneath the surface. The rate of motion decreases with depth. A wind current does not flow in the direction of the wind due to the force of the rotation of the earth or CORIOLIS EFFECT. Deflection by Coriolis force is to the right in the northern hemisphere, and toward the left in the southern hemisphere. Major ocean currents tend, therefore, to flow clockwise above the equator and counter-clockwise below the equator. The Coriolis force is greater in higher latitudes and most effective in deep water. Current direction varies from about 15 degrees from the wind along shallow coastal areas to a maximum of 45 degrees in the deep oceans.

The velocity of a wind-produced current depends on the speed of the wind, its constancy, the length of time it blows, and other factors. A wind blowing for 12 hours or more in the same direction will cause a surface current equal to about two percent of the wind speed. The SET and DRIFT of a current refer to the current's direction and velocity, respectively. The strength of a current is affected by:

CURRENT

Figure 4.22 Procedures for Current Diving

The following procedures are recommended for diving when currents are anticipated or present:

1. Always dive against a current and not with it unless trained, prepared and equipped to make a drift dive. Stay close to the bottom, pull yourself along and avoid unnecessary kicking, which can lead to overexertion and fatigue.

2. Descents should be made down a weighted descent line or down the anchor line. Free descents in currents should be avoided.

3. A TRAIL LINE at least 100 feet in length should be extended from the dive boat to assist divers back to the vessel if they surface downstream.

4. A qualified operator should remain on the boat at all times to facilitate assisting anyone swept downstream.

Note that the maximum sustainable swimming speed of a fully equipped scuba diver is about one knot. Swimming against a one knot current is, therefore, unwise because it will quickly lead to exhaustion.

DRIFT DIVING

Diving by drifting with a current is a popular activity in some areas, but training and supervised experience are paramount for safety. An orientation to drift diving is presented later in this book.

River Currents

Currents are also caused by gravity, such as when water flows downhill. Such currents can be extremely strong and hazardous. Sediment and other matter or bubbles on the surface can reduce visibility in rivers to zero.

Currents in rivers are strongest in the middle, at the surface, and on the outside edges of bends. The strength of the current decreases with depth and proximity to the shore.

The swift waters of rivers and varying bottom conditions can produce rapids, whirlpools, sucking holes, waterfalls, eddy currents and other unique and hazardous forms of water movement.

Special training, procedures and equipment are required for safe diving in swift-flowing rivers. Additional information on these subjects is provided in a separate section later in this book.

THERMAL CHANGES
Upwelling

During conditions of continuous, strong, offshore winds along a coast, warm surface water is blown offshore and replaced by colder, nutrient-laden water from beneath. This colder water, brought vertically to the surface from the depths, is known as UPWELLING. Certain areas with offshore drop-offs and seasonal winds are prone to upwellings.

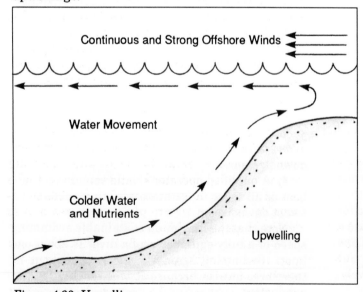

Figure 4.23 Upwelling

An upwelling initially results in colder, clearer water with increased amounts of nutrients which, in turn, increases the productivity of the food chain, resulting in increased fish activity. Good diving conditions prevail for a few days until the excess nutrients cause plankton to begin to multiply and reduce visibility.

Thermal Stratification

During summer months, the surface waters of lakes and quarries are warmed by the sun and form a layer of water called the EPILIMNION. Beneath this, a cold and dense layer of water, termed the HYPOLIMNION, remains. The surface may reach a temperature of 70 degrees F. or more, but the bottom temperature, in a typical deep lake remains approximately 39.2 degrees F, the temperature of maximum density for fresh water. Between the two layers is a zone of rapid temperature change called a THERMOCLINE. Thermal changes with depth are also present in oceans, but usually not as pronounced as in fresh water.

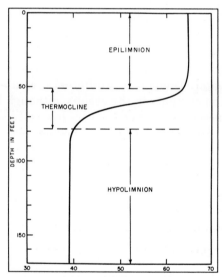

Figure 4.24 Lake Temperature Profile

During the fall months, the surface waters of lakes cool. When the water temperature is about 43 degrees F, wind-caused circulation is sufficient to destroy the thermocline and mix the entire water column, producing an ISO-THERM (same temperature) condition. This isothermal condition (fall turnover) exists until late winter when the lake has cooled to about 35.6 degrees F. Further cooling then produces sufficiently less dense surface water with a temperature of near 32 degrees F. This lighter water forms a stratification sufficient

THE DIVING ENVIRONMENT

to prevent circulation of the deeper water and a REVERSE THERMOCLINE is developed.

As the spring sun warms the surface water, the spring turnover begins. This mixing continues until the surface water exceeds 39.2 degrees F, producing a less dense upper layer and initiating the summer stratification period.

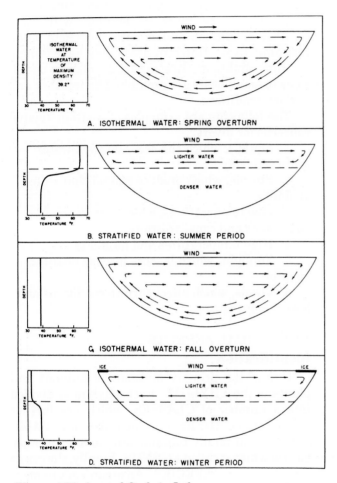

Figure 4.25 Annual Cycle in Lakes

Thermal stratification in lakes affects the amount of oxygen in the water and, therefore, fish distribution. The temperature also affects plankton populations which, in turn, affect visibility. In many lakes, isothermal conditions present the best times for diving unless wind action disturbs sediment and reduces the visibility.

Halocline

A HALOCLINE is a horizontal boundary between waters of differing salinity. In some situations where fresh water comes into contact with sea water, the waters remain separated in layers due to differences in density. At the boundary where the two layers come into contact, a mixing occurs. This boundary, which can be several feet deep, affects your vision as you pass through it, and can produce a feeling of disorientation. Avoid lingering in a halocline if you should encounter one while diving.

Bottom Conditions

The bottom type of the diving area affects visibility, aquatic life, navigation, dive planning, necessary equipment and more.

Coral bottoms usually offer good visibility, warm water, abundant fish life and exciting diving. Hazards include coral cuts, marine life stings, and exceeding planned depths due to clear water. Wear protective clothing, avoid contact and monitor your depth gauge frequently.

Rocky bottoms exist in colder seas and usually offer many of the benefits of coral reefs. Visibility varies from area to area and from season to season. Hazards include slippery algae growth on rocks at entry and exit areas, surf, currents, and marine plants.

Sandy bottoms are found everywhere and offer varying visibility, depending upon the amount of water movement. This environment may look like a desert to some divers, but many animals make their home here. Diving on sandy bottoms requires that you maintain neutral buoyancy and minimize fin action near the bottom to avoid raising silt and that you avoid dragging your equipment—especially gauges and extra second stages.

Muddy bottoms vary in consistency from compact, firm clay to a semi-fluid silt. These types of bottoms are found everywhere, but are most common in rivers, lakes and bays. Many animals similar to those found in sand live in the mud. The visibility is generally poor because of the ease with which sediment can be disturbed. Muddy bottoms can significantly affect entries and exits. Beware of slipping and of sinking deeply into the mud.

Environmental Activities

Divers engage in many specialized activities created by the environment. Natural formations such as caves, caverns, sink holes and blue holes arouse curiosity and spark interest. People dive beneath the ice, in mountain lakes at high elevations, in the blue waters of the open sea and to depths in excess of 100 feet.

All of these environmental diving activities and more have something in common— they all require specialized knowledge, equipment and skills. Introductory information for many diving specialties is presented later in this book. This information will reinforce the need for specialty training.

Man-made Structures

Jetties, piers and wharfs can pose dangers from waves, currents, poor visibility, boats, fishing lines and hooks.

Submerged shipwrecks attract divers. Some wrecks are extremely hazardous. Serious dangers include entanglement, entrapment, and getting lost. Special training and equipment are essential.

Offshore oil rigs provide sites for excellent diving. Such rigs are located from one to over 200 miles off shore in depths exceeding 300 feet. Spearfishing is popular, and presents a danger, especially if visibility is limited. In addition, the area under and around a rig is a virtual junkyard of cable, pipe, etc. Caution must be exercised to avoid entanglement or injury.

Large underwater pipelines are common in some areas. Diving in the vicinity of active pipelines is discouraged because the lines may be discharging large amount of pollutants that can cause illnesses or may be intakes that can suddenly suck divers to their doom.

Figure 4.26 Common man-made structures encountered by the diver.

You may be attracted to the area around a dam. Diving in the vicinity of large dams is also discouraged because strong currents can literally grab and hold you underwater. You could also be swept through an overflow channel.

Weather Conditions

Weather is an important factor affecting diving operations. You must be familiar with local weather conditions and monitor forecasts when planning dives. Different areas may have unique weather conditions. In some areas, offshore operations in small boats are prohibited by weather and surface conditions.

The following are examples of weather-related concerns for divers:

1. Squalls, which can occur on open water quite suddenly.

2. Storms, which produce run-off that ruins visibility.

3. Low temperatures, which can freeze equipment and cause frostbite.

4. High temperatures and humidity.

5. Sunlight, which is more intense near the equator.

6. Winds, which affect surface conditions and lower temperature.

BIOLOGICAL ASPECTS
Identification

One of the primary divisions of animals and plants is the PHYLUM. Each phylum is divided into a number of CLASSES, which are further divided into ORDERS, and the orders into FAMILIES. Each family contains still smaller groups, each of which is called a GENUS. Finally, the genus contains several SPECIES. An organism's name is either Latin or Greek and actually describes the life form. Classifications are keyed externally to such features as color, scales, shape, skeleton, etc.

Ecological Overview

ECOLOGY is the scientific study of organisms in relation to their environments. Animals and plants occupy certain regions within a major environment, such as the sea.

The precise "micro-environment" of a species is called its HABITAT. Within any habitat there are different species with their own feeding habits and reproductive cycles. The position each species occupies in its habitat is called its NICHE. Niches of various species are determined by physical factors as well as relationships to other species in the same

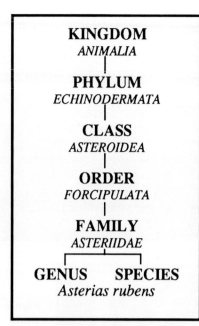

KINGDOM
ANIMALIA

PHYLUM
ECHINODERMATA

CLASS
ASTEROIDEA

ORDER
FORCIPULATA

FAMILY
ASTERIIDAE

GENUS   SPECIES
Asterias rubens

Figure 4.27 Classifications–This example is the common starfish.

habitat. Thus, the niches of species in a habitat are adjusted to each other and form an integrated community. Communities react to the non-living parts of the environment and vice versa to form a balanced ecosystem.

An example of a balanced ecosystem is a coral reef. Coral polyps secrete carbonates (limestone), which are bound together by calcareous algae. When man alters a natural environment by fishing, hunting, anchoring and polluting, this initial disturbance of the animals and plants may eventually disturb the entire ecosystem and eventually destroy it.

Zones

There are four basic plant and animal life zones:

1. INTERTIDAL OR LITTORAL– Plants and animals are adapted to withstand water loss, temperature extremes and strong water movement.

2. PLANKTONIC–Drifting and floating forms that are at the mercy of the wind and current. Many animals have planktonic stages in their life cycles. The most common "plants" in the oceans are the PHYTOPLANKTON, which are algae that use sunlight to produce carbohydrates. They represent the basic food source for all life in the oceans.

3. NECKTONIC–These are free-swimming forms, including fish, which rely on speed and streamlining for their survival. Some live at a constant depth in one area, while others prefer the open seas. Fish may live in schools for a greater chance of survival.

4. BENTHIC–These are bottom-dwelling organisms that are usually heavy so they can remain there. Crabs and crayfish have thick shells, and certain fish have no swim bladders. Seaweeds have no roots, but holdfasts to anchor themselves to the sea bottom.

Marine and Fresh Water Plants

Plants in water are like trees and shrubs on land. Without them, the underwater world would be an unattractive, barren place. The animals would have no place to hide, and their chances of survival in a world filled with predators would be slim. Many organisms depend upon plants for food. Most underwater plants lack a root system, do not require strong, woody limbs for support, and do not need a series of vessels to carry water to the plant from the roots. Water is simply absorbed. To remain in one place, the plants hold fast to the bottom with a root-like structure called a HOLDFAST.

Seaweed consists of a group of non-flowering plants and is properly called ALGAE. The three most important groups are green algae, brown algae and red algae. Seaweed makes rocks very slippery, affecting entries and exits. Divers can become entangled in algae, but this should not pose a serious threat. Panic is the diver's worst foe in a

Figure 4.28 Intertidal Region

Figure 4.29 Kelp Forest

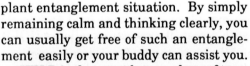

Figure 4.30 (Top) Eel Grass

Figure 4.31 (Left) Fresh Water Plants

plant entanglement situation. By simply remaining calm and thinking clearly, you can usually get free of such an entanglement easily or your buddy can assist you.

KELP is the great brown algae of temperate waters. Forests of kelp on the western coast of the United States grow from depths of up to 100 feet and abound with life just like the forests on land. Like their terrestrial counterparts, these undersea forests have a beauty that is unique. A tough holdfast anchors the algae to the bottom, while air bladders float groups of STIPES (strands) to the surface where the kelp spreads out to form a thick, floating canopy. It is much easier to swim under the canopy than through it at the surface, so experienced kelp divers save enough air to make excursions beneath the canopy at the end of a dive.

Surf grass or eel grass is a green algae found in the surf zone. Entanglement in this algae is not common. Surge may wash it over you, causing apprehension, but if you will be calm and patient, the grass will clear when the surge reverses direction.

Freshwater plants grow densely in some inland lakes and streams. You can become entangled in the plants and surfacing can be difficult. A calm, controlled procedure of freeing yourself is the best solution to an entanglement problem.

Food Chain

All living creatures require food to build new cells for growth, replace old cells and for energy to move about. With so many living creatures in the waters, what is the source of all their food?

The first link in the FOOD CHAIN is the one-celled plants. The PHYTOPLANKTON (called diatoms and dinoflagellates) exist in countless millions in the surface layers of the oceans and are eaten by the tiny animals called ZOOPLANKTON. These, in turn, are eaten by small fish. These are eaten by still bigger fish, and so the process goes. By the time you eat a fish, energy has been transferred through several organisms along a food chain of trophic (nutritional) levels in the marine community. The higher the trophic level of the organism, the fewer individuals will be found. This is because the organism concerned must pay the high energy costs of converting the food to the energy that is needed for respiration, movement and reproduction. The conversion of one form of energy to another, and the maintenance of the population, becomes more and more expensive as higher trophic levels are considered.

In the warmer waters of the tropics, there is not much plankton due to a lack of nutrients. Plankton thrives in colder, nutrient-rich water. Because of this, tropical waters are normally clearer than temperate waters. When conditions are right and plankton does very well, it may rapidly reproduce and form a BLOOM, causing a drastic decrease in visibility. An extremely heavy bloom is called a RED TIDE. Several types of organisms, mainly dinoflagellata, have a red pigment which turns the water reddish.

Figure 4.33 Diver with Game

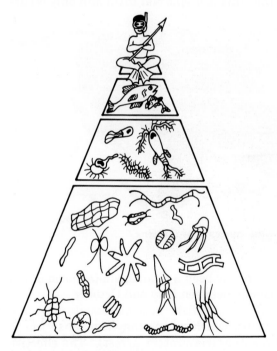

Figure 4.32 Food Chain

Some plankton produce a toxin and, if a bloom is heavy, can kill all the fish in an area. Some animals, such as clams and mussels, feed by filtering plankton and concentrate the toxin in their flesh without harm to themselves. If a human eats their flesh, the concentrated toxins can cause serious illness. Most of the concentrating organisms are bi-valves, such as the cockle clam. It is always wise to ask about the safety of eating local filter feeders.

Many places that do not have red tides have contaminated shellfish from polluters. It is prudent to avoid eating anything from a benthic habitat in

a bay where pleasure boats anchor. The boat toilets empty directly into the water and settle to the bottom. Many cases of hepatitis and diarrhea have occurred when people have eaten animals from such a bay. Awareness and avoidance are the best safety devices.

Conservation

Divers are generally conservation minded and understand the importance of maintaining a clean, unspoiled underwater environment. CONSERVATION is defined as the management of human usage of the waters so they may yield the greatest sustainable benefit to present and future generations. For conservation to occur, knowledge, commitment and action are required. There are many actions we can take to help preserve the world under water.

Knowledge is the first step. Read diving publications, newspapers, books and magazines. Obtain solid information to form opinions and inform and influence others.

Commitment to preserve the underwater environment is an essential, but individual matter. You must decide that you will do your part to protect the diving environment.

Action is commitment put to work. When you take game, take only enough for a meal. Filling your freezer, giving game away or helping others to get their limit are not consistent with conservation. When the limit on something is ten, it doesn't mean you should strive to take ten, it means that under no circumstances should you ever take more than ten. It is fine to take less if less meets your immediate needs.

Everyone has a tendency to place the blame on someone else when there is a problem. We have to take the responsibility for our environment. If we drop anchors on our coral reefs, the reefs will be severely damaged and lose their beauty. If we take large amounts of any organism from the waters, those organisms are going to become more difficult to find. If we dump pollutants into the waters, then the organisms that live there are going to either die, become poisonous to eat, or move away.

Some aspects of conservation we control by influencing others, some by our actions, and some by our vote. Without knowledge, we can control nothing. Continuing education is mandatory. Make part of your continuing education in the area of the environment. Have an informed opinion and take prudent action. You can make a difference.

HAZARDOUS ANIMALS–By P. Lynch

Just how deadly are various species of aquatic animals? How toxic or venomous are they? These are questions every modern underwater explorer needs to be able to answer if he or she is to remain safe.

The purpose of this section is to familiarize you with some of the more common injuries from aquatic animals without scaring the wits out of you and perpetuating any myths.

Poisonous animals are those creatures whose tissue, either in part or in their entirety, are toxic. In general, marine oral toxins are small molecules that are heat stable or unaffected by cooking. "Icthyosarcotoxism" is a term used for a type of poisoning identified with eating a specific type of fish.

Venomous animals are those creatures capable of producing a toxin in a highly developed secretory gland (venom sac) or group of cells and can deliver this material (toxin) through a sting or bite. These are the animals that have fangs, claws, stingers, spines or some other mechanism for delivering a toxin. Unlike the oral toxins, venoms are usually large molecules that are detoxified by heat or gastric juices. Toxins delivered by a venom apparatus are called PARENTERAL TOXINS.

Everyone knows there are large predators that are potentially dangerous because they bite.

We will now consider three separate topics of hazardous aquatic life: Oral toxins, parenteral toxins and predators.

Oral Toxins

As divers, we often get involved in gathering things from the sea to eat, either by spearfishing, crabbing or picking up shellfish.

Paralytic shellfish poisoning (PSP) is caused by chemical agents known as saxitoxin and neosaxitoxin. These agents are synthesized in microscopic plants known as fire algae (Pyrrophyta), specifically dinoflagellates (Gonyaulax tamarensis or Gymnodinium breve) commonly found in the marine plankton. These toxic dinoflagellates, occasionally in warm seas increase their numbers tremendously, causing what has become known as a "red tide". Shellfish, such as clams, oysters and mussels are filter feeders, ingesting large numbers of dinoflagellates, concentrating their toxins in the shellfish tissues. Man comes along, collects the shellfish, makes a chowder or eats the "critters" raw, with poisonous results. You should keep in mind that this is a seasonal toxin and only occurs

Figure 4.34 Potential sources of oral toxins

when there has been a dinoflagellate bloom or red tide, usually between May and October.

Paralytic shellfish poisons (saxitoxins) are neurotoxins, which means they can cause you to stop breathing (respiratory arrest). The effective treatment is to keep the victim breathing for the next 24 hours while the toxin is slowly destroyed in the body. Cardiopulmonary resuscitation may be life saving for the individual who has been exposed to a large dose of this phytotoxin. Getting them to a hospital respirator is essential. If you do not know CPR–learn it!

Fish represent a useful way of obtaining a high protein, low fat source of food for anyone following the American Heart Association guidelines for good nutrition. Most contain little or no cholesterol. Some of the more popular fish are becoming difficult to catch. The supply is dwindling, so we find ourselves eating species new to our palate. Fortunately, we are simultaneously becoming more so-

THE DIVING ENVIRONMENT

phisticated in our tastes, but in some cases, the demand for seafood is outgrowing the scientific information about specific species. Fish can be rapidly transported by air to areas of the world that never ate that species before. Along with this improved transport system, we are finding outbreaks of fish poisonings far from the sea, often to the surprise of the local health officials. There is an increasing consumption of fish and shellfish worldwide. Technological improvements have also increased the harvesting of traditional seafoods and new species. All of these factors contribute to a rise in the occurrence of illness resulting from fish toxins (ichthyosarcotoxism).

Ciguatera fish poisoning is probably the most common ichthyosarcotoxism found worldwide. It is a disease with both neurologic and gastrointestinal symptoms. Various reef dwelling fishes may transmit this poison or group of toxins known as ciquatoxin. Again, a dinoflagellate (Gambierdiscus toxicus) generates the toxins and finds itself in the food chain of many species of fish. The toxin does not seem to affect the fish who eventually concentrate the material in their tissues and become poisonous to man. As a generality, the larger the fish, the more toxic. Symptoms usually develop six to 12 hours after eating the fish; in some cases, within one hour after ingestion. The first signs of illness usually are gastrointestinal in nature; nausea, vomiting, cramps and diarrhea, soon followed by neurological symptoms; tiredness, itching, pain or weakness in the legs, painful joints (arthralgia), numbness around the mouth, hot and cold reversal of sensation, headache, muscle ache, chills, watery eyes, dizziness, tremor, sweating and a red rash. Clinical signs vary from minor complaints to coma and death. With proper and prompt diagnosis, ciguatera can effectively be treated by a physician with intravenous mannitol. Fish such as barracuda (sphyraeniadae), grouper (serranidae), red snapper

Figure 4.36
Always eat
fresh fish that
has been kept
cold.

(Lutjanus bohor), amberjack (Seriola dumerili) and surgeonfish (acanthuriidae) all can transmit ciquatoxin. Eating any affected fish, whether it is cooked or raw, may result in poisoning.

Another ichthyosarcotoxism is scombroid poisoning, which the Hawaiians refer to as mahimahi (dolphinfish) flushing syndrome or saurine poisoning.

Scombrotoxic poisoning generally results from eating fish from the families Scomberesocidae, Scombridae and Pomatomidae, which include tuna, bonita, mackerel and bluefish. Scombroid poisoning occurs when individuals eat fish that are partially decomposed containing high levels of histamine. Bacteria cause the breakdown of the tissue histidine into histamine and saurine at temperatures above 37 degrees centigrade. The spoiled fish frequently has a peppery or sharp taste, which to some people is not unpleasant. Signs and symptoms of scombroid poisoning usually occur within the first hour. The symptoms include diarrhea, hot flushed skin surface, bright red rash (face and trunk), sweating, nausea, headache (can be severe), stomach pain, vomiting, mouth-throat burning sensation, feverish, dizziness, tight chest, swollen face and respiratory distress. Cooking does not destroy the toxic substance in the fish flesh. Cimetidine (Tagamet®) has proved more useful therapeutically than antihistamines for treatment. The bottom line here is to always eat fresh fish that has been kept well refrigerated. If you catch or spear fish, keep them well refrigerated until you can eat or freeze them.

The most dangerous of all food poisonings is, without a doubt, those produced by tetrodotoxin–a very potent material found in the flesh of pufferfish, globefish, blowfish or swellfish–what the Japanese refer to as "fugu". Many people worldwide risk death by eating species from the Tetradontiadae family. Some describe this as "playing Russian Roulette with chopsticks". Eating these fish often produces a strange, warming sensation, or tingling over the entire body. In high concentrations, the tetrodotoxin can cause death in a few minutes by blocking the sodium channels of muscles and

Figure 4.35 Consumption of fish such as barracuda can result in poisoning. Always check with local fisherman to determine species that are safe to eat.

THE DIVING ENVIRONMENT

Figure 4.37 Pufferfish transmit the most dangerous of all food poisonings.

nerves. In other words, this is a potent neurotoxin that stops nerve functions. The victim stops breathing and dies. The toxicity varies from species to species and from organ to organ.

The liver and gonads are usually the most toxic parts of pufferfish. It has recently been learned that pufferfish raised in aquaculture (an artificial environment) do not produce tetrodotoxin. In their natural environment, pufferfish feed on algae that are covered with a bacteria of the genus Alteromonas which we now know produces tetrodotoxin. The northern puffer, Spheroides maculatus, which is caught along the east coast of the United States, is consumed in large quantities in some years and appears safe to eat probably, because the levels of toxin are in their tissues so low. The symptoms of "fugu" or tetrodotoxin poisoning include weakness, dizziness, pallor, tingling around the mouth, lips, tongue and throat, increased salivation, blood pressure falls (hypotension), vomiting (severe and frequent), victim turns blue (cyanosis), the heart slows (bradycardia), breathing becomes difficult (dyspnea) and is followed by shock symptoms. The onset of symptoms is rapid, from five to 45 minutes, and death may occur suddenly without warning. Treatment used: CPR, oxygen, intravenous fluids, atropine and saline stomach washes. Here, the bottom line is to avoid eating boxfish, cowfish, pufferfish and any unfamilar fish unless it is purchased in a reliable restaurant or seafood center.

Parenteral Toxins

Of course, it is easy to avoid marine oral toxins by not eating any seafood, but to avoid the parenteral toxins altogether means not venturing into the sea, which is an unacceptable proposition. It really is quite easy to reduce your chances of being stung by most creatures in the ocean. The first rule

is to always wear protective clothing (wet, dry or Lycra suit) whether you are diving in the tropics or temperate waters. Australian divers found that wearing "panty hose" was an effective protection from their dreaded sea wasp, Chironex fleckeri. A second rule would be to make sure you always wear gloves and boots, protecting your hands and feet, maybe that's still rule number one. Finally, a specific bit of advice is that you look at the bottom before putting your flippers down. In this way, you'll avoid a surprising confrontation with an electric-ray, sting-ray or scorpionfish.

As we progress up the phylogenetic scale, we find many animals that sting or have some form of introducing venom. From the most primitive of species to the more complex, venomous animals have developed some form of protective apparatus or a unique form of food gathering. Most venomous marine animals can be easily avoided. In some cases, you would have to go out of your way to be harmed by these creatures.

As a good example of this last statement, no member of the phyla Porifera (sponges) is going to jump off a rock or coralhead to attack you when you're underwater. On the other hand, if a diver should be stupid enough to squeeze a sponge without gloves on, he/she may be in trouble. Sponges have spicules or internal spines that are made of silica or calcium carbonate embedded in the animal's fleshy body. Only a few sponges are harmful to divers and then only if they come in contact with his or her skin. The red-beard sponge (Microciona prolifera), fire–or dread-red sponge (Tedania ignis) and the poison-bun sponge (Fibulila sp.) all can produce a stinging sensation. Other symptoms include a local sensation of severe burning, swelling (edema), red rash, muscle aches and joint stiffness (arthralgia). Physicians have treated these conditions with local hydrocortisones, systemic corticosteroids, aspirin and skin cremes. My advice, take pictures of sponges, but don't squeeze them.

Figure 4.38 Avoid squeezing sponges.

THE DIVING ENVIRONMENT

Moving up the phylogenetic scale, the next group that should be discussed are the Cnidarians (Coelenterates), which contain some of the most venomous animals known to man. One must keep in mind the vast majority are harmless. These animals are mostly marine, including true corals (Madreporia), soft corals (Alcyonaria), fire coral (Hydrozoan), jellyfish (Scyphozoans) and sea anemones (Anthozoans). These carnivorous animals are characterized by having radial symmetry,

Figure 4.39 Backlit photo of fire coral. Note the hair-like projections that contain stinging cells.

a gut with one opening and tentacles with stinging cells called nemotocysts. It is these nematocysts (or stinging cells) that deliver the venom. Some can penetrate human skin while others cannot. The amount of venom delivered by different species varies considerably. Consequently, some are harmless, others extremely dangerous. Fortunately, the more dangerous can be avoided with proper precautions: that is, full body suits, hood, gloves and boots.

The hydroids, which are a class of this phyla, contain three members particularly known for their ability to sting an individual; fire coral (Millipora sp.), the Portuguese man-of-war (Physalia, sp.) and stinging "seaweeds". Many members of this group of carnivorous animals look like innocent plants. The hydrozoans produce symptoms which range from a mild itching sensation to a severe painful sting. They produce a redness of the skin, urticarial rash (appear similar to hives), blistering vesicles and pustule formation. This may be followed by itching and skin erruptions. Victims of Physalia stings report an "electro-shock-like" sensation, followed by severe pain. This can be followed by systemic symptoms such as chills, fever, fatigue, headache, muscle cramps, nausea and vomiting.

Scyphozoans or true jellyfish are classified into three groups according to their ability to sting: 1),

relatively mild (Aurelia, Pelagica, Carybdea), 2) moderate to severe (Cassiopea, Cyanea) and 3) severe to highly dangerous (Tamoya, Chiropsalmus, Chironex). The symptoms range from a mild prickly sensation, itching to burning and throbbing, shooting pain. The skin becomes red and swollen (edema), has a rash, may blister, hemorrhage (petechial) and experience tissue death (necrosis) through its full thickness. In the more severe cases, one may find muscle cramps, difficulty in breathing, lung congestion (pulmonary edema), loss of consciousness and even death. Treatment of jellyfish stings include the use of household white vinegar, which prevents the nematocysts from most species from firing. Removing tentacles from the victim's skin may be dangerous. Always wear gloves and then wash off the gloves thoroughly. Pain relief may be obtained by giving aspirin. More severe cases may require CPR, morphine and eventually a hospital respirator. The four aims of treatment are to relieve the pain, deactivate the toxins, keep the victim breathing and control any shock symptoms.

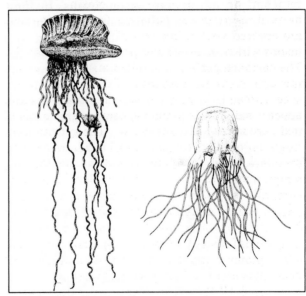

Figure 4.40 Portuguese Man-of-War (left) and Box Jellyfish (right). Both are extremely venomous.

The third group of Cnidarians that cause trouble for the unprepared diver are the Anthozoans, which include the stony corals and sea anemones. In general, this is a colorful, harmless group of animals, with a few exceptions. Every diver should know that he or she may be cut by shallow water corals like elkhorn (Acroporpalmata) or staghorn (Acropora cervicornis) coral. If you do receive a coral cut, wash it with warm soapy water and apply some antiseptic cream to the area.

Figure 4.41 Be careful to avoid cuts from corals.

Most people consider shellfish something to eat (clams, oysters, scallops, etc.) or something to collect, but few realize that there are venomous mollusk. The phylum Mollusca contains a class of gastropod shellfish known as Conus which contains a venom sac and a small poisonous dart capable of penetrating an ungloved human hand. These creatures feed on other gastropod mullusc, polychaete worms and fish. Consequently, they have developed a highly effective venom apparatus. If stung, the victim usually experiences immediate intense pain or a sharp stinging sensation, followed by a burning, then a numbness around the wound site. This may spread eventually over the entire body producing a muscle paralysis. CPR, a respirator and the treatment for primary shock are usually effective treatments. This envenomation is easily avoided by picking up any unknown shellfish with wet suit gloves.

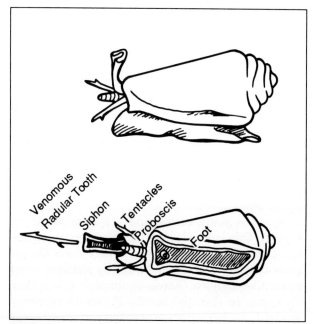

Figure 4.42 Cone Shell

Another mollusk that is known to have killed an individual through an envenomation is the blue-ringed octopus (Octopus maculosus). It has been discovered that this species contains tetrodotoxin in its salivary glands which it probably acquires through its foodchain. The symptoms following the bite of this octopus are similar to eating fugu, since this is a potent neurotoxin. In general, all the members of the octopus family (Cephalopods) are shy and not inclined to bite. The only time people have been bitten by these gentle creatures is when they handle them. Advice: look, take pictures, but do not touch.

Figure 4.43 Blue-Ringed Octopus

The last invertebrate group of animals that we should seriously consider are the echinoderms (Phylum-Echinodermata), which includes starfish, sea urchins and sea cucumbers. This is a group of exclusively marine bottom-dwellers with external skeletons, protruding spines, radial symmetry and a gut with two openings. Sea urchins have spines, some of which are hollow and brittle. They can penetrate the skin, breakoff and become irritating. Crushing the spines in the skin may fragment them and lead to the eventual absorption process with some fine-spined species. This practice should be avoided with thick-spined urchins; however, some spines may have to be removed surgically. Learn the best treatment for each type in each new area. Always keep the wound area clean to prevent infection. Some sea urchins have a special venom apparatus called a pedicellaria which can inject a venom causing some pain, swelling and joint stiffening. Don't handle sea urchins unless wearing gloves. One species of starfish also has stout poisonous spines: "Crown of Thorns" (Acanthaster planci). Wounds from these spines are extremely painful. This Pacific species is the only poisonous starfish.

126

Figure 4.44 Long-Needled Sea Urchins are a hazard in warm waters.

There are many venomous fish, such as sting-rays, scorpion and stonefish. They all have in common some general symptoms. First, as soon as the spines from these animals enter the skin, there is immediate, intense pain that may become excruciating over the next hour. The pain may persist for six to ten hours before diminishing. There will be a swelling (edema) and redness around the injury site. The victim may experience dizziness, weakness, cardiac arrhythemias, anxiety, sweating, muscle weakness, cramps, nausea and vomiting. This may be followed by primary shock, coma and death (rare). To treat victims of fish envenomation, first remove them from the water and immobilize the affected limbs. They will be in great pain. Reassure them. Place a wounded limb into hot, but not boiling water. The ideal temperature is somewhere around 50 degrees centigrade or 122 degrees Fahrenheit. As stated previously, all marine venoms are heat-labile, high-molecular weight proteins. Relieve pain and transfer patients to a hospital for further management.

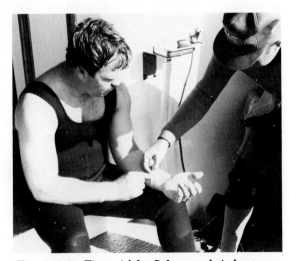

Figure 4.45 First aid for fish wounds is heat.

Another group of venomous marine animals is the sea snakes of the family Hydrophiidae, which are all poisonous. Aquatic inhabitants of the tropical Pacific and Indian Ocean, these reptiles have bodies more or less compressed laterally resulting in a paddle-shaped tail. Sea snake bites are often inconspicuous, sometimes painless and without swelling. Symptoms usually begin mildly and become progressively worse. The victim may experience a mild anxiety, drowsiness or even euphoria. Swallowing may become difficult as the patient's tongue swells. Muscle weakness may progress to a frank paralysis. Fortunately, there are anti-venoms, but they may not be readily available. Many consider the sea snake a docile animal, reluctant to bite, but one must remember that they are all poisonous and potentially lethal. The bottom line is that divers should always give them full and thorough respect. In other words, keep clear of them.

Figure 4.46 Sea Snake

Predators

This section deals with those animals that bite and are aggressive, specifically against man. Fortunately, this is an extremely small group and these are animals that, in general, can be avoided. We cannot include everything that is known about predators in this chapter. The better informed you are as a diver, in my opinion, the safer you'll be in the water. Read more in this area, become an informed diver.

Essentially, there are six principal predators found in the marine environment; barracuda, moray eels, large grouper, killer whales, sharks and poisonous sea snakes. One can say that they all have two things in common, 1) man is not their normal prey and, 2) they rarely bite man. This should be comforting, but if they do bite, the consequences can be devastating.

There are some things that can be done to prevent problems. Here are a few examples.

1. Do not swim or dive in areas with great concentrations of predators. If you can see a killer whale underwater, you are too close.

2. Do not spear fish. Wounded fish and fish blood are great attractions to sharks and barracuda. Do not spear large predators.

3. Do not feed wild predators such as sharks, barracuda, moray eels, groupers or killer whales.

4. Do not harass or handle predators.

5. Do not swim or dive alone.

6. Sharks feed on sea lions and seals. If you look like one on the surface or underwater, you may have a problem.

Figure 4.47 Predators deserve respect and should not be provoked.

These suggestions may seem to be just common sense, but many divers break all of these rules. If left alone, barracuda, moray eels and large grouper probably represent little threat to the diver. However, if molested, all of these animals are effective in biting man and producing serious wounds. The bite from a large shark or even a small killer whale could be severe and fatal. When these animals are spotted underwater, there is usually time to swim purposefully and slowly to a safe retreat. Most shark attacks have occurred in murky, shallow water. In general though, the surface appears to be the most dangerous location for a diver. Few authenticated shark attacks have occurred to a diver on the ocean floor. Don't set yourself up for a problem by provok-

ing a shark or other predator. The only problem with this information is that we are not sure just what provokes and bothers large sharks, so be cautious. Some areas of the world are riskier than others. Know your diving site.

Bites from sea creatures, whether severe or very moderate, should be handled with great respect. First, control the bleeding using large gauze pressure bandages. The wound or wounds should be filled with gauze and the material held in place with a flexible bandage and occasionally a splint to immobilize the limb. Once bleeding is controlled, treat the victim for shock symptoms. Then transport the individual as rapidly as possible to the nearest medical facility. The wounds should be cleaned as soon as possible and any necessary surgical procedures completed. The need for transfusions and skin grafting are common in many of these cases. These wounds can easily become sites for severe infections.

FRESHWATER LIFE HAZARDS

Compared to the oceans, freshwater streams, ponds, and lakes have relatively few forms of animal life that present specific danger to divers. The diver must, however, be aware of those few species that can inflict considerable harm.

Reptiles

The venomous cottonmouth water snake is found in lakes and rivers south of latitude 38 degrees north. This snake is probably the diver's most serious aquatic hazard. It predominantly inhabits stagnant or sluggish water, but has been observed in clear and moving water.

There has been a persistent notion that the cottonmouth would not bite underwater; however, two fatalities caused by cottonmouth bites have

Figure 4.48 Cottonmouth Water Snake

THE DIVING ENVIRONMENT

been documented. The cottonmouth is considered pugnacious, adamant, and vindictive when disturbed and will attack unprovoked. It does not show fear toward humans as most other aquatic snakes do; its behavior is unpredictable. Attack is more likely to occur in the evening.

Recognition is difficult since its color varies from jet black to green with markings absent or vaguely similar to the copperhead. Consequently, in areas where the cottonmouth is known to exist, it is advisable for the diver to regard any snake that does not swim away when encountered as a cottonmouth. The best defense is a noiseless, deliberate retreat. Wet suits afford reasonably good protection, but can be penetrated by larger specimens. Bare hands should be tucked under the armpits. The diver should never attempt to fight since this will probably only result in multiple bites. Although, evidence is inconclusive, it appears that the snake will not dive deeper than about six feet.

The timber rattlesnake is an excellent swimmer on the surface. Skin divers should be alert and avoid contact.

First aid for venomous snake bites includes:
- Keep the victim quiet and take measures to combat shock.
- If the bite is on an extremity, immediately apply a constructing band about one inch above the bite. This band need not be extremely tight. It should be loosened every 30 minutes for five minutes.
- Apply skin antiseptic over and around the bite and incise (about 1/4 inch long and not too deep) with a sharp blade.
- Apply suction with devices available with snakebite kits, if available.
- Seek immediate medical attention. An tivenom treatment may be required.

Turtles

Three species of aquatic turtles may be hazardous to the diver if provoked and mishandled, especially large specimens. Though not venomous, they may inflict serious, dirty wounds. The alligator snapping turtle found through the watershed of the Mississippi River, is vicious and aggressive when provoked. It has powerful jaws and sharp claws. The alligator snapper is recognized by three distinct, keel-like lines running longitudinally the full length of the upper shell. These are also wart-like projections about the head and forelimbs. The alligator snapper is extremely long and muscular, and can strike rapidly by extending the neck.

Figure 4.49 Snapping Turtle

The common snapper is smaller and similar in appearance to the alligator snapper. This species is considered by some authorities to be more vicious when provoked than the alligator snapper.

The softshell turtle may also inflict a serious wound. Contact with these turtles should be avoided or special precautions taken in handling.

Standard first aid for laceration-type wounds is recommended, as is Tetanus immunization.

Alligators and Crocodiles

The American alligator has been encountered by divers, but is not known to be aggressive or to cause injury. Yet, the potential of injury is present and divers should be cautious. In Central and South America, the crocodile may certainly constitute a hazard to divers, and in Africa, the crocodile is responsible for many human deaths each year. The saltwater crocodile of the coast of Queensland, Australia, is very large (up to 30 feet) and reported to be a vicious aggressor.

Mammals

The common muskrat is the only warm-blooded animal that will probably attack a diver in U.S. fresh waters. It attacks only in defense and the wound is usually minor. However, the possibility of rabies is present and serious. It is important for the diver to seek medical treatment if bitten and for the animal to be captured or killed for laboratory examination. If encountered while diving, the muskrat should not be provoked. If provoked into attack, escape is virtually impossible.

Fishes

The only freshwater fishes of noted hazard to divers are the freshwater sharks of Lake Nicaragua in Central America and the piranha fish of the Orient and South America. In U.S. waters, the only fish capable of inflicting serious injury are those of the catfish family, which are discussed in the section on venomous marine fish, and the gar. The gar fish commonly weighs in excess of 100 lbs. and if provoked by spearfishermen, has the capability of biting with needle-sharp teeth.

The previous discussion has concentrated on the freshwater life hazards of the United States. Certainly, it is only common sense for the diver to consult with local authorities prior to commencing diving operations when diving in other parts of the world.

Area Orientations

It should be readily apparent by now that diving in different areas requires different techniques and knowledge. Plant and animal life very greatly, as do water movement and conditions. Seasonal variations, local laws and regulations, local diving etiquette and customs also vary from place to place. Equipment needs and diving techniques may be unfamiliar to you. Your orientation is best provided by an instructor, guide or experienced diver from an area that is new to you.

Advance information on diving in a new area is helpful. Sources of information include:
1. Dive guide books
2. Magazine articles
3. Dive clubs in the area
4. Phone calls to dive facilities in the area
5. Handouts from dive facilities in the area
6. Letters to diving professionals
7. Boating books and charts
8. Pre-dive investigations when in an area
9. Presentations on diving in an area

Learning about diving in a new area in advance is helpful, but that alone will not fully orient you. Pay for some orientation dives in a new area. You will be safer, learn the area faster and make better use of your diving time than if you try to save money. Employ a diving professional for your orientation. Local instructors, divemasters and dive guides are available for hire. Ask questions. Find out where the best locations are. Learn about the plants and animals you see. Take advantage of the knowledge available to you.

Orientations to a new diving environment can be a lot of fun. They are needed for safety and to increase your enjoyment. You should avoid diving in any area or condition unfamiliar to you unless accompanied by someone who is qualified to guide and direct your activities.

Summary:

This section has briefly described some of the problems you can encounter in the underwater environment. We've also discussed how to avoid most of the problems with some simple rules for each section. **Oral toxins**: 1) avoid eating unknown species (fish or shellfish, 2) check local authorities for the safety of their species, and 3) do not eat shellfish collected from an area which has recently suffered a red tide. **Parenteral toxins** (the "stingers"); 1) always wear protective clothing while diving, 2) wear gloves even in the tropics, and 3) watch where you place both your feet and hands while underwater. **Predators**: 1) do not enter the water where sharks or other predators have injured man, 2) if you find yourself up to your armpits in predators - leave the water, 3) do not feed or molest predators, and finally 4) know your diving area.

Figure 4.50 It is always best to get a formal orientation from a diving professional.

DECOMPRESSION & RECOMPRESSION 5

The study of decompression and decompression sickness is one of the most fascinating aspects of diving. The complexity of the physics and physiology involved make exact answers difficult to find. As a result, after 80 years of research, there are different theories and tables around the world, each applying to different and highly specific circumstances. It is important to understand the background of some of the prevailing theories so appropriate techniques can be used for your diving situation.

Learning Objectives:

By the end of this course, you need to be able to:
1. Define and briefly explain tissue halftimes.
2. Briefly explain why NAUI uses the U.S. Navy Dive Tables.
3. Meet the dive table calculation objectives listed in this section.
4. Briefly explain the proper dive table procedures for:
- Cold or strenuous dives
- Ascent rate variations
- Less than ten minute surface interval
- Multi-level diving
- Omitted decompression
- Flying after diving
5. State the NAUI policy regarding mixed gas diving.
6. State the two primary advantages of using a dive computer.
7. List several uses for recompression chambers; contrast at least three different types of chambers used for diving injuries; and state at least two hazards associated with chambers.
8. Define altitude diving and list at least four procedural differences between diving at altitude and diving at sea level.
9. Correctly define the decompression and recompression terms presented in CAPITAL LETTERS in this chapter.

DECOMPRESSION THEORIES—

By P. Heinmiller

As you extend your diving range to foreign countries, you may have met other divers using tables unfamiliar to you. Supporting all of these tables is a decompression theory based upon historical and current research. All of these theories begin with the work of J.B.S. Haldane in England in 1908.

The Haldane Theory

Decompression sickness (DCS) was a problem which affected not only divers, but also caisson workers in bridge piers and tunnels. Those stricken by the disease tended to walk with a stoop (when they could still walk) similar to an affected posture called the "Grecian bend", popular with society ladies at the time. Their comrades, in harassing their afflicted fellows, nicknamed those DCS symptoms "the bends".

When you dive, the tissues in your body tend towards equilibrium with the surrounding gases. At the surface, your tissues are all at equilibrium, as much gas is going in as is going out, so the tissues have no net gain of gas. When diving, much more gas enters the tissues than leaves, producing a net increase in the amount of gas in the tissues. This continues until the tissues are once again at equilibrium with their surroundings, or until you surface, whichever comes first.

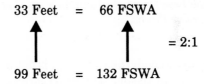

Figure 5.1 Summary of Haldane's ratio. As long as the calculated pressure in any tissue was no more than twice the pressure at the next dive depth, the diver could be allowed to proceed to the next dive step.

$$\frac{P_{tissue}}{P_{external}} \leq \frac{2}{1} \quad Safe$$

Figure 5.2 Haldane's observation of a 2:1 surfacing ratio applied to a change of depths without surfacing. If his theory was reasonable, a change of depth from 99 fsw to 33 fsw should also be safe.

Haldane observed that divers making dives shallower than 33 feet of sea water (FSW) could be brought directly to the surface without contracting "the bends". This observation implied that tissues at equilibrium at 33 FSW could surface without incident. Surfacing from 33 FSW is a pressure reduction of 50%. Extrapolating from this information, it was reasoned that tissues could always withstand a pressure reduction of 50%, whether from 33 feet to the surface, or from 99 feet (132 FSWA) to 33 feet (66 FSWA). This is the famous "Haldane ratio" of 2:1 pressure reduction.

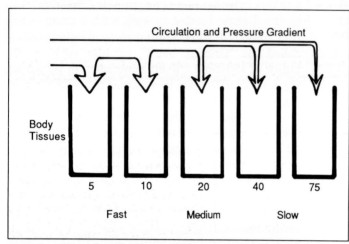

Figure 5.3 A half-time is the length of time it takes a specific tissue to become 50% saturated with nitrogen. Fast tissues, such as brain and heart tissue, saturate rapidly; while slow tissue, such as bones, saturates slowly. Times for each type of tissue have been established and form the basis for modern decompression theory.

The human body, as you know, is not made up of just one type of tissue. The heart, brain, muscles, bones, blood, gut, and fatty tissues are all part of the total picture. Each of the tissues behaves differently under pressure, taking up and giving off gases at different rates, but all headed for equilibrium. Rather than model the body directly, by measuring the gas uptake of human muscle and other specific tissues, a spectrum of theoretical tissues was established to span the range of human body tissues.

The speed with which a tissue takes up, or gives off, gases is measured by the HALF-TIME. The tissue half-time is the time required for the tissue to give up half of its excess gas. After the first half-time, half the gas would be gone and half remaining. After the second half-time, half the remaining gas would be gone for a total of 75% gone. After the third half-time, 87.5% of the excess gas has left the tissue.

After six half-times, more than 98% of the excess gas has gone, which is close enough to 100% for normal purposes.

Haldane and his co-workers used tissue half-times, called compartments, of 5, 10, 20, 40, and 75 minutes to model the body. During the course of a dive on paper, the pressures in the various tissues were calculated. If the absolute pressure in any tissue exceeded 66 FSWA, the diver would not be allowed to surface directly. For each diving depth, the maximum length of time before stops were required was established.

Haldane also proposed a method of "stage" decompression, where the diver would ascend to the shallowest stop possible without exceeding the 2:1 ratio. The diver would remain at the stop until enough gas left the tissues, so that he could safely surface.

Tables based on these principles were produced for the Royal Navy, and formed the basis for further work by other researchers.

American Theory

The U. S. Navy used the Haldane Royal Navy tables until their own were developed in 1937 at the U. S. Navy Experimental Diving Unit in Washington, D. C. The major difference was the use of different surfacing ratios for the different tissues. It was also decided that only the inert portion of the gas was important from a decompression viewpoint, because the oxygen portion was metabolized during pressure reduction. The third modification was the inclusion of longer half-time tissues in the model. By 1965, the U. S. Navy decompression model had evolved through research and use.

While the total pressure surfacing ratio is based on total tissue pressure, the nitrogen pressure surfacing ratio is only concerned with the tissue

Tissue half-time	Surfacing ratio
5 minutes	2:1
10 minutes	2:1
20 minutes	2:1
40 minutes	2:1
75 minutes	2:1

Table 5.1 Summary of the Haldane-Royal Navy decompression model used five tissues, with half-times ranging from 5 to 75 minutes, each with a surfacing ratio (Haldane Ratio) of 2:1.

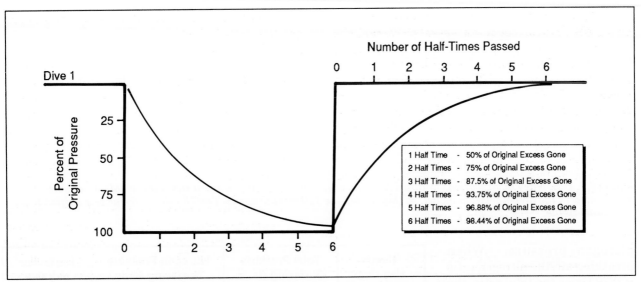

Figure 5.4 *Uptake and outgassing in an exponential tissue. After six half-times of gas uptake, the tissue is 98.44%*
saturated at the external pressure. Similarly, after six half-times of outgassing, the tissue is very nearly saturated at
the surface pressure, and the tissue has lost its memory of the dive.

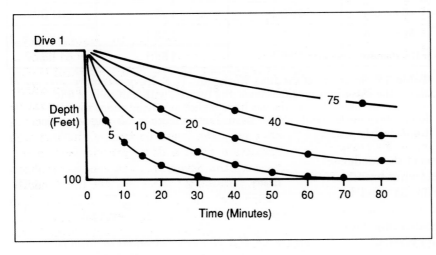

Figure 5.5 *Uptake of gas in Royal*
Navy model on a dive to 100 feet.
The five minute tissue is effectively
saturated at the dive depth after 30
minutes, six half-times. The 75
minute tissue, however, has barely
added gas after 30 minutes, and will
take a total of 75 minutes to just
reach 50 feet. Eventually, all tissues
will saturate, but this will take seven
and one-half hours, much longer
than a normal dive.

Figure 5.6 *Tissue pressures on a*
25 minute dive to 100 feet
according to the Royal Navy
decompression model. The first 25
minutes of the dive are not difficult
to calculate. However, upon
surfacing after 25 minutes, tissue
tracking becomes complex, as each
tissue has a different level of
pressure on ascent, and outgasses
according to its own half-time. It is
unrealistic to keep these equations
in your head, so tables
summarizing them are produced.

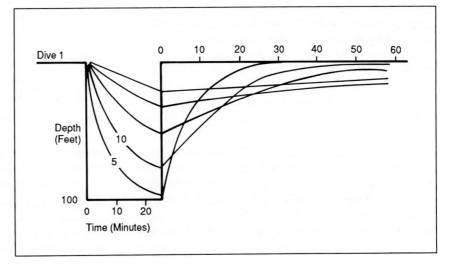

Longer Half-times

Figure 5.7 U.S. Navy modifications to Royal Navy theory. The U.S. Navy believed that longer half-times should be represented in the decompression model, so they added the 120 minute tissue. The 75 minute tissue was shifted to an 80 minute tissue.

nitrogen pressure. When breathing air, the nitrogen ratio is 0.79 times the total ratio, the gas fraction of nitrogen. It is easy enough to figure out the maximum allowable tissue nitrogen pressure by simply multiplying the nitrogen ratio times the 33 FSWA surface pressure.

A term used in the Workman model, which is quite often referred to when discussing decompression theory, is the M-value. The M-value is, quite simply, the maximum allowable nitrogen pressure in a specific tissue of the model. The nitrogen pressure surfacing ratio when breathing air is 0.79 times the total ratio, as used by Haldane. The surfacing M-valve is determined by multiplying the nitrogen pressure surfacing ratio times the pressure at the surface, 33 FSWA.

Therefore, when diving to 60 feet, where the nitrogen pressure is 73.5 FSWA, the 5, 10, and 20 minute tissues cannot exceed their maximums, regardless of how long you stay down. The 40 minute tissue will reach its limit after 60 minutes, producing the 60 minutes at 60 feet USN No-Decompression Limit (NDL). The 40 minute tissue is said to "control" this dive to 60 feet, since that tissue forced the end of the dive. The 40 minute tissue controls single dives using the U. S. Navy tables for depths between 31 and 60 feet.

The U. S. Navy made a major addition to the Haldane model with the concept of repetitive diving. Working surface supply divers stay on the work site until the job is finished. The decompression tables are their only limits, as their air supply is virtually unlimited. Only with the invention of

Tissue Half-time	Total Pressure Surfacing Ratio	Nitrogen Pressure Surfacing Ratio	Surfacing M-Value
5 minutes	4:1	3.15:1	104 FSWA
10 minutes	3.4:1	2.67:1	88 FSWA
20 minutes	2.75:1	2.18:1	72 FSWA
40 minutes	2.22:1	1.76:1	58 FSWA
80 minutes	2:1	1.58:1	52 FSWA
120 minutes	1.96:1	1.55:1	51 FSWA

Table 5.2 Summary of the 1965 Workman - U. S. Navy decompression model shows the U.S. Navy modifications. Six tissues, with half-time of 5 to 120 minutes are used. Faster tissues have higher surfacing ratios than in the Royal Navy model, while slower tissues ratios more in keeping with the Haldane 2:1.

$$\frac{P_{tissue}}{P_{external}} - \frac{2}{1} \qquad \frac{P_{TN}}{P_{external}} - \frac{1.58}{1}$$

Figure 5.8 U.S. Navy modifications to Royal Navy theory. The U.S. Navy believed that only nitrogen was responsible for the decompression problem, and modified Haldane's whole gas ratios accordingly.

scuba in 1943, did the scuba diver, bouncing up and down to change tanks, become important. The Haldane tables gave a diver no credit for time spent on the surface. As recently as 1972, British Sub-Aqua Club (BSAC) divers using the Royal Navy tables had to add bottom times or repetitive dives made within 12 hours of a dive to 30 feet or more. The total combined dive time and the deepest depth reached in either dive were used in the tables to determine decompression requirements. Once the diver had spent his 60 minutes at 60 feet, he could not return to that depth without stage decompression until 12 hours had passed. In the U. S. Navy

DECOMPRESSION & RECOMPRESSION

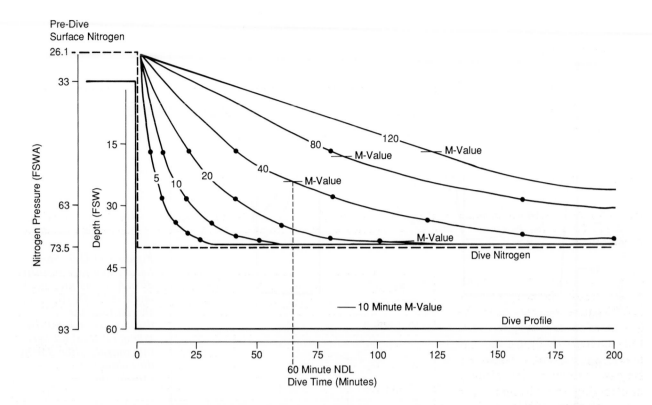

Figure 5.9 When diving to 60 feet, where the nitrogen pressure is 73.5 FSWA, the 5 and 10 minute tissues cannot exceed their maximums, 104 and 88 FSWA respectively, regardless of how long you stay down. The 40 minute tissue will reach its limit after 60 minutes, producing the 60 minutes at 60 feet USN No-Decompression Limit (NDL). The 40 minute tissues is said to control this dive to 60 feet, since that tissue forced the end of the dive. The 40 minute tissue controls single dives using the U.S. Navy tables for depths between 31 and 60 feet.

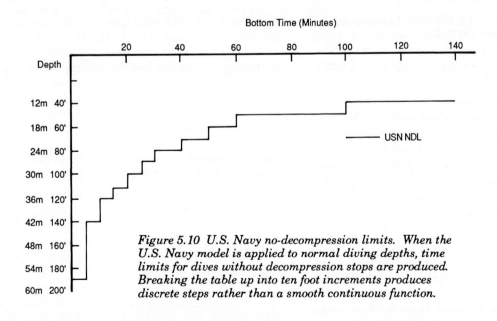

Figure 5.10 U.S. Navy no-decompression limits. When the U.S. Navy model is applied to normal diving depths, time limits for dives without decompression stops are produced. Breaking the table up into ten foot increments produces discrete steps rather than a smooth continuous function.

model, the diver, is assigned to a letter group based upon the pressure on surfacing in the 120 minute tissue, 2 FSW per letter. So, an "A" diver has between 33 and 35 FSWA total pressure, or 26-27.65 FSWA nitrogen pressure, in his 120 minute

tissue. While the diver remains on the surface, the nitrogen leaves the body, producing a reduced letter group. On returning to the water, the new letter group is used to determine the residual nitrogen time (RNT) at the dive depth. RNT is based on the

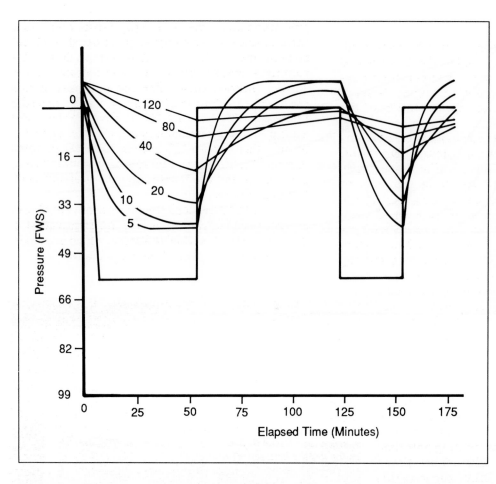

Figure 5.11 U.S. Navy tissues on a safe repetitive dive. A second dive can be made safely for dive times shorter than the no-decompression limits by taking residual nitrogen into consideration during dive planning calculations.

amount of nitrogen in the 120 minute tissue, and is measured in minutes to be considered already spent at the repetitive dive depth.

British Theory

The Royal Navy theory is also a descendant of the early Haldane-Royal Navy tables. The R.N. tables use more conservative surfacing ratios than their U.S. counterpart, providing less time at depth. They also provide an extremely conservative repetitive dive procedure, since all repetitive dives are combined and worked as single dives, regardless of surface interval. The Royal Navy tables were in use by the British Sub-Aqua Club as recently as 1972.

In the 1980 BSAC Decompression Table Workbook, the BSAC/Royal Navy Physiological Laboratory (RNPL) tables are taught. These tables are based on a more recent theory than the R.N. tables, and allow more time at depth than the R.N. tables and less time than the U.S. Navy tables. A technique has also been introduced to allow some surface interval credit for second dives, although more than two dives per day must still use the "multiple dive rule" of adding all bottom times and using the deepest dive depth. The BSAC/RNPL tables have

been produced with very easy to remember decompression stop times. Unlike the U. S. Navy tables, where the first stop over the NDL varies from two to ten minutes at ten feet depending on dive depth, in the RNPL tables the first stop over the limit is always five minutes at five meters for dives shallower than 20 meters, and always five at five and five at ten for deeper dives.

Swiss Theory

The Haldane theory also provides the origin for the Swiss theory as developed by the Laboratory of Hyperbaric Physiology at the University of Zurich. Swiss theory utilizes 16 tissues, with half-times of 2.65 to 635 minutes, to determine no-decompression limits for single and repetitive dives, as well as decompression requirements for longer dives. Unlike Haldane theory and its British and American descendants, Swiss theory is extended to altitude diving. The M-values, or maximum surfacing nitrogen pressures, are no longer constant, but rather are mathematical functions of atmospheric pressure. This further complicates an already complex situation, but tables and computers can be produced which are valid at reduced atmospheric pressures.

Canadian Theory

In contrast to the theories already mentioned, the Canadian tables published by the Defence and Civil Institute of Environmental Medicine (DCIEM), are not Haldanian in origin. None of these theories is an exact representation of the physics and physiology of the body in decompression, but rather a fitting of mathematical equations to a time-depth history and a symptom-free result. Haldanian equations utilize parallel tissues, each taking up and giving off gas from the ambient environment without regard to neighboring tissues. The DCIEM theory employs a set of serial tissues, the first of which takes up and gives off gas from the environment. The second and succeeding tissues take up and give off gas from the preceding tissue only, not from the ambient gas supply. This serial model has been designed to produce results which are conservative compared to the U. S. Navy tables. Tables produced from this theory are applicable to sport diving situations.

DSAT Theory

In 1987, Dive Science and Technology Corporation (DSAT) introduced a decompression model using the 60 minute compartment as the controlling or limiting half-time tissue, rather than the 120 minute tissue used by the U. S. Navy. DSAT suggests this is appropriate for recreational diving as opposed to the longer half-time tissue adopted for commercial and military diving operations. The number of repetitive groups for dive tables developed were increased by DSAT in an attempt to reduce residual nitrogen time penalties. Also, no-decompression limits less than the U. S. Navy limits were incorporated into the DSAT tables as a safety factor. The net effect of the DSAT tables is less no-decompression time for the first dive but longer bottom times for repetitive dives. And shorter surface intervals are required between dives. The DSAT tables have been tested, but concerns exist about the effects of multiple-day diving. The new concepts will have to withstand the test of time.

Dive Tables

In spite of the numerous dive tables available throughout the world today, NAUI still recommends the use of the U. S. Navy Dive Tables. More information and data is available for the Navy tables than for any other tables in existence. It is strongly recommended, however, that limits less than the Navy no-decompression limits be consid-

ered when using the U. S. Navy tables and that a three minute precationary stop at a depth of 15 feet be performed at the end of all repetitive dives. The stop time does not count as either bottom time or surface interval time. For the purposes of this course, the no-stop limit for a given depth will be the limits identified on the NAUI Dive Tables. For example, your no-decompression limit for 60 feet is 55 minutes (Group "I") rather than 60 minutes (Group "J"). The maximum rate of descent is 75 feet per minute and the maximum rate of ascent is 60 feet per minute.

As a NAUI Advanced Diver you should be able to correctly calculate repetitive no-required-stop dives using the NAUI Dive Tables, which are modified Navy Tables. You should be able to:

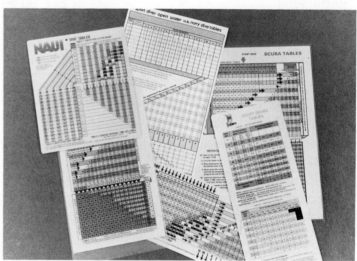

Figure 5.12 Various Dive Tables.

1. Determine the correct repetitive group designation for any single or repetitive dive schedule possible with the NAUI Dive Tables.

2. Correctly calculate the Adjusted Maximum Dive Time (AMDT) for a repetitive dive. For example, the AMDT for a Group "E" diver planning a dive to a depth of 70 feet is 19 minutes.

3. Correctly calculate the minimum surface interval required to make a repetitive dive of a given duration that does not exceed the maximum tmie limit. For example, the minimum surface interval required before a Group "H" diver may make a 30 minute dive to a depth of 60 feet is 2:24.

4. Correctly calculate the maximum depth allowable for a repetitive dive of a given duration. For example, a Group "F" diver who wants to make a 20 minute dive may not exceed a depth of 50 feet.

DIVE TABLES

RNT RESIDUAL NITROGEN TIME

+ADT ACTUAL DIVE TIME

TNT TOTAL NITROGEN TIME

(USE THIS FIGURE TO DETERMINE END-OF-DIVE LETTER GROUP.)

TABLE 1 - END-OF-DIVE LETTER GROUP

START DEPTH M	FEET											
12	40 ➤	5	15	25	30	40	50	70	80	100	110	(130) 150/5
15	50 ➤		10	15	25	30	40	50	60	70	(80) 100/5	
18	60 ➤		10	15	20	25	30	40	50	(55) 60/5	80/7	
21	70 ➤		5	10	15	20	30	35	40	(45) 50/5	60/8	70/14
24	80 ➤		5	10	15	20	25	30	(35) 40/5	50/10	60/17	
27	90 ➤		5	10	12	15	20	(25) 30/5	40/7	50/18		
30	100 ➤		5	7	10	15	20	(22) 25/5	40/15			
33	110 ➤			5	10	13	(15) 20/5	30/7				
36	120 ➤			5	10	(12) 15/5	25/6	30/14				
39	130 ➤			5	(8) 10/5	25/10						

00 MAXIMUM DIVE TIME (MDT)

00 / 00 DIVE TIME REQUIRING DECOMPRESSION — NO. MINUTES REQUIRED AT 15' STOP (5M)

TABLE 3 - REPETITIVE DIVE TIMETABLE

M.	12	15	18	21	24	27	30	33	36	39	NEW GROUP
FT.	40	50	60	70	80	90	100	110	120	130	
	7 / 123	6 / 74	5 / 50	4 / 41	4 / 31	3 / 22	3 / 19	3 / 12	3 / 9	3 / 5	◄ A
	17 / 113	13 / 67	11 / 44	9 / 36	8 / 27	7 / 18	7 / 15	6 / 9	6 / 6	6	◄ B
	25 / 105	21 / 59	17 / 38	15 / 30	13 / 22	11 / 14	10 / 12	10 / 5	9	8	◄ C
	37 / 93	29 / 51	24 / 31	20 / 25	18 / 17	16 / 9	14 / 8	13	12	11	◄ D
	49 / 81	38 / 42	30 / 25	26 / 19	23 / 12	20 / 5	18 / 4	16	15	13	◄ E
	61 / 69	47 / 33	36 / 19	31 / 14	28 / 7	24	22	20	18	16	◄ F
	73 / 57	56 / 24	44 / 11	37 / 8	32	29	26	24	21	19	◄ G
	87 / 43	66 / 14	52	43	38	33	30	27	25	22	◄ H
	101 / 29	76 / 4	61	50	43	38	34	31	28	25	◄ I
	116 / 14	87	70	57	48	43	38				◄ J
	138	99	79	64	54	47	**AVOID REPETITIVE DIVES OVER 100 FEET**				◄ K
	161	111	88	72	61	53					◄ L

TABLE 2 - SURFACE INTERVAL TIME (SIT) TABLE

	A	B	C	D	E	F	G	H	I	J	K	L
◄ A	24:00 / 0:10	24:00 / 3:21	24:00 / 4:49	24:00 / 5:49	24:00 / 6:35	24:00 / 7:06	24:00 / 7:36	24:00 / 8:00	24:00 / 8:22	24:00 / 8:51	24:00 / 8:59	24:00 / 9:13
◄ B		3:20 / 0:10	4:48 / 1:40	5:48 / 2:39	6:34 / 3:25	7:05 / 3:58	7:35 / 4:26	7:59 / 4:50	8:21 / 5:13	8:50 / 5:41	8:58 / 5:49	9:12 / 6:03
◄ C			1:39 / 0:10	2:38 / 1:10	3:24 / 1:58	3:57 / 2:29	4:25 / 2:59	4:49 / 3:21	5:12 / 3:44	5:40 / 4:03	5:48 / 4:20	6:02 / 4:36
◄ D				1:09 / 0:10	1:57 / 0:55	2:28 / 1:30	2:58 / 2:00	3:20 / 2:24	3:43 / 2:45	4:02 / 3:05	4:19 / 3:22	4:35 / 3:37
◄ E					0:54 / 0:10	1:29 / 0:46	1:59 / 1:16	2:23 / 1:42	2:44 / 2:03	3:04 / 2:21	3:21 / 2:39	3:36 / 2:54
◄ F						0:45 / 0:10	1:15 / 0:41	1:41 / 1:07	2:02 / 1:30	2:20 / 1:48	2:38 / 2:04	2:53 / 2:20
◄ G							0:40 / 0:10	1:06 / 0:37	1:29 / 1:00	1:47 / 1:20	2:03 / 1:36	2:19 / 1:50
◄ H								0:36 / 0:10	0:59 / 0:34	1:19 / 0:55	1:35 / 1:12	1:49 / 1:26
◄ I									0:33 / 0:10	0:54 / 0:32	1:11 / 0:50	1:25 / 1:05
◄ J										0:31 / 0:10	0:49 / 0:29	1:04 / 0:46
◄ K											0:28 / 0:10	0:45 / 0:27
◄ L												0:26 / 0:10

TIME RANGES IN HOURS : MINUTES

00 LIGHT FACE NUMBERS ARE RESIDUAL NITROGEN TIMES (RNT)

00 BOLD FACE NUMBERS ARE ADJUSTED MAXIMUM DIVE TIMES (AMDT) • ACTUAL DIVE TIME SHOULD NOT EXCEED THIS NUMBER

© **1990 NAUI**

89-0019

Figure 5.13
NAUI Dive Tables

Sample Problems

1. *A NAUI Advanced Diver dives to 99 feet (30 meters) for 20 minutes, surfaces, remains at the surface for an hour and 25 minutes, then dives to a depth of 50 feet (15 meters) for 35 minutes. What is the diver's repetitive group designation following the second dive?*

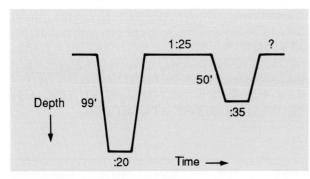

Figure 5.14 Question #1 Profile

Solution: 99'/20 = Group F. Surface Interval Time (SIT) of 1:25 = Group E. Residual Nitrogen Time for "E" to 50' = 38 + Actual Dive Time (ADT) of 35 = Total Nitrogen Time (TNT) of 73 = 50'/73 = Group "J".

2. *What is the AMDT for the second dive in question #1?*
Solution: AMDT for "E" to 50' = 42 minutes

3. *If the diver in question one wanted to make the second dive to a depth of 70 feet (21 meters) for 25 minutes, what is the minimum surface interval required to make the second dive a no-decompression dive?*
Solution: 70' for at least 25 minutes requires Group D. SIT to attain Group D from Group F = 1:30.

4. *If the diver in question one wanted to make the second dive one hour after the first dive, what is the maximum depth allowed with a no-required-stop dive time of 30 minutes?*
Solution: Group F with 1:00 SIT = Group E. First AMDT for Group E equal to or exceeding 30 minutes is 50 feet.

If you had any difficulty working the sample problems, please refer to Section Five of *The NAUI Textbook* for a review of NAUI Dive Table procedures.

SPECIAL DIVE TABLE PROCEDURES

Certain situations require special procedures for correct dive table calculations. The following list identifies the situations and the proper procedures.

Cold or Strenuous Dives

If a dive is particularly cold or strenuous, USE THE NEXT GREATER BOTTOM TIME to determine your repetitive group. For example, if you are cold during a dive to 90 feet (27 meters) for 20 minutes, consider the dive schedule as 90 feet for 25 minutes.

Ascent Rate Variations

Any delays in ascent during a no-decompression dive are simply added to the bottom time of the dive. Precautionary stop time is considered part of dive time as a margin of safety. With NAUI, dive time is considered from the time you descend until the time you surface from a dive. Ascent times slower than 60 feet per minute are of little benefit compared to a precautionary stop.

Surface Interval Less Than Ten Minutes

If the time between dives is less than ten minutes, the two dives are considered a single dive with a schedule consisting of the deepest depth of either dive and the combined dive times of the two dives. The surface interval is ignored. An example is a dive to 60 feet for 30 minutes followed by a dive to 50 feet (15 meters) for 25 minutes. The dive schedule for these dives is 60 feet for 55 minutes.

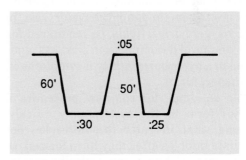

Figure 5.15 Less than ten minutes SIT

Multi-level Diving

The Navy Dive Tables are based on the concept of spending the entire time of a dive at the single depth, but recreational divers seldom remain at a constant depth while diving. You are then charged with more nitrogen than you actually absorb when diving at multiple levels. Procedures have been developed to manually calculate MULTI-LEVEL DIVES (a dive with varying depths) using the Navy dive tables, but use of these techniques is not recommended because they are complicated and errors are easily made. Those who wish to avoid the "maximum-time-at-maximum-depth" penalty when diving at varying depths are encouraged to consider the use of a dive computer which continuously calculates the exact depth and the precise nitrogen absorption by numerous tissues, thus allowing longer bottom times without decompression.

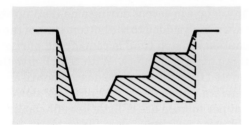

Figure 5.16 Penalty time for a square wave dive.

Omitted Decompression

The U.S. Navy procedure for omitted decompression, which involves recompressing the diver in water, has been updated based on conclusions reached by noted physicians and physiologists. The Navy procedure specifies decompression at depths of 40', 30', 20' and 10' with one minute between stops. This procedure has been replaced with the following: Divers who have missed decompression stops are to remain out of the water, rest, breathe 100% oxygen, drink fluids, be monitored for signs and syptoms of decompression sickness, and transported to a hyperbaric facility if symptoms of bends are suspected.

The rationale for the new procedure is that bubbles form in the system very quickly upon sufacing, that in-water recompression does not eliminate bubbles after they have formed, that decompression sickness can actually result or be aggravated by in-water decompression, and that breathing oxygen is more beneficial than the in-water procedure.

A diver who has omitted required decompression is to refrain from further diving for at least 24 hours even if no symtoms of decompression sickness are evident.

Mixed Gas Diving

The no-stop limits for various depths can be extended by using a gas mixture containing a higher than normal percentage of oxygen. Because less nitrogen is breathed, less is absorbed. Such diving is referred to as "Nitrox" diving, and is common in science and in the military. Special tables, tank filling equipment, and training are required for Nitrox diving, which NAUI considers at the present time to be beyond the scope of recreational diving. ATTEMPTING TO FILL OR PARTIALLY FILL SCUBA TANKS WITH OXYGEN IS EXTREMELY HAZARDOUS, CAN LEAD TO AN EXPLOSION, CAN PRODUCE OXYGEN TOXICITY, AND SHOULD NEVER BE ATTEMPTED.

Gas	%N$_2$	%O$_2$	%He	Max Depth
Air	79	21	0	130'
Nitrox I	68	32	0	130'
Heliox	0	32	68	200'

Table 5.3 Mixed gases for diving. Only air is recommended for recreational diving.

Additional Dive Table Problems

1. *Two hours after surfacing from a cold dive of 30 minutes duration to a depth of 80 feet (24 meters), you plan a dive to a depth of 70 feet. What is your maximum bottom time with no required decompression?*

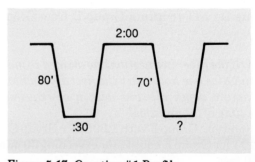

Figure 5.17 Question #1 Profile

Solution: 80'/30 = 80'/35 for a cold dive = Group H. 2:00 SIT = Group E. AMDT for E at 70' = 19 minutes.

2. *You spend the first ten minutes of your first dive of the day at a depth of 110 feet (33 meters), then spend another 20 minutes at a depth of 50 feet (15 meters). What is your total ascent time from the 50 foot level and your repetitive group designation at the end of the dive?*

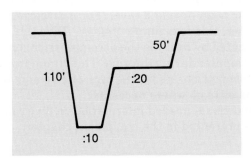

Figure 5.18 Question #2 Profile

Solution: 110'/30 = Group J. Ascent time = 7 mins. decom. + 110 seconds ascending = 9 mins.

3. *Your first dive is to 70 feet (21 meters) for 28 minutes, followed by a surface interval of 1:30. Your second dive is to a depth of 50 feet for 35 minutes, followed by a surface interval of nine minutes. Your third dive is to a depth of 45 feet for 35 minutes. What is your repetitive group after the third dive?*

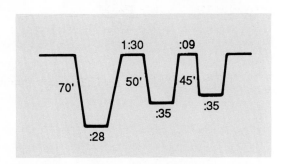

Figure 5.19 Question #3 Profile

Solution: 70'/28 = Group F. SIT of 1:30 = Group D. TNT for 50' = 29 RNT + 70 ADT (combine second and third dives because SIT was less than 10 minutes) = 99 minutes = 50'/100 = Group L.

4. *As a Group "D" diver, you plan a dive to 75 feet (23 meters). According to the procedures presented in this section, how many minutes may you spend on the bottom (not just underwater) during this dive?*

For this question, use a rate of 75' per minute when determining the maximum time you can spend on the bottom without exceeding the AMDT.

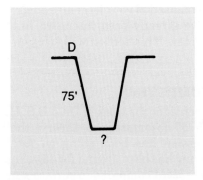

Figure 5.20 Question #4 Profile

Solution: Your descent should take 60 seconds (descent rate = 75 feet per minute), and your ascent should take 75 seconds (maximum ascent rate = 60 feet per minute). The precautionary decompression stop time is considered "neutral" time and is not counted. The AMDT for Group D at 80' = 17 minutes. Subtracting the descent and ascent times leaves a maximum of 14.75 minutes that may be spent on the bottom during the dive. This is hardly worth the effort, so a longer surface interval or a shallower dive should be considered. This example illustrates the need to plan your dives. If you actually spent 17 minutes on the bottom (including descent time), a decompression stop would be required rather than precautionay.

Aids to Decompression

There is a lot of equipment available to help you make decisions about decompression. None of the devices, however, can make decisions for you. It remains your decision how deep to dive and how long to remain at depth. We have seen that these two considerations are the most important when attempting to avoid decompression sickness. Although the devices mentioned here can give good advice, it is your decision to avoid pushing the limits that will keep you safe.

One of the most common aids to decompression, the tables, have already been discussed. U. S. Navy tables are available in a variety of formats on plastic cards to carry with you on your dive. An unused set of tables in your BC pocket is no excuse for an unplanned dive.

Aside from tables, there is a large variety of devices on the market. Capillary depth gauges, diaphragm depth gauges, oil-filled depth gauges, analog watches, digital watches, analog bottom timers, digital bottom timers, and dive computers can be purchased in your local dive shop. The other items have already been discussed in the equipment chapter. This section will focus on dive computers.

DIVE COMPUTERS

If we consider the work of Dr. J.B.S. Haldane as the birth of decompression theory, the study of decompression has been going on for 80 years. Scuba diving has been around for 45 years, which is relatively recent compared to surface supplied and breath-hold diving. The dive computer, less than ten years old, is the most recent advance in diving technology. Like all new ideas, it has taken time to become accepted, and now the diver is faced with quite a selection of dive computers. It can be quite a difficult task to sort out all of the available devices and select the one which is right for you.

Background

The U. S. Navy dive tables were designed to serve the needs of the U. S. Navy diver. Both the type of diver and the type of dive are present in the design of the tables. The recreational scuba diver population is different from the Navy diver norm, and is more varied than the Navy population. In general, the differences between the Navy population and the recreational population make the use of Navy tables by sport divers a non-conservative practice. Many divers compensate for this by adding time or depth when using tables. The typical leisure dive is different than the typical Navy operational dive. In general, pleasure divers are sightseers, wandering about, exploring the dive area, moving up and down at will or whim. Navy divers are typically working divers, moving to the work site and remaining until the job is completed. The Navy table's dependence on the "square dive" of the working diver is often much too conservative and restrictive for the sport diver.

The Navy tables are a simplified version of a general theory of decompression. The tables are arranged for ease of reading and use by typical Navy divers. In spite of this simplification, it is generally recognized that dive table calculations are one of the first learned skills from the entry level course which are forgotten by the diver in the field.

There are many simplified formats of the Navy tables available. Still, new divers lose their ability to work the tables.

The reason for building dive tables from decompression theory is the complexity of the decompression theory itself. It is unreasonable to expect you to keep six or more simultaneous equations running in your head during a dive. For a dive computer, however, this is a simple matter. Dive tables are eliminated by running the decompression model in the computer during the dive. This eliminates all of the assumptions about the type of dive and allows the diver to go where necessary.

Additional needed information on dive computers is presented in the equipment chapter.

Figure 5.21 Always consult the dive tables between dives.

RECOMPRESSION CHAMBERS—

By R. Rutledge

The treatment for serious diving injuries such as decompression sickness or air embolism is recompression, which is carried out in a recompression chamber.

Figure 5.22 Hyperbaric Chamber

Recompression Chambers and the Sport Diver

Chambers are often not covered in much detail in entry level scuba courses and divers usually have no first-hand contact with them until treatment is needed. As a diver, familiarity with chambers will alleviate some of the fears associated with them and better prepare you to deal with circumstances which may befall you or people you know. There are three general groups of scuba divers treated in recompression chambers. If you dive, you could fall into one of these groups. The three groups are as follows:

1. The first group are the divers with the "undeserved" hit. This is the statistically significant group of individuals who have been doing everything "by the book" and still suffer decompression sickness or air embolism. There will always be a small unpredictable number of incidences due to individual variations and undetectable abnormalities. This is the risk which all divers assume when they dive; although small, it is real.

2. The "over-the-limits" diver falls into a second group. These are divers who have taken their diving activities beyond their level of knowledge and training. In this group are novice divers who take up deep diving and repetitive diving without adequate guidance. The egotistical diver who, because of his experience, thinks he can "beat the odds" and liberalize or experiment with his diving activities belongs in this group. Divers using decompression computer devices without knowing their limitations may also be placed in this group.

3. The more common third group is the "inadequately trained" diver group. In this group are the totally untrained divers who use scuba with no instruction. Unfortunately, these divers usually require treatment for air embolism secondary to breath holding upon ascent. Another component of this group is the novice diver who knows enough to go diving, but not enough to monitor depth/time parameters and avoid decompression sickness. Whether this lack of knowledge is due to total ignorance or the inadequate development of good habits, it is irrelevant once the injury has occurred. Training must establish a general knowledge of what decompression is—an internalization of the importance of following decompression guidelines, and the ingraining of good habits which will optimize safety.

The following sections present an overview of chambers in general. They will familiarize you with some common vocabulary and start you on an exploration of what's available for treating sport diver injuries.

Descriptive Terminology of Chambers

Chambers are known by several different names. Usually the name is related to the particular task for which the chamber is used. All chambers share some common characteristics, can be used for multiple task, and therefore have several descriptive names.

Figure 5.23 This fairly large, portable chamber is on location at a popular New Mexico dive site.

Figure 5.24 Recompression chamber operators control treatment procedures.

Recompression chambers are used to place victims of decompression sickness or air embolism under pressure for treatment.

Hyperbaric chambers are used to place patients in oxygen breathing environments under increased pressure to treat various medical conditions.

Decompression chambers are used to provide commercial divers a means of decompressing out of the hostile water environment after a working dive.

Compression chambers are used in industry and research to increase atmospheric pressure around objects or subjects.

Altitude chambers (also called hypobaric chambers) are used in industry and research to decrease atmospheric pressure around objects or subjects.

These five different names all refer to a pressure vessel being used for a particular purpose. The chambers which might be utilized to treat divers have some general characteristics.

General Characteristics of Chambers

Chambers are pressure vessels: they contain a volume of gas which can be held at a pressure which is different from the surrounding ambient pressure. Chambers are usually cylindrical in shape with hemispherical ends. Some chambers used in commercial diving are completely spherical. These shapes allow hull strength to be achieved with

efficient use of structural material. There are chamber characteristics which are used for describing chambers.

To relate and compare one chamber to others, diameter measurements are commonly used. The 54 inch diameter chamber is often found in diving communities. It is a relatively small, economical chamber capable of treating victims with an inside tender and switching personnel during the treatment.

The 96 inch chamber may be found in large medical facilities where its large size allows many medical patients to be treated simultaneously. On the other hand, a 26 inch chamber may also be found in medical facilities where its small size allows one medical patient to be treated at a time in a cost effective manner.

In addition to using diameter denotations, chambers also described by their rated working pressure; usually expressed in pounds per square inch (psi) or atmospheres absolute (ATA). To immediately treat air embolism or life threatening decompression sickness, it is highly desirable to compress the victim to 165 feet of sea water depth (six ATA or 90 psi). The chamber for such a treatment must be "rated" to six ATA working pressure. Many chambers used for medical treatment are "rated" for three ATA pressures. They can be very useful for more common decompression sickness treatment; however, unless logistics mandate oth-

Figure 5.25 Large air systems and storage banks are required for a recompression facility.

DECOMPRESSION & RECOMPRESSION

erwise, they should be superseded by the nearest six ATA chamber for treatment of life threatening conditions.

Chambers can also be characterized by the number of compartments and "locks" which they possess. Locks are doorways or access openings which are pressure sealed when closed. Compartments are spaces which can be pressurized independent of each other and of ambient pressure. Compartments are really individual chambers sharing a common lock between them and are actually called "chambers" or "locks". A chamber with two compartments might therefore be called a multi or double lock chamber with inner and outer locks or inner and outer chambers. If capable of containing more than one individual in the inner chamber, it could also be termed a multiplace, multilock chamber. Some chambers have small compartments for passing supplies in and out. These compartments are termed "medical locks". The doors (locks) on medical locks commonly open outward and must therefore be bolted closed. The doors (locks) of the large occupancy chambers commonly open inward so that increased internal pressure works to seal the door closed.

Any given chamber will have a number of "penetrators" or sealed holes through which various tubes or wires penetrate into the inside space. During chamber design and fabrication, penetrators will be incorporated to meet the needs of the chamber's anticipated tasks.

To increase and decrease the pressure within the chamber, penetrators with valve systems input gas supplies and similar valved pipes are used to exhaust gases from the chamber. These pipes constitute the plumbing of the chamber.

Communications are established between the inside and outside of the chamber by wires introduced through a penetrator.

If present, lighting and electrical cables may also penetrate the chamber hull. (More on this later.)

Monitoring devices may also penetrate the hull to sense internal atmospheric conditions or to detect occupant status changes.

Medical patients in small chambers may need drugs and fluids or breathing assistance provided to them via special penetrators specifically designed for these purposes.

Compressors and Gas Sources

To pressurize chambers, compressors or sources of already compressed gas are needed. Backup systems, either compressors or gas cylinders, must also be present in case of primary source failure.

Pressures required for chambers are relatively low but the volumes of gas involved are usually quite high. A typical 54 inch chamber's inner lock is some eight feet long (the chamber is about 12 feet long overall) and has a volume of approximately 120 cubic feet. High volume low pressure air compressors are less expensive than high pressure compressors and are commonly used for chambers unless a high pressure compressor is already present for other reasons. Just as with compressors for scuba cylinders, chamber compressors must use special lubricating oils and air intakes must be guaranteed clean pure air. Proper maintenance is very important.

Cylinder banks of compressed air can be used as backup gas sources. Cylinder banks of compressed oxygen can be used to run or back up small chambers whose total pressurized environment is oxygen, or they can serve as sources of oxygen breathing gas in larger air pressurized chambers. Liquid oxygen sources are commonly used to supply oxygen gas for hospitals and will thereby be the primary oxygen source for most hyperbaric chambers.

Special gas supplies such as nitrogen, helium, nitrogen-oxygen or helium-oxygen mixtures find special application in the commercial diving industry. These special gases are usually stored in compressed gas cylinders and may be available for chamber use if needed.

TYPES OF CHAMBERS AND THEIR USES

There are a variety of chambers available in the market place. Choices are made on the basis of intended use and cost effectiveness.

In hyperbaric medical facilities, this usually translates into frequency of use or number of patients being treated at one time.

For the recreational diving community, this usually translates into pressure needs (6 ATA), size (room for inside tender and victim), and simplicity (get the job done at minimal cost). Because of infrequent use and little or no monetary reimbursement for treatments, chambers solely dedicated to treating recreational divers usually lose money or break even at best, even with volunteer help or local government support. Ideally, the recreational diver would be treated at a large medical or commercial facility if one is close by. However, the unpredictability and long treatment schedules for the injured diver can wreak havoc with routine scheduled operations. The "bent" recreational diver is not a welcome sight for anyone, including the diver. If the diver presents himself for treatment as soon as symptoms occur, outcome is usually good and treatment personnel get a lot of gratification from knowing they have returned an active individual to a happy, productive life. When this is not the case, no one wins and no one is pleased. Divers should know what type of recompression facility is available to them in their diving area, how to contact the facility for consultation, and how to get there expediently for treatment. The next section presents an overview of what might be available and what function it might normally serve.

Monoplace Single Lock

Small acrylic plastic one-person one-lock chambers are found at some medical centers. Their normal use is for hyperbaric medical therapy of various conditions. They use a total 100% oxygen environment at lesser pressure; *i.e.*, they are pressured to less than three ATA and are run using pure oxygen. These chambers can be used to treat the less severe cases of decompression sickness but are not preferred for life threatening decompression sickness or air embolism cases because of pressure limitations (see prior section). They are often used for follow-up treatment of decompression sickness in a fashion similar to their use in medical therapy.

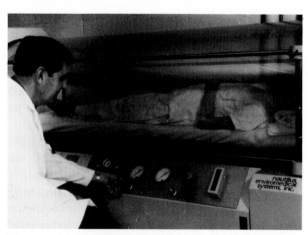

Figure 5.26 Monoplace Chamber

Small steel chambers rated at higher pressures (six ATA+) have been used to transport victims under pressure using a total air environment. To be useful, they must be capable of "mating" with the treatment facility's outer lock so that the victim can

be transferred, under pressure, into the treatment chamber. Conceptually, such chambers are a holding vessel used to inhibit deterioration of the victim prior to reaching a treatment facility. However, once locked into such a chamber, victims cannot receive hands-on care. A transport chamber which allows space for an inside tender would be a better choice if available. During transport, victims continue to breathe air and therefore continue to onload nitrogen, thus compounding decompression obligations. Generally, severely ill divers being transported will benefit more from hands-on care and surface oxygen administration than they will from being in these small chambers.

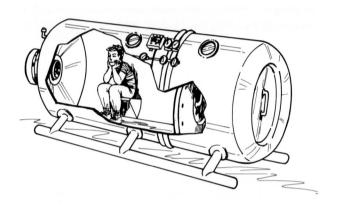

Figure 5.27 Multiplace Double Lock Chamber

Multiplace Double Lock

Large chambers with space for many persons and with both inner (occupant) and outer (passageway) compartments/locks can be found at larger hyperbaric medicine facilities. Their usual use is for the medical therapy of various conditions. Commonly, these chambers are pressurized with air at lesser pressures; *i.e.*, about two point four ATA. Patients wear 100% oxygen breathing devices which dump exhaled gases outside the chamber. Tenders usually breathe chamber air. Most of these chambers are rated for six ATA and, therefore, would be appropriate for treating life threatening scuba diving accidents (165 fsw breathing air), as well as less severe decompression sickness victims (intermittent oxygen breathing at 60 fsw and less). Treatment of decompression sickness victims in follow-up therapy would be similar to medical therapy usage at such facilities.

DECOMPRESSION & RECOMPRESSION

As mentioned previously, the 54 inch multiplace double lock chamber can be found in some locations as the treatment chamber for diving injuries. It is often subsidized by government and/or dive operations, staffed by on-call volunteers, and is mainly a public service operation in need of support and income. Some larger facilities have these chambers as back-up for their larger chambers.

Both small and large (livable) chambers are used in the commercial diving industry to provide surface decompression and/or habitat spaces for working divers and recompression of injured divers. Such facilities, if available, could also be used for treatment of sport diver injuries.

Divers seeking information about chamber facilities should be aware of the ever-changing status of availability. There are directories of chamber locations but, for a variety of reasons, a listed chamber may not be available for treatment of divers at a given point in time. Currently, the Divers Alert Network (DAN) is a source of more accurate chamber information. DAN is also a resource which should be used as a consultant for remote chamber operators and non-diving oriented physicians. DAN is only a phone call away and can serve as an excellent diver's advocate.

CHAMBER OPERATIONS, PERSONNEL AND SAFETY CONCERNS

At any chamber there are several tasks which personnel encounter during a treatment run. The number of actual personnel involved may vary from a few to several, but the tasks themselves fall into the following categories.

Supervisor

An overview of the entire operation must be ongoing. Someone must be monitoring compressed gas sources, the integrity of equipment, chamber pressure and gases, the status of operating personnel, and the status of the treatment subject. A supervisor must be ready to immediately intervene in the normal course of treatment, if necessary.

Timekeeper

Treatment schedules are based on depth and time, just like a dive. To insure proper treatment, the timing must be controlled. To document the treatment, activities affecting the subject or any change in subject condition must be logged into the time record. Because inside tenders are "diving", their depth and time profiles must also be logged.

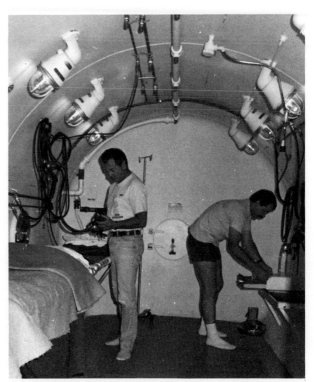

Figure 5.28 A large, double-lock recompression chamber. Note medical lock between two crew members.

The timekeeper logs all relevant events and times and keeps the treatment schedule on time. Commonly, the timekeeper is also responsible for communications with inside personnel and subjects.

Operator

Someone must monitor and control the chamber pressure. The chamber must be washed through with fresh gas periodically ("venting the chamber"), as dictated by the chamber schedule. This is the chamber operator's job.

Tender

Scuba diving accident victims can be very ill people. Often proper monitoring and care must be conducted with hands on contact. The inside tender is the hands on person taking care of the recompression subject. This individual needs experience in acute care and is often a paramedic, nurse, or physician. The tender is under pressure just like the subject and is "diving". On long recompression treatments, the tender has the potential of becoming a treatment subject if his own decompression obligations are not met. Chambers with multiple locks allow the switching of tenders, thereby enhancing both tender safety and subject care.

Physician Consultant

In remote sites on commercial diving operations, recompression treatments are often run by established company guidelines and physician consultation is not ordinarily needed. However, things do not always go as anticipated. When the standard protocols fail to yield good results, diving medical officers (physicians) are brought in to direct modifications of the treatment schedules or to "lock in" to assume monitoring and acute care of the subject. In the commercial diving industry, diving is well controlled and monitored and decompression sickness is usually detected early and treated immediately. Were the same true of the recreational diving industry, decompression sickness would be rare and treatment outcomes would be better. Because of all the variables involved with the recreational diver, a physician consultation is very desirable. This physician should be versed in the diagnosis and treatment of diving accident injuries and should have access to other consultants when necessary. Because of poor diving habits and delays in seeking or obtaining treatment, scuba diving accident victims can end up with protracted courses of treatment and the need for long term therapy and rehabilitation. Early physician involvement can sometimes improve outcomes.

Operational Procedures

Because treatment schedules for decompression sickness and air embolism are standardized in the U.S. Navy format (at least in this country), the operational procedures for most chamber facilities are similar. An initial victim assessment is made to establish the severity of the problem at that point in time. If the condition is life threatening, the victim is placed in the chamber and pressurized to six ATA (165 fsw) from where further evaluation and treatment will progress. If the condition is not life threatening, a more thorough history and examination are conducted prior to placing the victim in the chamber. A non-life threatening recompression treatment schedule will usually be run at 60 fsw pressure, utilizing intermittent oxygen breathing, alternating with air breathing periods. Typical treatments last between three hours (mild decompression sickness) to six hours (severe decompression sickness). Treatments may go even longer and can reach days of saturation in the commercial diving industry.

Specific Safety Concerns

Prior to beginning a treatment schedule, there are some safety concerns which are addressed.

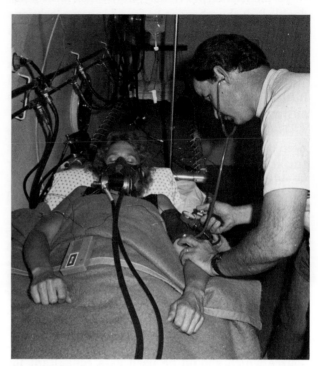

Figure 5.29 Treatment of a patient in a recompression chamber.

Fire

Fire is a potential hazard because of the use of pure oxygen, particularly at the increased pressures involved. If the total chamber environment is oxygen, as is the case in monoplace medical hyperbaric chambers, the problem is most significant. If an air filled multiplace chamber with oxygen breathing masks or hoods incorporating "overboard dumps" is involved, the problem is more of a potential concern. Chambers can be equipped with fire suppression systems to dowse fires, but the prevention of fires is the first priority. To create a fire, three ingredients must be present: a burnable substance, an oxygen like supporter of combustion, and an ignition source. To reduce chamber fire risk, as many of these factors as possible are controlled. Chambers and gas equipment and anything which enters the chamber is kept "oxygen clean", which is to say all greases, oils, etc., are eliminated. Combustibles are minimized within the chamber by special attention to clothing and supplies. Sources of ignition are eliminated by keeping electronic devices and electrical circuits outside the chamber or completely sealed. Lights are shone through port holes or fiber optic cables where possible. All who enter the chamber are "frisked" for potential hazards. In chambers where oxygen breathing equipment is used, overboard dumps are incorporated to direct exhaled gas out of the chamber, thereby keeping excess oxygen out of the chamber environment itself. In addition, oxygen analyzers are employed to monitor for any oxygen spillage into the chamber should it occur. In chambers where pure oxygen is used to pressurize and run the chamber, the other variables of combustibles and ignition sources are the only controllable factors.

Toxins

In addition to fire hazards, the pressurized gases which chamber occupants breathe can be toxic.

Oxygen at increased pressures can cause seizures. Usually, individuals can tolerate 100% oxygen at pressures of 60 fsw or less if they are resting. Any physical exertion increases the likelihood of a seizure, a rise in body temperature, carbon dioxide build up and mental agitation. Oxygen is used as a treatment gas for decompression sickness and air embolism victims. The dosage of oxygen is controlled by the total chamber pressure and by the time on oxygen. Very seizure sensitive individuals may not tolerate usual protocols, but such instances must be dealt with on an individual basis.

Carbon dioxide build up from the occupants' exhaled gases in the chamber can cause very minor symptoms all the way to death, depending upon the carbon dioxide levels. To eliminate the carbon dioxide build up problem, the chamber is vented periodically. To vent a chamber, fresh gas is blown into the chamber from the compressor or cylinder bank at the same time as chamber gas is exhausted to the outside. The gas flows must be matched or an overall pressure change will occur within the chamber. Venting is done periodically for short intervals based on a calculated schedule for any given chamber and number of occupants. In addition to cleaning the chamber of carbon dioxide, venting also helps control other occupant waste gases and humidity, thereby assuring overall comfort for those inside.

Carbon monoxide and other gas contamination can be a rare problem in chambers just as it is in scuba air. The key to solving this problem is good compressor inspection and maintenance. Air intakes should be inspected before each run to be sure that chemicals, solvents, paints, lubricants, etc. have not been used or placed near the intake. Compressed cylinder gases purchased from outside sources should at least be smelled and tested for oxygen concentration prior to use.

Victim Condition

One of the major concerns in any recompression treatment is the safety and welfare of the subject being treated. Even an individual with a mild case of decompression sickness can become disoriented, fearful, panicky, or (rarely) manifest combative behavior because of the chamber environment itself. Chamber personnel are aware of such possibilities and make every effort to inform, forewarn, and comfort individuals under their care. Progression (worsening) of a victim's symptoms during treatment is not a positive sign and often treatment schedules must be modified to regain control of the situation. Similarly, regression of the symptoms during attempted reductions in chamber pressure may necessitate schedule extensions or a move to a different schedule. As previously mentioned, oxygen can cause seizures. Should a seizure occur, the tender must remove the subject's oxygen mask and prevent injury. Oxygen seizures are usually brief and require no specific treatment other than removal of the oxygen. The inside tender is very important in severe diving accident cases, as he/she is the most sensitive monitor of subject status and the means of treating or controlling changing conditions inside the chamber.

Figure 5.30 An Australian "Paracel" portable chamber.

What Chamber Operators and Physicians Need From You

You, as a diver's friend or as a diving accident victim, can do a great deal to help the chamber personnel.

The first and most significant help is to plan for safe dives, including accident management plans for evacuation to the nearest recompression facility. Log your dives and know your options.

Second, simply seek aid when you even think someone (including you) may be bent or the victim of air embolism. Do not attempt to treat decompression sickness by returning to the water. In water recompression treatment using air is extremely dangerous and is not defensible. In water treatment using special equipment, special gas supplies and special expertise has been done. However, it is used only as a last resort, even by proficient persons prepared to do so in remote isolated dive operations. As a sport diver, you must seek chamber treatment. Oxygen breathing on scene and during transport to a chamber is the treatment of choice. (Please refer to other chapters for diagnosis of decompression sickness and air embolism.)

Third, cooperate with chamber personnel by doing what is asked of you. Be honest in all of your answers to questions. Don't let your ego or your image get in the way of good diagnosis and treatment. If you made one error, don't compound the problem with rationalization or denial. Be helpful to yourself by letting others help you.

Last, have understanding and compassion for chamber personnel and consultants. These people are trying to be helpful, often as volunteers, and they have stresses and tasks associated with their function that you may have little or no perception of during the course of the treatment itself.

Figure 5.31 Recompression chamber crews are highly skilled in emergency procedures.

What a Chamber Experience is Like

If you have the opportunity to take a "chamber ride", do so. There is nothing that will impress you more than being inside a chamber during pressurization, venting, and ascent. Most chambers active in treating divers will organize orientation sessions for interested groups. Although chambers differ, there are some elements which most experiences will have in common.

One of these is noise. Chambers are noisy places. Most chambers are steel "bells" which reverberate when struck by dropped objects and during general activities. Gases rush in through small orifices during pressurization and venting and, unless muffled, the noise can be too loud to talk over. In addition, as gas density increases with increasing pressure, voices become "weird" and sometimes difficult to understand.

Another obvious sensation is the rapid change in temperature and humidity during pressure changes. During pressurization, the chamber gets warm and feels stuffy. During ascent, the chamber gets cool and clouds of humidity can form.

If you're in a chamber for very long, the confinement and realization of loss of control over what is happening to you can get to you. However, if you're in chamber for treatment, these feelings will be outweighed by the feelings of concern and humanity which will surround the whole caring for experience.

A chamber ride is not a treatment, but it will yield an idea of what one would be like.

Summary

What then can be said about the scuba diver's relationship with chambers? They certainly need to be available. They come in various shapes and sizes. They often serve routine functions not related to treating the sport diving accident victim. They are complex entities requiring expertise to run and maintain. And, last, they are places you should seek out whenever you even think there is a need. Leave your ego and image behind when you seek aid.

ALTITUDE DIVING
—By Milledge Murphey, Ph. D.

While you may believe that you will never dive at altitudes above sea level, the potential for underwater experience using scuba at altitude is great. As transportation access increases, we may all be able to travel to moderate or higher altitude dive sites which are now known or may be discovered in the future. A high altitude dive may be defined as any dive which is conducted at an altitude greater than 1,000 feet. At present, there are many high altitude freshwater lakes, ponds, mine shafts, caverns, caves and rivers which are regularly dived by recreational scuba divers.

In this connection, NAUI has published a booklet by C. L. Smith, entitled *Altitude Procedures for the Ocean Diver* from which much of this chapter was taken and which you should read for additional information on this subject. As an advanced scuba diver, you should and will want to know the facts concerning diving at altitudes beyond sea level. Further, your safety and enjoyment are dependent upon your advanced ability to use the dive tables with error free ability. Make sure you are trained for altitude diving before you use the information included herein.

Perhaps the most significant differences which you will encounter when you dive at higher altitudes are the variances in buoyancy control, differences in use and types of dive tables, and variance in depth gauge readings. In addition, you should be aware of the special techniques and potential hazards involved in diving at higher altitudes. The purpose of this section is to provide information for your use in diving safely at sites which are above sea level.

Diving at Higher Altitudes

What are the primary differences which you face when participating in altitude diving and how can you safely deal with them? As all altitude diving is done above sea level, it differs from ocean diving in two important ways:

1. Fresh water (almost all altitude diving is fresh water) is less dense than sea water.

2. Atmospheric pressure at altitude is less than at sea level.

As your open water training indicated, the lower density of fresh water results in your being less buoyant, thus requiring less weight on, or in, your weight belt. Further, the lower density of fresh water causes your depth gauge to read differently than it does in sea water. The reduced atmospheric pressure at altitude adds to this variance in depth gauge readings (from readings taken at sea level). Finally, and most importantly, the lower atmos-

Figure 5.32 Divers taking a ride in a chamber. The group leader on the right controls the rate of descent via signals to the chamber operators.

pheric pressure at higher altitudes radically increases your susceptibility to decompression sickness should you not exactly follow special altitude dive tables.

The second part of the introductory question deals with what can/should be done to avoid the problems associated with diving at higher altitudes. Obviously, you should lower the amount of weight which you use to establish neutrality in the water. More important, however, is the mandate to avoid the problems associated with potential decompression sickness at altitude. In this connection you should have your depth gauges adjusted to compensate for increased altitude so that they will display the actual diving depth at the higher altitude. Since you are effectively heavier (when equipped with normal open water equipment) at altitude and in fresh water than when diving in the sea, weight must be removed if true neutral buoyancy is to be achieved. Typically, you'll need to remove two and one-half percent of your normal total sea water weight (usually three to eight pounds). If you dive without wet suit or weight belt in ocean water, you'll need to add air to your buoyancy compensator for altitude diving. To clarify this procedure; if, for example, you weigh 150 pounds and have 50 pounds of equipment on when prepared to dive at sea level in salt water, you'll need to remove five pounds from your weight belt to insure that you're neutral in fresh water.

Procedures for Altitude Diving

The procedures for altitude diving obviously vary from those used for diving in sea water and at elevations below 1000 feet. The differences in diving practice, however, are not as difficult to master as you might have imagined, and any qualified open water scuba diver can, with proper training and equipment, enjoy safe scuba diving at altitude.

A summary of necessary procedures for use by saltwater divers when diving at altitude is included in Table 5.4 below.

Having made these changes in preparation for your altitude diving experience, it is important that you clearly understand the effects of reduced atmospheric pressure at altitude.

Table 5.5 includes information regarding changes in atmospheric pressure at altitudes from sea level to 15,000 feet tabulated in increments of 1000 feet. You should be aware that the closed cell neoprene of your wet suit will expand as the suit is taken to higher altitude, making it more buoyant. This buoyancy increase is small but may be noticeable at higher altitudes.

It should be clear to you at this point that all altitude dives must be formally calculated, especially when diving at higher altitudes. In no altitude diving circumstance should you "guess", even though the dive is planned to be relatively short and shallow. An additional reason for you to be especially careful in dive planning and execution at higher altitude is that most dive sites are located at great distance from hyperbaric facilities. If an accident did occur, you might not be able to get to a recompression chamber in reasonable time.

Among the precautions you should take when you decide to dive at altitude are the following:

1. After diving, you should wait 24 hours before ascending to altitude. As in the "flying after diving" procedures which you learned in your initial open water courses, you must be aware of the potential problem of bends due to the lower cabin pressure in the airplane which transports you to the altitude diving site.

2. You should consider yourself to be in a repetitive dive situation (even though you have not made a dive) when you first reach any higher altitude dive site. This circumstance will require you to assume that you are in a higher group letter depending on the altitude to which you have flown. This is due to nitrogen accumulation in your body due to the altitude change and will require several hours to normalize. Information relative to this mandatory safety procedure is included in Table 5.7.

As can be seen from Table 5.4, you should treat any dive made within twenty four hours as a repetitive dive.

Procedural Change	Rule
1. Weight belt adjustment	Remove 2 1/2 % of total weight of diver and ocean gear from weight belt (3 to 8 lbs.).
2. Flying after an ocean dive	Wait 24 hours before flying following dives that do not exceed time limits and even longer following any dives requiring decompression.
3. Diving on same day as arrival at altitude	Treat as a repetitive dive. Adopt repetitive dive group letter G on arrival for elevations up to 10,000 feet. (See Section 6)
4. Decompression	• If dive is not too deep, use capillary depth gauge readings directly with the U.S. Navy dive tables to determine allowable bottom time. Use readings directly for 60 ft/min ascent rate and depths of any decompression stops. • If dive is deep or if capillary gauge is not available, use any other depth gauge and: - determine equivalent ocean depth, ascent rate and depth of any decompression stops from the altitude dive tables of Section 8. - apply the equivalent ocean depth to the U.S. Navy dive tables to obtain allowable bottom time, and decompress accordingly.
5. Depth gauge correction	• For capillary gauges, if above 3,000 feet, subtract 3% of reading per 1,000 feet of elevation.

Table 5.4 Summary of Procedures for Diving at Altitude

DECOMPRESSION & RECOMPRESSION

Altitude, Feet	Atmospheric Pressure PSIA
Sea Level	14.70
1,000	14.17
2,000	13.66
3,000	13.17
4,000	12.69
5,000	12.23
6,000	11.78
7,000	11.34
8,000	10.92
9,000	10.51
10,000	10.11
11,000	9.722
12,000	9.349
13,000	8.987
14,000	8.636
15,000	8.297

Table 5.5 Atmospheric Pressure vs. Altitude

Table 5.6 (Omitted)

Elevation, Feet	Group Letter On Arrival
1,000	B
2,000	B
3,000	C
4,000	D
5,000	D
6,000	E
7,000	E
8,000	F
9,000	F
10,000	G
11,000	G
12,000	G
13,000	H
14,000	H
15,000	I

Table 5.7 Repetitive Dive Group on Arrival at Altitude From Sea Level

As an example of the use of this table, consider the person who drives from sea level to a mountain lake at 7,000 feet and wishes to dive at once to a true depth of 60 feet. He arrives in group E and, applying this letter to Navy table 1-13, a corresponding residual nitrogen time of 30 minutes is found. The total allowable bottom time at that depth and altitude is only 40 minutes (80 feet equivalent ocean depth from the tables of Section 8). Thus, by diving immediately, the available bottom time is only ten minutes, a quarter of what it would have been had the diver waited until the next day.

3. You should never use the standard tables (NAUI, Navy or others) without modification(s) when diving at altitude. Further, you must have the information to correctly modify the tables so that you can correctly determine your allowable bottom time and ascent rate for the altitude at which you dive. There are no exceptions to this rule if you are to dive safely. All standard tables are based on sea water at sea level calculations and your altitude dive(s) are vastly different from the data on which the standard dive tables were based.

What then must you know in order to dive safely at higher altitudes? The answer to this question is clear:

1. The equivalent ocean depth of your dive
2. The allowable ascent rate of your dive
3. The depth of any (potential) decompression stops you may need to make.

Note: to determine changes in altitude decompression, you should use a capillary depth gauge on shallow to medium depth dives. Capillary depth gauge readings can be used without correction to determine your allowable bottom time and decompression stops. In addition, you can use the ascent rate indicated by the capillary depth gauge at any altitude and in any water density. As an example, at any altitude the capillary depth gauge reading of 40 feet may be interpreted as 40 feet of no-decompression time available on the first dive. Further, you may then read the gauge directly for any indicated decompression stops; *i.e.*, if a ten foot stop is required, you may correctly stop at the capillary depth gauge reading of ten feet to accomplish the necessary stop.

Should you choose to use a depth gauge of the non-capillary variety, a rather complex procedure is required to reduce the ascent rate (actual and gauge indicated) to less than 60 feet per minute. Table 5.8 yields equivalent fresh water ascent rates at altitude for the 60 feet per minute ocean rate.

The theoretical depth at altitude for actual diving depth in fresh water is included in Table 5.9.

Table 5.9 illustrates the tables developed by E.R. Cross for calculation purposes when diving at altitude. These calculations are based upon U.S. Navy tables and must be used with them for accuracy and safety. Decompression stops must be modified for fresh water and altitude. Table 5.10 provides information which allows you to cal-

Altitude, Feet	Proper Actual (not Indicated) Ascent Rate, Feet Per Minute
0	61.6
1,000	59.4
2,000	57.2
3,000	55.2
4,000	53.2
5,000	51.2
6,000	49.4
7,000	47.5
8,000	45.8
9,000	44.0
10,000	42.4
11,000	40.7
12,000	39.2
13,000	37.7
14,000	36.2

Table 5.8 Modified Fresh Water Ascent Rates Equivalent to an Ocean Rate of 60 Ft./Min.

Actual Depth	Theoretical Depth at Various Altitudes (in feet)									
	1000	2000	3000	4000	5000	6000	7000	8000	9000	10000
0	0	0	0	0	0	0	0	0	0	0
10	10	11	11	12	12	12	13	13	14	15
20	21	21	22	23	24	25	26	27	28	29
30	31	32	33	35	36	37	39	40	42	44
40	41	43	45	46	48	50	52	54	56	58
50	52	54	56	58	60	62	65	67	70	73
60	62	64	67	69	72	75	78	81	84	87
70	72	75	78	81	84	87	91	94	98	102
80	83	86	89	92	96	100	103	108	112	116
90	93	97	100	104	108	112	116	121	126	131
100	103	107	111	116	120	124	129	134	140	145
110	114	118	122	127	132	137	142	148	153	160
120	124	129	134	139	144	149	155	161	167	174
130	135	140	145	150	156	162	168	175	181	189
140	145	150	156	162	168	174	181	188	195	203
150	155	161	167	173	180	187	194	202	209	218
160	166	172	178	185	192	199	207	215	223	232
170	176	182	189	196	204	212	220	228	237	247
180	186	193	200	208	216	224	233	242	251	261
190	197	204	212	220	228	237	246	255	265	276
200	207	215	223	231	240	249	259	269	279	290
210	217	225	234	243	252	261	272	282	293	305
220	228	236	245	254	264	274	284	296	307	319
230	238	247	256	266	276	286	297	309	321	334
240	248	258	267	277	288	299	310	323	335	348
250	259	268	278	289	300	311	323	336	349	363

Table 5.9 Theoretical depth at altitude for given actual diving depth in fresh water.

DECOMPRESSION & RECOMPRESSION

Altitude,	Proper Actual Depth of Indicated Ocean Stop, Ft.		
Feet	Standard 10 Ft. Stop	20 Ft. Stop	30 Ft. Stop
0	10.3	20.6	30.8
2,000	9.6	19.1	28.7
4,000	8.9	17.7	26.6
6,000	8.2	16.5	24.7
8.000	7.6	15.3	22.9
10,000	7.1	14.1	21.2
12,000	6.5	13.1	19.6
14,000	6.0	12.1	18.1

Table 5.10 Modified fresh water decompression stops corresponding to standard ocean stop depths.

Altitude, Feet	Correction To Add To Gauge Reading, Feet*
Sea level	0
1,000	1.2
2,000	2.4
3,000	3.5
4,000	4.6
5,000	5.7
6,000	6.7
7,000	7.8
8,000	8.7
9,000	9.7
10,000	10.6
11,000	11.5
12,000	12.3

True depth is obtained by increasing the depth as corrected by this table by a further 3%.

Table 5.11 Corrections for Bourdon and Bellows depth gauges.

Altitude, Feet	Factor To Multiply Gauge Reading To Determine Actual Fresh Water Depth, Feet *
Sea level	1.026
1,000	.989
2,000	.953
3,000	.919
4,000	.885
5,000	.853
6,000	.822
7,000	.791
8,000	.762
9,000	.733
10,000	.705
11,000	.678
12,000	.652

Table 5.12 Capillary gauge corrections.

Figure 5.33 Wait at least 12 hours after diving before flying.

culate proper decompression stop depths which correctly correspond to standard ocean stop depths.

You should note that the only safe procedure for determining the depth of a required decompression stop is by use of a capillary depth gauge via reading it directly. No other gauge is inherently accurate enough at shallow depths for safe decompression stop determination. Typically, you'll need your depth gauge primarily for determining decompression information; however, some altitude dive tables require actual depth information. Should you use such tables, you will have to determine actual depth(s) which will require depth gauge correction.

How do various gauges differ from true depth when used underwater?

When using the capillary depth gauge to determine true depth you simply subtract three percent of the actual reading per 1,000 feet of elevation at the dive site. This correction is not needed at 1,000 feet elevation; however, it is accurate for use at sites located above 3,000 feet elevation.

For all other types of gauges you should add one foot per 1,000 feet of elevation, then add three percent of the gauge reading. While this procedure has a small, inherent error, it is useful for all routine altitude diving calculations.

To assist you in calculating true (actual) depths when diving in fresh water at high altitudes see Table 5.11 (corrections for non-capillary gauges) and Table 5.12 (corrections for capillary gauges) on the previous page.

Having read the foregoing and looked at the tables which clearly define the differences in diving at altitude, gauge types and readings, and other material, you can understand the need for special care when diving at higher altitudes in fresh water. Further, you should procure a capillary depth gauge in order to simplify your procedures for altitude diving. Finally, you should always observe the explicit altitude limits imposed by the tables included in this chapter, never guessing at any information regarding an altitude dive.

Diving at higher altitudes can be a challenging and rewarding experience for you if you will follow these guidelines. When contemplating such dives you should always contact instructors/dive businesses located in the area of the planned dive expedition in order to determine local rules and suitable sites.

Flying After Diving

Reducing ambient pressure below that of sea level by ascending in an aircraft after diving can produce symptoms of decompression sickness. The following procedures are to be followed when you plan to travel by aircraft after diving.

1. The altitude in an unpressurized aircraft in which you are flying should not exceed 8,000 feet, which is equivalent to the cabin pressure of a commercial airliner.

2. Wait at least 24 hours before flying following no-decompression diving (safety stops are not considered decompression for this procedure).

3. Wait more than 24 hours before flying following any dive with required decompression.

4. Shorter, deeper dives rather than long, shallow dives are preferred when flying is planned. Short, deep dives are limited by the fast tissue half-times. These tissues also outgas quickly, so your residual nitrogen is less when you fly than it would be for slow tissues which outgas slowly.

SECTION 2
INTRODUCTION

As an Advanced Scuba Diver you should be able to navigate using natural aids to navigation and a compass, to dive at night and in limited visibility, to find and recover lost items, and to dive at depths up to 100 feet. You should also be comfortable and relaxed while diving, proficient in the basic skills of diving, familiar with boats and boat-diving procedures, and better prepared to respond in the event of a diving emergency.

The purpose of this section is to introduce you to the techniques that will help you achieve the objectives described in the previous paragraph. It is important to understand that the limited supervised experiences provided during your advanced training are only orientations to specialty activities. According to NAUI Standards, upon completion of your Advanced Scuba course you will be considered competent to engage in advanced scuba diving activities in open water without direct leadership supervision provided the diving activities, the area dived and the diving conditions approximate those in which you were trained. Before participating in activities that are beyond the scope of your advanced training for a particular specialty area, such as search and salvage, completion of a specialty course for that activity is strongly recommended. In other words, you will be qualified to find and recover small and medium-sized objects after your Advanced course, but you should not consider yourself a "Search and Recovery Diver" because there is much more to learn about search and salvage than can be covered during your introduction to the activity in the Advanced class.

You have opportunities to experience various diving activities during your NAUI Openwater II and Advanced Scuba Diver training. The purpose of these activities is to acquaint you with various special interest areas of diving so you can determine which of them has the greatest appeal for you so you can then determine which specialty is right for you. Another purpose is to help you learn to relax and think underwater by requiring you to make the basic skills of diving secondary to those required for the activities. This makes you a better diver in general, which is one of the goals of advanced training.

Enjoy your introduction to the numerous techniques contained in the following pages. They can make your diving easier, safer and more enjoyable and can increase your opportunities to enjoy the wonders of the waters!

SAFE DIVING

TECHNIQUES

6

By Ella Jean Morgan NAUI #6945
By Erin O'Neill NAUI #6984

It is appropriate to begin this section with the assurance that diving is among the safest of the more venturesome sports. However, accidents do occur. The object of this chapter is to further reduce the chance of this happening to you. If you and your buddy are adequately trained and prepared, you will have a lifetime of safe diving in front of you, for the few accidents that do arise are usually preventable.

The major cause of diving fatalities is panic. There is always an excellent alternative to a panicked response. All you have to do is put it into action. This area of the book will focus on eliminating as many of the contributing factors to accidents as possible.

DIVE PLANNING

There is not much room in diving for impetuosity. Our sport demands care, attention to detail, and advance planning. The long-term planning begins as soon as you decide to make a dive. You make a commitment in terms of purchasing a spot on a commercial dive boat, make a date with your dive buddy for a shore dive, or perhaps purchase your plane tickets for your dive vacation. Now is the time to begin listing all the things you will want to accomplish prior to your dive. You will want to consider with whom, with what, when, where and how you will dive.

With Whom

Choose your dive buddy. Your choice will make the difference between having fun and not, being safe and not, achieving your purpose and not.

With What

Advanced planning will include the checking of ALL your diving equipment. Repairs will take some time, so you need plan ahead.

When

1. Time of the year is important wherever you plan to dive. Conditions will vary with the calendar. Locales that have no variation in dive conditions year round are very rare. Your purpose in diving will facilitate this choice. Lobster hunters prefer to dive during lobster season and photographers fancy

good visibility. Shore divers will be more wary of winter conditions than will boat divers.

2. The time of month is significant—full moon and new moon mean the tides will be higher. The resulting spring tides may or may not be significant—the determining factor will be the size of the swell. You may prefer to choose a quarter or three-quarter moon; this is the time of the neap tide when tidal changes are less dramatic.

3. The time of day is also important. Dive boats leave right on schedule. If you are not aboard at departure time, you will probably miss that dive. Leave enough lead time to drive to the dock, park your car, and unload your gear. This can consume quite a bit of time. Check the departure time—it may actually be the night before the dive.

Shore diving requires careful consideration of the time. High tide brings clean water into shore, but it also increases the size of the breaking waves. High tide may allow easier access to the water at a rocky shore or skimming over entangling aquatic plants lying just beneath the surface. Low tide invariably brings lowered visibility, smaller surf, and a more difficult rocky shore entry. The perfect time is the slack tide—between the tidal changes.

One last consideration—wind is often less in the morning. Increased wind chop on the surface of the water adds to the discomfort level of any dive. This is why most divers prefer to get an early start. Less wind translates into calmer water on the surface.

Where

This is not always up to you. If you are sharing a commercial dive boat with other divers, the choice will most likely be made for you. The intended dive location is important, but it is not always possible for the boat to reach this site safely and comfortably. You will be in the hands of the captain, crew and divemaster(s) on board. They will be cognizant of your safety, comfort and interests when they choose alternatives to the stated destination.

A shore dive puts the responsibility squarely on your shoulders and that of your buddy. There are many factors that will influence your choice:
1. Purpose for the dive
2. Access to the dive site
3. Rocky or sandy shore

4. Ease of entry and exit
5. Underwater terrain
6. Presence of longshore currents
7. Length of kick to the desired dive spot
8. Depth
9. Exposure to any undesirable water conditions
10. Skill level necessary to safely dive.

How

This refers to the means of transport to the dive location. The choices will depend on length of time available, expense involved, the location of the chosen site(s), the purpose of your dive(s), and many other factors. You may be fortunate enough to be able to choose between a commercial dive boat, a live-aboard dive boat, private boats of varying sizes, a ferry and, of course, your own legs.

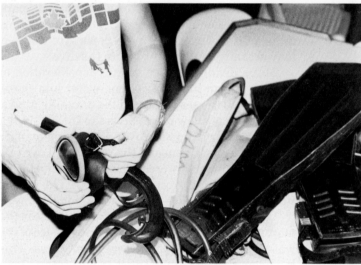

Figure 6.1 An inspection of equipment in advance of a dive trip can prevent frustration and embarrassment.

The final preparations go more smoothly if you leave enough time to comfortably accomplish all necessary tasks.

1. As the time for your planned day of diving approaches, you will pack your gear in the reverse order you will use it. Pack early enough to avoid last minute rushing, and pack with the aid of a written checklist. This will prevent forgetting a vital piece of equipment. Anything that will reduce stress at any point helps in the overall safety and fun of diving. It is a great help to make your own personal checklist and include such items as light chargers, cameras, spear guns, dive computers, sleeping bags, game bags, etc.

If you are packing for a plane trip, protect all your gauges sensitive to pressure changes. Do not allow them to go into an unpressurized luggage compartment unprotected. Either carry them aboard or place them in an airtight box.

2. Check the latest weather report and telephone any available source. Lifeguards, surf reports, marine forecasts, harbors, dive boats, fishing boats and stores, and waterfront establishments (restaurants, stores and hotels) are good sources of information.

3. Make certain you and your buddy are mentally and physically in good condition for diving.

4. Make certain you have emergency services information in case of any accident. Your knowledge of the process for notifying rescue and emergency personnel, either by telephone or radio, could save a life.

5. Do not forget the important items like lunches, drinks, dry clothes, carts, etc., not ordinarily found on a checklist.

Once you have arrived at the dive destination there are many tasks to perform before you dive.

A dive from the shore necessitates choosing a vantage point and assessing the diving conditions.

Watch the water long enough to determine the size, shape and duration of the wave sets and lulls.

Attempt to ascertain any longshore currents by observing floating objects, persons on the surface, presence of aquatic plants on the surface, and any other visible signs of water movement.

Look for rip currents by noticing foam, "dirty" water, silt or disturbances in breaking waves. Plan your entry and exit away from a rip current.

Assess the probable visibility by noting the color and clarity of the water.

Ascertain the best direction for your dive and the probable distance to the chosen spot.

Choose your entry and exit site and at least one alternate in case current, wind, injury or any unexpected situation eliminates your first choice.

Talk with the lifeguard, other divers, surfers and/or swimmers about the existing conditions.

Make certain this dive is well within your and your buddy's skill levels; do not consider any dive that requires greater strength and conditioning than you both possess. If either of you feel apprehensive, change to your alternate location or cancel the dive for this day.

2. Diving from a boat will free you from some of the tasks aforementioned. The captain and/or dive-

Figure 6.2 Always assess your dive site and try to have an alternate site.

hesitate to sit out a dive that you consider risky.

The dive plan is an essential part of all safe and fun dives. Whether you are diving from a boat or from the beach, once you and your partner have decided to make the dive, you will want to consult with one another on several key factors.

The intended depth and duration of the dive are essential, with contingency factors discussed.

The direction of the dive (always begin up current), and the type of compass course to be followed should be considered.

Each buddy should ascertain the air consumption rate of the other. Plan your turn-around time based on the consumption rate of

master will choose your dive location based on many factors, but primarily with safety in mind. It remains your responsibility, however, to ensure your own personal safety.

Again, it is not prudent to jump into the water without ascertaining the factors affecting your decision to dive or not to dive.

Be aware of the anticipated depth of the dive area and judge for yourself if this depth exceeds your personal limits.

Look at the water to determine the presence of a current. The boat will usually, but not always, align itself bow to stern in a current. Look at the stern to see if there is a small wake. Aquatic plants on the surface of the water indicate little or no current. If there is a current present, request a current line be let out in the water.

Notice the size of the ocean swell—it will indicate the amount of surge and the depth to which this surge will exist. Determine if this factor will affect your dive plans.

Ascertain any presence of wind and its accompanying surface chop. Decide if this affects your dive plans. Also, keep in mind the accompanying boat swing caused by the wind and how this will alter your exit plans.

The visibility will concern you. You may choose to cancel your dive for this site depending on the importance of this factor.

Be certain this dive is well within the physical abilities of both buddies and well within the skill level of both members of the buddy team; do not

Figure 6.3 A buddy check of equipment should be conducted prior to every dive.

the buddy with the higher rate. It will be more fun, easier and often safer to return to the boat or beach underwater and avoid a long surface kick.

You have spent a lot of time and energy in formulating your dive plan. Do not deviate from it, if at all possible. Dive your plan and you will stay safe.

A cardinal rule never to be broken consists of a thorough buddy check. This is fundamental, whether your buddy is a stranger or an old friend. The items of a good buddy check are:

1. Familiarization with your buddy's weight belt release

2. Proficiency in the inflation of your buddy's buoyancy compensator

3. Presence (or absence) of your buddy's safe second stage and its location

4. Procedure your buddy follows in an out-of-air emergency, whether that be buddy breathing with a single or redundant second stage

5. Presence and/or use of a reserve valve

6. Working pressure and existing pressure of your buddy's air cylinder

7. Hand signals.

Inform the lifeguard or the divemaster that you are entering the water, the direction you intend to take, and the intended time of your return. Notify them when you are safely back.

Recreational diving can be a very safe activity, but it is not safe for a diver with any of the following conditions:

1. Under the influence of alcohol, "street" drugs and some prescribed drugs.

2. A chest or head cold

3. An ear or sinus infection

4. Fatigued

5. Extremely fearful

6. Depressed

7. In poor physical condition

8. A smoker

9. An asthmatic

10. The dive is beyond his/her physical, emotional and educational limits.

COMMUNICATIONS

The more advanced your diving skills become and the more time you spend underwater, the more sophisticated your communicating skills need to be. The most fundamental of these skills relies on the use of hand signals. Take the time to become proficient at hand signaling and you will increase your fun and safety in the bargain. You and your buddy may enjoy developing your own special signals, as well:

Useful Hand Signals to Develop
• somewhat, more or less
• cold and cold?
• to kick or let's kick
• large
• small
• many
• few
• over, under, around
• level off
• buddy up
• question, query
• boat
• ear
• sinus
• tank pressure or tank pressure?
• on reserve or on reserve?
• turn around
• where?
• look around, search
• come here
• go back
• watch, see, look
• slow down
• speed up
• you lead, I'll follow
• yes, no
• tired or tired?
• I need help, assistance, or need help?
• understand or understand?
• I don't know or I don't understand

It is beneficial to utilize signals for various forms of marine life, for example:

• fish	• crab
• shark	• seal or sea lion
• eel	• dolphin or whale
• octopus	• ray
• lobster	• turkey fish

You use a different set of signals when you communicate by feel rather than by sight. These tactile signals are utilized during line work or when in physical contact with your buddy. You may be using a buddy line in low visibility, using a line in a search and recovery exercise, holding hands or simply touching. The number of times the signal is repeated is the key to its meaning, as follows:

1. Stop = one pull, squeeze, tap

2. O.K., proceed = two pulls, squeezes, taps

3. Surface, up = four pulls, squeezes, taps

4. Come here, help = five pulls, squeezes, taps

SAFE DIVING TECHNIQUES

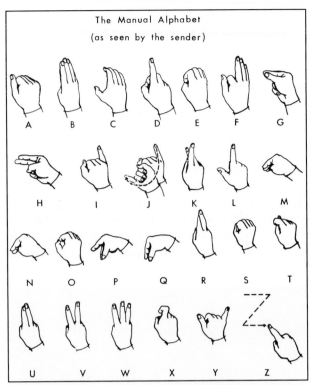

The Manual Alphabet

(as seen by the sender)

A B C D E F G

H I J K L M

N O P Q R S T

U V W X Y Z

Figure 6.4 Learning the sign language alphabet will immensely increase your communicating efficiency and enjoyment.

Note that three pulls is omitted as a signal. The purpose of this is to create a space between ordinary signals and the more urgent messages.

There are times when you will need to communicate or receive communications audibly. Many commercial dive boats use an underwater recall system that sounds like a siren. It is used in case of an emergency or when the boat needs to be repositioned. This sound requires that you immediately surface for further instructions. The divemaster or crew will tell you whether to hold your present position or return to the boat.

If there is not a recall system, apply the same rules as in the tactical system; *e.g.*, one sharp hand clap or rap with your knife against your tank translates to stop, two indicates go, and so forth.

Your buoyancy compensator should have a whistle attached for use on the surface. Do not blow it unless you are in distress. A whistle can be heard much more clearly than your voice and the lifeguard or divemaster on duty will respond when it is blown. Just as in the tactical signals, five blasts on your whistle means to come quickly, or help!

Written communication allows more complex exchanges or information. An underwater slate and a pencil can fully convey messages too compli-

cated for hand signals. A slate in your B.C. pocket ensures your ability to make yourself understood, whether to add to your fun or to your safety underwater.

Flags are employed when other types of signalling are impractical. Boats use three different types of flags:

1. Red/white—This is considered the sport diver flag. It is recognized internationally and it indicates there are divers in the area—stay clear for a 100 foot radius.

2. Blue/white—This is an international code flag. It indicates there is a diving operation underway—stay clear.

3. Blue/white (square)—This is an international code flag. It is used as a diver recall.

Divers leaving the immediate vicinity of their boat and those diving from the shore are vulnerable to injury by boat traffic. Under these conditions, use a diver flag and float. Stay within a 100 foot radius of your flag.

Voice communication has long been possible underwater. You may actually speak underwater, either through your regulator or not, but most divers are not easily understood. Good vocal communications require an air space around your mouth. Commercial divers are able to speak with the surface personnel through the use of full face mask or helmet systems. These are expensive and

Figure 6.5 Long range communications at the surface are possible with a whistle (left) or by using the mask as a reflector (right).

cumbersome, but there have been recent developments enabling sport divers to speak and be understood underwater.

1. Several manufacturers have various devices which fit over the regulator second stage, either outfitted with a small electronic speaker or providing the communication via cables. Each buddy must wear one to achieve two-way communications.

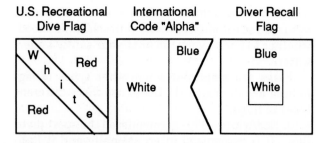

U.S. Recreational Dive Flag	International Code "Alpha"	Diver Recall Flag
White Red Red	Blue White	Blue White

Figure 6.6 Dive Flags

2. There is currently available an apparatus that allows a diver to be heard by several others in close proximity. Speech is transmitted through a small microphone to an external speaker usually attached to a diver's tank.

3. Another development in the communication field permits two-way conversation between the surface and divers underwater via cable.

Lights permit us to communicate more easily at night, both underwater and on the surface. Avoid shining your light in your buddy's face. This destroys the valuable night vision a diver has developed during the dive. Shine your light on your own

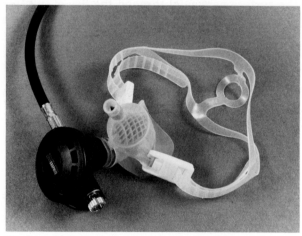

Figure 6.7 A regulator attachment that allows underwater communications at close range.

hand to communicate with hand signals. To signal with the light, the following signs are universally used: (illustrations)

1. O.K. is expressed by circling with your light

2. Distress is expressed by the rapid up-and-down movement of your light

3. Attention is conveyed by the back and forth, side-to-side motion of your light.

DIVING EQUIPMENT

Because of the environment, diving equipment is made from very sturdy materials and equipment failure is uncommon. However, you can help avoid the possible serious outcomes of equipment malfunction by ensuring that all personal equipment is in top operating condition. Periodically inspect your equipment, whether actively diving or not. Service your equipment before diving after a period of inactivity, and yearly.

Unserviced regulators can add considerably to diver stress; for example, a deteriorating mouthpiece can allow water to enter your mouth with each breath; increased inhalation resistance could lead to a feeling of air starvation during deeper or

Figure 6.8 Lights permit us to communicate more easily at night, both underwater and on the surface.

strenuous dives; a ruptured hose can quickly empty a tank at depth. Yearly service is highly recommended. Have your depth and submersible pressure gauges calibrated. Inspect your compass for air bubbles which could inhibit needle movement.

Tank valves and reserve levers should move easily without sticking and should not leak. Buoyancy compensators should be free of holes; the overpressure relief valve should function at maximum inflation; the inflator valve should operate easily. The inflator hose should attach and detach easily and should not leak. Check straps on masks and fins; check the purge valves in masks and snorkels. On wet suits, boots, and gloves, stop unraveling threads by knotting; patch holes with appropriate cements. Are your hoses free of pin holes and signs of breakdown? Never assume that because the equipment worked the last time you dived, it will work now. Check it!

SAFE DIVING TECHNIQUES

Some equipment was designed strictly with safety in mind. The weight belt with a quick-release buckle is now standard, but you may encounter a not-so-quick release system in some countries, as well as in used equipment purchases. It is not safe to attach your weights without being able to immediately dispose of same.

The submersible pressure gauge was developed so divers would always know the amount of air remaining in their tanks. It is of no use if it is not

Figure 6.9 Several items of equipment should be serviced or inspected annually.

constantly monitored. A safe diver allows enough air for a safe reserve, as well as starting for the surface with ample air in the tank.

The reserve valve provided safe ascents before the advent of the submersible pressure gauge. It was the only way a diver had of knowing when the air was running low. It is not considered safe now to dive without a pressure gauge, nor is it safe to rely on a reserve valve. The lever may have been inadvertently left in the off position before the dive or it may have been prematurely pushed down by accident during the dive. Either way, the diver will have less air than he/she thought was available.

Some simple equipment modifications can add to your safety. A clip on your console can be snapped to your buoyancy compensator to keep your instruments free from entanglement. An alligator or similar clip on your extra second stage hose can hold it in the center of your chest, readily accessible, yet out of the way. A short length of line will secure your dive tables to your buoyancy compensator and prevent accidental loss. Reduce the likelihood of entanglement by securing knives, lights (in a holster) and other instruments: locate them on the inside of arms or legs, in pockets in your suit, or on

your buoyancy compensator waist strap. Never hang any piece of equipment (including cameras) around your neck. Anything dangling from your wrist is an invitation for entanglement. Knives should be in good condition and capable of severing monofilament line. Turn fin and mask strap ends inward, or tape them in place; and avoid the practice of hanging easily-opened spring clips on your buoyancy compensator or weight belt (they can unintentionally become clipped to lines). Do not attach anything to your weight belt that is also attached to something else. This will prevent jettisoning of your weights in an emergency.

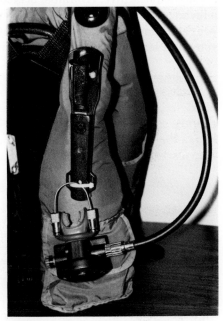

Figure 6.10 Some equipment modifications to add to your safety.

A safe second stage comes complete with a longer hose than does the primary second stage. If you intend to pass your primary second stage to your buddy in the case of an out-of-air emergency, switch the longer hose to your primary second stage and use the shorter hose on your safe second stage. You will also find this shorter hose length makes it easier to manage the safe second stage while it is not in use.

Divers do not usually have immediate access to medical attention. Carry a first aid kit and possibly oxygen, and be prepared to render first aid assistance.

As discussed earlier in this chapter, pre-dive planning includes inspection of equipment before the dive and checking its operation before entering the water. Uncomfortable incidents have been precipitated by as simple an oversight as a missing snorkel purge valve or a badly deteriorated fin strap. Verify operation of your primary and secondary second stages, buoyancy compensator inflator valve, submersible pressure gauge, reserve valve (if present), and compass before entering the water.

BUOYANCY CONTROL

Good buoyancy control is the mark of a skilled diver. The ability to achieve neutral, positive or negative buoyancy at will is essential to safe diving. A safe diver endeavors to be neutrally buoyant throughout the dive. A number of factors affect your buoyancy; some are personal, others depend on your equipment. To achieve buoyancy control skill, you must learn to control these factors.

Figure 6.12 *A properly weighted and trimmed diver will be horizontal, while an overweighted diver will swim at an angle with fins downward.*

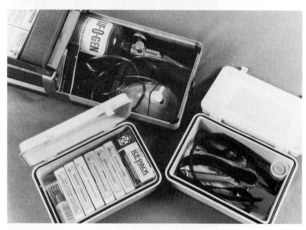

Figure 6.11 *In addition to your dive gear, a first aid kit, a spare parts kit, and oxygen are also recommended.*

The percentage of muscle, bone and fat in your body are major personal factors. Individuals with a large percentage of muscle and/or with large, dense bones, are negatively buoyant; those with a greater percentage of fat are positively buoyant. Be aware of changes during periods of weight gain or loss.

The amount of air in your lungs greatly affects your buoyancy. With practice, you will become skilled in controlling your vertical movement by changing this volume of air. By making long exhalations, you can retain less air, thereby slowing your ascent rate or assisting in your initial descent. Conversely, taking deeper breaths will slow a too-rapid descent by making you more buoyant. The difference between a full lung and an empty one can change your buoyancy by as much as eight pounds,

depending on your lung capacity. What's yours?

The other factors controlling your buoyancy relate to your equipment and objects you carry. Several items of equipment make you positively buoyant: your exposure suit, some buoyancy compensators (because of air trapped in the foam padding and between the inner bag and the cover), and some tanks (usually aluminum, but also some steel) when empty or nearly so. The amount of positive buoyancy from an exposure suit changes with depth because of the compression of the air or neoprene. You must determine the amount of weight required to neutralize this positive buoyancy individually in water; no formula will suffice. Your guiding principle, however, should be to use the minimum amount of weight which will provide neutral buoyancy at ten feet of depth with an empty buoyancy compensator and a near-empty tank. This ensures the ability to execute a safety stop at ten feet at the end of a dive without risking premature surfacing. Take the time to make the necessary determinations, perhaps at the end of your next dive.

Diving overweighted is dangerous: if you are excessively negative during your dive. The added pounds demand extra energy to move you and your equipment from one point to another above or underwater, more air is needed in your buoyancy compensator to achieve neutral buoyancy, and additional extra energy is needed to push the over-inflated buoyancy compensator through the water.

Overweighting constitutes unnecessary liability in the event of an occurrence requiring extra effort (long surface kick, increased currents, wind, buddy needing assistance, etc.). Because many women have a larger percentage of fat, they have high personal positive buoyancy. Consequently, they require more weight to achieve neutral buoyancy than a man of the same size and weight. With their smaller muscle mass, women are particularly susceptible to the higher energy requirements of carrying extra weight, and should make every effort to reduce their weights to the lowest amount possible.

The most common method of carrying the required weights is on a weight belt: standard webbing, shot-filled, or with pockets. Whichever you choose, basic principles apply. The belt should have a quick release buckle. The majority of the weight should be equally divided. Attach one of two weights just in front of your hips. Your tank constitutes a significant weight at your back, and better vertical and horizontal balance is achieved by the stated procedure.

The addition of ankle weights may be appropriate with dry suits. Ankle weights add a small amount of weight (usually one to three pounds and subtracted from the amount on your belt) to each ankle. However, ankle weights can also add significantly to the comfort of wet suit and other divers, especially those using light, floating plastic fins. Ankle weights keep your feet submerged for more effective snorkeling, and can actually help relieve the post-dive backache experienced by many divers.

Some systems employ weights integrated with the backpack and buoyancy compensator, thereby eliminating the necessity for a separate weight belt. The use of such a unit involves several important considerations. You should have training in its use and maintenance. You and your buddy must be thoroughly familiar with the weight release location and method of operation. Also, the weights (pellets or bars) require faithful maintenance, since salt buildup and corrosion can reduce the efficiency with which the weights can be jettisoned in an emergency.

If your upper body strength is on the lower end of the scale (most women, some men), you may find the handling of an integrated system difficult, since the weight of the whole unit (tank, buoyancy compensator and weights) usually exceeds 50 pounds.

An excellent safety skill to practice and maintain is the replacement of your weight belt while submerged. Loss of a weight belt at depth is not uncommon. A sudden increase in buoyancy without ascending should trigger immediate emptying of the buoyancy compensator and checking of the weight belt (see Emergency Ascents section that follows).

Items carried, such as cameras, tools, and game bags can add significantly to your negative buoyancy and drag. Be certain that you are able to support these items. Also, be aware that the release of such items will require immediate adjustments in your buoyancy.

The safest policy to follow is that of frequent adjustments in your buoyancy so that you are always neutrally buoyant.

BUDDY SYSTEM

Safe diving practices include adherence to the buddy system. The buddy system increases the fun of diving and can be a deterrent to accidents by providing assistance when it is needed (for example, during pre-dive equipment checks, entrapments/entanglements, out-of-air emergencies, medical emergencies).

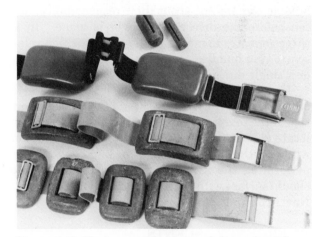

Figure 6.13 Various weight shapes, belts and quick releases. Note weight keepers.

Buddy diving usually occurs in pairs or multiples of two. For the system to work, the divers must be committed to its principles and willing to expend the necessary effort. Ideally, buddies position themselves shoulder to shoulder and retain the same position relative to each other during the entire dive. If it is necessary to proceed in single file, the leader must stop as soon as possible and wait for the follower to catch up. In pairs of unequal experience or individuals with differing interests, it is important that both individuals have an opportunity to make dive plan decisions, determine the pace, and have equal freedom to cancel the dive. Being a dependent diver is unsafe.

Figure 6.14 Frequent skill reinforcement enables divers to handle minor equipment problems, such as weight belt replacement, without difficulty.

Figure 6.15 Proper buddy system techniques include diving side by side and reminding each other about time and depth limits.

Threesomes are the most difficult buddy system to execute safely. Threesomes have been heavily implicated in recent fatal diving accidents. Divers are lulled by the presence of a third person and become complacent about their responsibility; often before the dive ends a diver is alone. In a threesome, try to maintain the same position relative to your buddies and never change to a twosome or a single during the dive.

If separated from your buddy, look around in a complete circle, look up, ascend a few feet and repeat the search, watching for bubbles. If you don't locate your buddy within a minute, start an ascent while continuing to circle. Your buddy should be performing the same search procedure and you should surface within a short distance of each other. Never continue your dive alone.

EMERGENCY ASCENTS

When faced with a problem, stop, think, then act. Problems such as loss of a mask or fin should be solved underwater and should not elicit a bolt-to-the-surface response.

An emergency ascent is one in which the diver ascends directly to the surface to avoid a life threatening circumstance, such as a medical condition, some mechanical problem, or an environmental threat. The most frequent reason for an emergency ascent among sport divers is an out-of-air emergency. An out-of-air emergency is preventable by adequate dive planning and instrument monitoring. A skilled, competent, advanced diver will consciously decide to eliminate this excessive risk by never allowing it to happen.

The out-of-air diver has gone through the last few increasingly-restrictive breaths and has ar-

rived at the no-air point after exhaling and attempting to inhale. Remind yourself firmly that no matter how it feels, there is air in your lungs and that amount of air is sufficient to start the emergency ascent procedure.

There are several choices facing the out-of-air diver. All involve pre-planning, conscious thought, avoidance of panic and a practiced skill. The skills learned in your entry level scuba class require continuing practice to retain efficiency. Being well versed in the emergency procedures to be applied is the single most important factor in avoiding panic.

You must now decide whether to go to the surface by yourself (INDEPENDENT ASCENTS), or contact your buddy for assistance (DEPENDENT ASCENTS).

Independent Ascents

There are some circumstances under which an independent method is preferred: you are unsure of your buddy's ability and willingness to render assistance, the surface is closer to you than your buddy, or you are in fairly shallow water (40 feet or less).

Redundant System Ascent

This ascent requires a second, independent source of air. Often consisting of a small tank and extra regulator, the redundant system provides enough air to make an emergency ascent and is probably the safest way to deal with an out-of-air emergency. The diver switches second stages, looks toward the surface, extends a hand overhead, uses the buoyancy compensator inflator valve to exhaust excess air and breathes normally while swimming directly to the surface at a normal ascent rate.

Figure 6.16 A controlled emergency ascent.

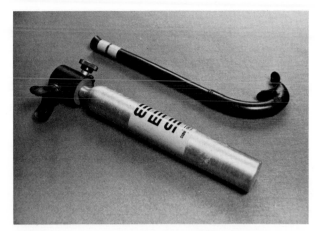

Figure 6.17 A small, redundant scuba system for independent, out-of-air direct vertical ascents.

Redundant systems are common among divers in the highly technical specialties such as cave, ice, deep, and wreck diving. These specialties all require additional training.

Emergency Swimming Ascent

The out-of-air diver knows that there is air in his/her lungs during ascent from 33 feet, the volume of air will double, and that the air is most likely sufficient for the 30 seconds that it will take to reach the surface. The diver retains the second stage, looks toward the surface, extends a hand overhead, uses the buoyancy compensator valve to exhaust excess air, and swims directly to the surface as close to the normal ascent rate as possible while exhaling gently all the way. Since scuba delivers air at ambient pressure, additional air becomes available to the out-of-air diver as ambient pressure decreases during ascent. Attempts to inhale should be made because additional air may be available. With training, a relaxed diver can execute the emergency swimming ascent from surprising depths. A neutral diver becomes buoyant upon ascending a short distance, thereby reducing the effort required to swim to the surface. Indeed, keeping the rate of ascent slow enough is the more common problem.

Buoyancy Compensator Breathing

The air contained in your buoyancy compensator is breathable provided you have not activated a CO_2 cartridge. With proper training, you will find this a viable way to obtain emergency air. To access this air, you must first clear any water from the inflator hose. Blow into the inflator mouthpiece while rolling from a face-down position away from the inflator hose over to your back. Look toward the surface, extend a hand overhead, and exhale into and inhale from the mouthpiece while holding the valve open. Breathe continuously allowing excess air to escape from your mouth or nose as you swim to the surface at the normal ascent rate. This method must be practiced under carefully controlled conditions before being added to your repertoire of emergency procedures.

Buoyant Ascent

A diver may elect to execute a buoyant ascent by removing the weight belt or retaining expanding air in the buoyancy compensator. Because control of the rate of ascent is very difficult, a buoyant ascent is considerably more risky and should be used only if you cannot swim to the surface. You may elect to start a buoyant ascent at the bottom or change an emergency swimming ascent to a buoyant ascent on the way up. Once the weights are discarded, the diver arches backward into a belly-up position, extends arms and legs horizontally (spread-eagled), and continues to exhale gently to the surface. Remember, expanding air from your regulator may become available to breathe as water pressure is reduced.

A skilled diver will practice assuming the buoyant ascent position, as it is useful in circumstances other than out-of-air emergencies; for example, accidental loss of weights or jammed inflator, exhaust, or over-inflated mechanisms.

Dependent Ascents

Dependent emergency ascents require a buddy who is trained, willing to assist, in the immediate vicinity, and has enough air for two. The procedures should be discussed with your buddy and rehearsed frequently until your response to an out-of-air sign is fast, automatic and elicits little or no anxiety on your part.

Shared Air Ascent: Alternate Air Source

The alternate air source may take several forms, all of which provide an extra second stage so that each diver has a source of air. The hose of one second stage is longer for the out-of-air diver's use. After the out-of-air diver receives a second stage, the divers hold firmly to each other with one hand, look to the surface, and ascend at a normal rate, while breathing normally and controlling buoyancy.

Because of the duplicate second stage, this ascent can be the most reliable of the dependent methods. However, the procedures must be clear and discussed between buddies before diving. Which second stage will be passed to the out-of-air buddy? Where will the extra second stage be located? The fastest response time requires passing the second stage from the mouth of the donor and may be of some psychological advantage to the needer. It is highly recommended that the extra second stage be mounted in the center of the chest for easy accessibility by both donor and needer. The mounting mechanism must be secure enough to hold the second stage with absolute reliability, yet release quickly enough for the minimum response time. Whichever second stage goes to the needer will, of course, be the one with the longer hose.

Shared Air Ascent: Buddy Breathing

The most complex of the shared air ascent methods, buddy breathing, requires the sharing of a single second stage. The donor takes a deep breath and passes the second stage to the needer who takes up to four breaths. They then alternate, taking two breaths apiece. Both individuals keep one hand on the second stage and firmly hold their buddy with the other. As soon as the breathing cycle is stable (within a few breaths), the ascent should begin. Because both hands are in use, maintaining control

Figure 6.18 Rebreathing air from a buoyancy compensator is possible, although complicated, and is not a primary emergency technique.

of buoyancy is more difficult. The ascent must be executed slowly and carefully. Good eye contact will assist in reassuring the person in need of air and reduce anxiety.

Constant practice in buddy breathing is highly recommended and necessary to retain your skill. Frequent practice sessions will add confidence and increase the chance of a successful execution in a real emergency.

The determination of which ascent method to use is affected by many factors. The best method for any given situation is dependent upon the circumstances. A controlled emergency swimming ascent is appropriate for shallow water, while an air sharing ascent is preferred for deeper depths.

While the safety of these procedures can be significantly enhanced by planning and practice, the avoidance of out-of-air emergencies is preferable.

REFRESHER TRAINING

The sport of scuba diving requires the development of very specific skills which are unlike those normally encountered in every day life. Constant reinforcement is required. Most experts agree that monthly dives are necessary to maintain diving skills at their highest level. A few month's leave from diving can degrade skills and should be followed by a personal review of the key subjects (such as medical aspects, dive table calculations and emergency and rescue procedures), a pool practice session, and a dive in highly controlled conditions.

A lapse in excess of a year may indicate the need for more formal refresher training. Contact a NAUI instructor for an evaluation of your status. Possible recommendations may include classroom review and testing followed by one or more refresher dives to return to your previous skill level or enrollment in the next higher class level or pertinent specialty class to renew and augment your skills.

Figure 6.20 Proper buddy breathing procedures. Note position of hands and small bubbles being emitted by donor.

Figure 6.19 Good technique for an air-sharing ascent where an alternate air source is being used.

NAVIGATION
FOR DIVERS

7

By Dennis Graver NAUI #1103L

To navigate means "to control a course through the use of calculations as to position and direction, etc.". To a diver, it means controlling a course while diving so you know where you are at all times in relation to a given point, such as an exit area.

Navigation has many applications for divers. The skill can be used to locate or to relocate a dive site, to conduct a dive pattern, for searching, and for environmental surveys. All divers have the need for navigational ability simply because even the best underwater visibility is insufficient to permit navigation by vision alone.

All navigation relies on references to surface positions. Navigational markers, landmarks, latitude and longitudinal references, navigational radio transmissions, charts, etc., are all useful references for the diving navigator. You need to become familiar with these resources and this chapter will help you do just that.

There are four basic items of information required for navigation: direction, depth, distance and time. When these components are known and applied to a reference, you can determine your location, which is what navigating is all about.

By the end of this chapter, you should be able to:

1. List at least eight items of equipment for diving navigation.

2. List at least five ways to measure distance for diving navigation.

3. List at least six aids to natural navigation.

4. Briefly describe how to take a "fix" on a position using natural aids to navigation and compass bearings.

5. Briefly describe the theory of compass operation.

6. List the basic types, features, selection criteria and procedures for the care of a diving compass.

7. Briefly describe how to determine and prevent compass deviation.

8. Briefly describe how to cope with underwater obstacles and water movement (currents).

9. Briefly describe the navigational terms which appear in CAPITAL LETTERS in this chapter.

Navigational Equipment for Divers

Among the most sophisticated equipment for underwater navigation are acoustic beacons and receivers. These are small, battery-operated devices that transmit and receive a high frequency signal when activated. A diver equipped with a receiver determines the direction of the beacon by slowly rotating in the water until the receiver produces an audible tone in a headset. A compass BEARING (the angular direction to an object expressed in terms of compass degrees from north, *e.g.*, a bearing of 270 degrees) is then noted and the diver swims toward the beacon until it is visually located.

The diving compass, watch and depth gauge are, for most recreational diving purposes, the simplest navigational devices available. The compass is used to maintain a HEADING (a course followed or to be followed). A heading may change from time to time. Progress is timed with the watch and the depth is noted.

Diving Compasses

There are two basic types of diver compasses: direct reading and indirect reading. There are various models of each type. Some compasses have

Figure 7.1 Various Diving Compasses

a needle which seeks magnetic north, while other compasses have a north-seeking disc called a COMPASS CARD. Diving compasses need to be equipped with a LUBBER LINE, a reference line which is aligned with the user to obtain and follow a course or a bearing.

Other desirable features of a diving compass include adjustable "index marks" to temporarily indicate a heading or a bearing, a low profile, a luminous dial, dampening of the compass needle, and the ability to operate accurately when tilted slightly from a level position.

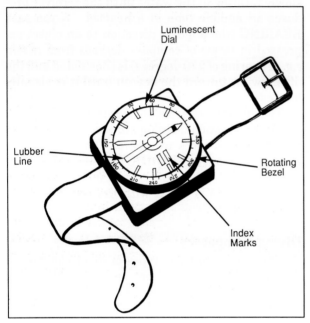

Figure 7.2 Parts of a Compass

A needle direct reading compass has a north-seeking needle and numbers on a rotating BEZEL (rotating collar on a diving compass equipped with alignment marks to indicate a course to be followed) that read zero to 360 degrees in a clockwise direction. A compass card direct reading compass reads zero to 360 degrees in a clockwise direction on a circular compass card but has no bezel. Both types have a lubber line for reference.

An indirect reading compass has fixed degree markings on the compass body which read from zero to 360 degrees in a counterclockwise direction. The compass also has a rotatable bezel containing only index marks. This type of compass was designed to combine the advantages of both types of direct reading compasses.

There are two basic uses of a compass: to establish a bearing to be followed to move in a

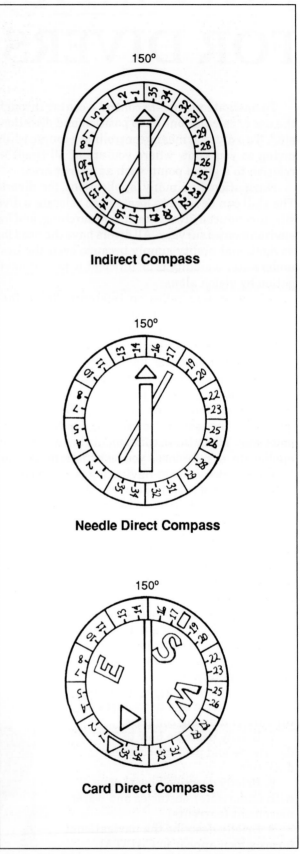

Figure 7.3 Direct and Indirect Reading Compasses

NAVIGATION FOR DIVERS

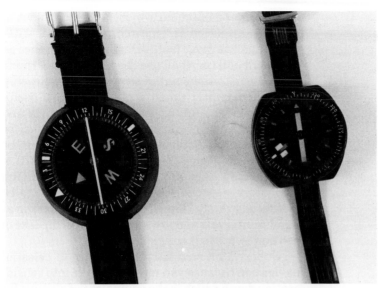

Figure 7.4 Establishing a bearing of 120° with a card direct compass (left) and with a needle indirect compass (right).

certain direction or to determine a bearing to an object. Let's determine how to perform each of these functions with each type of compass.

To establish a direction with a needle direct reading compass, align the desired direction on the bezel with the lubber line. Rotate the entire compass until the needle points to north or 0. The lubber line then indicates the direction of travel.

With the card direct reading compass, rotate the compass until the desired direction is beneath the lubber line. The lubber line then indicates the desired direction. There is nothing to set, and the course heading is indicated under the lubber line.

A needle direct compass has an advantage over the card direct compass because the desired bearing is located physically at the point of the lubber line and does not need to be remembered. With a card direct compass, the bearing needs to be mentally recalled or written on a slate.

To establish a direction with an indirect reading compass, simply set the index marks of the bezel to the desired bearing and rotate the compass until the needle is bracketed by the index marks. The lubber line will indicate the proper direction.

The advantages of both types of direct reading compasses are combined with the indirect reading compass. The selected bearing does not need to be

remembered, and the needle points directly to the actual course heading.

To determine the bearing to an object with a needle direct reading compass, point the lubber line of the compass toward the object, then rotate the bezel until 0 degrees is aligned with the needle. The bearing at the point of the lubber line is the bearing to the object.

Determining a bearing with a card direct reading compass also involves aiming the lubber line toward an object. The reading on the card at the point of the lubber line is the bearing to the object.

To establish a bearing to an object with an indirect reading compass, simply point the lubber line toward the object and the bearing to the object will be indicated by the compass needle. The bearing can be set simply by aligning the index marks with the needle.

The accuracy of any type of diving compass is improved with the use of a COMPASS BOARD, a board on which the compass is mounted and which extends the length of the lubber line.

Another type of compass which is useful for above-water navigation by divers is the HAND BEARING COMPASS, a special compass designed for the taking of accurate bearings. This compass is useful primarily for dive site relocation.

A MANEUVERING BOARD is an item of

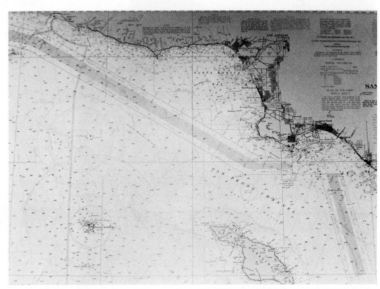

Figure 7.5 Charts

Figure 7.6 Compass Board

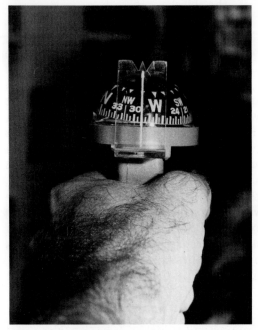

Figure 7.7 Hand Bearing Compass

Figure 7.8 Maneuvering Board

navigational equipment which can be useful when precise navigation is required, as in underwater mapping. The diver plots direction and distance on the board and can then use the board to determine the bearing to the point of origin at any time.

An underwater timer or dive watch is a useful piece of navigational equipment. When time and speed are known, distance can be calculated, or when time and distance are known, speed can be determined.

Measured lines are frequently used by diving navigators, especially when distances need to be measured exactly. The lines are usually marked at regular intervals and are stored on a reel for ease of use and to prevent tangling.

Underwater navigation is similar to celestial navigation because you must also take into consideration depth which is the equivalent of altitude for an aviator. Underwater navigation, therefore, requires the use of a depth gauge.

Finally, diving navigation can be enhanced by the use of CHARTS, which are the aquatic equivalent of a map. A chart depicts the coast and the offshore bottom, indicating the depths of water.

Distance Measuring

Divers must be able to measure distance reasonably well under water in order to navigate accurately. Distance measuring may be accomplished in a number of ways, ranging from rough approximations to extremely precise measurements.

Approximations of distance can be achieved with tank pressure readings at a constant depth. If a dive team uses 500 psi of air while swimming in a given direction, the return distance will be about the same for 500 psi of air provided the depth, swimming speed and water movement remain constant.

Figure 7.9 Measuring lines are valuable for accurate distance measuring.

NAVIGATION FOR DIVERS

Figure 7.10 Kick cycles can be used to measure distance. Count the number of "cycles" it takes to swim a measured distance.

Figure 7.11 Arm spans are an accurate way to measure distance under water.

KICK CYCLES can also be used to approximate distance. The cycle of a kick is from the time a fin kicks downward until that same fin kicks downward again when swimming using a flutter kick. A diver needs to know the distance traveled with each kick cycle when swimming at normal speed. This can be determined by counting the number of kick cycles required to swim a known distance and then dividing the number of kick cycles into the distance. For example, if 30 kick cycles are required to swim 100 feet, the distance covered with each kick cycle is about 3.3 feet.

Time and speed can also be used to measure distance. You should know how many seconds are required to swim a given distance under water at a constant depth and an easily maintained speed. This information can then be used in conjunction with time to determine a distance covered. If 60 seconds are required to swim 100 feet, the following formula may be used to determine your swimming speed:

$$\frac{D}{S = T} \quad \frac{100'}{S = 80} \quad = \quad 1.25 \text{ feet per second}$$

Where S = Speed, T = Time and D = Distance.

When speed and time are known, distance may be estimated. If you swim for 140 seconds at normal speed, the distance may be determined with the following formula:

D = ST   D = 1.25'/sec. x 140 secs. = 175 feet

Where D = Distance, S = Speed and T = Time.

When visibility is limited, when the situation requires starting and stopping, or when very accurate distance measurements are required, arm spans may be used. The exact length of the span of the arms—measured with the arms extended in line with the body rather than perpendicular to the body—is needed. You can then measure distance underwater by extending one arm backward and placing the fingertips on the bottom, extending the other arm forward in the direction of travel, moving forward while pivoting on the fingertips of the extended hand and keeping that hand stationary, then bringing the trailing hand forward, etc. The distance can be measured by multiplying the length of the arm span times the number of spans required.

Another means of distance measuring underwater is with a measured line. One end of the line is secured to a stationary object or held by your buddy while you unreel the line and swim the distance to be measured. Beware of line that stretches.

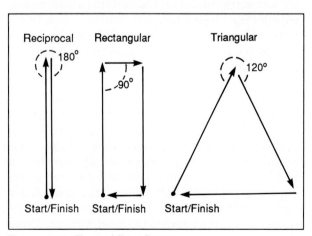

Figure 7.12 Typical Dive Patterns

Means of Navigation

You may navigate by using natural aids to navigation, by using instruments for reference or by using all of these in combination. When your location is confirmed with visual check points, you are navigating by PILOTAGE. When your location is an estimation based on distance and direction, you are navigating by DEAD RECKONING. Divers frequently use both pilotage and dead reckoning for underwater navigation.

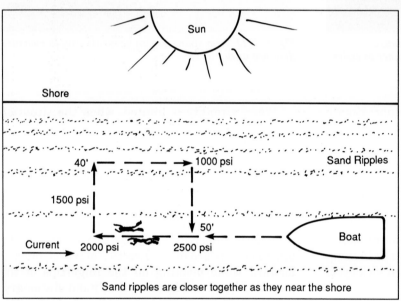

Figure 7.13 Using natural aids to navigation.

Natural Navigation

There are many aids to navigation in the underwater environment. A good diver can estimate his or her approximate location reasonably well by means of natural aids to navigation. Such aids include sand ripples on the bottom (which usually parallel the shore), sun and shadows, direction of water movement, orientation of certain stationary marine life (such as sea fans), bottom contour and depth, formations, and underwater landmarks (such as a wreck).

Another key to natural navigation is the use of a DIVE PATTERN which is the total course or dive path to be followed on a dive. The pattern may be square, rectangular or some other shape. The configuration of the pattern is not as important as buddies agreeing upon it prior to a dive and adhering to the general pattern during the dive. A dive pattern with square corners is easiest to perform, while a circular pattern is the most difficult. Circular patterns are not recommended.

When natural aids to navigation are used in conjunction with a dive pattern, reasonably accurate navigation is quite possible. Imagine a dive with a square dive pattern where you begin diving at the anchor of a boat, against the current, parallel to shore, with the sun on your right and at a depth of 50 feet. With 2,500 psi of air in your tank upon reaching the bottom, you and your buddy move slowly, but steadily, for 500 psi against the current and parallel to sand ripples on the bottom. You then agree to make a 90 degree turn toward shallower water on the right and are aided by the sand ripples on the bottom. With the sun in your face and the current coming from the left, you move into 40 feet of water during the next 500 psi, then agree to another 90 degree turn to the right. You again parallel the sand ripples on the bottom, the sun is on your left, and you are moving with the current. 500 psi later you and your buddy agree to your final right-hand turn. The sun is now to your back, the current is on your right, and you are swimming perpendicular to the sand ripples. As you approach a tank pressure of about 500 psi and a depth of 50 feet, the anchorline of the boat comes into view and you begin your ascent.

Strict adherence to a dive pattern is not essential for effective navigation. Temporary deviations from a heading to investigate points of interest are acceptable as long as the general direction is maintained and some pace of forward progress is maintained or the distance is measured.

Another form of natural navigation can be used to identify a position at the surface. A position can be determined from the observations of terrestrial objects. When the direction and distance to two or more land-based objects is known, the resulting position is known as a FIX. Direction is established by natural means through the selection of objects that align with one another, such as a phone pole that is in line with the edge of a house. Two such sets of in-line objects result in a very precise fix. The angle between the two directions should be as great as possible. Notes and simple drawings of a fix should be made.

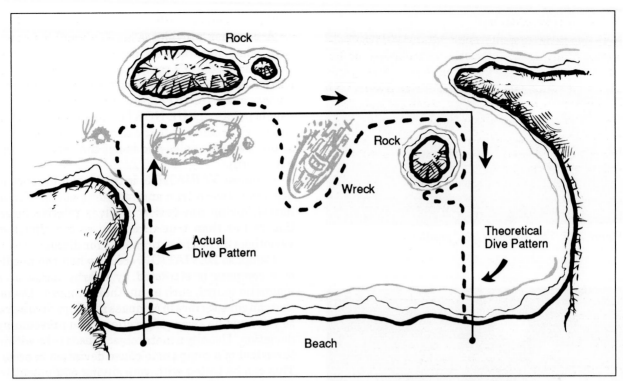

Figure 7.14 For increased accuracy in natural navigation, follow a general course while diving.

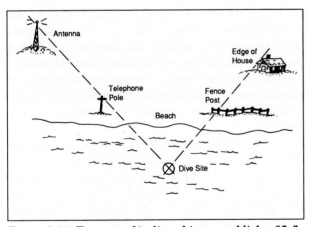

Figure 7.15 Two sets of in-line objects establish a "fix".

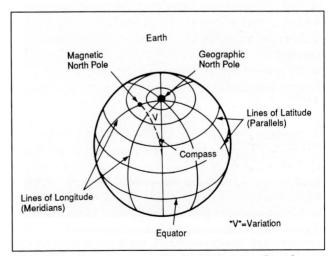

Figure 7.16 Earth with true and magnetic north and variation.

Figure 7.17 The "compass lock" position.

Figure 7.18 Extension of the compass with two hands is more accurate than having the compass mounted on the wrist.

Figure 7.19 Navigation with a console-mounted compass is generally acceptable, but is not as accurate as other compass-lock positions.

Compass Navigation

A compass provides a navigational reference even when natural aids are not available. The magnetic needle of a compass aligns itself with the earth's magnetic poles. MAGNETIC NORTH is a point near the North Pole towards which a magnetic needle points. TRUE NORTH is a geographical location with reference to the earth's axis rather than to the magnetic poles and is not the same as magnetic north.

Compass VARIATION is the local difference in degrees between true and magnetic north. Fortunately, diving navigation involves relative direction rather than true direction, so the effects of variations do not pose problems for divers.

Compass DEVIATION occurs when the needle of a compass is attracted by nearby metal or a magnetic source, such as another compass. Deviation can cause errors in compass readings for divers, so you must be aware of its effects and prevent any deviation. Usually a metal object needs to be within three feet of a compass to cause deviation to occur. This can be tested with your diving equipment by placing your diving compass on a floor, noting the needle reading, then passing your other equipment past the compass and seeing if deviation occurs and, if so, at what distance.

A popular type of diving compass is the indirect needle type with index markers on a rotating bezel. This section will explain how to use this type of compass. Manufacturer's instructions will explain how to use other types. No matter which type of compass you select, there are procedures for the use and care of a compass with which you need to be familiar.

To set a heading with your compass, point the lubber line of the compass in the desired direction of travel and align the index marks so they bracket the compass needle. To follow a heading, simply keep the lubber line aligned with your body and keep the compass needle between the index marks.

Keeping the compass aligned with the centerline of your body is very important. If the compass is worn on the wrist, good alignment can be obtained by fully extending the arm without the compass and grasping the elbow joint of the extended arm with the middle finger of the arm equipped with the compass.

An even more accurate way to align the compass is to hold it in both hands extended in front of the diver.

A console-mounted compass can be aligned by holding the console in both hands with the elbows

NAVIGATION FOR DIVERS

tucked against your sides. This method is not as accurate as the two other positions described.

The most accurate way to use a compass is to mount it on a compass board which is held in both hands and extended in front of the diver. The extended lubber line on the compass board increases the accuracy of the compass itself.

You should sight across a compass when following a heading rather than looking down on the instrument. As you look across the compass, select an object ahead that is directly in line with the course you wish to follow. You can then make your way to the object without having to watch the compass continuously. When the object is attained, use the compass to select another object on the heading to be followed. Simply repeat the procedure for as long as you desire to follow the heading.

Your compass can assist you in conducting very precise dive patterns. You can swim a square pattern by swimming the first leg on a heading of 0 degrees, the second leg on a heading of 90 degrees, the third leg on a heading of 180 degrees and the fourth leg on a heading of 270 degrees. An out-and-back pattern is referred to as a RECIPROCAL COURSE which is always 180 degrees or exactly opposite that of an initial heading. If you swam away from a boat on a heading of 10 degrees, your reciprocal course to return to the boat would be 190 degrees.

A compass can also be used for surface navigation to fix a position when in-line objects are not available. Compass bearings to various terrestrial objects can assist you with the relocation of a dive site, although a compass fix is not as precise as a fix which uses two or more sets of objects which are aligned. Position relocation from a boat using a hand bearing compass can also be quite accurate.

Care of your diving compass is required to keep it functioning properly. The instrument should not be dropped, shocked or abused. Leaving a compass in the sun for prolonged periods can cause the liquid inside to expand and a leak can result. The instrument should be rinsed after use. The bezel should turn freely, but should hold a setting.

Combining Navigational Techniques

Effective diving navigation employs all of the techniques presented thus far plus a few others which will be presented. Both natural and compass position fixing techniques are used to locate a dive site. If swimming from shore, you swim along a course indicated by a set of in-line objects (such a course is called a RANGE), or along a reciprocal course indicated by a compass bearing from an object on shore. This heading is maintained until the course intersects another line of direction that fixes the desired position.

Figure 7.20 More accurate navigation is possible with a compass board than with a compass alone.

A compass heading is selected and set prior to descent. The heading frequently uses the shoreline as a reference so you will know if you are swimming toward or away from shore once you are on the bottom.

Upon reaching the bottom, landmarks are noted to indicate your point of departure, especially if you intend to return to that point at the end of the dive. Other natural aids to navigation are noted.

Turn yourself to align your centerline with the starting bearing of the compass and take a sighting on a distant object on the course you wish to follow, then move in that direction. Distance is estimated and your heading is changed as is appropriate to maintain your planned dive pattern. Natural aids to navigation—depth, shadows, water movement,

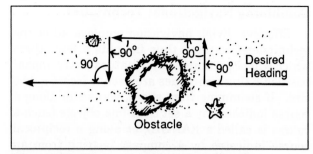

Figure 7.21 Circumnavigation of an obstacle.

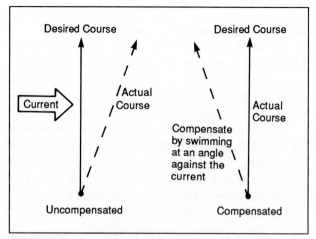

Figure 7.22 Compensating for leeway.

etc.—are noted all along the way. Frequent reference to your compass and depth gauge allow you to navigate more accurately than by the use of natural aids only.

You take pride in returning to your exact starting point at the end of a dive without surfacing. Your combined navigational skills have made your dive easier and more enjoyable. Not only that, if anything of note is discovered on a dive, you are confident that you can relocate it because you employed good navigational techniques throughout the dives. At times it is easier to find a small reef or wreck by following a bearing from a known point on a larger reef than it is to try to descend directly onto the smaller site.

Navigational Problems

Two problems you will encounter in underwater navigation are obstacles and currents. An obstacle will interrupt your dive pattern or distance measuring. A current will affect your speed when swimming with or against the water movement, and will cause LEEWAY, which is side-slippage in the direction of a current when you swim across a current. The error produced by leeway can seriously affect a dive pattern or even a heading.

An obstacle can be circumnavigated by modifying your dive pattern. By swimming perpendicular to your intended course while measuring the distance from your course until you are clear of an obstacle, you can then swim past the obstacle and swim a reciprocal course back to the original intended line as depicted in the illustration. This is one situation where effective distance measuring, such as kick cycles, is very useful.

There are several ways in which to handle the effects of leeway underwater. First of all, navigate close to the bottom where the water movement is at its minimum. Next, navigate from object to object along a heading. If visibility is poor or no objects are available for visual reference, angle yourself in the direction of the current to compensate for the lee-

way. Practice and experience will enable you to make reasonable estimations on how much to compensate for side-slippage in a current.

It is possible to measure the strength of a current and to calculate complex vectors to navigate accurately in currents, but such complicated approaches are beyond the scope of recreational diving and are rarely, if ever, used.

Use of Charts

Charts can be useful for diving navigation. Charts contain information on depths, formations, wrecks, bottom composition, landmarks, bearings, distances and more. Because divers typically cover very small distances in relation to those on charts, and since corrections for variation are required when using a chart, these coastal "maps" may not allow divers to navigate as accurately as they desire.

Charts establish position and measure distance by means of LATITUDE and LONGITUDE. You are probably familiar with the grid-like lines on a globe that extend around it horizontally at the equator and vertically from the poles. Latitude is the angular distance in degrees north or south of the equator, while longitude is the angular distance in degrees east or west of Greenwich, England. A line of longitude is also referred to as a MERIDIAN. Such lines of latitude and longitude appear on charts, and are used to establish position as well as to provide an accurate scale for distances on a chart.

The interpretation of charts and the proper use of them requires training. Such training is readily available through Power Squadron and other boating courses. These courses are inexpensive and recommended. The navigational techniques learned are applicable to diving navigation.

NAVIGATION FOR DIVERS

LIMITED VISIBILITY

DIVING

By Milledge Murphey, Ph.D. NAUI #7179

8

While most recreational divers prefer diving in water which is clear, there are times when lower visibility diving can be equally challenging and enjoyable. Further, you may have a specific diving interest in mind which is usually pursued in low visibility water. Two types of low visibility diving quite popular are night diving and cavern and/or cave diving, both of which are considered in other sections of this book. In this section, some of the many other types of reduced visibility diving will be discussed, as will procedures for safely and comfortably enjoying this unique and challenging diving environment.

What is limited visibility diving? Underwater visibility is considered limited when you cannot see another diver at a distance of 10 feet or less in a horizontal direction.

Why would one ever want to dive in water with a horizontal visual limit of less than 10 feet? There are so many reasons why you might want to dive in limited visibility water that only a small portion of the available answers will be mentioned here. Among the reasonable answers are: the only water in the area is of limited visibility, to explore wrecks located in such water, to earn the NAUI limited visibility specialty rating, to search for lost objects, to explore a previously undived site, artifact hunting, to locate clearer water at greater depths, to examine marine life (which may be abundant in such water), and for many other equally valid reasons. Whatever your personal requirements, make sure that you have had adequate advanced training before diving in any limited visibility setting.

What causes turbidity or lack of good visibility in water?

Among the causes for low visibility water are darkness (night) or extreme overcast during daylight hours, overhead environments which limit the available light (cavern zones, caves, or the interior of sunken wrecks), silt or debris being stirred up (many times by the divers themselves), suspended silt, mud, tannic or polluted water. In the case of diver-induced low visibility water conditions, simply being trained in anti-silting swimming techniques can mean clearer water, and thus more enjoyable, clearer water diving.

Other causes of turbid water are related to a variety of matter being suspended in the water which cause a reduction or loss of visibility. Among the causes are:

1. Surface winds stirring the bottom
2. Rain falling and creating particulate runoff into the water
3. Offshore currents and waves stirring the bottom near shore
4. Tidal changes stirring the bottom
5. Thermoclines wherein the colder denser layer of water will hold particulate matter in suspension (the water above a thermocline may be quite clear)
6. Pollution of any kind
7. River outflow into the ocean
8. Upwelling of colder, plankton loaded water toward the shore
9. Plankton-rich water causing reflected light to scatter and lower visibility
10. Algae bloom in fresh water

From this listing it can be seen that you should choose dive sites which lie upcurrent from entry points of streams and rivers. Obviously, diving on calm days or nights will enhance your chances of finding clearer water. Your best potential visibility will occur around reef areas away from the shore. You should avoid cove or bay areas which will usually have lower visibility. Further, the lee shore is usually clearer, as are drop-offs or rocky shoreline areas. Periods of tidal change are to be avoided as the radical movement of the water during these times usually creates more suspended matter, with consequent lower visibility.

Thermocline interface areas may sometimes be multi-layered, under which conditions you may find layers of clearer, warmer water sandwiched between colder, more turbid layers. The fresh water algae bloom may affect your diving visibility most during the spring and summer months. It will commonly occupy from the surface to 40 feet deep water. Usually, the water below 40 feet is clear of algae. Little algae is found during the colder winter months, as it is sensitive to colder temperatures and lower available sunlight.

Techniques for Low Visibility Diving

Many of the specific techniques used in low visibility diving are also appropriate for use in normal open water diving settings. All divers would enjoy all types of diving more if they would consistently avoid stirring up the silt and sediments which form the substrate of almost all open water diving sites. Even in very low visibility water, it is still important (for both safety and enjoyment) to minimize the addition of visibility limiting substances to the water. Thus, the first consideration for all is, don't make it worse than it already is by using poor diving techniques which churn up the bottom and reduce visibility even further.

The major increase in risk caused by low visibility diving is the reduction in your ability to communicate and interact with your buddy underwater. You can, however, compensate for this reduced ability to communicate with your buddy and mitigate the increased risk imposed. Among the most important factors to consider are visibility, navigation or direction of your swim, and careful dive planning.

As you descend, light is absorbed by the water (especially in fresh water), causing the diving environment to become darker. If particulate matter is not too great, you may choose to use a dive light; *i.e.,* tannic stained fresh water is sometimes low in suspended particulate matter and thus, even though the visibility is low, a light may dramatically increase your visibility under such conditions. In water with a high concentration of suspended particles, your light may be reflected to the point that it becomes of little or no use. To use a dive light most effectively, you should hold it to the side and above the object you're attempting to see, as this will minimize the scatter problem caused by the intervening suspended materials.

Buddypersonship

While correct use of a dive light may or may not improve your visibility (depending upon water conditions), there are other techniques essential to your safety while diving in reduced visibility. Buddypersonship, that is, remaining within touching distance of your buddy, is a necessary skill to be mastered. Staying in sight of your buddy, constant visual buddy, referencing and, in very low visibility conditions, actual contact with your buddy, are important considerations.

It is also important to recognize that stress increases as water visibility decreases, as does your

Figure 8.1 If particulate matter is not too great, you may choose to use a dive light.

personal task loading. You should plan your low visibility dives for shorter durations and less mobile, shorter distance swims. In addition, it is a good idea to monitor your instruments and direction more frequently than in clearer water diving. If you'll swim slower than usual, the increased tasks can be accomplished in a timely manner and you can enjoy your dive more.

If, in spite of your slower, more regulated pace, you become separated from your buddy, simply follow the rules of open water lost buddy protocol. Look, circling slowly with your light for one minute, then surface, continuing to slowly circle with your light at the surface. Your buddy will replicate your actions and once you're together on the surface, you can briefly discuss the cause(s) for your underwater separation, make plans to avoid reoccurence of the separation, and resume your dive.

Diving Lights

Use of diving lights implies courtesy, so never aim your light directly at your buddy's face. Light signals are covered in the Night Diving chapter of this book; make sure you read it. Always aim your light at any hand signals which you give, not at your buddy. Don't give non-illuminated signals. Use of one or more back-up lights is advisable under low visibility conditions. Should your primary light fail, you can continue the dive using your backup. If all lights fail, you and your buddy should surface and terminate the dive.

Buddy Lines

When water conditions produce visibility near or at zero, you should consider using a buddy line (a three foot length of line clipped to both buddies or hand-held by both). This will enable buddies to remain in direct contact and signal each other by a prearranged series of tugs or hand squeezes. You should be aware that use of the buddy line introduces an additional potential entanglement hazard and take appropriate precautions to avoid underwater difficulties. Practicing use of the buddy line in clear water will greatly enhance your success in using the line in actual low visibility conditions. Finally, use of buddy lines in confined underwater spaces is unwise as this increases the danger of entanglement or the line becoming ensnared with a fixed object.

Tether Lines

When current is present and visibility is near zero, you should consider use of a tether or lifeline. Diving under such conditions is a very advanced situation and should only be engaged in by properly trained divers. The tether is a line from the diver to the surface and should be placed on the body beneath all scuba equipment and secured by a bowline knot which will produce a circle that will not slip.

Use of tether techniques requires a fully dressed safety diver at the surface and a number of other prearranged safety procedures and rope tug signals. In most instances, the tethered divers are in increased jeopardy of line entanglement and, consequently, knives must be carried and located in easily accessible positions in the divers' equipment configuration (chest or arm mounted knives are recommended).

Orientation

As you enter turbid water, you lose the surface references of light and the pull of gravity, and thus, your spatial reference. This sensation can be pleasurable if you are in total control of the situation. You may, due to light changes, experience brief tunnel vision or visual vertigo. You can control both potential problems by remaining vertical and grasping an object (anchor line, rock, etc.). Should the problem(s) persist, you can surface using depth gauge, watch, and slightly positive buoyancy to make a safe controlled ascent. Buddies should stay close together, as the visual reference of the buddy can lessen the impact of potential disorientation problems.

On your first dives in low visibility water, you will want to dive in a known area or with a buddy who has been in the area before. This will minimize the natural tendency to be anxious under new conditions and will enable you to practice and rehearse all techniques before you enter the low visibility underwater conditions. Further, your task loading will be increased, as you must keep close track of your rate of descent, depth, and buddy location.

It is always a good idea to use the anchor line or a drop line for a controlled descent and ascent. Under near zero visibility conditions and in moderate current, the buddy team using a buddy line may also choose to use an underwater reel so that a continuous line may be run from the anchor or dropline point of attachment throughout the dive. Control is assured, although you must be vigilant to avoid line entanglements as you increase the number of lines used. In some areas, permanent

Figure 8.2 A buddy line should be held, not tied, and kept taut.

lines are available for divers to follow and should be used in open water areas when provided.

Horizontal control can be maintained by use of a reel, line and depth gauge or by use of depth gauge and compass. As in flying, you must, in low visibility, trust your compass and follow its directions. How you "feel" under these conditions is not an accurate method of determining direction. To enjoy diving in very low visibility conditions, you must be a competent underwater navigator.

You can use several other methods for insuring proper direction referencing, including:

1. Reel and line (be trained and practice these skills before attempting to use them in actual low visibility conditions)

2. Time your trip out and follow a timed reciprocal on the return

3. Reference objects or bottom slope, reversing the sides they appear on for the return trip

4. Be aware of depth changes and current direction

5. Use surface light direction (if some surface light is available)

6. Remember that ripples on the bottom usually occur parallel to shore

As has been stated previously, avoid silt on the bottom, especially in fresh water or under no current conditions Use of protective gloves (to avoid being cut by objects which you don't see), as well as exposure suits is important in low visibility diving. In zero conditions, one hand held well out in front of the mask may protect it from breaking in the event you accidently run into an unseen stationary object. The other hand may be placed beneath you as you swim in a slow, neutrally buoyant, fins-off-the-bottom fashion during the dive. The dive knife should be arm or chest mounted to insure easy access should you become inadvertently entangled in a submerged line or rope. In this connection, a smaller dive knife is recommended for use in low visibility. This will enable you to mount it on the arm or chest and thus enhance your access to it in case of a low visibility line entanglement.

Diving in limited visibility water can be an exciting and challenging addition to your diving skills repertoire. Differing conditions, location of submerged objects, hunting and collecting, artifact and river dives are among the activities which are frequently pursued in lower visibility conditions.

As you improve your limited visibility diving skills, your ability in clearer water will be enhanced by the increased awareness and anti-silt techniques which you develop.   Further, you will broaden your diving potential by developing the ability to dive in more diverse dive sites. Finally, you will be a safer, more skilled, and more competent diver under all possible diving conditions.

NIGHT
DIVING

9

By Ted Boehler NAUI #2699

Diving is a collection of amazing experiences. Your first open water dive, the first eel you saw, the thrill of a wreck dive (even if it was only a '58 Chevy at the bottom of the local quarry), all occupy a special file in your memories. And, if you haven't ever made a night dive then, well ... save room, you have some wonderful memories ahead!

The Rewards

So, why dive at night? For the excitement, for lobster crawling around in the open, for phosphorescence bursting off the tips of your swim fins, for the gentle stroking of giant parrot fish or sleeping sunfish, for a once-in-a-lifetime dive with millions of mating squid. Dive at night for the fun, for the adventure, for the soul-filling joy of it!

Night diving has a way of focusing your attention, of making the things you encounter more interesting, more colorful. And, of course, using a light source undiluted by the blue filtering effect of the water makes those colors more vibrant than you have ever seen them in the daytime. You will also encounter creatures you have never seen on midday dives and find the timid daylight ones amazingly approachable in their nocturnal stage.

Indeed, while it may seem that your range of vision will be limited in the night, you will find, as other divers have, that the reward is a newfound appreciation in the microcosm, You will find that your air probably lasts longer as you limit your attention to a small and interesting section of the reef or bottom, as opposed to hurrying by, oblivious to some of the most fascinating sights. Even the most mundane dive sites seems to make a Cinderella transformation after the sun goes down.

The Preparations

Rewards have their way of demanding tribute before they can be collected. Pay your dues by becoming completely comfortable in the water with your skills and your equipment before making a night dive.

Dive the area in daylight first. Choose an area with easy entry, calm, shallow water, and prominent landmarks. Remember that orientation and judgment of distance are difficult at night. Arrive before dark, if possible, to re-orient yourself and to prepare your equipment for the dive.

Figure 9.1 *It is possible to get much closer to animals at night than it is during the daylight hours.*

Keeping Track of Where You Are

A compass is a must. So is a depth gauge. Even more helpful is a pre-night dive orientation to the spot to key in on specific underwater landmarks. A neat trick is the use of two "range lights" set up in a line to show you the path back to your exit point after surfacing. These can be two lanterns on the beach or a similar alignment of battery powered lights or small emergency flashers. Don't have the misfortune of using a porch light or street light for a return reference only to have it turn off before you get back to shore!

Another handy idea is to use a chemical light stick (cyalume) attached to your gauge console or tank to make it easy for you and your buddy to keep track of one another.

You will also notice that it's helpful to avoid hovering just above the bottom to prevent the sand or silt from clouding the water. Many divers prefer to adjust themselves to slight negative buoyancy on the bottom to avoid floating unaware toward the surface.

The Three Hand Complex

Clearly, human beings have been given too few hands to efficiently night dive. How do you adjust your BC while holding your light, while reading your depth gauge, while carrying your camera? For

Figure 9.2 Lining up shore lights to form a "range" is an excellent means to help divers find the exit point.

Figure 9.3 Waterproof, pressure proof chemical light sticks can be used for a variety of purposes on a night dive.

your first few night dives, limit extraneous equipment, use gear you are familiar with. Your first experience is truly not the place to try out a new mask or buoyancy pack.

As to the extra hand? The answer is buddy cooperation. You hold the light while your partner reads the depth gauge and maintains the reference ascent rate. Your buddy holds the light while you make camera adjustments. One holds the bag while the lucky one puts in lobster!

The Equipment

As night diving has become more popular, manufacturers have made equipment improvements to make the activity easier. Many gauges now glow in the dark, allowing easy readability even without direct light.

Small mini-lights are a great back-up in case of primary light failure. They allow a check of gauges during ascent to get you safely back to the surface. But the star of the equipment show is the powerful underwater lights that brighten the way and the wonders of the evening.

What to buy, what to buy . . . the bottom line is get the brightest light you can afford. Your enjoyment of night diving is directly tied to how comfortable you are and how much you can see. While relative "foot candle" ratings are useful for comparison of different models, the best demonstration is to turn the light on in a darkened room. Check the pattern on a wall. If it is too wide, the light doesn't reach very far underwater. If it is too narrow, it may not light a reasonable area during, say, your search for lobster. Remember also that water causes significant attenuation (loss) of the light. Even the

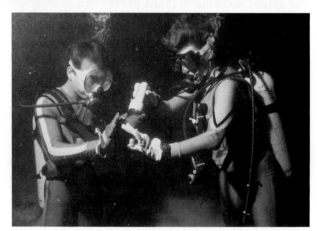

Figure 9.4 Hand signals must be given and acknowledged in front of a light when diving at night.

most powerful dive lights only reach about 20' or so unless the water is extremely clear.

To Charge or Not to Charge

If you spend a lot of time in remote locations away from power, or if your budget is bare, a regular battery light is in order. Otherwise, the most cost effective light is a rechargeable system. At $6 -7 a trip for batteries, you'll find that the rechargeable light quickly becomes a good investment. Follow manufacturers' rules carefully on charging cycles. Some lights can be damaged by overcharging, or charging too fast.

You'll also want to pick up a couple of extra battery packs to sustain you on vacations where night dives come in multiples.

More About Dive Lights

A stretchable lanyard should be attached to your dive light to prevent loss. The stretchable feature is important so your hand can pull free in case the light becomes caught.

In addition to dive lights, you will need lights for above water use. These include lights to use for dive preparations as well as surface lights to mark the entry/exit location. It is a good idea to use regular flashlights for above water use. This conserves the batteries and bulbs in your dive lights. Also, some dive lights will overheat unless cooled by immersion in water. It would probably be wise for your flashlights to be waterproof in case they fall in the water.

Lights to mark the entry/exit point can be anything from a lantern to a roadway flasher. The main idea is for them to be distinctive so they won't be readily confused with other lights in the dive area. Be careful to avoid the use of lights which might resemble navigational aids, especially flashing red, green or white lights. Amber or yellow are good alternatives.

A Few Words About Maintenance

There is nary a diver so tearful as one with a flooded light. Take extra precaution to seal the light in a well illuminated area before the pace gets hectic. Preferably, do it before you change to dive. Check and carefully clean the o ring. Use a pencil eraser to clean any metal contacts.

Apply a light film of silicone grease to the o ring. Be sure all wires or foreign matter are clear of the sealing surface. Carefully screw down the lens or snap the sealing latches evenly. Examine the look of the light. Does everything seem even, flush, properly positioned?

Avoid banging the light unnecessarily, especially when it is turned on. Banging tends to make the bulk filaments fail. Use a rubber strap to retain the light on your wrist. Occasionally, you need to have your hands free to deal with an equipment problem.

The Dive!

If possible, pick a calm, familiar, shallow spot for your first dive. Avoid kelp, big surf and wash rocks at night. Stick to open water areas. Boat dives to shallow or protected reefs are excellent. You've checked the area earlier in the day, and your gear is ready. Take a moment to go over the dive plan with your partner. Set up your return light(s). Don your gear and do a last minute check in a lighted area.

When entering the water from shore, lay down and swim in shallow water. This will prevent you from falling down or getting knocked down. Activate your "chem light" before entering the water. Take bearings on the point where you wish to exit before submerging so you can navigate during the dive to finish near your exit point.

Check with your buddy once you reach the diving area, and descend together. You may experience disorientation or vertigo from lack of a point of reference during the descent. Shining your light on your bubbles or using a descent line helps prevent this. Once on the bottom, be alert to surge and current lest you be swept into unseen obstructions. Move slowly and stay together, looking not only from side to side, but up and down as well. Do not shine a light into your buddy's eyes, but on the chest instead. Agree on an attention gaining signal — rapid wiggling of the light, covering and uncovering the light, or line pulls. A buddy line may be used.

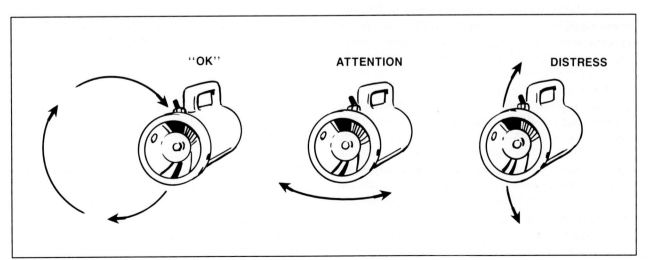

Figure 9.5 Light signals used for night diving.

Figure 9.6 Examples of lights for above water use on night dives.

If you should become separated, stop, turn slowly and look for your buddy's light or bubbles. If you do not locate them after two revolutions, surface. Your buddy should do the same. Leave your light on after reaching the surface. When your buddy is sighted, signal by making a large "O" for OK on the air with your light. Your buddy should return the signal. Descend again after getting back together and checking your references.

During ascent, shine your light on your bubbles and gauges to judge the rate of ascent. Keep one hand over your head as protection against surface obstructions. If you have navigated correctly, you should be near your exit point upon surfacing at the end of the dive.

Night diving can be safe, fun and adventurous. There is a great deal to see and experience in the dark, mysterious waters of the sea at night. Know the area, your buddy and your gear well; plan the dive and then dive the plan. You will find night diving can be rewarding and exciting and increase your confidence in your diving ablity. Give nocturnal bubbling a try.

SEARCH &
LIGHT SALVAGE

By Leonard Greenstone
NAUI #2336

10

As a diver you may need to find a lost object underwater and bring it to the surface. You or a friend might lose some item from a boat, and you may be asked to recover it. As a NAUI Advanced Scuba Diver, you should be able to select and perform an appropriate basic search pattern to locate an object and then salvage the object, provided its weight is less than 100 pounds.

Objectives

By the end of this section, you should be able to:

1. List at least five items of special equipment recommended for search and light salvage.

2. List the three general steps to be followed when searching for an item underwater.

3. Illustrate and describe at least three underwater search patterns and explain under which circumstances each should be used.

4. List at least three safety rules for diving salvage.

5. Briefly describe the procedures for salvaging an object using a lift bag.

6. Briefly describe the search and salvage terms that appear in boldface in this chapter.

Organization

Most people quite mistakenly believe that finding something underwater is not difficult. Locating an object underwater is often equivalent to parachuting into a dense fog on a vast desert and initiating a search!

Many factors affect the outcome of an underwater search. Factors include visibility, depth, bottom contour and composition, aquatic vegetation, accessibility, water movement, information provided to the searchers and the organization of the searchers. Of all these factors, only the organization of those who will be searching can be controlled. Organization is, therefore, very important.

The basic rules for organizing an underwater search are:

1. Define the area to be searched.
2. Select and conduct a search pattern best suited to the area.
3. Keep track of the areas searched.

When defining the area to be searched, consider dividing a large area into smaller ones.

When selecting a search pattern, consider the number of searchers available, their training and experience, the available equipment, the water and bottom conditions, and the above-water conditions.

When trying to keep track of areas that have been searched, consider the ways in which this can be accomplished. A number of surface markers or marker buoys will probably be required.

If several divers are to participate in a search, each should understand exactly what the other members are supposed to do. With this information, a minimum of communication will be required underwater. A dry run practice of the chosen search pattern or procedure on land prior to attempting it underwater can save a great deal of time and confusion when the actual diving begins.

Hazards

Search and light salvage when done in murky water can be very hazardous. Broken glass, metal, barnacles, coral, fishhooks and other sharp objects will injure you unless you are careful. It is not uncommon to have to search for items in harbor waters which have a layer of oily black silt on the bottom. This silt rises very easily and can rapidly reduce visibility to zero, increasing the difficulty of the search. When groping along a harbor bottom, bare hands are needed to maximize your tactile

Figure 10.1 Search and Salvage Equipment

sense. Your hands, therefore, are subject to cuts, so move them slowly. After exiting from this type of search, bathe your hands in alcohol. It is also a good idea to rinse your ears with a solution of half vinegar and half water followed by a solution of half alcohol and half water.

Currents, submerged trees, aquatic vegetation, fishing line, search lines and boat traffic pose additional hazards. Only training and experience enable you to minimize these hazards during search and salvage operations.

Some controllable hazards include hypothermia and decompression sickness. When you become cold, stop searching. Do not let the excitement of the search encourage you to push the no-decompression limits.

Equipment

Besides your basic diving gear, special equipment may be needed for search and light salvage operations.
1. Surface floats/Marker buoys
2. Anchors and search lines
3. Dive lights
4. Compass board
5. Diver's sled and tow line
6. Tool kit
7. Spare parts kit
8. First aid kit
9. Lift bag

Search Procedures

Gather as many facts as possible. Your chances of success are much better if the search area and the lost object are well defined. Find out what was lost, how it was lost, where and when it was lost, what the water conditions are like, and what the bottom topography and composition are like.

One person needs to be in charge of a search. Everyone involved must agree to follow the instructions of the search leader.

Establish an operational timetable as well as depth and time limits for the search and salvage operations.

Discuss and agree upon emergency procedures for accidents that may occur during the diving operations.

Select and practice a search pattern. Information on search patterns is included in this section.

Be prepared to mark the location of an object when it has been located. An item can become lost quickly after it has been found if the location is not marked.

Figure 10.2 Maintain positive buoyancy while searching so silt and sediment will not be stirred up.

Everything possible must be done to avoid disturbing the bottom and stirring up silt. Do not wade around in the water. Avoid treading water in a vertical position near the bottom. Use positive buoyancy to ascend rather than swimming upward from the bottom. Avoid contact with the bottom as much as possible. Slight positive buoyancy that requires you to swim with your fins slightly above a horizontal plane is desirable.

Search Patterns

An underwater search is usually conducted by swimming a definite pattern. The two fundamental types of search patterns are straight line and circular. All accepted search patterns are simply variations of these two basic themes. Different patterns lend themselves better to one type of search than others, depending on the type of bottom, depth, obstructions, and the base of operations. Several search patterns will be described. An imaginative combination of two or more of these basic patterns will usually prove effective in almost any instance.

All search patterns involve distance measuring. This can be accomplished by using measured lines, by counting kick cycles, by swimming for a measured time, or by counting arm spans when visibility is limited. Skill in the areas of navigation and distance measuring are prerequisites for underwater searching.

The Contour Search

When the probable depth and approximate location of an object lost offshore are known, a CON-

TOUR SEARCH can be very effective. This is where the contour of the bottom along a shoreline is followed at a constant depth. This method is not a true "pattern", but rather a search technique. The search is initiated about 100 feet down the shore from the estimated location and at a depth slightly greater than the estimated depth. You follow the contour of the bottom, which means you maintain a constant depth, until you are about 100 feet up the shore from the estimated location. You then turn at a right angle toward shore to a shallower depth. The distance you move toward shore and the new depth will be determined by the visibility. You then turn parallel to shore again at the new depth and parallel your first course in the reverse direction. Successive sweeps at shallower depths are conducted until you either find the object or conclude it is not in the area being searched.

Figure 10.4 Searching for an item dropped overboard.

Circular Search

The first true search pattern is the CIRCULAR SEARCH, which is popular because it is simple and effective in many situations. This pattern is most useful when there are no underwater obstructions in the area being searched and when visibility is reasonably good.

One end of a line is secured firmly in the center of the area to be searched and serves as a hub. One member of a buddy team remains at the anchored end of the line, while the other diver holds onto the line and keeps it taut while swimming circular sweeps to search for the lost object. After each complete circle, the searching diver lets out more line and repeats the sweeps in ever-widening circles until the object is located or the circles become too large for effective use of the line. The anchored end of the line can then be moved in a predetermined direction and the search repeated. The areas being searched should overlap each other somewhat to ensure that the entire area is searched.

The starting point for a circular sweep must be marked so the searching diver will know when a full sweep has been completed. This can be done by either the diver at the tethered end of the line or by the searching diver.

Semicircular Search

A variation of the circular sweep is the semicircular search, which is used from a shoreline, pier or jetty which form the extremes for a semicircle. A line is anchored in the center of the search area and along the straight edge. The line may extend from shore or be anchored at the bottom. Searching is conducted in the same manner as the circular sweep except you reverse direction at the end of each semicircular sweep.

In addition to use from shore, a version of the semicircular search is useful when searching for objects that have fallen overboard from an anchored boat. A boat at anchor swings in an arc on the anchor, especially when there is a wind. An object falling into the water at a certain position relative to the boat will probably not be where you think it is due to the lateral movement of the vessel. A line attached to the anchor can be used to sweep back and forth in the area transversed by the boat, thereby increasing the chances for success by employing an appropriate methodical searching method.

Figure 10.3 A circular sweep is an effective flat bottom pattern.

Straight Line Search Patterns

Straight lines form the basis for the majority of search patterns. These patterns are very adaptable to a variety of conditions and situations. Straight line searches can be conducted in several ways:

1. A compass or a compass board may be used to navigate along straight lines to methodically search an area.

2. A line can be strung in a straight line along the bottom and used as a reference for a straight line search, then repositioned to allow methodical searching.

3. A grid of rope or PVC pipe can be spread out on the bottom.

4. A planing board or diver's sled can be towed along a straight line course by a boat.

The use of a compass to conduct a search pattern is not easy. There may be no landmarks on a featureless bottom, and you may even believe you are going in the wrong direction at times. You cannot effectively navigate with the compass and search simultaneously. One member of a buddy team should be responsible for navigation and swimming a search pattern. The other team member should maintain buddy contact and thoroughly scan the surrounding area continuously for the object being sought. More accurate patterns can be achieved with a compass board than with a compass by itself.

A buddy team can double the effectiveness of a tethered line sweep by searching side by side on each side of the line, first in one direction, then in the other. This allows twice as much area to be searched on either side of the line.

The use of a **Planing Board** (sea sled) or a tow bar behind a boat is reserved for use when a large

Figure 10.5 Buddy team doing compass search.

object, such as a wreck, is being sought and the search area is very large. There are hazards associated with the use of a planing board, and use of a sea sled is discouraged unless you have training and supervised experience in the use of one.

A **Grid Search** is useful when looking for small objects in a well-defined area. The grid is constructed of rope or of PVC pipe and is spread out on the bottom. A very minute search can be conducted. If the bottom is soft and the item being sought is small, sifting the mud or sand square by square may be necessary to recover the lost object.

Light Salvage Procedures

When the object of your search has been located, the next step is to recover it. That can be as simple as picking it up or as complex as breaking the suction of a moderately heavy object that is embedded in the bottom.

In addition to the previously listed gear needed for salvage work, you must also be equipped with specific knowledge and skills for the task. The following principles and procedures are important and should be studied carefully.

Requirements for Safe Light Salvage

1. Knot tying and rigging—You need to be able to properly tie the following knots when rigging objects to be lifted: Bowline, sheet bend, clove hitch, and a round turn and two half hitches.

2. Lift bag use—You must be able to estimate the correct size of the lift bag, inflate it using an independent air source, and maintain complete control of the lift as it ascends.

3. Breaking suction—You need to be able to safely break the suction of an object embedded in the bottom. This can require a force that is as much as ten times the weight of the object. The use of lift bags to do this is dangerous. Acceptable methods include the use of a tidal lift or a surge lift. A **Tidal Lift** is a line extended tightly at low tide from an object on the bottom to a large surface float or boat. The incoming tide then pulls the object free from the bottom so it can be raised. A **Surge Lift** works on the same principle, but uses the changing height of waves passing overhead to pull the object free.

4. Thinking—You must be able to remain calm, think, analyze and act to minimize or correct errors.

Controlling a Lift

The capacity of a lift bag must not exceed the weight of an object to be lifted by a great deal because the air in a lift bag expands during ascent. If a 200-pound lift bag is used to raise a 50-pound object from a depth of 66 feet (20 meters) the lift will

Figure 10.6 The control of expanding air in a lift bag during ascent is important.

dump valve on the lift bag, and the other should remain beside and in contact with the object being lifted to watch it and to help control it if necessary. If the lift bag being used is not equipped with a dump valve, a line should be attached to the top of the lift bag so it can be pulled to force air down and out of the bag as required. If a lift rises faster than it should and becomes uncontrollable, release it and swim away from it. If you release too much air from a lift and it begins sinking, let it go; follow it to the bottom and start over. Swimming to support a sinking lift is dangerous because the lift becomes heavier as its volume decreases with increasing depth.

When an object has been lifted to the surface, it can be pushed to the exit point and pulled out. If the object is to be removed from deep water, a line should be secured to it before lifting by the bag so it will not sink if it falls.

Figure 10.7 The use of a "round turn" around the object is recommended to attach securely to the lift bag.

gain 100 pounds of buoyancy during ascent. This will cause the lift to rise rapidly and dangerously out of control. It can come completely out of the water when it reaches the surface, spill its contents and drop the lift back down on the divers below. The first important step in light salvage is to closely match the capacity of the lift bag to the weight of the object to be lifted.

A lift bag should be inflated with air from an independent tank, not from the tanks of those filling the lift bag. The purpose of this is not to conserve air, but to ensure that your regulator or hoses do not become entangled in the lift as it begins to ascend.

If a lift bag is inflated until the object begins to rise, you have probably put too much air into the bag. It takes time to overcome inertia in water. Add air to the lift bag bit by bit and test the lift from time to time by raising it from the bottom. Your lifting will tell you how much additional air is required and will help overcome any inertia the lift may have.

When the lift begins to ascend, both you and your buddy must clear the area beneath the lift and should ascend with it. One of you should control the

Specialty Training

Search and salvage is a specialty area. You are only introduced to the activity in this NAUI Advanced class. Search activities requiring further training in a specialty course on the subject include gang sweeps involving many divers, special zig-zag patterns employing lines, special techniques for searching in swift-flowing rivers and around marina docks, proper use of a diver's sled and more. Salvage training includes the use of larger lift bags and drums, the use of winches and block and tackle devices, and detailed calculations pertinent to salvage operations. If you have a need to be involved in search and salvage or an interest in this activity, learn what you need to know by completing the NAUI Search and Recovery specialty course.

DEEP DIVING

11

By Pat Scharr NAUI #4593

Now that you've learned how to drive that neat, wrap-around underwater vehicle, you are looking for the road to high adventure; or should I say "deep adventure?" This chapter is your road map for getting acquainted with a new area. But you should really consider going on this exploration with a pro—someone who knows all the ins and outs (ups and downs). Your instructor, in the format of a deep diving specialty course, can show you just how safe and enjoyable deep diving can be.

Before we get started on this adventure, let's look at the legend on the map for some important definitions.

Deep: in the depth range of 60 to 130 feet.

Profile: time and depth parameters which are at least one repetitive group within the no-decompression limits.

Precautionary Stop: refers to a non-required decompression stop (three minutes at 15 feet) made as a safety precaution at the end of your dive.

All deep dives and repetitive dives should incorporate these factors.

There are two general areas in which diving can take place. The most popular locale is warm, tropical reefs, wrecks and walls in areas like the Caribbean, North America's playground. Hundreds of thousands of diving tourists make safe, enjoyable deep dives here under the supervision of professional dive operators. Spectacular panoramas,

encounters with large marine life, and fantastic photographic opportunities abound.

Another popular locale (often closer to home) is in colder waters of the east, west or middle coasts.

Whether in the oceans or the Great Lakes, ship wrecks, silent sentinels of days gone by, lie quietly waiting to unfold their mysterious secrets. Note well, however, that you'll need special skills and equipment in either case. And the risks are higher. So, why, you ask, do people want to deep dive? Why are you reading this chapter?

Reasonable purposes to dive deep may include exploration, photography, marine life identification, and ship wreck mapping. Inherent in all of these is ego challenge. It's worth taking a minute here to look at our greatest asset and biggest danger.

Our egos are the essence of our quest for adventure. A healthy ego gives us confidence, persistence, creativity and flexibility and is vital to the ability to manage stress. But over-confidence (or an unhealthy ego) can lead to errors in judgment or diving beyond limitations. It is exhilarating and satisfying to participate in well planned, well executed deep dives. It is macho and ignorant to take crazy chances with excessive depth. Hopefully, as you read this chapter, you will analyze your own motivation and ego and integrate these common sense concepts.

Jack McKenney photo

Chuck Allen photo

Figure 11.1 Two general deep diving situations include warm, tropical waters and colder, darker waters.

DEEP DIVE PLANNING

There are five factors that must be considered when planning deep dives: Environment, Personnel, Equipment, Profile and Emergency Procedures.

Environment

The first step in deep dive planning is to select and analyze the environment in which you are going to dive. Of course, it's much easier and safer to rely on the expertise of a dive industry professional familiar with the proposed area. Nevertheless, these questions must be answered:

1. What is the basic topography of the area? (Depth of reef bottom? Depth of wall? Is the wreck intact, broken up, penetrable? Are there caverns and gorges? What is their bottom depth?)

2. What types of free swimming (pelagic) creatures are frequently found in the area? (Sharks, rays, barracuda, dolphins, etc.?)

3. What types of bottom dwelling marine life are frequently found in the area? (Corals, sponges, etc.?)

4. What is the average water temperature? What type of exposure suit is necessary?

5. What is the average visibility?

6. What type of water motion is common? (Currents, swells, upwellings, surge?)

7. Are there any single hazards or combination of hazardous factors which might cause you to cancel the dive? (Weather, dangerous marine life, wreckage which might cause entanglement, large amounts of silt—which if stirred up might reduce visibility?)

When you've done your homework and answered all these questions, you are at a crossroad—you may choose not to dive due to environmental conditions, or you may want to go on with the dive plan.

Personnel

Your next step is to select personnel—your dive buddy and your support personnel.

When you are selecting a buddy, look for someone who has equal or greater experience. It's a good idea to have made a few shallow dives with this person to ensure good communication and compatibility. You and your buddy will also need to make a mutual commitment to personal preparedness (*i.e.*, be well rested, well fed, consume no alcohol for 24 hours prior, be pre-checked equipment and procedures).

Figure 11.2 Support personnel are recommended for deep diving activities.

Because deep diving involves greater risk, including increased exposure to decompression sickness (a longer way to the surface in case of emergency) the possibility of impaired mental and physical function due to the effects of partial pressure of Nitrogen (ppN_2), it is recommended to have support personnel (*i.e.*, divemaster, dive guide and safety divers).

The divemaster has overall responsibility for the entire dive, including:

1. Final confirmation of dive site with safe, acceptable conditions (*i.e.*, currents, visibility, weather).

2. Supervision and direction of divers and support staff.

3. Inspection of divers' equipment and safety equipment.

4. Determination and recording of profiles.

5. Development and implementation, if necessary, of emergency procedures and accident management.

The divemaster generally stays at the surface and supervises all aspects of the diving activity.

The dive guide, sometimes referred to as an underwater tour guide, is generally a person familiar with dive sites. Dive guide responsibilities include:

1. Supervision of divers during entry, descent, stabilization (which includes establishing neutral buoyancy), the excursion, ascent, simulated decompression stops and exiting the water.

2. Navigation and identification of special points of interests.

3. Recognition of and assistance with any problems divers might encounter.

The dive guide goes in the water with the divers. At many Caribbean destinations, the role of divemaster and dive guide are fulfilled by the same person.

Safety divers are advanced divers trained in search and recovery and diver rescue techniques applicable to a given area. Their function is to:

1. Maintain a state of readiness while diving activities are in progress.

2. Assist the divemaster as directed during any emergency.

This type of safety diver is generally employed in advanced levels combining specialties like deep diving and penetration wrecks and ice or cave diving.

As you can see, it takes a lot of expertise to plan a deep dive safely, and we're only halfway through. Participating in organized diving activities with trained professionals will increase both the safety and enjoyment of your dive.

Equipment

Now, let's talk about our neat, nifty, necessary wrap-around underwater vehicle—our diving equipment. After all, you can't go diving without it!

Hopefully, by the time you become interested in deep diving, you already own your own wrap-around underwater vehicle. It's very important! Why? Well, there are three reasons in particular:

1. Comfort—You should have properly fitting, comfortable equipment. Rental Roulette never guarantees you proper, consistent fit. Also, you may not be able to select exactly what you need. When you put your hard-earned bucks down to purchase equipment, you buy specifically for your own needs and comfort.

2. Adaptability—Most experienced divers modify/personalize their equipment to make fit and function easier. Strap adjustments, addition of brass utility clips or rings, systems for tethering dangling hoses and consoles are common examples. Owning your own gear allows you to modify it just the way you like it.

3. Familiarity—Your equipment, *i.e.*, your life-support system should become second nature to you. You should be able to locate and operate every item with either hand with your eyes closed (although you will have to open your eyes to read gauges).

When you own your gear, you will become totally familiar, and therefore, more comfortable while diving.

Owning your own equipment is one mark of a serious, competent diver. Comfort and equipment familiarity are definite prerequisites for deep div-

Figure 11.3 Deep dives require additional equipment considerations.

ing. Specific modifications recommended for deep diving include:

1. Specific location and tethering of octopus regulator.

2. Tethering of console and streamlining of equipment to minimize chance of equipment getting snagged or entangled.

3. Tethering of additional equipment like lights or cameras in case dropped.

Additional equipment recommended for deep diving includes redundant timing device, depth gauge, dive computer, waterproof dive tables, slate, pencil and light.

It is generally accepted that each diver must have a timing device and depth gauge; theoretically, your buddy's gear is your back-up system. In deep diving, however, there is much less margin for error. Many Caribbean divemasters who dive to depths of 100 feet daily use two or three depth gauges and timing devices. Such redundancy gives you increased accuracy and dependability. Depth gauges with maximum depth indicators and pressure activated timing devices are recommended.

The advent of dive computers and multilevel diving has revolutionized thinking about deep diving. These computers, when used according to the manufacturer's directions, actually give you more valid information and safer profiles, as they constantly record your depth and time and calculate profile based on a more conservative set of tables than the standard U.S. Navy Tables. It is recommended, however, that these be used in conjunction with standard instrumentation and that dive plans be predetermined and actual profiles accurately recorded.

You may also want to carry a light. In clear tropical waters, plenty of daylight filters down, but section of brownish, greenish wall and paint a riot of bright reds and yellows.

Exposure suits, from lycra suits to dry suits, can be chosen according to environmental conditions. Thousands dive in just bathing suits every year in the Caribbean, while others choose shorty jackets or full 1/8 inch suits. Cold water deep diving necessitates dry suits. You should learn how to operate a dry suit and make several shallow dives in one to develop fine-tuned buoyancy control and equipment familiarity.

In summary, in addition to your personal gear, you should have redundant instrumentation for time, depth and tables. Dive computers are recommended, as well as dive lights and some type of exposure suit.

There is a second category of equipment necessary for deep diving—safety support equipment. Standard equipment, including first aid kit, oxygen, backboard, communication equipment (VHF or CB radio or phone), and transportation equipment should be available at the dive site. In addition, there should be stable, designated, decompression stops, additional air supply and surface support station (boat, unless shore is very close to drop off. How close is very close? How long a distance can you, or do you, want to tow your dive buddy in case of emergency?).

In any body of water where there is surface wave motion, decompression on an anchor line is not recommended. The passing of a wave overhead at a ten foot stop can change your depth by the height of the wave. A much safer situation exists when a shot line or decompression bar is suspended from mid-ship. This ensures your depth relative to the surface, eliminates anchor line jerking and provides a stable, designated decompression stop.

Another necessary item of equipment is an extra air delivery system that makes compressed air available at the ten foot stop. This may be accomplished with a hang tank and regulator assembly or by running 20-25 foot octopus hoses from a tank on board.

Let us re-emphasize the importance of a surface support station, preferably a boat equipped with all emergency equipment listed above. This not only simplifies procedures and supervision, but allows for much more efficient accident management.

Profile

Planning your dive profile should involve a little more thinking than just choosing a time and depth. Here are the guidelines:

1. Plan the dive not to exceed the Maximum Dive Time limits of the NAUI Dive Tables. These time limits are more conservative than the U.S. Navy no-decompression limits.

Figure 11.4 A weighted decompression bar is preferred over a line.

2. Make sure the profile is realistically tailored to the underwater terrain, depth and contour.

3. Select a profile that is feasible, considering your air supply and air consumption rate and your buddy's.

4. Take an underwater slate with you, with your primary and contingency profiles written out.

5. Dive your plan.

6. Do the deepest part of your dive first and work progressively upward.

7. Allow both time and air to make a slow controlled ascent rate with safety stops.

8. Perform a precautionary decompression stop at a depth of 15 feet for at least three minutes at the end of every dive.

Emergency Preparedness

Due to the increased risks in deep diving, a fine-tuned emergency procedure is necessary. After all, your life may depend on it. Doing your deep dives through organized courses, PRO-Facility outings or NAUI DREAM Resorts, supports you with highly trained professionals and a fine-tuned emergency procedure. Here's what to look for:

1. Trained professional staff—currently certified Divemasters and/or instructors with current Dive Rescue, CPR and first aid training specialized in diving-related problems.

2. Rescue equipment, including O_2 kit, first aid kit, backboard, etc.

3. Communication equipment which may include UHF radio, CP radio, telephones to alert medical support, if necessary.

4. Information and an access plan for evacuation of a victim to the nearest chamber.

5. Transportation by boat and/or vehicle—car, truck, ambulance for evacuation.

Remember—good accident management is no accident. It take a serious amount of training, experience, and dedication to produce competent, efficient emergency procedures. Your piece of mind is worth a few extra dollars on the cost of your diving to dive with professionals.

Potential Hazards

When, for various reasons, things do not go according to plan during a deep dive, you need to be prepared to deal with decompression-related problems that may occur. Five such problems are listed below along with instructions for dealing with them.

1. Emergency Decompression: If the no-decompression limits are unintentionally exceeded, it is recommended that you perform a precautionary decompression stop for three minutes at a depth of 15 feet.

2. Omitted Decompression: The U.S. Navy procedure for omitted decompression, which involves recompressing the diver in the water, is no longer a viable option. In-water decompression has been eliminated as an acceptable procedure based upon recommendations by noted physicians and physiologists. If required decompression is missed, remain out of the water, rest, breathe 100% oxygen, drink fluids, and be alert for signs and symptoms of decompression sickness. If bends are suspected, proceed at once to the nearest hyperbaric facility for medical examination and possible recompression. In-water decompression does not eliminate bubbles once they have formed and can make the situation much worse than it would otherwise be. A bent diver requires medical attention and recompression in a controlled, air environment.

3. Rapid Ascent Rate: If, for some reason, your rate of ascent is too fast and you are able to arrest it at a depth greater than 20 feet, simply pause for the estimated length of time it should have taken

you to reach that depth if ascending at the proper rate. If an uncontrolled ascent takes you all the way to the surface from a depth greater than 30 feet and you feel no symptoms of decompression sickness upon surfacing, re-descend at once and carry out the procedures for omitted decompression.

4. Cold or Strenuous Dives: If a dive is particularly cold or strenuous, use the next longer bottom time schedule. If a dive is cold and strenuous, use the next greater depth and bottom time schedules.

5. Instrumentation Failure: If your instrumentation providing information about your decompression status fails, you should ascend to a depth shallower than 30 feet and then perform precautionary decompression appropriate for your best estimate of your decompression status. If, to the best of your recollection, you are well within the no-decompression limits, a simple precautionary stop may suffice. If, on the other hand, you are uncertain about your decompression requirements, extended decompression is recommended. The more nitrogen you feel you have, the longer the precautionary decompression should be. After surfacing, diving activities should be terminated for the day.

There have been several references to the increased risks involved with deep diving. Let's take a look at what they are and how to minimize them.

Effects of Increased Pressure

The obvious effects of increased pressure are that increased exposure to higher ppN_2 can cause decompression sickness and/or narcosis. The risk of decompression sickness will be minimized greatly by staying above 130 feet and planning your dives conservatively to within the no-decompression limits. More subtle, but nonetheless important, minimizing factors include common sense things like getting a good nights sleep, eating a good breakfast, and drinking plenty of fluids (non-alcohol).

Insufficient Experience

This is a major factor in diver distress situations for deep diving in the Caribbean. Whether the insufficient experience is due to lack of mastery of basic skills or infrequent diving activities, this problem manifests itself in overweighting ("gotta have enough to get down"); lack of buoyancy control ("gotta wear these knee pads"); and lack of equipment familiarity. These most common hazards can be minimized by your participation in ongoing continuing education programs and organized diving activities. Owning your own equipment will also minimize these hazards.

Increased Stress

There is an increased amount of stress on divers during deep dives. These situations create a task-loading, which may include some combination of the following:
1. Lack of familiarity with dive environment.
2. Lack of familiarity with dive buddy.
3. Lack of familiarity with dive equipment.
4. More exact time limit.
5. More exact depth profile.
6. More gauges to watch.
7. Effects of narcosis.
8. Less available light.
9. Extra tasks like photography.
10. Anxiety about air consumption.
11. Unexpected currents/changing weather.
12. Use of more sophisticated equipment.
13. Greater buoyancy fluctuation.

This task loading can be minimized with proper planning and participation in a comprehensive deep diving course, which intentionally and gradually exposes you to greater depths, more refined procedures and increased task loads.

Another related hazard which results from a combination of task loading and possibly some narcosis, is a lowering of diver awareness levels. Increased stress build-up can result in both mental and perceptual narrowing.

Diver Ego

This last and potentially most serious hazard is often the most difficult to perceive and control. Novice and experienced diver alike can be affected by this hazard. It can lead to unnecessary risk-taking and/or errors in judgment. The best way to minimize it is to participate in organized diving activities, under the good judgment of diving professionals. In such programs, trained professionals have a responsibility to control dives for maximum safety and enjoyment.

Procedures

You've followed the map through the various steps of deep dive planning. Now, you are ready to go for a ride in our (modified for deep diving) wrap-around underwater vehicle.

Preparation and Procedures

1. Review environment for any last minute changes in weather or water conditions. (It really helps to have someone familiar with the site to advise you.)
2. Confirm buddy, support personnel and their state of readiness.

Figure 11.5 Be prepared in all ways for deep dives.

3. Check all equipment for last minute adjustment and full functioning.
4. Review dive plan and hand signals with buddy and divemaster.
5. Confirm emergency procedure plans. Be sure proper equipment is present and functioning. Check to see that channels of communication are open and functioning.

During the Dive

1. Dive your plan.
2. Frequently monitor instrumentation for time, depth and air supply.
3. Continuously confirm site orientation and location of surface support station.
4. Drive carefully—reef bound fender benders may only scratch your equipment, but they can destroy hundreds of years of coral growth.
5. Follow the dive guide—they know where the neat stuff is.
6. Take only pictures. Leave only bubbles. Removing wreck artifacts, coral or shells leaves less for others to see.
7. Use a slower than normal ascent rate and follow ascent instructions from your dive computer.
8. Make a precautionary stop at 15 feet for three minutes at the end of every dive.

Post Dive Checklist

1. Log dive with buddy and divemaster.
2. Replace fluids and warm up in the sun.
3. Check with buddy on how you feel.

DIVER RESCUE

12

By Dennis Graver NAUI #1103L

Thus far in your diving education you have learned to surface an unconscious diver and to administer in-water artificial respiration. You have been encouraged to acquire the skills of first aid and cardio-pulmonary resuscitation (CPR), and you have learned the basics of first aid for various diving maladies and injuries. You need to know more and be able to do more in order to respond to and manage diving accidents. This section will increase your knowledge of rescue and accident management techniques, but you will need to complete the NAUI Dive Rescue Techniques course to develop the skills needed in the event of a diving emergency.

Rescue Techniques

A RESCUE is the prompt act of removing a person from imminent danger. A rescue begins when a danger to an individual is recognized and ends when the person has been freed from the situation. As applied to diving, a rescue usually ends when a victim has been removed from the water. At that point, first aid and accident management begin.

Problem Detection

The ability to identify a dangerous situation as early as possible is invaluable. Seconds saved via early detection of a problem can save a life. Whether you are in the water, aboard a boat or on shore, be alert for signs of distress.

When you are in or under the water, the following signs may indicate an imminent rescue situation:

1. Shallow, rapid breathing (continuous bubble trail).
2. Upright position with pumping knee action and "dog-paddling" hand and arm movements.
3. Quick, jerky, fumbling movements.
4. Wide, fright-filled eyes.
5. Mouthpiece abandonment.
6. Bolting for the surface.

If you are observing divers at the surface while out of the water, watch for the following signs:

1. Treading high in the water with no air in the BC.
2. Abandonment of mask and mouthpiece.

Figure 12.1 Diver in Distress

3. Lack of response to signals or verbal communications.
4. Chin barely above water and gasping.

An interesting note is that divers in distress at the surface seldom call out for help or signal for assistance.

Rescue Preparation

You can't simply jump into the water and go to the aid of a distressed diver when you recognize a dangerous situation. The better prepared you are to effect a rescue, the greater your chances of success. The following ways in which you can be prepared should be carefully considered:

1. Have the recommended dive rescue techniques training.
2. Don enough equipment to be able to rescue a diver. The minimum recommended equipment consists of mask, snorkel, fins and—if a thick exposure suit is worn—a weight belt so you can descend if necessary.
3. Take some flotation with you that can be extended to the person in distress. A BC, a life preserver, a surface float, or even a cooler chest are good examples of items you can carry along.
4. Instruct nearby divers to don scuba gear and follow you on the rescue attempt. If the victim should sink and you are not able to reach him or her,

the scuba divers right behind you could reach the victim quickly.

5. Instruct nearby observers to point to the victim's location continuously and to help guide you to him or her.

6. Instruct a nearby observer to standby to summon medical assistance if needed and to make ready the emergency equipment.

Entry and Approach

Enter the water in such a way that allows you to maintain visual contact with the victim. Swim with your head above water so you can keep the victim in sight. Using your arms to swim may make keeping your head up easier. Swim quickly, but not as fast as you can, or you will experience a severe oxygen debt just about the time you need to assist the person in distress. Pace yourself and conserve energy for the actual rescue.

As you approach the diver in distress, quickly assess the situation. Your goal is to get the diver buoyant. If you can get the victim to establish buoyancy, that is the best action; but if the victim is panicky, cooperation is unlikely. The next best course of action is to extend flotation to the person in distress. If this cannot be done, position yourself behind the victim and establish buoyancy by inflating the diver's BC or ditching his or her weight belt. As a last resort, make yourself buoyant and make contact with the victim.

Figure 12.3 Inflation of another diver's BC should be done from behind.

If it appears a diver is on the verge of exhaustion and is not buoyant, do not delay in your approach. Make contact as soon as possible and establish positive buoyancy. Do everything possible to prevent the diver from losing consciousness and sinking.

If the victim does sink before you reach him or her, swim to the spot where the person disappeared from view, then surface dive straight down and try to reach the victim. If you are unsuccessful, surface, look for others to assist you, call for assistance, and try again. Without wasting time, try to take a "fix" on your exact location while you are catching your breath between dives.

Assists

If you go to the aid of a diver in distress and are successful in getting the diver buoyant, your work will be much easier. Only two additional steps are involved:

1. Get the diver to rest, breathe deeply, and recover. Do not insist that the diver breathe through a snorkel or regulator until they have overcome their respiratory distress.

2. Assist the diver to shore or boat. Use the transport techniques you learned in your previous diver training courses. Maintain eye-to-eye contact with the person you are assisting and reassure them periodically.

Figure 12.2 Extending buoyancy to a distressed diver is often all that is required to prevent a panic situation.

DIVER RESCUE

Recovering a Submerged Victim

The paramount concern for an unconscious, non-breathing diver underwater is to get the individual to the surface. Establish buoyancy on the victim any way you can and get the person up. Not only is it is not necessary to tilt the victim's head back during the ascent, you may actually make the situation worse by forcing water that is in the mouth into the throat. Expanding air will escape from an unconscious person regardless of the head position. It is only difficult to get air into a person who is unconscious.

In-Water Artificial Respiration

Get the victim buoyant and in an horizontal position at the surface. Call for help. If the person is wearing a wet suit and the weight belt has been discarded, additional buoyancy may not be required at this point. Avoid excessive inflation of the victim's BC. This often interferes with your efforts to ventilate the victim.

Remove the victim's mask and your mask. Open the victim's airway and listen for breathing. Often this action is all that is required to allow a diving victim to breathe on their own. If the person is not breathing, turn his or her head toward you, drain any water from the mouth, look and feel to make sure the mouth and throat are clear, and begin artificial respiration, which consists of two full breaths initially, then one breath every five seconds. If you are wearing a weight belt, it should be discarded at the first opportunity after the victim is at the surface and buoyant.

Do everything possible to keep water from entering the victim's mouth and nose. Position your back to surface chop, use mouth-to-nose rather than mouth-to-mouth ventilations if the water is not calm, and cover the victim's mouth and nose if a wave passes over him or her.

In-water artificial respiration is very demanding. You will approach exhaustion in a very few minutes unless you make yourself buoyant and remain as low in the water as possible.

Rotate the victim's head slightly toward you, then tread higher in the water only during inflations. Lower yourself back into the water and rest as much as possible between breaths.

Resuscitation

RESUSCITATION is the combination of external cardiac compressions and artificial respiration. CPR cannot be performed in the water. If you suspect cardiac arrest, transport the victim to the shore or boat as quickly as possible while continuing ventilations, remove the victim from the water, and place him or her on a firm surface; then commence CPR.

Figure 12.4 When surfacing an unconscious diver, the most important consideration is getting the diver to the surface.

Figure 12.5 In-water artificial respiration. The rescuer opens airway, to see that the mouth and throat are clear, and simulates ventilations by sealing on the cheek of the victim.

Equipment Removal

If the distance to the shore or boat is only a few yards, do not concern yourself with equipment removal until you are in contact with the bottom or the boat. If you must transport the victim a considerable distance while performing artificial respiration, the following suggestions should be kept in mind:

Figure 12.6 Equipment removal is accomplished in small steps between ventilations.

1. Weight belts and masks are removed first.
2. If you are wearing a scuba tank, it should be removed as soon as possible because it pulls down and back when you administer in-water artificial respiration.
3. Removal of the victim's scuba unit is affected by several factors. Is it the only source of buoyancy? How far do you need to transport the victim? How easy is it to get the unit off, and can you do it alone without interrupting ventilations?
4. Your fins should be removed only when you can stand in shallow water or are in contact with a boat.

Removing the Victim from the Water

One of the most difficult aspects of diver rescue is getting an unconscious, non-breathing victim out of the water with the minimal interruption of artificial respiration. The techniques are as numerous as the situations. Different procedures are needed for shallow, sloping beaches, surf exits, deep water shore exits, piers and wharfs, and boats. You will learn various egress methods in your NAUI Dive Rescue Techniques course, but for now you should give some thought to how you could accomplish this for the situations in which you dive.

Accident Management

When an unconscious, non-breathing diver has been removed from the water, initiate first aid procedures and manage the accident if you are the most qualified person to handle the situation.

First aid procedures are presented elsewhere in this section.

Accident management involves many actions. Here is a partial listing of possible tasks that need to be handled:

1. An accounting must be made of all divers involved in the diving activities. Divers need to be recalled and a roll call taken.
2. Locate the victim's buddy as soon as possible. If he or she cannot be found, have a search conducted immediately in the area where the first victim was recovered.
3. Control the group and any observers.
4. Assign someone to summon medical assistance, to give information on how they can be reached if additional information is needed, to

Figure 12.7 Sub-surface weight belt removal is a good method of establishing buoyancy for a panicky diver.

report when aid has been summoned, and to then stand by the phone or radio in the event of a call for additional information.
5. Station someone to meet and direct emergency medical personnel traveling to the scene.
6. Assign someone to keep a time log of all activities and events.
7. Assign someone to locate the victim's identification and any medical history or medical alert information.
8. Monitor the victim continuously, even if he or she regains consciousness and indicates a feeling of well being.

Figure 12.8 Techniques for landing a victim.

9. Assign someone to prepare a list of all witnesses to the accident. The list should include names, addresses and phone numbers.

10. Secure the victim's equipment. Do not test the gear. Turn off the air, but do not remove the regulator from the tank. Rinse the equipment with fresh water and hold it for release to the proper authorities.

As you can see by now, there are many things to manage during a diving accident. If you are administering first aid, the task of accident management is even more difficult. Try to identify trained and qualified individuals who can administer first aid to the victim while you manage the situation.

You should also be acutely aware by now that additional training is essential in order to effectively perform the rescue of a diver, administer first aid, manage the accident, and coordinate the evacuation of the victim. Only the fundamentals of these topics have been addressed in this section. Get the recommended training so you will be prepared. Know what to do, how to do it, and decide in advance that you will act if an accident occurs.

BOAT
DIVING

By Eric Hanauer NAUI #3318

Boats are an integral part of diving. In pursuing this activity, you are likely to encounter any type and size of dive boat, from a tiny inflatable all the way up to a luxurious live-aboard. All dive boats have certain elements in common, along with some basic differences. Techniques used to dive from them can vary as well.

You can dive from almost any boat, but some are better dive boats than others. What do you look for in a dive boat? Basically, they all share three elements: deck space, stability, and power. Diving is an equipment-intensive sport, and all that gear has to go somewhere. Furthermore, people need room to set up tanks and suit up. A well laid-out inflatable or runabout can be better than a cabin cruiser if the larger ship lacks sufficient deck space. Diving activities also require a stable platform. Too much rock and roll is detrimental to tanks as well as people. Finally, it takes a strong engine to effectively move any heavily loaded vessel. This doesn't necessarily require top speed, but power. Dive boats can be considered the "pickup trucks" of the boating world.

In this section we will examine the different types of dive boats, and discuss techniques appropriate to each. There is a bit of overlap and, to avoid repetition, procedures common to all boats will be covered in the final section on charter boats. Techniques unique to a certain type will be covered in the section for that type.

Inflatables

Don't confuse inflatable boats with rubber rafts. Today's inflatable is a high-performance boat, as safe and rugged as any comparably sized hard-hull craft. They are easily stored in limited space, transportable in small vehicles, and require less fuel than hard-hull boats of the same size. When the oil crisis hit the United States — along with the trend toward smaller cars and smaller homes — sales of these vessels took off. It wasn't long before Asian manufacturers came in to pick up a piece of the action. As a result, divers today have a wide — sometimes confusing—choice of inflatable boats, at very competitive prices.

What should a diver look for in an inflatable boat? First, some sort of hard floor and a keel are necessary. Soft, fabric-floored boats are intended primarily as dinghies or tenders, and will not stand up to the abuse of diving. They accept only small engines, which would be hard pressed to move the extra weight of diving equipment.

Figure 13.1 Boat diving can provide new worlds of underwater adventure.

Always look with skepticism at advertised carrying capacity. Rated capacity should be cut by 40 to 50 percent where divers are involved. If a boat is rated for eight passengers, it will accommodate four to five divers with equipment. An inflatable should be at least 11 feet long to accommodate two divers. Boats from 11 to about 14 feet are easily transportable or can be carried and assembled by two persons. They are usually best for offshore runs to local reefs, up to 10 miles round trip.

Fifteen to 16 footers belong in the next category. These boats are usually stored on trailers, permanently set up. They will accommodate up to six divers, and are appropriate for open water runs up to 30 miles. Anything larger than 16 feet is generally considered a commercial boat rather than a sport boat. These can be quite large. A 60-foot inflatable was built in France to carry Jacques Cousteau's Diving Saucer.

Originally, all inflatable boats were made of nylon impregnated with neoprene and hypalon.

This required a lot of hand labor in assembly. Recently, manufacturers have changed over to plastics for lower cost, greater durability, and for more automated assembly methods.

There are three types of keels for inflatable dive boats: inflatable keels, wood keels, and fiberglass hulls. Inflatable keels are light, easy to transport and set up. They are the least likely to get damaged when running over rocks or obstructions. However, they tend to bounce more in swells and wind chop, resulting in a harsher ride. Wooden keels impart a

Figure 13.2 Inflatable Dive Boat

firmer shape to the bottom material, allowing the boat to cut through chop more effectively and turn with less skidding. However, they require more care and assembly, make the boat more difficult to transport assembled, and are heavier than those with inflatable keels.

The third type of boat has a fiberglass hull, mated to inflatable tubes. They are called RIBs, or Rigid Inflatable Boats. These offer the best performance and the smoothest ride, but sacrifice two of the primary advantages of an inflatable: compact storage and light weight. Why would someone buy one of these instead of a comparable sized hard-hull boat that costs less? Performance. The light weight of RIBs results in more speed and power with smaller engines. Also, their inflatable tubes make them more stable than conventional boats, and virtually unsinkable.

Regardless of which kind of inflatable you choose, look for maximum deck space. Avoid boats with intricate consoles, seats, and remote steering that sacrifice storage capacity. All that diving gear has to go somewhere. This is an important factor to consider in any type of boat for serious divers. If this is going to be primarily a dive boat, some creature comforts may have to be traded off for deck space.

Diving procedures for inflatables are primarily the same as for any small boat. Be sure to fly a Diver's Flag; it is required when diving off any boat, regardless of size. Since space is at a premium, tanks, regulators and backpacks should be assembled before leaving the dock. Everything on deck will probably get wet, so divers should wear wet suits and boots for the trip. Anything that has to remain dry—like wallets, fishing licenses and lunch—should be packed in a waterproof container. Trim is important in any boat. Arrange passengers and cargo to balance the vessel fore and aft, as well as port and starboard. If the total weight approaches the engine's capacity, the craft might not plane until some passengers move forward temporarily. Thus crew members can serve as moveable ballast.

Upon arrival at the dive site, tanks should be put overboard, attached to a line. This will open a lot of deck space for final suiting up. A major advantage of an inflatable is its stability; more than one person at a time will be able to move around.

Entry should be a backward roll or slip-in, then don the tanks in the water. Don't forget to check the anchor on initial descent. Failure to do so could result in acute embarrassment, and a long swim if the boat slips anchor while you are underwater.

When returning to the boat after the dive, remove the tank in the water and attach it to the line. In a strong current, hook the tank to the line first, then take it off and pull yourself back to the boat. Bringing the tanks back on board should be the last thing done before the anchor is pulled.

Figure 13.3 Diving from an open boat.

Open Skiffs

Boats that are designed for fishing often make the best dive boats. Those designed for touring or water skiing are the poorest, because of reduced space and stability. Most skiffs are made of fiberglass, many with foam sandwiched between the layers to provide buoyancy. Hull design will determine the boat's riding characteristics. Flat or cathedral hulls are generally very seaworthy, but have a harsher ride due to bounce in short-interval chop. Deep vee hulls cut through the waves more smoothly, but can be less stable at anchor and, because of their higher profile, harder to board.

Welded aluminum boats with deep vee hulls are rapidly gaining acceptance, owing to their lower cost. Weight must be carefully arranged in these boats to keep the bow down, especially in high wind. Any metal boat also requires protective measures against electrolysis.

The most popular sizes for open skiffs range from 16 to 21 feet, although both smaller and larger ones are available. There is generally more room than an inflatable, but they also ride wet, so it is best to suit up before leaving the dock.

Diving procedures are almost identical to inflatables, but in some larger skiffs it may not be necessary to don tanks in the water. However, many divers prefer to remove them, along with weight belts, before climbing back on board. The outboard motor can often be an effective stepladder for climbing back in.

The engine should usually be shut off before anybody enters the water. Occasionally, however, currents, sea conditions, or lack of an anchorage make it necessary to drop off divers while the boat is moving. This is called "liveboating". The divers should be ready to exit as soon as the skipper announces arrival at the site. Then the engine is placed in neutral and, on command, the divers execute a backward roll. They should immediately swim clear of the boat to allow the skipper to move out of the area. Before returning on board, swim well clear of any shallow reefs or obstructions, because boarding will take longer than exit. The boat is vulnerable to running aground while drifting without power. Do not approach the boat until the skipper informs you that the engine is in neutral. Remove your tank, hand it to someone on the boat, then climb aboard quickly as soon as you are given the order.

Runabouts, Cabin Cruisers, and Yachts

Runabouts come in a wide variety of layouts and sizes, from 20 footers with rudimentary cuddy cabins to 28 footers (the largest size that can be trailered) with many of the amenities of home. As is the case with skiffs, boats designed for fishing generally make the best dive boats. For ease in

Figure 13.4 A good dive boat has enough room topside to prepare for the dive.

boarding, there should be no rail around the rear portion of the deck. (On larger boats with inboard engines, a step-through gate is desirable.) Most runabouts are powered by automobile engines, converted for marine use with an outdrive (referred to as an inboard-outboard). Because of their seaworthiness and greater fuel capacity, the effective range of these boats extends to over 50 miles offshore. They are dry riding, allowing divers to travel fully clothed, in comfort, to and from the dive site.

The owner will have many important decisions to make regarding deck space versus creature comforts. A bewildering array of options is available that can quickly deplete a budget. However, some are essential for a serious dive boat. These include a VHF radio (required on boats this size), a good fathometer to find the reefs, and a swim step to make it easier to get back on board. Also highly recommended are trim tabs to compensate for overweighting that is almost certain to occur (and make the ride smoother). Another desirable accessory is a LORAN navigation unit, using electronic coordinates to help you return to favorite dive spots without long fathometer runs.

Although there is more room to move about on this sort of boat, the deck has a tendency to shrink when it's time to dive. It might be necessary to dress in shifts. Even on boats this size, it usually helps to put tanks overboard before the divers suit up.

Choices in the category of cabin cruisers, yachts, and sailboats are so varied, and dive procedures so similar to charter boats, that diving from them will be covered in the next section. Because of difficulties in maneuvering and anchoring larger vessels, the actual diving on these boats is often done from tenders or skiffs. This is especially true of sailing craft.

Charter Boats and Live-Aboards

These boats can range from converted fishing boats barely longer than runabouts, all the way up to luxurious yachts of more than 100 feet. But diving procedures are essentially the same for all. Over the years, a code of "dive boat etiquette" has been developed by skippers, instructors, and crew. It is based on courtesy and respect for others. Regardless of the size of a vessel, the key to effective boat diving is cooperation. If you know the basic rules, you will feel at home on any boat anywhere, from California's Channel Islands to the Red Sea. The following is adapted from materials developed

Nick Craig photo

Figure 13.5 Live-aboards are the most luxurious form of boat diving.

by skipper Roy Hauser of Truth Aquatics, Santa Barbara, California.

Preparation: Pack your dive bag the evening before the trip, working with a checklist to make sure nothing is missing. Don't forget spare straps, o-rings, dive log, certification card, and fishing license. Make sure your equipment is marked to avoid confusing it with someone else's.

On board: Anything left on deck will probably get wet, so all non-diving gear should be stored below, in the galley or the bunkroom. Many skippers will allow wet suits to be worn in the galley, but no hard gear. In the bunkrooms, everything should remain dry. Check with the crew as to procedures on your boat.

If seasickness strikes, go up on deck and feed the fishes to the lee. Getting sick indoors—including in the head—is considered a serious breach of boat etiquette.

When it's time to suit up for diving, work with your buddy and help each other. Stake out your own area on the deck, centered around your dive bag. Always work out of your bag, taking out items only as you need them, and returning them to the bag immediately after the dive.

Never leave a tank standing unattended. If it isn't secured in a rack, it should be lying down. Never walk on a rolling deck with fins on. To avoid holding up other people at the exit gate, finish all preparation and buddy checks before heading for the gate. The fins should be the last things to go on, and this is done just before entering the water.

Entry: One of the hardest concepts for some divers to grasp is that a boat at anchor is a moving platform. Many live-aboards have high profiles and are extremely sensitive to the wind. At anchor, they will swing in a very predictable arc. If you jump off at the wrong time, the boat can swing right over you. Many skippers will put out a swing buoy at each end of the boat's arc to use as a reference. Use the port exit while the boat is swinging to starboard, and vice versa. After the dive, wait near one of the buoys and let the boat come to you. If conditions allow, the skipper will set a stern anchor to eliminate the swinging.

After jumping in, swim away from the exit area so the next diver can follow closely behind. It's usually a good idea to descend along the anchor line. But be sure to stay about an arm's length away from the line at all times. As the boat bounces on the waves, the line will become slack, then tighten again. If you are too close, it could hook around your tank valve or other equipment and give you quite a jerk.

In the water: Many boats have an emergency underwater recall system that sounds like a police siren. If you hear it during a dive, surface as soon as it is safe, and look toward the boat for a signal to stay clear or to come aboard.

Figure 13.6 Using a line upon return.

If there is a strong current, begin your dive up-current. In case you are swept beyond the boat on return, look for the current line. This is a long line with a float at the end, trailing behind the boat. Swim for the line instead of the boat, then pull yourself back hand-over-hand, either face down or on your back. To avoid bunching up the line in front of you and becoming entangled, bring the pulling hand well past the waist before letting go.

Return: When reboarding the boat, watch the movement of the swim step as it bounces in the swells. Time your climb when the ladder or step is at its lowest point. This not only saves effort, but will prevent being hit by it coming down. Once on the swim step, remain on your hands and knees. If you sit on the step and the boat pitches or rolls, you will flop on your back, out of control. Be ready to hand your camera, game, or speargun to the crew member at the ladder. And make sure the speargun is unloaded.

Immediately after the last dive of the day, store all equipment in your gear bag. When showering, save some for the divers coming after you by making it a Navy shower. Turn off the water while you lather up, because hot, fresh water is always in short supply.

Be sure to settle up your bills before returning to port. And don't forget a deserving crew. Like most service workers, they are underpaid and depend on tips for their livelihood.

Diving from a boat opens a world of opportunities for divers. By following the suggestions outlined here, your experiences on board will be safer and more enjoyable.

BOATING & SEAMANSHIP 14

By John Kessler NAUI #3590

Expanding your diving knowledge and water skills through continuing diving educational programs will allow you to participate safely in a wider range of diving activities. One of the most rewarding of scuba activities is diving from boats.

Boat diving has many advantages. One is that you can access locations that are generally not divable from shore. Secondly, boat diving usually provides better visibility, as well as more game and plant life.

Knowledge of boats and how to operate them is an important skill for every diver. Whether you own your own boat, aspire to own one, or plan to dive from boats, the following information will give you a basic understanding about:

1. Your responsibilities operating a boat
2. Basic seamanship
3. Introduction to rules of the road
4. Anchoring and preparing for diving
5. Basic marlinspikemanship

Because no one chapter can inform you of everything you need to know to be a safe (diving) boater, the information presented here is intended primarily for small, personally owned power-driver boats. For more in-depth information, further programs and courses, contact the U. S. Coast Guard, U. S. Coast Guard Auxiliary, U. S. Coast Guard Power Squadron, and professional maritime academies.

Responsibilities

Can you operate a boat? Do you need to be a licensed captain? If you own your own boat, can you let your diving friends help pay for expenses?

There are no regulations required to operate your own boat. However, you most likely will be required to pay boat registration fees, etc.

Being a good dive buddy is an excellent prerequisite to being able to operate a boat safely. If you perform impeccable dive planning procedures, equipment, safety and pre-dive checks, you are well on your way to becoming a responsible boat operator.

Aside from being a responsible dive buddy, you are now responsible for the safety of every person (diver and non-diver) on your boat. You also become responsible for the safety of your boat and other boats around you, including swimmers, snorkelers,

Figure 14.1 A license is not required to operate a boat, but training is recommended.

surfers, sailboarders and jet skiiers. In short, you are responsible for the safety and well-being of practically everyone and everything around you.

Responsibility means your boat is properly equipped. Just as certain equipment is necessary for safe diving, specific safety equipment is required for your vessel. A personal dive boat will most likely fall into one of these classifications of motor boats: under 12 meters, or under 20 meters. The Coast Guard requires specific lighting, bells or whistles, and emergency equipment such as life jackets. (Diving buoyancy compensators do not qualify!)

You do not need to be a licensed captain to operate your privately owned recreational boat! However, the moment you take anything of value from anyone for services (compensation or reimbursement) you need to have a licensed boat operator on board at all times or be one yourself.

Anything of value can mean money: sharing fuel expenses, launching or trailer parking fees, supplying food and refreshments, buying meals, gifts, etc. When you fall into the category of having a licensed captain aboard, your boat will most likely be reclassified, be required to undergo other inspections, and need to carry additional equipment.

Basic Ship Handling

Before trying to pilot a boat, you must understand and use proper nautical terminology.

Left	Right
Port	Starboard
Red	Green
Odd*	Even *

Remembering is easy. All the larger words are
on the same side, and all the smaller words
are on the other side.
*Numbers on channel buoys.

Bow - forward section of the boat
Stern - rear section of the boat
Port - left side (facing the bow)
Amidship - middle of the boat
Forward - toward the bow of the boat
Aft - toward the stern of the boat
Galley - kitchen
Head - bathrooms

Figure 14.2

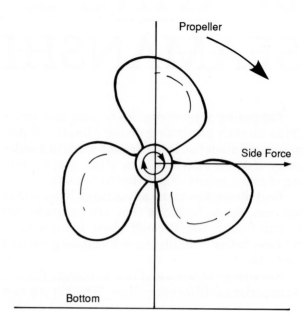

*Figure 14.3 Propeller spin causes a sideways
movement of boat.*

In order to operate and safely steer your boat,
you must have an understanding of six basic forces
that act on your boat. These forces react differently
during various speeds and conditions. The following overview and definitions of these forces will help
you become a more competent ship handler:

1. Propeller Thrust: Your boat moves forward
through the water because the pitch of the propeller creates a low pressure area in front of the
propeller and a high pressure area behind it. The
boat will move forward toward the low pressure
area.

2. Rudder Force: When you turn the rudder to
one side, a high pressure area is created on the
leading edge side of the rudder, and a low pressure
area develops on the trailing edge side. The stern of
the vessel will swing (or turn) toward the low pressure side. This is why the stern will swing to the
opposite side from which you turn the rudder.

3. Side Force: Side force is the direction your
boat moves in relation to the direction of the spin (or
rotation) of your propeller. If you have a right-
handed propeller (facing from the stern to the bow)
your propeller turns clockwise and the stern of the
boat will swing to the right. Visualize, as the propeller turns, that the tips of the blades of the propeller
"walk" along the bottom. Side force is much more
pronounced at slower speeds.

4. Pivot Point: The pivot point (where it turns)
on your boat varies with the speed and how the boat
is loaded. On most boats, the pivot point is one-third

the distance back from the bow when the boat is
moving forward.

5. Bank Cushion: When passing close or near
another boat or seawall, the bow of your vessel will
be pushed away. When moving ahead, water is
funnelled back along a narrow channel which
causes the bow to be pushed out or away. The
opposite happens in reverse.

6. Bank or Bottom Suction: As your vessel
moves forward water is pulled (or sucked) from
ahead of the propeller and discharged astern. When
you move into shallow water (a harbor or reef), a
bottom suction effect is caused and the stern of the
boat will sink lower into the water.

The above basic six forces affect your boat when
going ahead or astern, fast or slow. These forces
must be taken into account when casting off from a
dock, docking the boat, leaving and approaching
harbors and piers, and when meeting and passing
other boats.

Introduction to Rules of the Road

Without doubt, the three worst emergencies
that might occur while at sea are:

1. Collision with another vessel
2. Sinking (usually caused by #1)
3. Fire (which usually causes #2)

The purpose of this section is to learn to prevent
collision with another boat.

Similar to our freeway systems, there are specific waterway rules governing when and where

boats are allowed to maneuver. The international collision prevention regulations (abbreviated COLREGS) apply to coastal waters and the high seas. These rules were designed to prevent "risk of collision". You will find it extremely difficult to convince the Coast Guard or a judge that "risk of collision" did not exist when two vessels have collided. Ironic as it may seem, most collisions occur during daylight hours, in open seas with unlimited visibility.

Before we discuss the basic rules of the road, you need to have a basic understanding of the buoy system to insure that you enter and exit harbors safely and correctly. Basically, when coming in from sea to the harbor, the red channel buoys are kept to your right (starboard) side. The three "r's" will help you remember: red, right, returning.

Who has right of way? It is generally assumed that sailboats have right of way over power-driven vessels. For the most part, this is true. However, there are power-driven boats, due to the nature of their work or other circumstances, that have preference over sailing vessels!

Simple Collision Avoidance

1. When meeting another boat head on (bow to bow) both boats should alter course to starboard (right), if possible.

2. Crossing: The vessel ahead of you and on your starboard has right of way. You are the "give way" vessel and must slow or turn to starboard and pass behind. The "stand on" vessel should maintain course and speed.

3. Overtaking or Passing: Any boat that is being overtaken, or passed from astern, is always the most privileged. If your power boat is being overtaken by a sailboat (although embarrassing) you are the most privileged and have right of way. You must, however, maintain course and speed.

4. Day Shapes and Signal Lights: Who should you watch out for and keep well clear of? As mentioned above, certain boats, due to the nature of their work, are more privileged and, therefore, are given the right of way. Such vessels will display day shapes during daylight hours, and signal lights at night. There is a chain of command, or pecking order, for who is first, second, third and so on. (See figure 14.5.) You must stay well clear of those above you in this chain of command. Dive boats will fall into categories two and six.

Let's take a quick look at what these boats are, why they are privileged, and what day shapes and signal lights they display. Memory phrases for the signal lights will assist you in remembering these

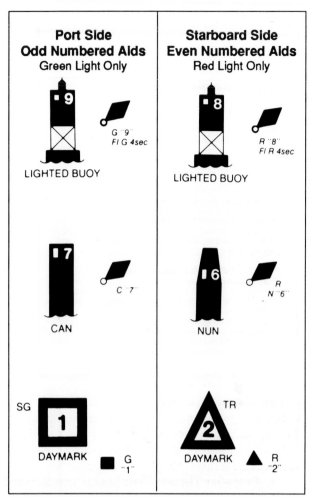

Figure 14.4 A standard system of buoys provides valuable information to boat operators.

lights. Day shapes and signal lights will be displayed on the mast.

Not Under Command

The night signal is two all-round red-over-red lights in a vertical line where they are best seen. Memory phrase: "Red over red. Should've stayed in bed". The day shape is two black balls in a vertical line.

These vessels are normally broken down in some capacity. They often have steering and or engine difficulties and cannot maneuver easily.

Restricted In Maneuverability

All-round red-white-red lights in a line. Memory phrase: "Restricted with reason". During the day, ball-diamond-ball shape sequence.

These vessels cannot maneuver easily due to the nature of their work. They include dive boats or

New Unified Rules of the Road

Rule of Good Seamanship*
Don't fail to comply with the rules or precautions governed by good seamanship or special circumstances.

General Prudential Rule*
If all else fails, the rules may be broken in order to avoid immediate danger.

CAUTION: Stay well clear of lights you don't understand.
*Now combined in "Responsibility" rule.

Steering and Sailing Rules
1. Risk of collision exists if another vessel's compass bearing doesn't change or changes very little relative to you.
2. To avoid collision: Avoid crossing ahead.
   —take early and positive action
   —make obvious course and speed changes
   —slow, stop or reverse if necessary
3. **If in doubt:** Between crossing and head-on, assume head-on; or between crossing and overtaking, assume overtaking and act accordingly.

In Restricted Visibility (Fog, Rain or Snow)
1. Proceed at a safe speed.
2. If you hear a fog signal head, slow to minimum speed or stop. Then proceed with caution unless you've determined that risk of collision does not exist.
3. If you take avoiding action based on radar:
   —take early action; avoid course changes to:
   - port for a vessel ahead except when overtaking, or
   - toward vessels abeam or abaft your abeam.

Right of Way

stand on vessel*	**maintain**	**course speed**
give way vessel		**keep well clear**

*Shall take action if give way vessel does not take timely, sufficient and appropriate action to avoid collision.

If you are: vessel below line, give way

1. Meeting head on: pass port to port.

2. Crossing: Starboard vessel has right of way over / port vessel

3. Overtaken from more than 22.5° abaft the beam / Overtaking (includes sail overtaking power)

4. sailing: starboard tack / port tack on same tack leeward / windward

5. • not under command
   • restricted in maneuverability
   • constrained by draft (international only)
   • fishing
   • sailing
   • power driven
   give way to vessels above you on this list.

6. in narrow channels vessels restricted to channel / vessels under 20 meters, or fishing or sailing

Figure 14.5

underwater operations (laying cable or pipe), aircraft carriers (launching or landing only), mine sweepers and buoy tenders.

If a tug boat is pulling a tow, it will also display a day shape and two or three white signal lights.

Deep-Drafted Vessels

The night signal is three all-round red lights in a vertical line. "Rudder rubbing rocks" is the memory phrase.

It is unlikely you will encounter a super tanker displaying a black cylinder day shape (optional) or three red lights. If you do encounter one, you'll quickly understand its right of way because of the enormous size. Deep-drafted vessels displaying day shapes and signal lights can barely manuever in the confines of a narrow channel due to their size and draft.

Fishing Vessels

While stationary and fishing, they show an all-round red-over-white light. "Red-over-white—fishing at night" is the memory phrase.

A boat with nets out behind it is considered a fishing vessel. A boat with nets dragging behind or alongside is also considered a fishing vessel. They are occupationally restricted and will display a basket (if under 20 meters) for a day shape. A fishing vessel at night will display red over white signal lights; trawlers will display green over white. A sport fishing boat that is trolling (lines behind the boat) is: 1) not occupational, 2) shows no day shape or signal lights; and, 3) deserves no preference in the right-of-way pecking order.

Sailboats

The light signal is all-round red-over-green. "Red-over-green—sailboats are seen" is the memory phrase.

You now can see that sailboats do not always have the right of way over a power-driven boat. A sailboat has the right of way over a power vessel only if she is solely under sail. If the sailboat is motoring, it should display the cone down day shape. The sailboat using her engine is now considered a power boat and treated accordingly.

Power-Driven Vessels

Recreational boaters and sailboaters constitute the greatest number of other boaters you will encounter. Unless you are being overtaken (passed from behind), you must stay well clear and give right of way to anyone higher than you are in the pecking order.

Sound and Fog Signals

Many commercial vessels communicate their intentions (turning port, starboard, backing down) by radio. Most vessels still use internationally recognized sound signals.

Flags and Signals

What should you display during day and night dives? Let's look at the rules. First, the day shapes and lights are required for vessels over 12 meters in length.

Rule 27 (E (II): A rigid replica of the international code "A" flag not less than one meter in height is to be displayed. Measures shall be taken to insure its all round visibility.

Note: The international code flag "A" is blue and white. It is not the scuba diver's red flag with a white diagonal stripe that is familiar to recreational divers and boaters. The international meaning of this blue and white code flag as found in the international code of signals is "Diver Down, Keep Clear". A rigid replica of the code flag "A" is authorized for use aboard small vessels (less than 12 meters) that may not be able to carry or display all of the required day shapes and light signals for vessels engaged in underwater operations. The other flag is not authorized by the rules. The flag must be one meter in height. Rigid replica means a wooden or metal reproduction or a flag that does not bend or flap in the breeze and would remain visible even without a breeze. All-round visibility means it can be seen from anywhere. A flag painted on your boat doesn't meet the above criteria.

Many states, however, require beach divers and boaters to use the recreational diver's red-with-white-stripe flag. Therefore, you should check your state's regulations. You may be required to fly both the code "A" flag, and the red-with-white-stripe flags.

For night boat diving, the same rules apply. However, the red-over-white-over-red signal light is best used by itself. Anytime you use your anchor light it infers that "This is a safe anchorage. Come on over here and drop your anchor on my divers' heads". If you anchor without signal lights, make sure that you:
1. Hoist your "divers down" flag(s)
2. Illuminate the flag(s)
3. Show a spotlight in the direction of the divers.

International Sound Signals Legend

Whistle

Prolonged blast four to six seconds	—
Short blast one second	•

Bell	B
Gong	G
Rapid ringing of bell five seconds	BBBBB
Rapid ringing of gong five seconds	GGGGG
Clear ringing of bell five times	▲▲▲▲▲

Restricted Visibility, Every Minute

Under 100 meters

Anchored	BBBBB
Aground	▲▲▲▲▲▲BBBBB▲▲▲▲▲

Over 100 Meters

Anchored	
Bow	BBBBB
Stern	GGGGG

Anchored	
Bow	▲▲▲▲▲▲BBBBB▲▲▲▲▲
Stern	GGGGG

Restricted Visibility, Every Two Minutes

Power vessel underway	—
Power vessel underway but not making way	— —
Limited or restricted in maneuverability	— ••

Good Visibility

Turning starboard	•
Turning port	••
Backing down	•••
Danger	•••••
Approaching a bend where visibility is obscured or Backing out of a slip, overtaking, narrow channel	—
May I go starboard?	— — •
May I go port?	— — ••
Yes	— • — •

Figure 14.6

Anchoring

Ground tackle is the broad term that includes all the gear used in anchoring. Regardless of the size of your boat, general procedures and criteria are required to safely anchor your boat. These are:

1. Water depth and bottom characteristics
2. Effects of wind and current
3. Locations of established channels and harbor entrances
4. Existing traffic patterns
5. Submarine cables and pipelines

Properly "dropping the hook" is done by slowly lowering the anchor until it has reached the bottom, letting out scope (anchor line) and slowly pulling the anchor when in reverse to insure the anchor "sets".

The three main reasons that anchors do not hold are:

1. It was dropped incorrectly causing anchor, chain and the line to tangle.
2. Not enough scope. It is recommended that you have a scope (length of line) of a minimum of five to seven times the depth of the water for ideal conditions, and a minimum of seven to nine times the depth of the water for rough weather. Ideally, the anchor and chain should lay on the bottom and pull parallel.
3. Using the wrong anchor. For the majority of recreational boats used for diving, the lightweight Danforth anchor is the most widely used and the most effective. With the proper amount of anchor line and chain, the Danforth will hold 17 to 1,000 times its weight, and in larger sizes, eight to 30 times its weight.

Anchoring and Preparing for Diving

The procedures for anchoring for diving are similar to normal anchoring. However, certain procedures must be followed to inform other boats that you have divers in the water. The proper display of flags, day shapes and signal lights protect your divers.

The best way to anchor a boat for diving is to be able to tie off to a mooring buoy which preserves the environment and saves time and energy. Unfortunately, mooring buoys are not always available.

The procedures for anchoring a dive boat are:

1. Slow down before you reach the dive site. If there are other boats in the area, they may have divers already in the water. (Everybody doesn't always fly the proper flags!) Secondly, if boating near shore, shore divers may not have a float and flag.

2. Look for bubbles before "dropping the hook" to insure it doesn't land on and injure a diver.

3. Try to anchor in the sand whenever possible. Although coral holds an anchor better, every time coral is touched by an anchor, hands, or fins, it is damaged. Preservation and conservation are important. It is highly recommended you have an anchor line buoy or float. In the event a diver gets down current and is in need of assistance, you will be able to tie off the anchor line to the float. This is faster, leaves a reference for other divers, marks the anchor, and saves precious time in recalling all of the divers and pulling the anchor. Note: This procedure must be explained to all divers, as well as whatever recall system will be used.

4. Hoist your diver down flag(s). Next, put out a trail or current line. A trail line is usually a minimum of one and one-half times the length of the boat. A float with another divers down flag on the trail line is also very useful.

5. Prepare your divers down line (divers shouldn't use the anchor line). The down line is usually located mid-ships.

6. If you are anchoring for repetitive dives and/or deeper diving (over 60 feet), put out your decompression trapezes for safety stops. An extra tank, regulator and dive tables are also recommended.

KNOTS

Perhaps the most mystifying of all the nautical skills is the tying of knots. Of the over 2,000 kinds of knots known, you can comfortably and safely get by with 11 basic knots. The ability to know which knot to tie for the proper application is an important and admired nautical skill. Your knot tying abilities are useful above as well as below the water. The following explanations of these knots describe the knot, as well as when and where to use each one.

Only practice will make you a good knot tyer. Since many of these knots are used underwater as well as above, it is a good idea for you and your buddy to practice tying these knots underwater while wearing your diving gloves.

Overhand Knot

Of little use by itself. Might be used temporarily to keep the line from unlaying or running through a block, but may jam so tight you have to cut it.

Figure Eight Knot

Better for the uses listed above. Will not jam.

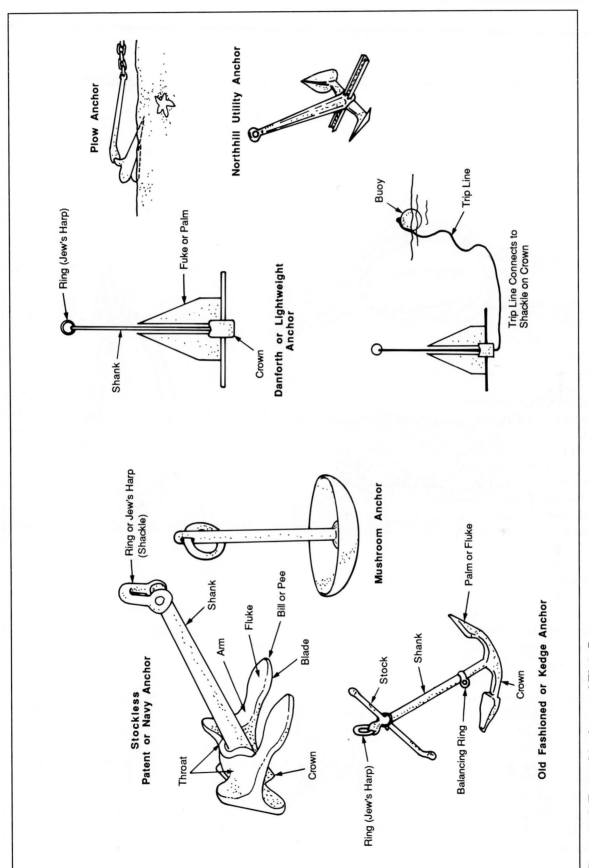

Plow Anchor

Northhill Utility Anchor

Ring (Jew's Harp)

Fuke or Palm

Shank

Crown

Danforth or Lightweight Anchor

Buoy

Trip Line

Trip Line Connects to Shackle on Crown

Stockless Patent or Navy Anchor

Ring or Jew's Harp (Shackle)

Shank

Arm

Fluke

Bill or Pee

Blade

Throat

Crown

Mushroom Anchor

Palm or Fluke

Stock

Shank

Crown

Ring (Jew's Harp)

Balancing Ring

Old Fashioned or Kedge Anchor

Figure 14.7 Types of Anchors and Their Parts

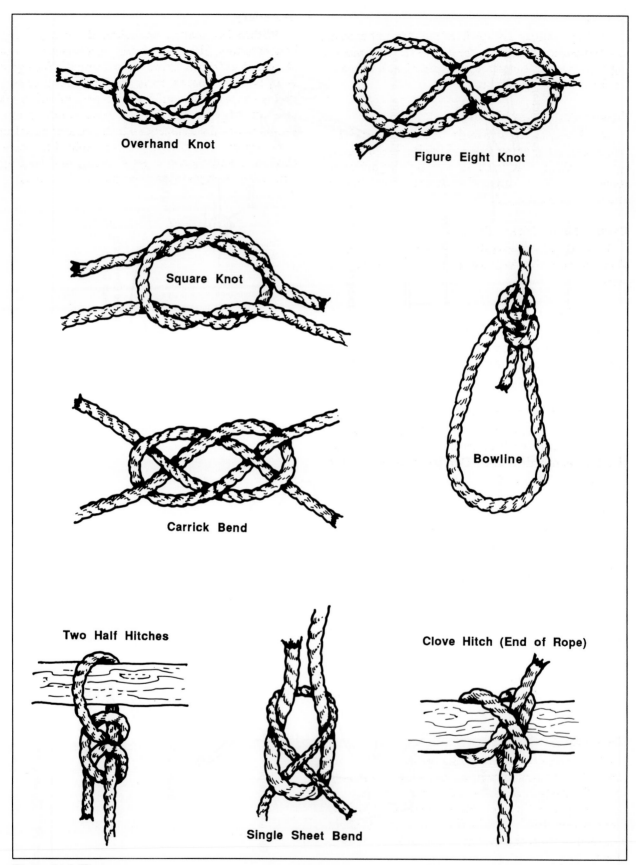

Overhand Knot

Figure Eight Knot

Square Knot

Bowline

Carrick Bend

Two Half Hitches

Single Sheet Bend

Clove Hitch (End of Rope)

Figure 14.8 Knots

Bowline

Makes a temporary eye in a line. Might be used as a temporary substitute for an eye splice in mooring line. One of the strongest, practical and most useful of knots you will use.

Square Knot (Reef Knot)

Quick way to join two ends. Is secure only if the two lines are the same size and the knot is pressing against something, such as the rolled part of a reefed sail. May "capsize" and come apart under strain if not supported.

Becket Bend (Sheet Bend)

Used to join two ends when knot must stand alone in "mid-air." Will work with lines of different sizes.

Carrick Bend

Useful for joining large lines (same size) for heavy work such as towing. Will not jam if ends are seized to standing parts. Double Carrick Bend performs the same job.

Round Turn and Two Half Hitches

Quick way to make fast to anything of any shape. Remains secure with or without strain and with strain from any direction. Can jam and be difficult for you to untie.

Clove Hitch

Quick to make and will not jam. Secure when made around cylindrical object and strain remains steady, but can loosen if standing part goes slack or strain comes from varying directions.

Rolling Hitch

Quick, secure, and adjustable. Knot can be slid along spar or line without loosening.

Bowline On A Bight

Handy if you need an eye but the ends are not available.

Sheepshank

(Theoretically) used to take up excess slack or strengthen a weak spot in a line. Will hold if very carefully made and strain is absolutely steady.

When you cut a line, you notice that it tends to come unraveled. "Whipping" is twine that is wrapped around the end of a line to keep it from unravelling.

Summary

Within the marine industry, there are many boat captains. However, there are a select few who stand out as "captains among captains." Your goal is to become known as a "diving boater among diving boaters." The information presented here is only an introduction to small boat handling and seamanship. It was intended to introduce you to the very basics. Hopefully, you will take the above challenge and continue your diving and boating education through more programs and courses.

SECTION 3
INTRODUCTION

Specialty Diving Activities

The purpose of this section is to familiarize you with various specialty activities that are not usually part of Advanced Diver training. An understanding and appreciation of the potential hazards and considerations associated with these activities is part of the knowledge that you need to have as an Advanced Diver. You need to be informed about altitude diving, drift diving, cave diving, etc.

You will find the following articles interesting and informative, and you will enjoy learning more about many interesting activities. These articles are not intended to teach you the techniques and procedures for the specialties, but are presented for orientation and introduction to the activities. Supervised, sanctioned training is strongly recommended before participating in any highly specialized aspect of diving. A wide range of specialty training is available from NAUI Instructors in your area. If the instructor who teaches your advanced course does not teach a particular specialty in which you become interested, he/she can probably refer you to an associate who does.

We hope you find gaining insight to the activities described in this section as fascinating as the authors do. Diving offers a wide range of adventure and excitement that can meet the inner needs of every diver. See what turns you on, then obtain the necessary specialty training and maximize the pleasure of diving through some never-to-be-forgotten experiences!

RIVER DIVING

TECHNIQUES

15

By George Swan NAUI #4258

Rivers throughout the world vary in size, turbidity, and in the terrain through which they flow: diving conditions will vary with the river.

As an example, the Columbia River is the longest North American river, about 1,200 miles long, flowing into the Pacific Ocean (Figure 15.1). In volume of flow, it is the second largest in the United States. Annual flows average about 200 Kcfs (thousand cubic feet per second) and range normally from about 50 Kcfs in winter months to well over 300 Kcfs during spring freshets. The Columbia River flows from its headwaters in the Canadian Rocky Mountains of British Columbia to about 450 miles down from the United States boundary. After crossing into north-central Washington, it flows 750 miles through the semi-arid Columbia River plateau, Cascade Mountains, and coastal plain to the Pacific Ocean.

Within the United States, the Columbia River is a series of reservoirs behind hydroelectric dams, with the exception of the reach from the mouth to Bonneville Dam and about 52 miles of the relatively free-flowing Hanford Reach located upstream of the confluence with the Snake River (U.S. Army Corps of Engineers 1977). Water depth in the main river channel ranges from about 10 to well over 200 feet. The current varies between near zero, in portions of the reservoirs, and over 10 fps (about six knots), in the Hanford Reach. Underwater visibility varies from zero feet, during the heavy sediment loads of the spring runoff and the algae blooms of late summer, to about 12 feet or better in the winter. Water temperature may range from the lower 30s to 70° F.

A considerable amount of recreational, commercial and scientific diving takes place year-round in the Columbia River. You can apply most or all of the diving techniques used by Columbia River divers to your particular river environment through good common sense in planning, training and preparation. With a little time and effort, additional local information can be obtained from a literature search through libraries, museums, and govern-

Figure 15.1 The Columbia River is a series of reservoirs behind hydroelectric dams.

ment offices for topographical maps, NOAA charts (if available for your area), and government publications which include depth contours, aerial photos, and depth and bottom profiles.

Figure 15.2 A large pump intake, typical of the water withdrawals found in the Columbia River Basin.

As with planning any standard dive, inexperienced divers or those unfamiliar with river diving techniques should seek the training advice and guidance that local, experienced river divers can share. Nearly all divers learn to dive in still water and acquire experience in currents later. Therefore, before making your first river dive, additional instruction by a nationally certified instructor is highly recommended. You should begin river diving in the safest and least threatening situations and take on more difficult diving tasks at a comfortable rate, gradually building your experience level. Snorkeling in slow shallow stretches of rivers or streams is not only a safe introduction to river diving, but can be a very interesting confidence builder.

Current is the most distinct characteristic of a river. Swift water can be regarded as any water where the current is running so fast that a diver cannot swim against it. Generally, fast, turbulent water indicates a shallow and rocky run, whereas a smooth, calmer appearing surface suggests deeper and slower water. The velocity of a current is usually highest in the middle or main channel of a river near the surface and lowest near the shorelines and the bottom, due to frictional resistance. Thus, the scuba diver can avoid some of the high velocities encountered by the skin diver.

Current is generally greatest at the outside of a bend in a river, and currents can be wind-aided or slowed. The velocity of a current increases when the channel becomes narrower and/or shallower.

Rivers carrying large amounts of sediment, either normally or as a result of recent rains or snow melt, will be extremely dark, in terms of light penetration. In some instances, the sun will appear only as a red glow when the diver is just under the surface and looking skyward. When ascending, use safe ascent techniques to avoid overhead objects. Other sources of reduced visibility include: algae blooms, disturbed sediments (caused by wave action or other divers), and reduced surface light due to shadows, clouds, fog or lower angle of sunlight in northern temperate zones. Diving with underwater lights in turbid waters is not of much help because the light is attenuated by the particles suspended in the water. Care must be exercised in relatively clear rivers with mud or silt deposits on the bottom. You should use a restricted kick and avoid stirring it up; position yourself so that the current will carry any clouds of sediment away from the dive site. Another difficulty in a fast-flowing stream is the blocking of light by bubbles. In or under white water, it may be almost dark. Diving in river pools and reservoirs when visibility is low can be accomplished if you move slowly and exercise caution. You will virtually feel your way. However, diving in fast current with low visibility is discouraged unless special techniques are utilized.

Most hazards found with river diving stem from the effects of currents, eddies and/or poor underwater visibility. Any river should be studied thoroughly and conditions known before the dive is planned. Log jams are a hazard, as are submerged objects such as sharp rocks, trees, limbs, old cars, barbed wire, lost or abandoned rope and cable, and the ever present monofilament fishing lines, nets, and lures and hooks. Debris tends to accumulate on the inside or at the ends of islands. A sharp diver's knife is a mandatory equipment item. You must beware of current carrying you from a deep calm run or pool into rapids or over waterfall (Balder 1968). Rapids or steep river bottom profiles are hazardous because a diver may be swept over, slammed against or between rocks or a submerged object, and sustain serious injury or be held by the current. Due to the above hazards so readily encountered in river diving, snorkel or scuba diving should never be performed alone, and ropes should never be attached to a diver's body while that person is in the water, except in special types of "elevator diving" (straight up and down diving in low current and low visibility situations). Hand-held buddy lines may be

Figure 15.3 As a river diver, you must beware of the potential for current carrying you from a deep run or pool into rapids.

Figure 15.4 Greater Wenatchee Irrigation District. An example of a water withdrawal site that is attractive to recreational divers, but may harbor many underwater hazards.

surface elevations exceed 1,000 feet above sea level.

Equipment for river diving is basically the same as that required for salt water diving, with a few exceptions and modifications. Wet suits are standard diving dress in all but the warmest waters. Dry suits are recommended for safe and efficient diving in colder waters, especially if the diver will be immersed for periods of an hour or more. Dry diving suits can also provide buoyancy and protection against sunburn and skin abrasion. A buoyancy compensator should also be worn.

used in some situations. On larger rivers, small boat, river barge, tug and even ship traffic, must be monitored and avoided. Diver-down flags, both the blue and white international alpha and the red and white recreational diver's flags should be displayed; but remember that many boaters have no idea what they mean (especially on inland waters) and may even approach them out of curiosity. A surface tender in the dive boat should accompany the divers, at a safe distance, to alert and ward off other boaters. A chase boat, to recover divers, is highly desirable on larger rivers with swift current or long surface swims. Inflatable boats are preferred by many river divers due to ease of exit and entry. Recreational divers should avoid low-head dams and water diversion structures for irrigation canals and water withdrawals such as pump intakes and siphons due to the uncertainty of approach and intake velocities and underwater structures and debris. Diving in the vicinity or immediately downstream of industrial waste water and domestic sewer outfalls could subject divers to concentrations of chemicals which may be hazardous to their health, as well as their equipment.

Most river dives are no-decompression dives. However, you should be aware that decompression tables are calibrated at sea level. Atmospheric pressure is reduced as you move to higher elevations, thus the no-decompression limits, and depths are shorter and shallower, respectively. Depth gauges should be adjustable for elevation and barometric pressure. Consult local divers or diving instructors to acquire the proficiency to determine safe diving limits and depths in areas where river

Although wet suits are standard diving dress for river diving in all but the warmest waters, dry suits make for safe and efficient diving in colder river waters when used with adequate weight. A sharp knife should be worn on the inside of the leg and possibly a spare knife on the arm. The tank pressure gauge can be held close to the body by attaching it to the shoulder strap with elastic tubing or a bungee cord. Any excess equipment prone to snag should be eliminated.

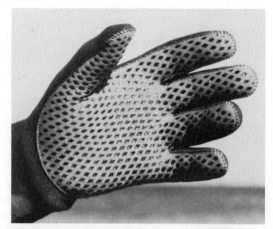

Figure 15.6 Flexible gloves provide dexterity for grasping handholds on the river bottom with less cramping of the fingers. The special surface provides a positive grip and longer wear.

Dive equipment modifications for river diving begin with removal of all excess gear, including snorkel, compass, and goody bag (unless absolutely required). All remaining equipment items that present any potential for hanging up or snagging on lines, obstacles, or the bottom, must be carefully secured. Excess portions of straps and pockets should be removed or taped. The knife should be worn on the inside of the leg (or arm). Some river divers wear a second knife on the chest or inside of the arm. Gloves should be flexible to prevent cramping and provide dexterity for grasping ropes, cables, or rocks. Textured surfaces provide a positive grip and longer wear.

A minor inconvenience in calm water, such as snagging, losing, or dropping a piece of equipment or having a weight belt come loose, can become a life threatening problem in a strong, swift current. Consequently, special precautions are required. Elastic or neoprene rubber weight belts conform to the waistline as your diving suit compresses with depth and prevent the weight belt from slipping around the body. Buckles of the wire latch design are less susceptible to accidental release from crawling on the bottom. Divers should be aware that more weight is usually required when diving in currents than in quiet water and excessive amounts of weight may be required to perform stationary diving in current. Low volume BCs produce less drag and are not as apt to snag. However, adequate buoyancy compensation to remain positively buoyant at the surface must be assured. A second quick release weight belt or special weight attachment system is sometimes used for the additional amount of weights. Masks with low volume and profile and a firm skirt will stay in position best and are less susceptible to flooding. Mask straps that cover a large area on the back of the head and can be drawn tight after donning are desirable. Use of fasteners with spring clips lacking locks is not advised. Carabineers or thumb operated clips help prevent accidental hooking or opening and loss of necessary equipment. Loss of fins can be avoided by running the fin straps through the buckles so that the ends are inside next to the foot. Fin keepers are highly recommended. The use of vented fins is not recommended because objects can pass through the vents and hold a diver.

The potential for air hoses to catch on objects is high. Regulators and tank pressure gauges require special treatment to prevent entanglement. Avoid long hoses that form loops. Small, streamlined gauges can be held close to the body by a short elastic cord attached to the tank shoulder strap. Special precautions should be used to secure octopuses or special alternate air sources. Current may cause a venturi effect across the second stage, resulting in free flow. Flooding or free flowing potentially resulting from velocity rolling back the exhaust valve may be prevented with special mouthpiece plugs.

The riverbed offers many good handholds by which the diver can maneuver from place to place. However, due to faster currents and some river bottom materials, the diver may need something to hold onto other than rocks on the bottom. One device which can help in such situations is shown in Figure 15.7. This device, referred to as a creeper, is used by lifting and moving the corners forward in alternate turns as shown; it also can serve as a diver anchor when not moving. In mild currents, a diver may move about using a weighted hand rake or claw to grip soft bottoms or a weighted bar which can be walked one end at a time.

Figure 15.7 Close-up of creeper.

RIVER DIVING TECHNIQUES

The key to diving in swift water is to strive for harmony with the water—not confrontation. In a swift current, entering the water can be difficult. If practical, enter the water at an area of shoreline protected from the current and remain close to the bottom, swimming against the current to approach a particular underwater site; the return swim, with the current, will relieve some of the fatigue acquired during the dive. From a boat, one technique for entering relatively clear, swift water is to attach a line to the anchor with a handle (similar to those used by water skiers) on the other end. The diver can grasp the handle end and, with appropriate changes in body position, can descend letting the current do most of the work. Descent also can be made using the anchor line, but this requires considerably more effort.

Where there is considerable surface current, diving in large holes may be done by dropping directly to the bottom. At some distance below the surface, the diver may be surprised to find either no current or one going slightly toward the head of the hole.

If caught in unusually strong currents, relax and ride with it while swimming diagonally toward shore or boat, much the same as dealing with a rip current. Multiple and easily identifiable exit points must be available for swift water dives. (A pick up boat simplifies this task.) Set a cutoff point of remaining air for terminating the dive. You must face downstream, or perpendicular to the current, in order to see hazards and respond accordingly. It is possible to stop by ducking in out of the current behind current breaks, but dive buddies must have ample warning or rapid separation of divers is imminent.

Diving in swift rivers can be classified in two categories: 1) Drifting with the current or "free running", or 2) Remaining stationary to complete a work task or observation. Drift diving or free running with the currents can be a very rewarding experience because you can cover a large distance with a low expenditure of energy and air supply. Stationary diving in currents is the most exhaustive form of river diving, as you must not only maintain position in the current while overcoming the tremendous forces applied to you by the water velocity, but also expend energy to complete the work task.

If you observe fish in high velocity rivers and streams, you will note that they only venture out into the fast currents for short periods of time, but mostly stay in the low velocity areas found close to the bottom and behind a current break such as a large rock. A descent line attached to the bottom will enable the diver to arrive on the bottom at a known location. Lateral or up or downstream movements can be facilitated by laying cables or lead-core ropes on the bottom. Ropes that can float up from the bottom are entanglement hazards. Prior to entering the water, all excess air should be removed from the BC and/or the dry suit to enable rapid descent through the current to the bottom and to avoid being hampered by excess buoyancy. Unwanted buoyancy in this situation requires ex-

DIVING SLEDS

A two-diver maneuverable sled complete with a "watershield" (the counterpart to a windshield) that deflects the velocity away from the divers, allowing them to remain in high currents for longer periods of time with less stress and fatigue.

The "cockpit" of a two-diver sled. The observer lies prone on the starboard side and grasps a solid handle while the pilot occupies the port side and operates the controls.

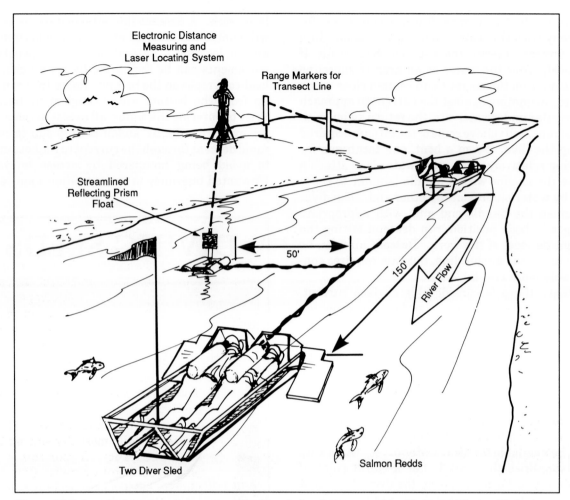

Electronic Distance
Measuring and
Laser Locating System

Range Markers for
Transect Line

Streamlined
Reflecting Prism
Float

50'

150'

River Flow

Two Diver Sled

Salmon Redds

*Figure 15.8 A typical two-man maneuverable dive sled technique used by National Marine Fisheries
Service research divers to survey salmon spawning in the Columbia River.*

tra energy expenditure to stay down out of the current. You must keep your head down in high currents to prevent excess drag on mask and body.

Research and search and recovery divers have employed various types of towed sleds in rivers. The sleds have varied from relatively simple designs, such as an aquaplane (Miller 1979), a board that, when tilted downward or sideways provides a dynamic thrust to counter the corresponding pull on the towing line, to complex, such as a two-place maneuverable sled. Especially with these techniques, divers operating the sleds must avoid abrupt changes in depth. There should be two crew members in the tow-boat; a boat operator and a lookout/tender to watch for boat traffic, the surfacing divers, and to keep the tow-line from fouling in the boat propeller. In rivers with considerable current, the sleds are not actively towed, but trailed in the current from the tow-boat and maneuvered by the divers.

Rivers offer a wide variety of possibilities for diving activities. Observations of fish and other aquatic life can be very exciting and interesting when viewed firsthand in the natural underwater environment, especially during spawning seasons. Gold dredging can be an adventuresome and sometimes rewarding hobby, but check on laws and regulations before trying it. Throughout history man has been attracted to inland waters. He camped and built his settlements on the riverbanks; therefore, rivers became one of man's primary dumping grounds. Thus, it is possible to find historically valuable artifacts.

River diving safety considerations are considerable, but not insurmountable. The keys to safe river diving are training, progressive experience, good physical fitness and common sense. To some extent, a diver's instinct is the best regulator.

DRY SUIT DIVING

TECHNIQUES

16

By Steven Barsky NAUI #2076

If you haven't been trained to use a dry suit properly, it is unrealistic to assume that you can make one work. Without training, you will probably find a dry suit to be uncomfortable and possibly dangerous. Dry suits are not difficult to use but proper instruction in the correct techniques is essential.

There are many contrasts between wet suits and dry suits and their use. Most divers are surprised at the ease of dressing into a dry suit compared to a full quarter inch wet suit. On the surface, a dry suit is much more comfortable during cold, rainy weather than a wet suit. On hot days, however, a dry suit can rapidly become too warm topside, and divers must be careful not to overheat.

By design, wet suit material is very buoyant, while most dry suit material has no buoyancy. If your suit is damaged to the point where it will not hold air, you must regain positive buoyancy by ditching your weight belt and inflating your buoyancy compensator.

Wet suits are only effective over a narrow temperature range. Modern dry suits can be used over a wide temperature range by varying the amount of insulation worn beneath the suit itself. A single dry suit can actually be used in every environment requiring exposure protection, from the tropics to the Antarctic.

Although dry suits create more drag than wet suits, due to their greater surface area, your bottom time per dive will be longer. You will also be capable of more dives per day in a dry suit due to less fatigue from the effects of cold water.

Figure 16.1 Proper instruction in use of your dry suit is essential.

While dry suits require higher maintenance than wet suits, to keep wrist and neck seals in optimal condition, the life of a dry suit usually far exceeds that of a wet suit. Wet suits suffer loss in insulating capacity after approximately 300 dives. Dry suits suffer no loss in insulating capacity due to diving activity.

Finally, while the risk of a loss of buoyancy control is high for an untrained diver in a dry suit, actual buoyancy control is much more precise for the experienced dry suit diver. Dry suit divers can hover horizontally, upright, or inverted with more control than wet suit divers can ever achieve. Think of your dry suit as an envelope of air which surrounds your body. This volume of air allows very precise buoyancy adjustments.

Figure 16.2 With the minimum volume of air in your dry suit, it's easy to right yourself from an inverted (upside down) position.

The most important safety aspect of dry suit diving is understanding the concept of minimum suit volume/minimum weight. Don't make the common mistake of wearing too much weight with your dry suit. Extra weight must be neutralized by adding a large column of air to the suit. The excess air inside the suit will not create a problem as long as you remain in the head up or horizontal position underwater. However, if you turn upside down,

either intentionally or accidentally, the air in your dry suit will rush to your feet and can make it difficult to recover to a "heads-up" posture if you have not been trained in this technique. Since most dry suit exhaust valves are located on the upper torso of the suits, you can't vent air from the feet.

If you are properly weighted and invert, recovery to a normal swimming attitude poses no problem. If you are positively buoyant and invert, this is not an emergency unless you allow yourself to get out of control. There are several methods used to return to an upright position. Recovery with slight positive buoyancy requires you to tuck your body into a ball and roll to upright. Greater buoyancy demands a concentrated effort to swim hard towards the bottom, compressing the air trapped in the suit, and either pushing off the bottom with your hands or bending at the waist to re-establish a normal heads up posture. Once you have salvaged this situation, immediately vent your dry suit to prevent any further unwanted ascent.

To compensate for additional weight acquired during a dive (such as for lobsters or abalone), air should be added to your buoyancy compensator, not your dry suit. Upon ascent, both your dry suit and BC must be vented as the air inside them expands. This procedure requires coordination and should be practiced under the supervision of a diving instructor. Heavier objects, such as anchors, should only be raised with lift bags.

A dry suit diver in a vertical upright position will experience a pressure differential between his neck and feet which may be as much as two psi., depending upon his/her size. This is known as an "under-pressure". As air migrates to the upper part of your suit, it can create uncomfortable pressure on the carotid artery. Use your BC during surface swimming, and vent all of the air from your dry suit to avoid unnecessary pressure on your neck. You may also consider wearing additional insulation from the waist down if you are an underwater photographer and spend much of your time kneeling on the bottom. This added layer of insulation will compensate for the compression and loss of warmth experienced with a single layer of underwear.

Another potential dry suit emergency which might be encountered is an inflator valve stuck in the open position. The simplest method to deal with this problem is to disconnect the inflator hose, the same way you would your BC power inflator.

In the event your dry suit exhaust valve jams shut, air can be exhausted from your suit through the neck seal or the wrist seals. Of course, if this action is taken you will get wet. If you become

DRY SUIT DIVING

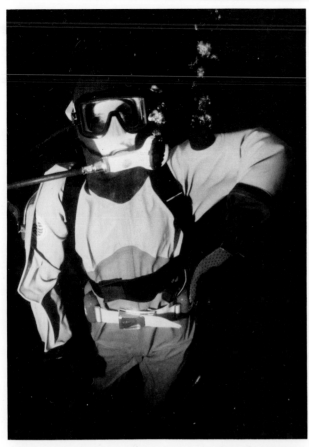

Figure 16.3 Your dry suit should be equipped with an automatic exhaust valve.

positively buoyant and are unable to regain control of your ascent, "flare" your body to create drag and slow your movement through the water.

Small leaks of water into your dry suit will not normally require you to terminate your dive unless the water temperature is so cold it causes you to be very uncomfortable. Most leaks are due to "diver error", such as a failure to tuck the neck seal properly, rather than damage to the suit itself. It is very rare for a dry suit to completely flood and fill with a large volume of water. Most leaks do nothing more than make the underwear damp.

Dry suit diving will extend your diving season and add immensely to your diving pleasure. If more instructors would teach divers to use dry suits properly, there would be far fewer drop-outs due to cold water discomfort.

Figure 16.4 In the event of the loss of buoyancy while wearing a dry suit, ditch your weight belt and inflate your buoyancy compensator to return to the surface.

By Marcel Lachenmann NAUI #2024L

Why Go Ice Diving?

The usual responses to your announcement of going ice diving are either "WHY?" or "ARE YOU CRAZY?"

There are three basic and sane reasons for ice diving:

First is the clarity of the water. The reduced sunlight and the lack of turbulence combine to produce water clarity that might approach the Caribbean or Florida springs. If you are a photographer, you will get to desire rather than dread winter.

Second is the availability of the diving. If you lack the finances and/or the time to travel, ice diving is the only alternative to giving up diving during the winter.

Third is the distinct thrill and romance of ice diving. Imagine the response as you discuss your weekend adventure. Ice diving allows you to be an astronaut on earth...when was the last time you were able to walk across the ceiling?

The argument that the water is too cold does not apply, since the temperature of northern inland water below 40 feet is constant year round. The major differences in ice diving are the air temperatures and that you do not have the option of surfacing at just any location.

Organization of An Ice Dive

Ice diving is a team sport. For safe ice diving you should have a minimum of 6 people. Two are the initial divers, two are safety divers, and two are line tenders. Positions may be exchanged if exposure does not compromise safety.

Ice and Its Inherent Problems

A true ice dive occurs when the ice is both thick enough to prevent you from surfacing and can support your line tenders and safety team. Ice that is about 1" (2.5cm) thick is difficult to break through from beneath; but it is inadequate to support persons on the surface. A minimum of 6" (15cm) is desirable. Before you venture out onto the ice, you should use an auger or ice pick to check the thickness. ICE IS THICKEST NEAR SHORE and thus should be more than 6" before venturing out on the ice. Also, you should realize that current will thin

Figure 17.1 Ice diver about to enter.

the ice. You must exercise special care when diving in lakes that have a flowage.

Once you have determined the ice is safe, move your hole cutting equipment out to the dive site. A toboggan or sled is very helpful at this point. As you walk out onto the ice, you may hear cracking. This is especially true if the temperature is quite low. The ice is contracting with the cold and cracking. It is unnerving, but not dangerous with sufficient thickness.

Cutting the Hole

The shape of the dive hole should be triangular. The only easy way to get a somewhat circular hole is to have a heavy buddy walk on thin ice. A rectangle has four sides to cut. A triangle has 1 less side than a rectangle and thus saves considerable time and effort in the cutting effort. Also, the sharper angles (less than 90 degrees) make it easier for you to pull yourself out of the water.

Figure 17.2 Cutting the ice with a chain saw. Notice the water surfacing during the cut.

The actual cutting of the hole depends upon what type of equipment you have available. The slowest method is with an ice pick, the fastest is with a chainsaw. Some divers have been able to purchase old hand ice saws. . . used to harvest ice in the winter for use in summer. Most divers today use chain saws. In addition to the usual precautions when using a chain saw, you should make your individual cuts as deep as possible without cutting through the ice. When you penetrate the ice, the cuts will fill with water and the saw will throw it up. You should have waterproof clothing on at this point. You should also auger three holes at this time. . . two into the block and one about eight feet from the triangle. You now have a problem of disposal.

Ice is both heavy and buoyant. For a six-foot triangle, consider the following figures (rounded off to units):

ICE THICKNESS	WEIGHT OF BLOCK	BUOYANCY FORCE
.5 ft.	442 lb.	40 lb.
2.0	1769	159
3.0	2653	239

Obviously you cannot lift out the block, so you will need to push it under the ice. Once under the ice, the block is very easy to push about. . . unfortunately, too easy. It could move back into the hole and imprison you under the ice!

One hole in the block and in the surface ice are lined up and a rope with a stick attached is pushed through. This will serve both as an anchor and as a point to attach your guide ropes.

The second hole in the block allows you to put a line in the block so that you can pull it back at the end of the dive. A large open hole on a lake is courting disaster for snowmobilers and others. You will not have much difficulty in pulling the block back, as it melted during the dive. The water under the ice is warmer than the ice and thus the block will get smaller during the dive.

While the hole is being cut, snow lines can be shoveled in a pattern radiating from the hole. These lines are quite visible under the ice and can serve as guides back to the hole. By including "V", lines you can indicate the direction back to the hole. If there is no snow cover, lines can be chipped or sawed into the ice.

Figure 17.3 Block of ice partially pushed under surface. Pallet will be used for tender.

While the work on the hole is going on, others can be bringing down equipment.

Line Tender

The line tender is the most important part of this dive. One of the major differences in ice diving is that you must exit at one point. You use lines to accomplish this; thus the line is your means to a safe and enjoyable dive. A line tender cannot function well if uncomfortable with freezing hands. Wet ice is also very slippery and could cause a bad fall. One of the best approaches is to have wooden pallets for the tender to stand on. They should also have very warm and waterproof boots and most especially warm and WATERPROOF gloves. For the sake of both the tender and divers, you might consider sprinkling sand around the hole for better footing.

Ropes

The actual rope used is often a personal choice. It should be strong, not very heavy in water and resistant to tangling. A common choice is a 3/8" non-floating polypropylene rope. Heavier lines can be used; but remember, the diver must pull the rope along and heavier ropes do not carry hand signals as well. Thinner ropes tend to tangle. No matter what rope you use, it should be checked for weak spots before each dive.

The length of the rope is also one of preference; but for safety's sake, it should not exceed 100 to 150 feet. For novice divers, a shorter rope can be used.

This rope should be stretched out on the ice before the dive as this eliminates tangling.

Figure 17.5 Preferred Double "Y" Line.

The safety diver rope should be FLOATING polypropylene in a bright color and at least 50% longer than the divers' rope.

Another worthwhile rope is a shot or anchor line. The use of a 10 ft. anchor enables a diver to descend slowly and hold onto something while waiting for a buddy. This also allows a very slow decent to check equipment and ears. This line is pulled up after the diver leaves the area to avoid tangling.

Fastening of Lines

Without question, safe ice diving demands the use of a harness. Merely tying a line around a diver is going back to the Dark Ages! The style of harness chosen is personal. It should be noted that a recently designed harness also functions as a weight carrier.

The lines can be fastened to the harness D rings in a variety of ways. A preferred method is with scissor snaps. These snaps are easy to put on and to remove even with mitts on and yet they will not pull open from strain.

Many divers prefer a combination attachment with a harness plus a modified hangman's knot around the wrist. The knot is made with less than 13 loops and is thus easier to loosen. The knot can be brought back between the thumb and the hand and thus the diver is always ready to signal if the need arises.

Lines and Buddies

This is an area that is open to discussion. Some divers feel that each diver should have a separate line and tender. The author has seen too many lines become entangled with the result that neither diver is safe. A better method seems to be a "Y" line. Both buddies are controlled by one tender. They are separated by a short line and thus can take photographs of each other. They can never get separated and they are close to offer aid if needed.

Figure 17.4 Diver with both hand and harness attachment. The harness has a special design to also work as a weight belt. Notice the knife sheath position.

Signals & Rope Handling

Line signals should be SIMPLE! You should not need a cue card to remember them. These are the ones commonly used:

Every five minutes the tender will give one pull and the diver should return one pull. This guards against the line snagging and diver numbness. The pulls should be long and strong—not short jerks.

The line tender must keep the rope taut enough to feel signals; but not too taut to hinder the diver. In short, the tender must be attentive at all times. The job is definitely not for the disinterested person in the group!

Flags

A diving flag should be flown to warn snowmobilers. In addition to the standard sport diving flag, many groups also fly the "I" or INDIA flag (yellow with a black dot) to signify ice diving in the area. The India flag is very visible on ice.

Entries and Exits

The best entry is done sitting down at a corner of the triangle and then turning around and lowering yourself into the water. This entry is often called a "reverse slither". It has the advantage of total control and no splashing.

The best exit is exactly the reverse of the entry. Just be sure to do your exit at a corner.

Equipment—Regulators

The major problem with regulators is either first or second stage freeze-up.

First stage freeze-up occurs because the air is expanding when it leaves the tank and thus, gets colder (Charles' Law). The problem occurs at two times: (1) the diver gets in the water and then comes out into the colder air, or (2) the diver uses an excessive amount of air, and causes ice to form. For this reason, once you have gotten the first stage wet, stay in the water. If you are hyperventilating, try to relax and control your breathing. If you can't stop being nervous, stop the dive and don't endanger yourself or your buddy.

Figure 17.6 Avoid freeze-up! Keep regulators and power inflators in warm water between dives. Also notice the proper carrying position for the knife in ice diving.

Second stage freeze-up usually occurs under very cold air conditions. The diver checks the breathing of the regulator in the usual correct way—by inhaling and exhaling—and the moisture-laden, exhaled air causes a freeze-up. To prevent this, do not breathe from the regulator until you are in the water.

If you intend to do several dives, you immerse regulators in hot water to prevent a freeze-up. The hot water can also be poured on regulators that have frozen without pulling the diver totally out of the water.

At least modern regulators will tend to malfunction by releasing air; older regulators tended to stop delivering air or burst the hoses!

Using a submersible pressure gauge and following the practice of starting back when your tank is half full, you should always be able to reach the hole with a totally free-breathing regulator.

Regulators used in ice diving should all be equipped with extra second stages (octopus) and power inflators.

Buoyancy Compensators

Buoyancy compensators are important for not only their usual role but as an aid in finding lost divers. An inflatable dry suit does not function as a buoyancy compensator.

All buoyancy compensators should be equipped with power inflators. One of the first parts to get numb from cold will be your lips. Movement of a regulator in and out of your mouth will increase heat loss. A power inflator keeps the regulator where it belongs—in your mouth!

	From Tender	**From Diver**
1 pull	Are you OK?	I am OK
2 pulls	Need more line?	I need more line.
3 pulls	No more line.	Take in line; coming back
4 pulls	EMERGENCY***PULL ME BACK!	
4 pulls repeated	NEED HELP! SEND SAFETY DIVER!	

Table 17.1 Ice Diving Line Signals

Before leaving home you should make sure that the BC is totally drained of water. Ice forming inside a BC will often prevent total inflation; it may also prevent the use of the power inflator. If you intend to do several dives, heat the power inflator with hot water to melt any ice just before entering.

Figure 17.7 Diver checking seals by squatting down and compressing suit.

Full Face Masks

The problem of numb lips leads to the solution of a full face mask. There are several on the market and the choice is yours. Remember that a full face mask is almost impossible to buddy breathe with, so you must have an octopus. You should also try your full face mask under pool conditions before going under ice. The clearing is different and some masks must be completely clear in order to breathe. In short. . . know how to use your equipment!

Snorkel and Knife

The snorkel is of no use in ice diving! Contrary to what you may have heard, there is not a layer of air under the ice, nor is it possible to shove your snorkel through thick ice to breathe.

On the other hand, a knife is **mandatory**. A knife should be carried on any dive involving lines.

I suggest testing your knife on a sample of the line that you plan to use. When your line is tangled, it is a bad time to find that your knife is suitable for cutting only limp spaghetti. Keep your knife sharp; it may save your life.

Exposure Suits

The most common form of exposure suit is the wet suit. As you realize, it allows water next to your skin and restricts the flow of water over your skin.

To prevent the instant chill upon entering, you should consider priming the wet suit with hot water. Prime the suit just before entering.

To restrict the flow of water over your skin, there are several tricks you can employ:

1) Wear clothing under the suit—lycra dive suits, underwear, socks, etc.
2) Use plastic garbage bags over your legs to help get the suit over clothing. The bags will also make putting on/removing boots very simple. They also restrict water entry.
3) Use duct tape over the junctions of boots and gloves.
4) Use a wet suit without zippers in the arms and legs.
5) Use a hooded vest instead of the normal bibbed hood. Water that enters around your neck will simply pass between the hood and your jacket and will not enter your pants.

Unquestionably the warmest suit is the dry suit. The choice of a dry suit is personal; but you should learn how to use it before going under ice.

Air is put into a dry suit for insulation. . . not for buoyancy! Many divers try to use a dry suit as a BC and find that dumping air on ascent can sometimes be quite difficult; especially if it gets into your legs and you end up ascending upside down!

Before entering the water, make sure your zipper is closed and your seals are tight. You will always see experienced ice divers crouching down to compress their suit and check for leaks before entering.

Gloves again offer choice. The coldest are five finger gloves; the warmest are two finger mitts. Before diving with mitts, you should practice with them. Under ice is no time to find out that you cannot grasp things as you thought you could. Dry suit gloves can be made even better by putting a plastic tube between the glove and wrist seal. This allows the glove to become air filled and prevents squeeze.

Lights

A snow cover of six inches makes almost an opaque covering. . . it's dark down there! A light becomes a necessity when there is snow cover. As batteries tend to be less efficient when cold, make sure they are fresh/fully charged.

Chemical lights can be used as additional aids. In addition, small flashing strobe lights can be hung by the hole to aid in locating it.

Figure 17.8 A custom lighting system for ice diving keeps hands free.

Safety Procedures

The first basic rule of ice diving is that **You Never Go Under The Ice Without Being Attached To A Line!** Accidents have occurred when a diver was going under "just to check the visibility" or "to push the block".

What should you do if somehow you lose the line?

1. You ascend and if you see the snow lines, you can follow them to the hole. This accident tends to occur when divers are on separate lines and might get entangled.

2. If you cannot see the hole or the lines, inflate your BC and stay under the ice with your legs pointing down; for this reason, do not drop your weight belt.

3. As soon as the tender realizes that the line is lost, the safety divers enter the water. They swim out in a straight line to the end of their longer rope and then commence swimming a circle while keeping the line taut. Eventually, they will make contact with the diver as the line floats and the lost diver has his legs down.

When contact is made, the lost diver grasps the rope and signals with three pulls (take-in line). The tender then pulls the safety divers to the lost diver and then all three move to the hole. The buddy of the lost diver should have already been brought to the surface.

Medical Aspects

One of the major problems facing the ice diver is psychological. In this respect, ice diving is akin to cave and closed-wreck diving. You know that you cannot just surface anywhere. Never force or browbeat a person into ice diving. **Panic Kills!**

Another problem is hypothermia—you get **Cold!** The first area that often gets cold is your lips. Numb lips cannot hold a regulator in place. Cold also numbs the senses and you are not as responsive. This is why the tender checks on your responses at regular intervals.

Cold also has other effects on your body. In order to maintain your interior temperature, your body uses more energy. One major waste product is water. A cold diver often ends up with a filled urinary bladder. Urine is quite warm and will warm up a wet suit; but the aesthetics of swimming around in urine might not appeal!

Cold also increases mucus production and thus makes ear equalization more of a problem. Asthmatics should not consider ice diving, as the cold can trigger attacks.

Upon surfacing, you must consider frostbite. Immediately upon surfacing, try to get dry and warm. Do not neglect your head. . . cover it. Your head radiates the greatest proportion of heat from your body.

Use hot foot or liquids to warm up after a dive. **Do Not Use Whiskey.** Alcohol is a vasodilator and will actually increase your heat loss. Hot chocolate, hot tea with honey, chile, bean or noodle soup, are rich in heat and energy.

End of the Dive

Once you are warm and dry, the only thing you need to do is pack up the equipment and **Close the Hole!** Be careful driving home. . . you have a much greater chance of getting hurt while driving home than while ice diving!

CAVE

DIVING

By Jeffrey Bozanic NAUI #5334L

Cave diving has typically been considered one of the most extreme and hazardous forms of recreational diving available. The reasons for this are many, not the least of which is the vast amount of publicity that accidents in underwater caves get from the various media. Like sport diving, though, diving in caves and caverns need not be unduly hazardous if proper training has been pursued and a few simple rules are followed. This chapter will outline some of the fundamentals cave divers follow while pursuing their activity. It is not intended, however, to present all the information which would be covered in a complete cave diving course. Nor is it intended that you participate in this activity without the training by a qualified cave or cavern diving instructor.

Accident Analysis

The basis of cave and cavern diving instruction, as outlined by most of the major agencies in the United States today, centers around accident analysis. This is an analysis of cave diving accidents that have occurred over the last 20 years. It was primarily done by the National Speleological Society Cave Diving Section in an effort to prevent these unfortunate accidents. To date, nearly 400 cave and cavern diving accidents and near accidents have been analyzed to determine why people have gotten into difficulties. Regardless of the wide range or experience levels—divers ranged from people who were not certified to open water diving instructors—they found that all accidents had several things in common.

In all events, just five reasons explained why these accidents occurred. These accident causes have been rewritten to form the five safety rules for cave diving and will be further explained in more detail.

1. Be trained in cave and cavern diving.
2. Always utilize a direct continuous guideline to the surface.
3. Always reserve a minimum of 2/3 of your air for exit.
4. Dive no deeper than 130 feet.
5. Carry a minimum of three lights per person.

Being trained for cave and cavern diving is the most important rule for the prevention of accidents. NAUI Instructors may teach an instructor-specified course in cavern diving which normally lasts two or three days; or two levels of courses in cave diving—cave diving and advanced cave diving. These courses last an additional two and four days, respectively. Cave diving without this specialized training is like flying a plane with only a driver's license—you cannot do it safely with only an open water certification card. The majority of people who have died in underwater caves had no training at all in either cavern or cave diving. Hence, they were not knowledgeable of the special hazards involved, nor of the special safety precautions that they could

Figure 18.1 A typical cave diving setup.

Figure 18.2 Sign placed by NSS-CDS as a public service warning in Devil's Ear Spring, Florida.

follow to alleviate those hazards. After reading this chapter you will have a brief understanding of these things, but not the ability to participate in these activities on your own.

The primary direct cause of accidents in underwater caves is the failure to use a continuous guideline to the surface. A continuous guideline is utilized for many reasons — it prevents the divers from getting lost in the cave, allows them to find the entrance in silty conditions, and even enables them to get out if all lights fail.

The second direct cause of accidents in underwater caves involved air management. Cave divers use the "Thirds Rule". They use 1/3 of the air supply for penetration, 1/3 of the air for exit, and reserve 1/3 of the air for use in emergencies. Emergencies might include getting tangled in the line, getting stuck in a rock passage, or any type of air supply failure where their buddy would breathe the last remaining 1/3 of air to effect a safe exit. Air management is one of the critical techniques that cave divers use that requires a great deal of planning and instruction to apply properly.

The primary reason experienced cave divers have died in caves is depth. Diving certification agencies, like NAUI, recommend a maximum safe diving limit of 130 feet. Many caves, however, extend much deeper than that. During the course of their exploration, some very proficient cave divers have experienced difficulties because of narcosis, extreme decompression and cold.

The final cause of cave diving accidents is failure to carry at least three lights per person. Carrying

multiple lights insures the dive team will have a spare should they experience one or more failures. Any light failure is cause for a cave dive to be terminated.

Environment

Caves are found in all parts of the world. There are many different types of caves, each of special interest to divers. Sea caves form along shorelines. Waves beating against rock erode the softer layers, making caves. They also form at areas of natural weakness, like faults or joints. Most sea caves are shallow and simple systems.

Coral caves are found in areas of abundant coral growth. These form as living corals, joined together at the top of narrow canyons. The passageways created may extend several hundred feet in depths extending to more than 100 feet. Typically, the passages are not completely closed at the top, allowing light to enter. This makes it very easy to swim down these passages without realizing that it is impossible to exit at any point during the dive.

Lava tubes may be found in volcanic areas, like Hawaii and Oregon. These tubes formed as volcanos erupted, spewing forth molten rock. As the lava flowed downhill, it cooled and channeled itself, forming tubes. When the volcano stopped erupting, the tubes were left behind. Sea level then rose, flooding some of the passageways. Lava tubes can be as long as five miles and be more than 100 feet from floor to ceiling. An average lava tube is typically about 15 feet in diameter and is generally a simple, long tunnel.

The longest caves in the world are formed in limestone. They form as slightly acidic groundwaters dissolve away the easily soluble limestone. They may be very complex. Large underground rivers found flowing from limestone bedrock are called springs.

Rivers flowing into the ground are called syphons. Because the flow in syphons pushes the diver into the cave, diving in them is not recommended. Due to their maze-like complexity, limestone caves have many dangers not associated with other types of caves.

Diving in underwater caves has many hazards not experienced in open water. Foremost, is the inability of the dive team to surface immediately from any point in their dive. The rock ceiling forces them to swim horizontally to the entrance before surfacing. This is the reason cave and cavern diving are considered advanced specialty courses.

Cave diving hazards can be typically grouped into two broad categories — hazards which affect diving visibility and those which are caused by passageway configuration problems. We will first look at the visibility grouping of problems.

Visibility in caves often ranges in excess of 300 feet. However, many factors can reduce visibility. In the simplest sense, failure of your lights may cause visibility of 300 feet to be reduced to zero because there is no light in the cave by which to see.

Most caves have easily disturbed sediments on the walls, ceiling and bottom. Kicking these sediments up or knocking them down with your exhaust bubbles is called "silting" and may reduce visibility to just a few inches. The degree to which silting is a problem in any given cave is a function of the currents found in that cave and also the quality of the sediments in the cave. The finer the sediments, the more likely it will be for you to disturb the silt. Finer sediments are more hazardous because they remain suspended for a long period of time. The primary cause of visibility loss in caves is diver error causing silting.

Some caves near shoreline areas have water masses of different salinities. In the shallow parts of the cave you may be swimming through drinkable fresh water, while deeper you may be swimming through brackish or marine waters. At the boundary of these different water masses is a sharp gradient of salinities called a HALOCLINE. When mixed, the waters may remain perfectly clear, but visibility be reduced to just a few feet. There is a blurring effect similar to that seen when mixing oil and vinegar in a salad dressing.

Dissolved chemicals can also cause visibility loss. Chemicals may include tannic acid or humic acid, formed as vegetable matter decays. Another chemical is hydrogen sulfide, which gives the water an odor resembling that of rotten eggs. Hydrogen sulphide, also formed by decaying vegetable matter, can be very unpleasant and as debilitating to divers.

In all caves it is possible to become disoriented or lost. While it may seem impossible in some simple cave systems, it remains a real possibility when you consider that in even the shortest system you could lose all visibility due to light failure or silting. The longer and more complex a cave system, the greater the potential for becoming lost. There are no natural navigational aids in most caves to assist you in finding the exit.

Many caves have areas which are difficult to swim through. These small passageways are called "restrictions", and are defined as any area through which two divers cannot comfortably and easily pass while sharing air. They may be likened to small doorways, through which it would be difficult for more than one person to squeeze through at a time in an emergency. Restrictions require divers to carry specialized equipment.

Another passageway problem is potential rock fall. Rock fall is generally a problem in unexplored caves and is avoided only by exercising good judgment. This is one reason that exploration of new caves should be left to experienced cave divers.

Passage configuration poses another concern to cave divers. If the guideline is improperly placed, it may be dragged into a narrow crack or crevice too small to swim through. If you then need to exit the cave by following the line, you are unable to do so. If the cave is completely silted out, you might not be able to see the wider part of the passage. Proper line laying is a very important technique taught during a cave diving course.

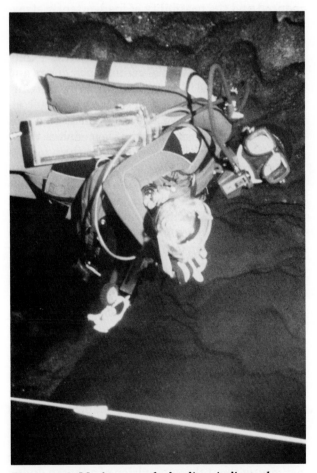

Figure 18.3 Markers attached to lines indicate the direction of the entrance of a cave. Disorientation can occur easily in a cave.

CAVE DIVING

Caves vs. Caverns

Cavern diving is a much simplified version of cave diving. Because penetration is limited, equipment requirements are much less stringent. A strict definition differentiates caves and caverns. You must remain within the following six environmental constraints to be considered in a cavern environment. These are as follows:

1. Daylight must be visible from the entrance of the cave. The sun replaces the diver's primary light and provides the primary navigational aide. A guideline is always used in cavern diving as a backup navigational tool. Because daylight must be visible, there is no cavern diving at night.

2. Maximum linear penetration of 130 feet. You must always remain within 130 linear feet from the surface at your point of maximum penetration. This is why cavern diving reels have only 130 feet of line.

3. Maximum depth of 70 feet. At depths greater than 70 feet the time available to solve problems is reduced and the possibility of inadvertently straying into a decompression profile is greatly increased.

4. No-decompression. Decompression diving imposes an "impenetrable" ceiling upon divers and may be considered to be very similar to cave diving.

5. No restrictions. Cavern divers are not allowed to pass through any type of restriction in a cave or cavern passageway. Cave divers carry specialized equipment which enables them to pass narrow points safely.

6. Minimum visibility of 40 feet. If visibility falls below 40 feet, it is very easy to lose sight of daylight from the entrance without being aware of that fact. It is also very easy to disturb visibility by silting to the point where you lose sight of the exit. If, at any point during a dive, visibility is reduced to less than 40 feet, the dive should be terminated by exiting the cavern.

The major advantage of participating in cavern diving as opposed to cave diving is that it allows you to experience much of the new without the concurrent hazards and requirements that are necessary for cave diving. In fact, cavern diving may be safely enjoyed with minor additions to standard open water equipment and with some simple techniques which may be learned in a cavern diving course. Remember that cavern diving **does** require additional training and you should not participate in the activity without the supervision of a cavern diving instructor.

Figure 18.4 Cave Diving Equipment

Figure 18.5 Buoyancy control, trim and anti-silting techniques are all essential skills for cave diving.

Figure 18.6 One third of your air is used to enter a cave, one third to exit and one third is kept as a reserve.

19

WRECK DIVING

By Ken Heist NAUI #1036L

Shipwrecks and diving have been closely related throughout history. Non-divers invariably equate diving with shipwrecks and sunken treasure. In reality, while very few divers ever find sunken treasure, all divers can treasure the joy of diving on a sunken ship. Whatever the cause of the shipwreck, be it weather, navigational error, war, or even intentional sinking to create an artificial reef, wreck dives offer the opportunity to explore history and to share the experience with others through underwater photography or archaeology. In addition, ocean wrecks offer abundant marine life. Fresh water wrecks, especially those in colder water, are often very well preserved.

In some areas, wreck diving is very popular diving activity. This includes the Atlantic coast and the Great Lakes. Resorts, while best known for their coral reefs, often have wrecks. Truk Lagoon in the Pacific Ocean, with many World War II wrecks, is a popular destination resort for wreck divers.

Wreck diving requires certain skills and training. This chapter is only an introduction and should not be a replacement for training and practice. With the variety of wreck diving locations, there is a corresponding variation in wreck diving techniques. In many areas, laws also affect wreck diving. Local instructors or dive stores can help divers avoid difficulties. Destination resorts often offer wreck diving training or guided wreck dives. It is far better to learn from the experience of others than by trial and error. The NAUI Wreck Diving Specialty course is an excellent introduction.

Regardless of the location, there are a number of items that all wreck divers should consider. Except in very sheltered water, shallow wrecks are often quickly destroyed by surface waves or intentionally destroyed as hazards to navigation. As a result, most wrecks are in water over 60 feet deep. At these depths, proper dive planning is very important. Wreck divers must be aware of underwater currents and surges that could result in abrasions or cuts from the wreck itself. Despite these challenges, with proper training, equipment, and planning, a dive on a shipwreck is a unique experience.

As with most diving specialties, the wreck diver needs proper equipment to best cope with the environment. This typically includes thermal or abrasion protection, an air supply suitable for the diving depth, instruments, dive lights, and knives. These primary pieces of equipment are described below. For divers engaged in special activities, including the taking of marine life or underwater photography, additional equipment is needed.

Thermal or abrasion protection—All wreck divers require some form of abrasion protection. In warm waters, a nylon skin suit may suffice, but a thin wet suit is generally preferred. Colder waters require increased thermal protection, either with a thicker wet suit or a dry suit with proper underwear. Nothing will ruin a wreck dive more than being too cold. Dry suits, while being extremely comfortable, require special training. This training is best done in confined water before venturing out to a wreck.

Air supply—Proper dive planning is a must. This includes having enough air for the dive. Tanks are now available in many sizes. By knowing air

Figure 19.1 Most wrecks are in water over 60 feet deep.

consumption, divers can select the tank with the capacity to meet their needs. For deep wrecks, double tanks are often used. Regardless of tank selection, it is important to plan for an adequate safety margin. A good practice is to surface with at least 1/3 of the air supply remaining. For example, with a 3,000 psi tank, plan to surface with at least 1,000 psi remaining.

Proper buoyancy is important. Different size tanks have different buoyancy characteristics. Dry suits also affect buoyancy. Overweighting is a common mistake. This results in an over-inflated buoyancy device and significantly reduced swimming efficiency at depth. By establishing correct buoyancy in advance in confined water, the diver will avoid difficulty on the wreck dive.

Instruments—As with any dive, instruments to monitor the dive plan are a must. This includes a tank pressure gauge, an accurate depth gauge, and a watch or timing device. A back-up watch or timing device is recommended. Many divers now use an electronic dive computer as one of their instruments. A proper understanding of how it works and its limitations is very important.

Dive lights—To really "see" a wreck, the diver needs a good dive light. Much of the marine life (fish, lobsters, crabs, shrimp) hides in the nooks

Figure 19.2 Wreck divers carry a small, back-up light in addition to a larger primary light.

and crannies of the wreck. The light makes it possible to see these creatures. There are many good dive lights on the market. In waters where the visibility is limited, a large bright light is best. Look for a light with either a sealed beam, or a halogen or krypton bulb. Make sure the batteries will power the light for the entire dive. Movie and underwater video lights, while bright, often only operate for minutes before the batteries must be replaced or recharged. Because dive lights often fail when least expected, a small back-up light is recommended.

Knives – Wrecks in salt water are inhabited by fish which, in turn, attract fishermen. The almost transparent monofilament fishing line they leave on the wrecks can easily entangle a diver. Similarly, commercial fishing nets that accidentally snare a wreck can also be a hazard. A good sharp dive knife helps to avoid entanglement from fishing line. On wrecks where fishing line is a known problem, carrying two or more knives is strongly recommended. If the primary knife is worn in the traditional spot on the leg, put the back-up knife in a totally different location, such as the arm or instrument console. If the leg gets tangled to the point that the knife cannot be used, the second knife in its separate location can be used. Small stiletto type knifes are ideal back-ups.

Of course, the best protection against entanglement is still the buddy system. It is far easier for a buddy to extract a diver from a predicament. It also helps to be streamlined in the water. Streamlining includes mounting the knife on the inside of the leg, taping mask and fin straps, and not tying or hooking non-life support equipment (lights, catch bags, etc.) directly to the diver. Keep this equipment on a wrist lanyard. If it becomes entangled, it can be easily ditched.

With the emphasis on back-up equipment for wreck diving, a back-up breathing system is recommended. This can take several forms, including octopus systems and dual regulator valves (often used in cave diving). A popular back-up system for many wreck divers is the pony bottle and regulator. The pony bottle is a small 10 to 15 cubic foot air tank with its own separate regulator. This system has all the advantages of the octopus and dual regulator valves with the added advantage of being suitable for an out-of-air situation for both the diver and his or her buddy. The disadvantage of the pony bottle system is the increased bulk of this extra tank. Regardless of the back-up system being used, it is important that diving buddies be thoroughly familiar with all primary and back-up air systems. This includes practicing for out-of-air situations.

In some locations, there may be additional equipment to consider. Each piece of this equipment must be considered for its ability to make the dive safer, more enjoyable, or comfortable.

Generally, wrecks are only accessible by boat. Most wrecks are not marked and require a skilled and properly equipped boat crew to be located. Dive instructors, stores, clubs and resorts often arrange wreck diving boat trips. At the wreck site, the anchor is often dropped into the wreck. Other wrecks may have a permanent mooring for dive boats. Either way, they provide convenient descent lines to the wreck.

Figure 19.3 It's important that diving buddies be thoroughly familar with all primary and back-up systems.

Before making an entry, the diver must check to see if there is a strong surface current. In some cases, the boat crew will run a line from the anchor line to the diver's entry point. Upon making the entry, divers should move quickly to the anchor line, meet up with their buddy and descend to the wreck. Upon reaching the wreck, check again the anchor or mooring to see that it is properly hooked to the wreck and the line to the surface is not rubbing on the wreck. This is also an ideal time to check again that instruments are functioning and for an underwater buddy check.

The diver is now free to explore the wreck. Divers should plan to return to the anchor line with an adequate reserve. If there is a current running, divers should swim into the current for the first half of the dive. This makes the return trip to the anchor line much easier. Near the wreck, divers must be aware of currents, which often flow swiftly along the top or ends of the wreck. Often, there is a surge that moves the diver back and forth on the bottom. If the surge is heavy, the diver should explore the wreck from a safe distance to avoid being bumped into the wreck.

Underwater navigation on all but the most intact wrecks is best learned through experience. On a metal wreck, a compass is inaccurate and should not be trusted. On the other hand, a compass can help the diver navigate to a wreck near the shore. Most wrecks are not intact and, on first inspection, may seem hard to navigate. With repeated dives on the same wreck, the diver will soon notice distinguishing features that aid navigation. In extremely limited visibility, a line on a reel can help the diver return to the anchor line.

Many divers visit wrecks for the fish and other marine life that can be found. In many areas, this includes lobsters. While underwater hunting on wrecks is popular, there are often laws that control this activity. This includes size and catch limits, licensing requirements and, in some areas, a total ban on taking anything from the water. Check with your instructor, divemaster or boat captain for what is allowed.

Wrecks offer many opportunities for excellent still, motion picture and video photography. Wide angle lenses allow you to capture

Figure 19.4 Wreck dives should be planned so divers return to the anchor line with adequate reserve.

Figure 19.5 Wrecks are artificial reefs that provide havens for many forms of underwater life.

Just as divers are tempted to enter wrecks, they are also often tempted to dive deeper than is safe. In some cases, this can be by accident. Often one part of a wreck will be in relatively shallow water, while another part of the same wreck is in very deep water. Divers have become so fascinated by exploring the wreck that they don't properly monitor their depth and exceed their planned dive. On a wreck, gauges must be constantly checked.

Other divers are tempted to visit wrecks that are clearly out of bounds to recreational divers. Diving magazines, which often feature articles on these very deep dives, don't help this situation. What they often don't say is that these deep dives have significantly increased risk. Below 100 feet, bottom time is significantly reduced. Air consumption at these depths usually requires an increased air supply. Divers who exceed the no-decompression limits significantly increase their decompression sickness risk. Once the no-decompression limit is exceeded, safety is no longer at the surface. The best divers know their limits and stay within them.

Wrecks are artificial reefs and, like their coral cousins, can be enjoyed day and night. In a salt-water environment, a night dive is a chance to see marine creatures that are hidden in daylight. Like any wreck dive, proper planning is imperative. This includes back-up lights. Chemical lights are an excellent and almost foolproof back-up. Many consider them mandatory for a night dive. With the absence of ambient sunlight, it is easy for the diver to accidentally get under an overhang, or enter the wreck without knowing it. A flashing strobe light on the anchor line is an easy way to maintain visual contact with a safe path to the surface. Wreck

identifiable objects and divers on the wreck. Close-up and macro lenses allow you to photograph the fish and other marine life that lives in the wrecks. Photography allows the diver to show the wreck and its marine life in its natural environment without detracting from future divers' pleasure.

While most wreck divers enjoy exploring wrecks from the outside, some wreck divers will venture inside sunken ships to continue their exploration. This type of diving, called penetration diving, is similar to cave or ice diving in complexity. Inside a wreck, safety is no longer directly above, so special care must be taken. The risk of getting lost in passageways and compartments, along with the hazard of reduced visibility caused by silt, are major concerns. While the water may look clear on the way into a wreck, it is easy to kick up silt and reduce the visibility for the return trip. Inside a wreck, back-up systems are mandatory. This includes extra dive lights, an alternate air source, and the use of lines to guide the diver back to the wreck entrance. These all require special training.

J. Prosser photo

Figure 19.6 Penetration diving requires specialized training and equipment.

WRECK DIVING

Figure 19.7 Wreck divers can help archaeologists locate and preserve history.

selection can also avoid this problem. Many wrecks are very broken up and have no "insides" that can create a night dive problem.

Because wrecks are often associated with history, knowledge of the ship and the story of its sinking increases the enjoyment of the dive. While this information is readily available on many wrecks, others require some research. Maritime museums, naval archives, historic societies, and old newspapers (often available in library microfilm files) are excellent sources of this information. Many divers have successfully identified wrecks by comparing what they see underwater (ship construction, size, and other distinguishing features) with what they find in their research.

Wreck divers can help archaeologists to record and preserve history. Historical societies, universities, and government organizations often have underwater archaeology opportunities. Working with scientists, divers record detailed data on historic wrecks. This data allows a reconstruction of the ship and its people. In some areas this may be the only way to visit some particularly historic wrecks — as local laws may prohibit recreational diving on these sites. Most underwater archaeology is hard work, but the rewards can be tremendous.

Wreck diving offers excitement and a chance to explore history. With proper training, equipment, and planning it is both an enjoyable and safe experience.

DRIFT DIVING

20

By Jeff Bozanic NAUI #5334L

Drift diving is a specialized form of boat diving which allows you to drift with the current throughout the entire duration of your dive. This gives you several advantages. First of all, it makes the dive much more enjoyable because you never have to fight the current. You are always using it to move where you want to go. It also allows you to cover a great deal of territory in a very short time. However, like other specialty forms of diving, drift diving requires an orientation and training by a NAUI divemaster or instructor who is familiar with the drift diving techniques used in the area. There are several styles of drift diving and many different safety precautions to be followed. These will be the basis of the information to be covered.

DRIFT DIVING STYLES

Float Drift

Float drifts are the safest and most common form of drift diving. A float is used with a down line or drift line that always lets the boat captain know where the group is. The group leader holds the end of the float line while the rest of the group follows. The boat captain and crew are then able to follow the float on the surface. When practicing float drift diving, it is typical for the group to meet at the surface to adjust their equipment prior to descent. This helps ensure that the entire group will remain together during the descent. If the water is especially rough, it may be easier for the group to hover at a depth of 15 to 20 feet prior to going to the bottom. This, again, allows everyone to adjust their buoyancy and make minor equipment adjustments prior to starting the dive. The entire group moves down the line together.

Group size should generally be limited to 8 to 14 people depending upon the experience of the instructor or divemaster leading the dive. In this manner, the entire group stays together. It is the responsibility of each of the individual group members to maintain contact with the group leader holding the end of the dive line. The person holding the float line oftentimes has the tendency to move faster than the remainder of the group because of the stronger current at the surface pulling the float and consequently, him, along at the end of the float

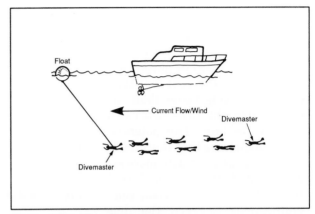

Figure 20.1 Float Drift Diving

line. As key members get low on air, they will ascend by buddy teams up the drift line to the surface. During this period, they should not be pulling on the line, but should maintain a very light grasp to ensure they do not pull the line from the leader's grasp.

Upon reaching the surface, they should inflate their BCs, give a long distance OK sign to the boat crew, and let the current pull them away from the drift float so that the boat can back up to pick them up. Safety decompression stops while float drift diving should be done by the entire group. It is often very difficult for dive teams to conduct a safety decompression stop while on a float line since the current will be dragging them to a far greater degree than it will the group on the bottom. Thus, the only time safety decompression stops should be done while float drift diving is when the entire group remaining in the water does it together with the dive team leader.

Anchor Line Drift

Anchor line drifting is another form of drift diving that is generally used if there is very little or no bottom current at the site being dived. With an anchor line drift, surface currents or windage on the boat are used to pull divers along. With an anchor line drift, a weighted down line or the anchor line is used as a tow rope for the divers during the dive. As the boat is pulled along on the surface by the current, or blown along by the wind, the dive team members hold onto the line and are pulled across the bottom where they have the opportunity to explore a large territory with very little effort.

This type of diving, however, has inherent hazards that are not encountered during float drifts. The primary additional hazard is that the divers must hold onto the anchor line for the duration of the dive. If the divers release the anchor line, they may be quickly left behind, since the boat will typically be drifting faster than the diver will be able to swim to catch up with the line. This potential problem dictates that this type of diving only be done with more experienced drift divers and that there also be very efficient communications between the dive team members left on the line and the boat crew on the boat. In this event, the boat crew can make arrangements to pick that diver up either by having the entire group ascend the line and then circling back for the diver or by having a trailing line which a diver can use to get back to the boat. In all cases, if communication is lost with a diver, the dive should be terminated and the entire dive team brought back on board the boat, which then circles back for the lost diver.

Another potential hazard of this type of diving is that it can be awkward for divers to ascend and descend up and down the line because they are going beside or over other divers who may be above them sequentially on the line. This is another reason why this type of diving should only be pursued by more experienced divers. It is best done with very small groups. A maximum size of six is recommended. This type of diving makes decompression stops easier, since the down lines are already down and divers are continuously in contact with the vessel from which the diving is being done.

Live Boat Drift Diving

Live boat drift diving is used in areas where float drift diving is not practical. This generally occurs when you're drifting with currents through areas that have a large number of obstructions in the water column, for example, in kelp beds or other areas where there are either surface or underwater obstructions which may entangle the line. For this type of diving, the divers drop to the bottom as a group and drift along the bottom throughout the dive. The dive boat crew follows the dive team by

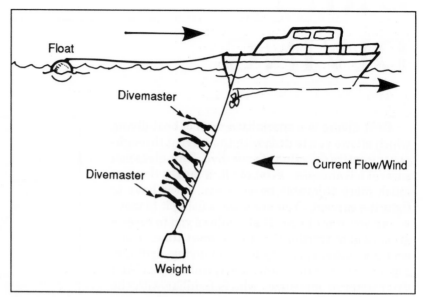

Figure 20.2 Anchor Line Drift Diving

following the bubbles at the surface. It is imperative for the divers to stay together throughout the dive so the volume of bubbles is great enough for the boat crew to follow.

This is a much, much more hazardous form of diving than either float diving or anchor line drift diving as previously described. This is because there is no communication with the boat crew. Because of this, only very experienced divers and a very experienced boat crew should attempt to perform this type of diving together. Smaller groups - generally less than six to eight—are far preferable for this type of drift diving. If there is any doubt as to the amount of experience or the conditions that might be encountered throughout this type of drift diving, the dive should be aborted.

Environmental conditions which might cause cancelling this type of drift dive would include, for example, a high degree of surface chop which would make it impossible for a boat crew to be able to see the bubbles from the dive team below. There should be some kind of an auditory signal between the boat crew and the dive team below to allow the boat crew to terminate the dive should conditions degrade to the point where they can no longer follow the dive team.

Night Drift Dives

Night drift dives add another dimension to drift diving. Any of the described techniques may be used although, obviously, the float drift type method is the safest and the best to follow. In this particular instance, a light should be used on the float and on the divers to enable the boat to follow the float in a far easier manner. A light on the dive leader allows dive team to follow him or her. In some instances, colored chemical lights might be used on the dive leader as well as on the dive float to make it easier for them to be followed. Night boat drift diving should be attempted only if the visibility is excellent so the boat crew can easily see the dive lights of the dive team members on the bottom.

It is important during all types of drift diving to mark the dive team leader well so none of the dive members can confuse the leader with any other person. For night drift diving this is especially important. It enables the group to maintain coherency in an environment that is oftentimes confusing, even without the additional stresses of drift diving and extra equipment. Obviously, participating divers should have experience both in drift diving and in night diving prior to trying to combine the two skills during a more advanced dive.

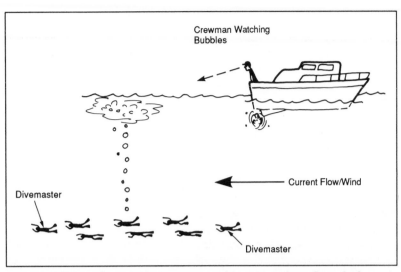

Figure 20.3 *Live boat drift diving is used in areas where float drift diving is not practical. For example, in kelp beds or other areas where there are either surface or underwater obstructions which may entangle the line.*

General Safety Procedures and Precautions

There are a variety of specialized safety procedures and equipment to make drift diving a far safer activity than just jumping in the water and making the dive. There also are precautions that should be taken to obviate potential hazards. The hazards, precautions, equipment, and procedures should be learned during a drift diving specialty course.

Conclusion

Drift diving can be a very relaxing, enjoyable, and lazy way to dive. By allowing the currents to drift you along the bottom, you can cover vast areas without having to kick a fin or expend any energy. However, in spite of its relative physical ease, drift diving is an advanced form of boat diving requiring specialized training and equipment. In areas where drift diving is a common activity, you may wish to consider enrolling in a NAUI drift diving specialty course. Given this degree of experience and a few simple pieces of equipment, drift diving can open new horizons and vistas to further your enjoyment of the underwater environment.

EQUIPMENT

By Richard Jacoby NAUI #2987

Bring Back the Pleasures of Diving

How often have you tried to explain the emotional high of diving, flying through three dimensions inhabited by creatures that appear more Martian than terrestrial? To give people a feeling of what diving is like requires more than words. You need pictures, still or moving, to do justice to the strange world beneath the sea.

Choices: Photo and Video

The kind of equipment you choose depends on the pictures you want to show.

1. Build a scrapbook of memories. A small-format still camera captures candid diving experiences that family and friends enjoy. Photos are easy to show, keeping memories alive with the flip of a cover.

2. If your bent is to freeze on film a moment that expresses your feelings, choose a 35mm still camera. A rich, red flame scallop trailing translucent tendrils makes a stunning image, either as a slide projected on a screen or as a print hung on your wall. So does the fascinated look on your buddy's face as he or she stares down a pugnacious fish.

3. Impart the feel of diving. A video lens explores underwater the way a diver sees it, whether swimming through kelp in the Pacific or water plants in a local lake or quarry.

4. Capture thrilling images with the least trouble. Videotaping is the easiest way to get underwater images worth looking at. The biggest challenge is limiting the amount of tape you shoot.

5. Sell pictures. A Nikonos or housed 35mm single lens reflex camera captures everything from tiny creatures to a diver swimming over a wreck.

6. Produce videotapes for sale. Videography's state of the art is beginning to reach the point where home production approaches the quality necessary for broadcast or sale of videotapes.

7. Expense of a camera is a major consideration. It is a worthwhile purchase, however, if one considers that it prolongs a diving trip with visual memories to which one can return years later. Considered in this way, the "street price" of camera equipment compares favorably to the cost of a diving vacation.

Canon, Hanimex, Minolta, Nikon, and Sea & Sea make 35mm cameras designed for in-water

Figure 21.1 Nikon's Nikonos—sturdy design, an assortment of excellent lenses, and a wealth of accessories.

shooting. Among them, Nikon's Nikonos is universally accepted. Its appeal lies in a sturdy design, an assortment of excellent lenses, and a wealth of accessories.

WATER'S EFFECTS ON LIGHT

Shoot Close

In underwater photography and videography, the name of the game is to get rid of the water! This rule alone makes the difference between pictures that are worth looking at and those that are not. Add the myriad particles through which you swim, and it is not surprising that shooting underwater images is a little like looking through the bottom of a soft drink bottle.

Simple methods exist to overcome problems connected with reduced contrast, dull color and focus. We will address the problems first, then describe methods to solve them.

Problems of Contrast

Even in the clearest tropical water, where visibility extends over 200 feet, light becomes diffused over short distances. Illumination is shadowless and without apparent direction, making everything appear diffuse and hazy. Images turn dull and undefined. As first-time photo buffs discover, the result is boring pictures.

Problems of Color

A fish's world contains a fraction of the sunlit palette of our world. Snorkel on the surface, and your view of a landscape only 30 feet below appears dull blue-green. Or, watch the brilliant red on your buddy's BC fade as he or she descends. At 15 feet, nearly all red, the hue image-makers prize most, has disappeared. Orange is lost by 30 feet, and by 60 feet, yellow is gone. From there on the diver's world darkens from blue-green to deeper shades of gray.

Happily, contrast and color are less important in underwater video. The three-dimensional action of divers and fish absorbs viewers' attention, so they do not expect the same image quality from a television set that they are accustomed to seeing in a photograph.

Problems of Focus

Water's density contributes to another deception. Because it is 800 times more dense than air it focuses light waves so that images are fuzzy to both your eyes and a camera. To correct focus for divers, a mask plate separates the water from their eyes. Additional methods are used in camera lenses.

How to Improve Contrast and Color

A simple, effective method to increase contrast is to compose the subject against the sun. Such backlighting creates high-contrast photographs and video.

You can achieve colorful, sunlit photos by taking advantage of midday sunlight in tropical water. To make the best use of this available light, photograph within 10 feet of the surface and as close to the subject as possible.

Special underwater filters extend the depth at which you can achieve acceptable contrast and color. Unlike above-water filters, they are designed for special characteristics of water's color and contrast. Use them on sunny days. At depths of 30 feet and more, you photograph more color with a still camera than you actually see. Improved contrast and color are possible with video at even greater depths.

To get the most photographic color and contrast, you will need an electronic flash. The flash acts as a miniature artificial sun that delivers sharp defini-

Equipment	Cost as fraction of $1,000 vacation in 1988 dollars
Basic disc system	1/10
Flexible housing for existing camera; use above 30 feet	1/10 to 1/5
Basic underwater 35mm camera limited to use above 100 feet	1/5
Housing for your present 35mm SLR plus flash	1/2 plus
Nikonos and flash	3/4 plus
Video and housing	1 1/2 plus

Costs listed represent minimum expenditures. Additional costs are:

Accessories to a Basic System
- Adding or upgrading a flash
- Extra optics
- Top-of-the-line SLR and housing
- Motor drive
- Advanced video camcorder
- Video lights

Table 21.1 Considered in this way, the "street price" of camera equipment compares favorably to the cost of a diving vacation.

tion, directionality, and color—the crisp images you expect from a picture taken on a sunny afternoon.

Video's emphasis on action reduces the need for artificial light during daytime shooting. A water correction filter usually is enough to improve color and contrast. Use a video light to bring out colors and fill in shadows when shooting small subjects in shaded locations.

Size and Distance

While the same problems are common to both optical systems, different methods are employed to focus still and video cameras. We will discuss focus of still cameras in this section. Focusing methods for video cameras are described in the Video section of this chapter.

How far away is your subject? The distance of a shellfish appears the same to you and the camera; to a tape measure the distance is a little further. Suppose a shellfish looks like it is 12 inches away; its actual distance would be 16 measured inches.

Because you and your camera share the same kind of viewing, in most cases you can focus underwater in the same manner you do in air. Set your camera at the same distance you see the subject. If a fish looks like it is three feet away, set the focus at three feet. It is that simple!

How to Judge Underwater Distance

To avoid miscalculating distance, photographers like to double-check their estimates with a measuring device. If you do so, keep in mind the difference between "apparent" and "actual" distance.

Let the length of your arm act as a standard measurement: if you are a six foot adult, the distance between fingertips and your eye is approximately 32 inches—two apparent feet in front of you. Set your focus at two feet and shoot.

Suppose your camera lens focuses no closer than three feet. To double-check whether the subject really is three feet away, reach out and touch it, then back away an extra one-half arm length. To photograph your buddy four feet away, reach out and touch his or her extended arm. In all cases,

Figure 21.3 Focus distance can be deceptive under water.

STILL PHOTOGRAPHY

Film Selection

Because print film allows the greatest latitude for exposure error, select it over slide film if your camera does not allow control of aperture and shutter speed. More sophisticated cameras also accommodate print film, but experienced photographers usually select slide film for richer colors and sharper images.

Choice of film also depends on a compromise between brightness of the scene and quality of the image. Select daylight film that can be exposed in low light (ISO 400 or higher) when taking pictures that are illuminated only by the sun's filtered rays.

Choose less sensitive daylight film when you brighten the scene with a strobe. Film rated at ISO 100 is a good all-round choice. Films with lower ISO ratings—64, 50 or even 25—result in finer images. For excellent quality in close-up pictures, select film rated at ISO 25.

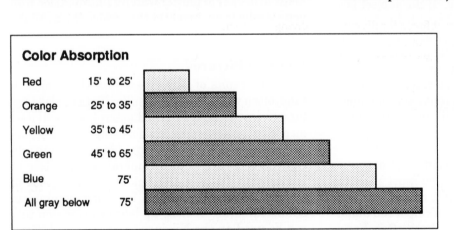

Figure 21.2 Warm colors are lost due to absorbtion, but can be regained with a flash.

focus your camera at the apparent distance, not the actual number of inches your arm has measured.

Extending your arm to check distance works even when photographing skittish creatures that won't let you touch them. In such cases, substitute an inanimate object—a rock or piece of dead coral, for example—for the fish you want to shoot. Memorize the distance you have measured, then turn to your actual subject, adjust your physical distance accordingly, and shoot.

Location and Control

Once your camera is loaded and tested for leaks turn everything off and locate a suitable site for the kind of pictures you want to take. Like a photographer's studio, components of your "studio in the sea" help you take good pictures.

Requirements of an Underwater Studio

- Attractive setting
- Natural habitat for fish
- Assistance from your buddy
- Comfortable location
- No backscatter
- Lighting control

For an attractive setting, avoid distractions such as dead coral or tangled tree branches. If the bottom is barren, find a man-made object. Pilings near shore create simple backgrounds for small animals and divers.

Open water makes the best all-round background, especially when the subject is framed by a small part of the environment. Low camera angles allow you to include at least one-third open water in the composition. When taking close-ups of very small objects select a background of open water or a solid-colored surface.

Look for a spot in which you can exercise control over the subject. A cleaning station where a grouper pauses to let tiny fish pick its body clean functions as a buffet table of photo possibilities.

Use your buddy as a photographic assistant and model. To pose the grouper, he or she drops half-inch-square chunks of fish a few inches in front of where you want the fish to pose. If the subject is a bottom dweller, have your buddy get behind it and "herd" the animal towards you.

Find a comfortable location. It may be necessary to wait 15 minutes or more for your subject to pose. You will know when the moment is right. Then click off a dozen photographs at different camera angles and exposures. The wait will be worthwhile. Chasing fish too often creates wasted "rear-end" shots.

Steady yourself against current. Lie down or brace yourself on the bottom. If you must shoot in mid-water, hold onto something to control vertical motion. A projection on a wall or a kelp frond make good parking places. Photographers often hang onto an anchor chain while photographing schools of mid-water fish.

Move slowly and with little fin motion to avoid kicking up particles that cloud pictures. To further reduce this cloud of backscatter, position yourself down-current from the subject so particles you stir up are swept away from the picture area.

Consider using bounce-lighting and sunlight in order to reduce hard shadows. When choosing a setting, look for a light-colored surface close to your subject but just outside the picture area. Then bounce a strobe's flash off the light surface onto your subject.

Figure 21.4 Experienced diving photographers devise creative lighting techniques.

Avoid large areas that reflect light, such as a sandy bottom. When illuminated with a strobe, the bright sand bleaches out the images.

In clear, shallow water sunlight illuminates background not exposed by a strobe. Sunlight also helps in deeper or darker water if illumination from your strobe is not brighter than twice the available light.

Close-up Pictures

Photographs of tiny objects are the easiest to take, often with stunning results. To take close-ups (or extreme close-ups, called macro), you will need an optical system capable of focusing on a subject no further than 18 inches away. Many housings designed for 110 and disc cameras accept close-up lenses that fit over the outside port. Close-up systems also are available for some amphibious 35mm cameras. A close-up lens or extension tube can be used on the Nikonos or on a housed 35mm camera.

Take your first close-ups of non-moving subjects, such as coral polyps, egg sacks, or kelp fronds. To aid focus and composition attach a framer to an extension tube or close-up lens. Compose the subject inside the metal frame, away from the wire edge.

Make camera settings in advance. If you use a close-up lens, follow the manufacturer's instructions. With an extension tube, set the lens to its smallest aperture, focus at the closest distance, and aim a small strobe from above your camera into the framer.

CAMERAS & VIDEO EQUIPMENT

Fish Pictures

Find subjects for fish pictures according to instructions in the Location and Control section of this chapter.

Photographs of fish usually are taken with a strobe no further than three feet from the camera. To help keep the subject in focus, and if your lens permits, adjust aperture and focus to allow the greatest possible depth of field. (Depth of field is a range of focus in front of the camera in which objects appear to be sharply defined in the finished picture. Lens scales on single lens reflex and Nikonos cameras show depth-of-field information.)

Aim the strobe at the fish's actual position, rather than where it appears to be. To do so, point it slightly beyond the spot where you see the subject.

Your approach may frighten the fish, so expect to wait several minutes for them to return. Remain in the same place until you are sure you have the shots you want. If you are unable to pose your subject attractively, move to another location.

Pictures of Large Subjects

Suppose that you want to photograph a coral landscape during a summer vacation. You desire bright, colorful pictures, but do not own a strobe. Such pictures are not difficult to take, providing you select a shallow location in clear water.

In the Caribbean, beautiful stands of coral grow within five or 10 feet of the surface. To name only three of many locations, ideal conditions exist, weather permitting, at John Pennekamp State Park in the Florida Keys; Buck Island National Park in the U.S. Virgin Islands, and Turtle Rocks near Bimini.

Determine exposure with a built-in metering system or a separate light meter. If your system does not include a meter, increase exposure one f-stop beyond the setting recommended in information packed with the film. (An f-stop represents the size of a lens opening that admits light to the film. The larger the opening, the more light strikes the film. F-stops are symbolized by a series of numbers on a lens. A small number represents a large opening; conversely, a large number represents a small opening. Low-cost cameras may not offer a choice of f-stops.)

When silhouetting divers and other large objects, frame the picture so only a tiny bit of the sun peaks out behind the subject. Compose the subject first. Then, point an auto-exposure camera or light meter towards the sun, check exposure and increase it by one stop. If you have no meter, set exposure for surface sunlight according to information packed with the film. Unlike the previous example, do not revise settings for underwater lighting.

For colorful front light, you will need a wide angle lens and a strobe with comparable coverage. Visibility should be at least 25 feet, and the main subject should be no further than 5 feet away. Set exposure according to information packed with the strobe.

Figure 21.5 Video is a popular, easy way to capture images.

VIDEO

The Camera

The history of underwater video equipment is much like going on a diet: results are less weight and sharper and better images. With housings, early VHS and Beta models weighed up to 100 pounds. In recent years manufacturers combined the camera and recorder into a single package called a camcorder. Including the housing, many of today's systems weigh less than 20 pounds, yet produce surprisingly good pictures.

You will find small video systems extremely easy to use. As of this writing, 8mm and Super VHS-C are the systems of choice. Both offer lightweight convenience and high-quality pictures.

With its many improvements over older VHS, Super VHS-C produces excellent video images. Quality is especially good when played back on television monitors that are designed to take advantage of its features. Two recording modes are available: 20 minutes and one hour. Twenty minute mode produces the best image resolution.

Housed 8mm models are the smallest and lightest available, and their image quality is unusually good. Several weigh less than 15 pounds, including the housing. All systems are weightless or slightly negative when taken underwater.

Advantages of 8mm for Underwater Videography

- Lightweight
- Low light capability
- Good resolution
- Vivid underwater images
- One hour high quality recording
- Good audio quality
- Simplified editing

8mm systems employ different technology than half-inch camcorders. The camera's "film", hundreds of thousands of tiny electronic light sensors compressed on a chip less than one inch square, records scenes in dim underwater light. Because the recorder section requires high quality metal tape and employs an electronic frequency that approaches professional systems, color and sharpness of the recorded images are greatly improved over earlier VHS and Beta systems. A side advantage of the new technology is that its circuitry makes underwater images appear even more vivid and colorful than that recorded by other systems. The video image often looks better than what your eyes see!

FOCUS

On a sunny day you should be able to tape action at varying distances in front of the lens without stopping to make adjustments. While underwater video systems require very little focusing, you need to know how to establish focus and make occasional adjustments. There are three main methods.

Method 1

The easiest way to focus is found in a dedicated underwater system; the lens in the camera and optical port in the housing are designed to work together. As of this writing, Sony Corporation's Handicam Pak 8 and its underwater housing function in this manner. The camera has no zoom control; you won't even find a focus control on the housing. Except in very dim light, subjects appear in focus from about a foot to more than 10 feet away from the lens.

Method 2

A second method takes advantage of a macro focus feature found on many zoom lenses. By turning the zoom to its widest focal length and then releasing a switch, you can focus on subjects only a few inches from the lens.

Macro focus allows you to focus on an image of the scene created by the dome port just in front of the housing (see the definitions that follow). To focus, gently adjust the housing's zoom control until the image becomes sharp in the finder. Image sharpness is improved by affixing a wide angle adapter to the zoom lens. With the aid of its increased depth of field, only slight changes in focus will be necessary as you and the subject move back and forth.

Method 3

The method just described works only when the zoom lens is set in macro which is at the wide end of the lens' focal length. Using the zoom to shoot at narrower focal lengths requires attachment of a +4 diopter close-up lens. Like macro focus, the close-up lens focuses on the virtual image created by the dome. Addition of a wide angle converter between the zoom and close-up lens further widens and sharpens the image.

Technique: Tell a Story of Actions

Select sequences that show the diver's active relationship with the underwater environment; animals, wrecks, scenery, and other divers. Video also captures close-ups as well, especially when motion is involved.

Some steps to good underwater video:
1. Plan sequences
2. Stabilize yourself
3. Anticipate action
4. Limit pans and vertical swings (tilts), especially when performed quickly
5. Change point of view
6. Limit shots to less than 15 seconds
7. Begin and end above water

Before entering the water, plan your shots and discuss details with your buddy/model.

The simplest way to capture action is to kneel on the bottom and let it unfold in front of the camera. Select the location first, then aim the camera at an interesting scene and let the action happen. For example, shoot five seconds of a shipwreck; then, without moving the camera, have your buddy swim into the scene.

Change the camera's point of view during a sequence of three or four shots. Instead of a single shot, relate your buddy to the shipwreck by shooting a sequence of five shots: wide, medium, close-up, medium, and again wide.

Add to the viewer's feeling of action by putting the camera into motion with a dolly shot. For example, inject a mid-water shot after take #2 in the above sequence. First adjust buoyancy for mid-water swimming. Then retrace your buddy's swim while the camera is running. The viewer partici-

Power	Control on camera and housing	A switch that turns on the camera. One system turns itself off if it has not been operated for three minutes.	Required
Start/Stop	On camera and housing	Begin and end actual recording.	Required
Zoom Control	Control on camera and housing	A zoom control changes the lens' focal length*, thereby expanding or contracting the lens' coverage of the scene. With zoom you can shoot a wide angle shot that covers much less area. "Zooming" the lens during a take is less desirable; shots appear artificial, and if there is no external mike, the sound of the zoom motor is audible on the tape. Because you can swim your camera into and out of a scene you rarely need to zoom while the tape is running.	Required unless camera and housing are dedicated for underwater focusing without a zoom (See Macro Control)
Filter Control	Control on camera and housing	Adjustment of the camera's internal filter prevents colors from jumping between blue and harsh red. A control on the housing that connects to the filter switch is handy if you expect to use a video light during the day. It also helps if you want the option of attaching an underwater filter to the outside of the housing.	Optional
Iris	Control on camera and housing	The camera's auto-exposure system performs satisfactorily under average lighting conditions. However, manual control of the iris through the housing allows compensation for too much exposure. By closing down the iris you can prevent washed out images if dark and light objects occupy the same area or if video lighting dominates sunlit exposure.	Optional
Finder	On camera and housing	The camera's finder should be located so it can be viewed through the rear of the housing. Minimum size of this miniature black and white TV screen should be no less than 2/3 of an inch on the diagonal. Other housings employ a gunsight finder.	Strongly recommended
Finder Magnifier	Attachment to finder	As an accessory to some housings, miniature magnifiers spread the finder's image over a wider area. A magnifier significantly improves viewing through the small eyepiece.	Strongly recommended
In-Water Microphone	Attached to housing	When enclosed in a housing, a camera's microphone picks up normal noises associated with the camera's operation. The camera records cleaner sound if an underwater microphone is built into the housing.	Optional

*Note: Numbers on a zoom lens describe the focal lengths to which it can be adjusted. A small number means that the lens covers a comparatively wide view; larger numbers represent narrower fields of view. On a zoom lens advertised as "12-72", for example, a 12mm setting would cover six times the picture area as the 72mm setting.

Table 21.2 Satisfactory operation of an underwater video system depends on a few important features. Other optional features offer increased flexibility.

Take	Action	Coverage
1	Take a wide shot of a large section of the wreck.	Wide Shot
2	Move in close to show an interesting piece of wreckage while your buddy swims in view.	Medium Shot
3	Show a close-up of your buddy's face as he or she looks at the wreck.	Close-up
4	Show the wreck from over your buddy's shoulder.	Medium Shot
5	In a final wide shot, show your buddy swimming out of the scene.	Wide Shot

Table 21.3 Sample Sequence

Dome or Optical Port	Attached to the housing	Video housings incorporate either a dome or special lens to act as an interface with the water. Both enable the camera's zoom lens to focus sharply with the same coverage for which it was designed on land. At the same time, the dome refocuses everything beyond it into a virtual image less than 10 inches in front of the port.	Required
Macro Control	Part of a camera's zoom range and a housing control	A common method of focusing requires that the camera's zoom control be operated at the macro end of its range.	Required if a wide angle adapter is used (See Zoom Control)
Wide Angle Adapter	Accessory lens	When the housing incorporates a dome port, a supplementary lens called a wide angle adapter increases coverage while permitting an extra margin for focusing error. If the scene is bright, once focus is set, adjustments are rarely necessary. This lens is fastened to the front of the camera's lens and focus is achieved by adjusting the camera's macro control.	Required if macro focusing is used
Close-up Lens	Accessory lens	Remember that virtual image the dome creates just in front of itself? Because zoom lenses normally focus no closer than three feet, a close-up lens with a diopter power of +4 is required to bring the virtual image into focus. The lens may be used with a wide angle converter, either built in or attached to the front of the converter.	Required if you do not use macro focus with a dome port.
Wide Angle Converter	Accessory lens	A wide angle converter increases sharpness and widens coverage when changing lens coverage with the zoom control. It must be used with a close-up lens, either as a separate component or built into the converter. Focusing is necessary to shoot extreme close-ups when the macro control is not used. It is also recommended for slight adjustments when light is dim.	Optional
Focus Control	On camera and housing	Focus adjustments are critical when you want to zoom and change distances in dim light. Assuming the camera is not pre-focused in its housing, a focus control lets you sharpen the image. Turn off the camera's auto focus before closing the housing.	Strongly recommended if you want to zoom to various focal lengths.

Table 21.4 Video Accessories

CAMERAS & VIDEO EQUIPMENT

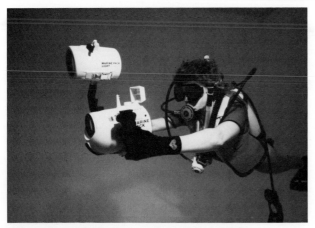
Figure 21.6 Underwater video is easy and fun.

pates in the action as the camera is propelled through scenery and towards the wreck.

Assemble a series of sequences that tell a complete story. Building on the shipwreck example, begin when your buddy enters the water, then follow his or her descent with other divers.

On the bottom, follow your buddy's travel near the wreck. Set up shots that include the diver, wreck, and local fish. Show your buddy's return to the boat, followed by excited talk about the dive as everyone strips off gear.

Plan a Complete Show

Establish the story with pre-dive surface sequences. Begin with a scuba tank being filled. Your camcorder will pick up the sound of air entering the tank. Follow with shots of divers carrying equipment onto the dive boat. Shoot the boat's wake as you travel to the dive site, then show someone on deck setting the anchor. Get two or three shots of your buddies as they dress for the dive. Just before the diving sequence, tape your buddies as they enter the water. Make these shots short, no more than three seconds each.

After the dive, complete the show with a sequence of divers relaxing and discussing their experiences. Begin with a wide shot of the water while the diver's voices are heard off camera. Pull back to include the divers,then cut to close-ups of individuals reliving their dive. Vary close-ups with a medium shot of an individual speaker taken from over the shoulder of a listener. End the sequence as your buddy turns towards the water; then zoom back to include his or her silhouette against the open sea. If the sun is setting, so much the better.

The resulting production should last between 5 and 15 minutes. It will entertain you and your friends for years to come.

Conclusion

In underwater photography and videography, enjoyment comes with knowledge. To help you grow in these exciting diving activities, NAUI offers courses in Underwater Photography, Underwater Video, and Underwater Modeling.

HUNTING & SPEARFISHING 22

SPEARFISHING

By Ron Pavelka NAUI #4860

Underwater hunting and spearfishing are very similar to hunting on land. Armed with the correct knowledge of the local laws, safety and the proper techniques, underwater hunting can be a truly enjoyable and rewarding activity you can incorporate into your diving interests.

Education is the single most important aspect of underwater hunting. The diver must not only know about the particular area in which he is diving, *i.e.*, the weather, currents, rip tides, depths and reef structures; he must also know the local restrictions for what species may be taken, quantity that may be possessed and size limits.

For more information on where to obtain the rules for fish collection in your locale, please refer to the Appendix.

Lastly, underwater hunters take only what they need for their immediate consumption. Remember, we would like to have our children and their children enjoy hunting beneath the surface of our waters.

Spear Gun Safety

The safe and proper use of a spear gun should be the primary concern for any underwater hunter. The spear gun or pole spear are weapons and should be treated as such. When your weapon is out of the water, there are many rules that you must not forget to ensure safe transportation.

Whenever your spear gun or pole spear is out of the water, the tip or point should be covered. Most local professional dive stores should have covers available for purchase. If a cover is not available, try pressing the spear tip into a tennis ball, beverage cork, or wrap a cloth around the spear tip and secure it with tape. With your spear tip properly covered, you will have much less of a chance of inflicting injury to yourself, fellow divers, the headliner of your automobile or your buddy's inflatable boat.

Upon arrival at the dive site, prepare your spear gun for use. When walking with your weapon, be sure to have the spear tip pointed forward where you can see it. When entering the water from a boat, have your buddy hand you the weapon after you

Geri Murphy photo

Figure 22.1

enter the water. If you enter the water from the beach, point the weapon outward in front of you and do not load it until you are well outside of the surf zone.

Many divers prefer to load their spear guns while resting on the surface. This is done so they will be "ready" to confront the big one on their way down. Other divers would rather load their spear gun on the bottom (more on techniques later). Whichever technique you employ, remember to make sure that all divers and objects, *i.e.*, boats, are clear (never load above the surface) and the safety must be in the ON position. The only time the safety should be released is just before pulling the trigger.

Figure 22.2 Be sure to always cover your spearpoint while transporting your speargun.

Once the spear gun is loaded, NEVER point it at any other diver, boat, or creature that you have no intention of spearing. Do not attempt to make any adjustments to the spear point or any other accessory on the spear gun once its loaded. Unload it first. Upon surfacing, unload your spear gun before you enter the surf zone or begin swimming back to the boat. Never hand a loaded spear gun to anyone on a boat.

Think Safety First!

Do not forget that the spear gun should be in good working order. Prior to any dive or dive trip, inspect the spear gun thoroughly. If anything looks suspicious, take it to your local dive store to have them check it over or return it to the factory.

Spear Gun/Spear Pole Selection

Selecting the proper weapon for your specific underwater hunting needs takes much consideration and research. As stated in the beginning of this section, underwater hunting is very similar to hunting on land. A weapon which works well in one area may be totally useless in another. Many hunters, both on land and below the surface, find it necessary to have a collection of weapons for various conditions, areas, terrain, and types of fish sought.

There are three basic categories of spearfishing weapons available with a few sub-categories. Upon examining the three basic categories, we find the pole spear, bang-stick, and the spear gun. Before looking further, let us arrive at an understanding of what each type of weapon is, what it is used for, and whether is it suited for your needs.

The Pole Spear

Many people still incorrectly call this the "Hawaiian Sling." The Hawaiian Sling was a product found in the 1950-60s and generally is not used today. Today's pole spear is much easier to use and usually less expensive than any of the other types of underwater hunting equipment. The pole spear can be one solid piece of either flexible fiberglass or rigid aluminum tubing, varying in length from 4 feet to 7 feet. The travel pole spear is gaining popularity because it can be "broken down" for each transportation. The travel pole spear can also be customized for length by adding or deleting sections. This enhances the use of the weapon. A pole spear is recommended for divers taking small fish up to (6-8 pounds), schooling fish or fish found above the reefs close to the surface or free swimming.

The Bang-Stick or Powerhead

This is a limited-use weapon and is not widely accepted by the diving public. This product was popular during the 1960-70s; however, most of the manufacturers have ceased production on this product for various reasons. The powerhead utilized a standard rifle, pistol or shotgun cartridge which is slipped into the powerhead and usually threaded back onto the main body. The powerhead can be attached to either a spear gun or pole spear and is generally used on larger or predatory fish. Most of these weapons have a manual safety switch which must be removed before firing. Once the spring-loaded unit strikes its target, a firing pin similar to that in a pistol strikes the cartridge and the projectile is on its way. The bang-stick or powerhead should be used only by a properly trained diver and all safety precautions should be read and thoroughly understood.

Spear Guns

This category has the wider selection than the previous two discussed. We can eliminate many of the spear gun types which were prevalent in the 1950-60s and concentrate on today's preferred weapons. In the past, spear guns used springs, CO_2 cartridges, pistol ammunition and even air from the diver's tanks to propel the shaft from the gun. If any of these spear guns are found at second-hand stores or handed down from your uncle who used to dive, they are best hung on your office wall as relics.

The most popular spear guns used today are the "band gun" and the "pneumatic gun". The band gun is the simpler of the two types of guns and has been regarded as the standard for many years. Until recently, the popularity of pneumatic guns was limited; however, with today's technology, the newer pneumatic boasts faster shaft speed, greater accuracy and easier loading.

In determining which spear gun is right for you, you must decide on a few simple factors—cost, maintenance, and types of fish to be taken. Pneumatic spear guns usually cost more than their band-powered counterparts. If you are spending a lot of time in the field where you have little or limited access to a repair facility, take a close look at a pneumatic gun before you choose it. Most band guns can be easily repaired while in the field with only a screw driver and a pair of pliers. As stated before, the pneumatic gun produces more muzzle velocity. That is, the spear shaft is exiting the gun at 250 mph. This means it will reach its target faster than most band guns. As far as accuracy, both types of spear guns compare favorably; it is on rare occasions that you can say one type of spear gun is more accurate than the other.

If you choose to hunt large migratory or free-swimming fish, a band gun is recommended. Most pneumatic guns are smaller in length, which diminishes their accuracy over long distances. For hunting larger fish that will not come in close to you, a longer gun (usually only found in band guns) is recommended.

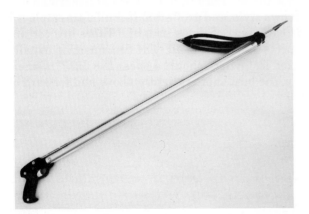

Figure 22.3 The Band Gun

Power and range can generally be determined by the length of the spear gun and the shaft, as well as by the diameter of the shaft. You will find two shaft diameters in use today: the 5/16" and 3/8" shaft. The 5/16" or thinner diameter shaft is usually faster because of less resistance in the water and lighter

Al Bruton photo

Figure 22.4 Proper way to cock gun.

weight. This could be compared to a 22-caliber bullet vs. the 3/8" diameter shaft being a 357 magnum. The larger shaft, like the larger bullet, can be slower traveling, but it will pack a lot more punch because of its weight if it is powered properly.

The length of the shaft (within reason) will help determine the accuracy over a larger distance. A larger gun does not necessarily mean larger fish. A long gun would be used to reach out to those fish that are too stubborn to get in close to, like your pelagic fish, i.e., Jacks or the Tuna family. A small gun is excellent in tight areas such as around reefs, wrecks, holes or rocky areas. A gun with a total length of no greater than 36" with a 24-28" shaft would be an excellent choice for the underwater hunter in this type of situation. A spear gun of this size should be reasonably accurate at a range of approximately 7 feet from the end of the gun.

For larger reef and bottom fish (bass, lingcod, halibut, grouper, or snapper), a spear gun with an overall length of 42-48" with a 36" shaft, preferably with a 3/8" diameter shaft, would be suitable for the job and assist you in landing the BIG ONE.

With all of the information about accuracy, the spear shaft will only travel as far as the shock line. If the shock line is only 6 feet long, your spear gun is only accurate to 6 feet. It can travel no further.

Power settings are standard on many of the pneumatic guns. If you are shooting at distance, you have the option of setting the power to HIGH. If you are shooting in close quarters around the rocks, at your discretion, you can simply reset the power to LOW with the flick of the switch. On your band powered spear gun, you have the ability to change the power by changing band lengths or diameters. Bands are made of surgical tubing and, according to studies by the manufacturer, the black tubing has the same elasticity as the amber-colored tubing. This material is found in three sizes that are recommended for band spear gun use — 1/2", 9/16" and 5/8". Manufacturers will usually put 1/2" or 9/16" bands on your gun. If your spear gun is equipped with a smaller diameter shaft (5/16"), do not use the heavier bands. This will cause the shaft to whip as it is released and will greatly affect your accuracy.

Figure 22.5 Various sizes of surgical tubing are available for various "power settings" on band guns.

Apply the 5/8" bands only to the longer shafts with the larger 3/8" diameter. The length of the bands is also important. When you purchase extra or replacement bands for your spear gun, use what the manufacturer has recommended. If you wish to get extra power, you might try going to the next diameter band, but make sure the length is the same as the one you removed. If you want to use the same size diameter band, you can generally use a band which is 2" shorter than the one which you removed.

If at anytime you have questions regarding replacement parts, modifications of your existing spear gun, or you wish to purchase a new spear gun and need some additional guidance, consult your local professional retail dive store.

Spear Point Selection

Selection of the proper spear point is as important as the selection of the proper gun for game sought and terrain to be dived. Nothing can be more frustrating to the spear fisherman than the use of a wrong point in the wrong place. The sharpness and edging of a spear point are important factors. Sharp, thin edges are not best while hunting in rocky areas, while a rockpoint, which is blunt, will do the job. It is recommended that you use sharp, thin-edged points for fish with larger scales or tough skin where penetration is difficult. The length of spear point wings must be determined by the game you are seeking. Generally, the faster, stronger or bigger the fish, the greater the wing length needed. The use of spinner points is highly advantageous for small-to medium-sized fish, as they prevent the spear point from spinning off the end of the shaft. A fixed point can be spun off and lost. For larger and stronger fish, the break-away point or slip-tip would be the proper choice. Selection of the proper break-away point for a specific gun is important. A large point on a small gun can severely affect the shaft speed and direction. The three-prong point is most often used with a small gun for flat fish and small fresh water fish. The paralyzer tip is designed primarily for use on a pole spear and is highly effective in rocky areas for close-range shots.

There is little doubt that the spear fisherman using the proper equipment can have spectacular results.

Spear Fishing Techniques

It is difficult, at best, to identify an exact technique to use. Each individual spear fisherman has his own style, and a different technique is employed for each type of game sought. There are certain aspects that apply to all. The first question usually asked is, "Where should I spear the fish?" Generally, the best shot is slightly above and forward of

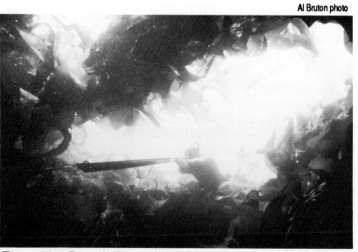

Figure 22.6 Diver hiding in kelp.

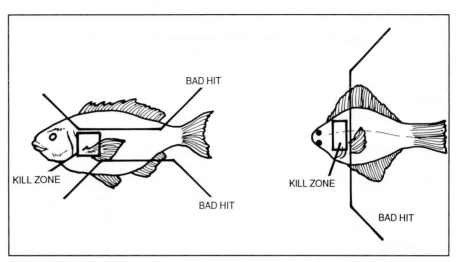

Figure 22.7 Kill Area

the pectoral fin in the gill plate area. Any shot from the eye back to the pectoral fin is usually a good shot, except in the upper area behind the eye. On a large fish, the bone structure in this area is sufficient enough to prevent penetration and can break a tip or bend your shaft. If a fish is shot in the soft gut area, it will usually work itself free. A technique used in the Gulf of Mexico for large fish is to spear the fish forward of the caudal fin to limit its swimming ability. The use of scuba is another important factor. As a rule, the noise of your bubbles will chase fish away, so patience must be especially applied. Pelagic fish can almost never be taken when using scuba.

When approaching a free-swimming fish, keep your body profile in a non-threatening position. Approach from below or even with the fish, not from above, except for bottom fish, such as halibut or sole. In stalking a fish, try to be fluid and smooth in your motions. Avoid rapid, jerky movements.

Aiming your spear gun is just like firing a land weapon. The arm which holds the gun should be fully extended so you can sight down the barrel. The other hand is usually placed on the butt of the gun to hold it securely. In this position, the gun becomes an extension of your arm; the trigger should be squeezed, not pulled or jerked. Each spear fisherman will have his own adaptations to this format, but success depends upon a rigid, extended gun with a smooth firing motion, as long as the line of sight is direct.

Rubber slings tend to lose 25% of their power in about 10 minutes when cocked, so many spear fisherman with multi-band guns will leave one sling uncocked and periodically rotate cocked slings.

Patience is a major part of successful spear fishing, but some techniques do exist to attract fish to you. One method, which is most popular for attracting bottom fish, is to chum for them by either bringing bait into the water with you or breaking up edible materials found in the area. A method used to attract pelagic fish is to run your hands up and down the gun barrel to make a squeaking noise or to strum your bands like a guitar string. Slapping your fins on the surface will also attract attention. And yet another common method is to learn where the fish pathways are. That is, find the routes of travel most popular for the fish sought. A common technique used in areas such as the California kelp forests is to hide in the middle of the surface canopy, be as still as possible and let the natural curiosity of the fish bring them to you. Divers around oil rigs will often try to come up under the fish or hide in the middle of the rig and shoot outward, away from the rig, towards their target. The diver in a reef area will hide where he has a clear shot of a pathway between the reefs.

The more serious or advanced spear fisherman will adapt his gun for a variety of specialized needs. The most common will be the addition of a line reel to enable him to play a large fish as the pole fisherman does. Many spear fisherman place a small light, such as a SUPER Q LITE on the barrel to sight the gun at night or for searching through large crevices in a reef structure. Often guns are rigged with stainless steel cable for use in rocky crevices around wrecks, and especially near oil rigs, to prevent a speared fish from fraying the shock line and breaking free. Many Gulf spear fishermen use a technique called "free shafting" in which the shaft is completely detached from the gun after firing. A kill or stoning shot is almost essential; however, if the fish is not stoned, it will generally "hole-up" for easy retrieval by the spear fisherman. Once a fish has been speared, it should not be removed from your shaft until it has been placed on a stringer, placed in a surface float, or returned to your boat.

Of course, the goal of spear fishing is to bring home dinner for all to enjoy. And, while we all enjoy a good fish story, the proof of the pudding is the actual fish. Once caught, you need only use a good fillet knife, a cutting board and a few minutes of your time to have the ingredients for a good fish dinner. Then it's down to the basics—a well prepared fish dinner by the spear fisherman for loved ones and good friends.

Al Bruton photo

Figure 22.8 Always rinse your equipment in fresh water after a dive.

Spear Gun Maintenance

Your spear gun is just like any other piece of diving equipment. It should be thoroughly rinsed in fresh water after each dive. With proper maintenance, a spear gun will last a lifetime and be ready to perform as it was intended to.

Beyond rinsings, silicone spray should be applied to the rubber slings to prevent cracking and prolong their longevity. It wouldn't hurt to apply a small amount of silicone spray to your shock line rubber as well. Before each use, check the shock line for fraying or knotting at the muzzle or slide ring. Inspect your spear point and look at the wings to see if they turn freely. The point itself should be sharp and can be filed to bring it back to it's original sharpness; be sure it is securely attached to the shaft. You can use either Teflon tape on the threads of the shaft or a few small drops of Loctite on the threads of the spear point to secure it to the shaft. Avoid over-torquing the spear point when threading it onto the shaft, as this might cause the end of the shaft to break.

Pneumatic spear guns should be pressurized periodically to ensure maximum power when needed. It is also recommended that every two years you have your pneumatic spear gun serviced by the factory. They will generally replace the seals, make any adjustments necessary, and send you back a spear gun ready to keep that big one instead of letting it get away.

Don't forget, you are a DIVER FIRST! Even while you are chasing the fish that your buddies won't believe you actually saw, you must always abide by the rules you learned in your entry-level scuba course.

RESEARCH DIVING

TECHNIQUES

By Dan Orr NAUI #5612

This segment is designed to familiarize the qualified recreational diver with the preparation and procedures necessary to participate in a submerged research project. Unlike recreational diving, the focus is not on the enjoyment of diving but the collection and retrieval of information. Diving skills are simply a vehicle by which research divers can cope with the potentially hostile environment while collecting the artifacts, living specimens and other types of valuable scientific data from a submerged site. As a successful research diver, you are the one who is best suited, by virtue of skills, abilities and temperament, to assist professional scientists (biologists, geologists, archaeologists, etc.) in their quest for knowledge.

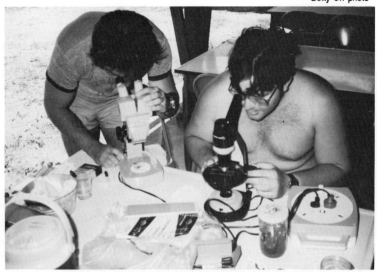

Figure 23.1 Research diver students conduct preliminary analysis of freshwater organisms during a water quality study.

Diver Training and Qualifications

You must have achieved a level of proficiency allowing you to focus your attention on the successful completion of an underwater task. Improper research or collecting techniques could invalidate the efforts of even the most careful and methodical scientist. In traditional diver education programs, this level of proficiency is not reached until you have completed at least advanced-level training.

Research Dive Organization

Research divers are an integral part of an overall research team involving the primary researcher, the diving coordinator (or diving officer), surface support personnel and research divers. Regardless of the apparent simplicity of any project, an operational unit must never consist of fewer than three (3) people; one buddy pair of well-qualified research divers and one surface support person. If the operation is being conducted from a boat, the surface support individual must be boat operator qualified. Organizational schemes depend upon the complexity and magnitude of the project.

Equipment Standards for Research Diving

Considering the important role equipment plays in the overall outcome of the scientific investigation, equipment and maintenance standards must be established and enforced. Each piece of equipment must be evaluated and its performance considered in the worst case scenario. You must not sacrifice any equipment simply for convenience or the sake of personal preference.

The Regulator System

All components of the regulator system (i.e., the octopus) must be able to provide a maximum air flow consistent with the expected workload of a working diver with a minimal amount of breathing resistance. A properly functioning regulator system is the key element in the successful conduct of any submerged research project.

The Buoyancy Compensator

The B.C. with redundant inflation systems including oral inflation, power inflation and the CO_2 cartridge quick inflation system, should be considered essential for each diver working in the open water.

There may be conditions where the use of the B.C. must come under additional scrutiny. One such situation involves those working under saturation conditions where an ascent without appropriate decompression would result in decompression sickness. This type of working condition precludes the necessity to maintain any type of surface orientation. Even in a rescue situation, the stricken diver must be returned to the habitat and maintained under pressure.

The Scuba Cylinder (Tank)

Your choice of a cylinder is largely dependent upon the air volume necessary to complete the required diving. Cylinders may be utilized as singles or in tandem (doubles). Certain working conditions may dictate the use of tank valves (or manifolds, for double tanks) which can accommodate dual regulator systems such as under ice, cave, wreck or deep diving. The use of a slingshot valve for single cylinders and the Benjamin manifold for double cylinders allows for a malfunctioning regulator to be deactivated via a valve while permitting the remaining air to be available through the secondary regulator. Some research divers prefer the use of the pony (or small volume) tank and regulator or the emergency breathing system (EBS) which incorporates a small volume tank with a mouthpiece/valve. These provide sufficient air for you to safely return to the surface in an out-of-air emergency.

The Exposure Suit (Wet or Dry)

The type of exposure protection you choose as a research diver is a function of the local environmental conditions, the time you expect to be underwater and the expected workload. The continued loss of body heat (Hypothermia) can result in losses in mental acuity and significant reductions in manual dexterity, grip strength and affect other motor functions. These impairments can reduce your effectiveness and reliability. Exposure protection can include thin, leotard-like Dive Skins ™, the wet suit and the dry suit. The dry suited research diver should have extensive dry suit experience prior to use in a working condition and must be proficient in procedures necessary to cope with dry suit emergencies. Your personal qualifications and the environmental conditions should be considered in the choice of exposure protection.

Masks, Snorkel and Fins

The choice of these items is largely a matter of your personal preference and the ability of the equipment to perform under the rigors of the work site. For example, silicone masks with nearly transparent skirts, may allow so much light into the mask as to form distracting images on the lens when working in a face-down position. Fins may also affect research diver performance. If you are expected to move materials along the bottom, you may elect to remove the fins and put them in a

secure place until the work is done. Some divers have elected to remove a portion of the blade so that they may walk on the bottom without completely sacrificing swimming ability. Your ability to quickly and successfully handle emergencies should never be sacrificed for convenience sake.

The Weight Belt (Weighting System)

The weight belt or weighting system you use must provide adequate compensation for the exposure suit without significant overweighting. Weights must be distributed to assist in maintaining the appropriate swimming or working position. This is best accomplished by positioning the bulk of your weights at or slightly forward of the hips. This position will reduce the likelihood of weight belt shift during exposure suit compression.

Dive Knives or Tools

Knives and other accessory equipment must be attached in such a position so as not to interfere with the safe use or removal of any other equip-

Betty Orr photo

Figure 23.2 Research diver conducting dry suit evaluation. Note pony tank used for emergency breathing and suit inflation and weight position.

RESEARCH DIVING TECHNIQUES

Figure 23.3 Research diver inspects anchor for marine growth.

ment. Hand tools should be tethered by a short lanyard to prevent loss during use and facilitate quick recovery if dropped.

Dive Flags and
Emergency Recognition Signals

Flags or signals should conform with local, national and international laws and regulations. When away from the protection of the dive or work boat, you should utilize a dive flag and float to assist in identification of your position to the surface support team and approaching watercraft. The flag/float also provides a buoyant platform for support of a tired or injured diver and in the holding of collected artifacts or specimens. A system should be devised whereby you could be notified in case of a diving or surface emergency (rapid weather changes, underwater or topside injuries. etc.). Signalling against the inside of a boat hull has been shown to be effective. If you spend considerable time on the surface as part of your in-water assignments, surface recall flags or some sound signal (i.e., a bullhorn) may be of value.

Miscellaneous

This category would include such things as watches or other reliable timing devices, a recently calibrated depth gauge (which could be useful in the development of a bottom topographical map of the site), a compass and a slate (for recording data).

If dive lights are considered as standard equipment, some thought must be given to the use of mask-mounted dive lights. They enable the working diver to maximize the use of hands but may also create difficulties when looking at the dive buddy (i.e., the eradication of night vision adaptation). Chemically-activated lights should be used as a backup light source for emergency signalling if the primary light fails.

Dive Preparation and Execution

The preparation and execution phases of a research diving experience are categorized as follows:

Buddy Selection and Assignments:

There must be complete compatibility between divers in order to accomplish any underwater task. Compatibility increases productivity and potential success of the project.

Dive Planning:

No amount of scientific knowledge can replace a human life. When planning all dives, safety is paramount. Working in depths greater than 30 feet, the possibility of decompression sickness must be considered. A decision must be made as to which dive profile will fulfill the objectives of the project without jeopardizing the divers. Along these lines, a new genre of automatic decompression computing devices is available which may significantly increase the diver's bottom time, especially if the research is conducted at a variety of depths during a single dive. Since these electronic devices relate changes in working depth with the "no-decompression limits" every few seconds, the researcher is able to make adjustments in dive plans to accommodate for changes in experimental conditions while remaining within the limits.

Preparatory of Simulation Dives:

Depending upon the difficulty, complexity or hazards involved in a planned diving project, it is advisable to conduct preliminary dives under controlled, simulated conditions. The simulation should be conducted in conditions similar to those found at the project site and require you to use all skills necessary to complete the actual working dive. This will allow you to familiarize yourself with the general conduct of the dive, reinforce buddy compatibility, review individual dive assignments, identify and correct mechanical or procedural problems related to the dive, gain confidence in all aspects of the overall diving evolution and reinforce familiarity with equipment and diving skills. It makes little practical sense for a researcher to

Figure 23.4 Research diver student inspects the draught marks etched into the bow of the Sweepstakes in Tobermory, Canada.

spend months in dry land preparation just to risk damage to the site by an out-of-control diver or dive team.

Pre-Dive Briefing & Hazard Identification:

The pre-dive briefing, conducted by the diving officer, gives the individual team members an opportunity to discuss problems and to consider all possible options in the event of changes in working conditions. The diving phase of the project should not be initiated until you know the tasks to be performed and how they relate to the entire project. The briefing should: 1) outline individual, team and project objectives; 2) delineate specific task assignments ; and, 3) review the dive profile. Part of the comprehensive pre-dive briefing is the identification and discussion of hazards.

Hooks, Snap Rings, Carabiners, Etc.:

In certain working conditions, equipment or accessories may be attached to you via a hook, snap ring or carabiner. You must carefully consider the application of any gear which may result in entanglement or entrapment. If you must use a snap ring or similar device, have it open inward, oriented in such a fashion as to eliminate the likelihood of entrapment from wires, cables or ropes or use a locking carabiner and do not wear anything you can't handle underwater.

Out-Of-Control Gear:

To the research project, out-of-control equipment is, potentially, one of the most serious problems. If the project requires a grid or other similar device, an errant SPG or additional second stage

(octopus) can become entangled, endangering you and possibly destroying weeks of work. Prior to active participation in the submerged research project, you must carefully consider the placement and control of all equipment. The SPG can be threaded up through the interior of a chest-mount B.C. or under the arm of the jacket-style so that it will be in front of the diver instead of trailing behind, or it can be placed behind the leg when maneuvering around the research site. Some thought must be given to the quantity of equipment you carry. Research divers should only carry equipment necessary to maintain basic diving safety and to complete the tasks required. Unnecessary gear will increase the hazard and reduce your effectiveness.

Breakdown of the Buddy System:

The buddy system is one of the tenets of diving safety. The buddy relationship, in the context of safe diving, begins with the preparatory phases and continues through the post-dive activities.

A highly efficient dive team should reinforce each other's abilities and compensate for any weaknesses. The productivity of an effective buddy pair should be greater than the sum of their individual productivities. If, however, the buddy team does not function efficiently, its productivity will suffer.

Hand Protection is Essential:

Since the research diver uses the hands for much of the work, protection from cuts, scratches, abrasions and stings is essential. Seemingly minor wounds, left untended, can worsen and reduce your working effectiveness.

The Entry

You should choose an entry procedure which will minimize the potential danger to the diver and the possibility of lost or displaced equipment. From a boat, whether using a back roll or giant stride entry, all equipment must be under control. Prior to the entry, as much air as possible should be removed from the B.C. Excessive buoyancy, coupled with wave action and currents, may cause the diver to be drawn into the boat hull after entering.

The Descent

You must begin the descent from a head-up/feet-down position. Head-first surface dives while diving should be avoided because rapid pressure

RESEARCH DIVING TECHNIQUES

changes make clearing difficult; the head-down position reduces the effectiveness of the buoyancy compensator's inherent air elimination systems, and the effort required creates an unnecessary workload. During the descent, alter your position to horizontal or parallel to the bottom, finally reaching the bottom or site in a slightly head-down position. This position will protect the site from disturbance caused by fin-generated water movement.

Work on the Bottom

You should reach the bottom neutrally buoyant and in such a position that movement around the bottom will not disturb the substrate. Out-of-control fins can do much to render a site useless by introducing material from outside the research area, drastically reducing visibility, and significantly increasing the risk to all divers in the vicinity. You may "finger walk" through the site to minimize disturbance of the substrate. You must be constantly aware of the position of your legs so that kick-generated water movement is away from the focus of the investigation. If numerous samples or artifacts must be removed to the surface for analysis, a system should be developed to send samples to the surface independent of the dive team. This will minimize physical and procedural problems brought on by multiple ascents.

The Ascent

You must be in control of your physical attitude during the ascent so as not to jeopardize your welfare, that of your buddy and the data or artifacts you have collected.

The Proper Exit

The best exit is one which combines ease and safety. A cavalier attitude toward exiting could result in serious potential risk to you or your buddy if you slip or fall back into the water.

The Post-Dive Debriefing

The overall success of the project sometimes depends as much upon post-dive activities as pre-dive preparation and diver performance. The debriefing should be used to:

Identify Research and Diving Objectives

The identification and reporting of completed and upcoming diving and research objectives will minimize duplication of tasks and reduce the likelihood of overlapping between individual divers and dive teams.

Pre-Dive Preparation

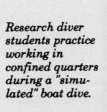

Research diver students practice working in confined quarters during a "simulated" boat dive.

Pre-dive preparation is conducted by each individual diver to assure readiness for open water diving. An integral part of this procedure is the buddy check. The buddy check should include anything that has the potential to reduce the safety or effectiveness of the research diver and should continue through all phases of equipment donning and various stages of the diving sequence in order to identify minor problems which may prove hazardous if left uncorrected.

Prior to commencing any underwater work, you should conduct a short pre-dive review. This should include:

1) Review hand signals. This will help refresh the memory and identify the use of "pet" or regional hand signals that may not be a part of each diver's manual vocabulary.

2) Review the dive plan. This review will prevent dive team members from being on incorrect or different dive plans.

3) Review emergency procedures. You should spend a few moments practicing complex emergency skills, such as out-of-air emergency procedures. These critical skills must be practiced regularly to be an effective part of the diver's safety repertoire.

All dives should be planned so that each dive team can brief the next team as to progress of the research effort, environmental changes and other factors so that dive team members can be prepared and ready to improvise.

Identify Potential Problems
and Develop Solutions

All errors or problems should be identified and discussed to assure that the appropriate response was used. No problems are insurmountable if given the appropriate amount of time for thought and the proper application of sound common sense. It is important that problems not be perpetuated and their seriousness compounded by neglect.

Any research project at a submerged site presents the principal investigator and research diver with challenges not found in any other realm of diving or scientific investigation. This section of the Advanced Technology Manual is designed to provide information which can be used to assist you in becoming a research diver and help you to develop procedural methods that will maximize the potential for success, scientific validity and the safety of all concerned.

COMMERCIAL DIVING   24
TECHNIQUES

By Steven Barsky NAUI #2076

Commercial diving is a career choice which crosses almost every sport diver's mind at some point.   The fantasy of the commercial diver, his work and his lifestyle, are something out of a Hollywood movie.   While the fantasy of a commercial diver's life might seem "romantic", the realities of the diving industry are harsh.   The realities of commercial diving are: rusty barges and lousy plumbing, surly, unwashed men, greasy diesel machinery, steel decks, and diving in cold, muddy, zero visibility water. Commercial diving involves simple things like hauling 50 pound sacks of sand for hours on end to stabilize offshore drilling rigs resting on shallow bottoms in rough water.

Figure 24.1

valuable to a potential employer. No one will hire you just because you can go underwater and blow bubbles. You must be able to perform as part of a commercial diving crew, topside and underwater. You must have reasonable mechanical ability. Skill areas considered valuable by commercial diving companies include welding, diesel engine maintenance and repair, rigging, explosives, non-destructive testing, plumbing and pipe fitting, mechanical drawing, technical report writing, photography, and electronics. As a diver, you are expected to be familiar with each of the above mentioned subjects.

Most commercial diving done today is performed in the service of the offshore oil industry, a tough business subject to the boom or bust cycles of petroleum supply and demand. Divers work for diving contractors who sub contract to offshore construction firms, drilling firms, or directly to oil companies. There is little employment for commercial divers outside the offshore oil fields.

The 1960s and 1970s saw tremendous growth in the numbers of oil field divers. Since then, with the world oil glut and improvements in underwater robotic technology, the demand for divers has declined, despite the advertising claims by commercial diving schools. However, there will always be jobs for commercial divers who possess a professional attitude with the skills to perform a wide variety of underwater tasks.

Training is the key to employment in the commercial diving industry. No reputable diving firm will hire you unless you have graduated from a recognized commercial diving school. It is also essential to develop other abilities to make you

Upon graduation from commercial diving school, you can expect to be employed as a diver's apprentice or "tender". While you are attempting to get hired as a tender, you must be willing to go wherever there is work. Most commercial diving work in the continental U.S. is still in the Gulf of Mexico, specifically Texas and Louisiana.

Tenders are expected to "pay their dues" over a period of time ranging from one to four years. While working as a tender, your wages will be low, only a bit above minimum wage.

During the bust cycles in the petroleum industry, when the price of oil is depressed, there may be periods when both divers and tenders go without work for weeks or months on end. Only truly dedicated tenders will have the determination to stick it out until the work picks up again. Survival means falling back on other skills, part-time work, and unemployment benefits.

During a good year, tenders and divers can usually expect to work offshore between 150 and 200 days. This time may be broken up into periods lasting anywhere from one day to several consecutive months. In the United States, divers and tenders, like doctors, live with a "beeper". When the beeper goes off, you go to work. You are on call 24 hours a day while you are on shore. On overseas jobs, the time offshore is usually 30 days, followed by 10 days of leave. While offshore, the normal work day is 12 hours on, 12 hours off, seven days a week. There is no such thing as a holiday offshore. Every tender and diver misses important family events (birthdays, anniversaries, etc.) many times throughout his career. Offshore, you will be living with many different people under confining and unpleasant living conditions. How you get along with others is often more important to your advancement in the profession than the actual skills you are able to demonstrate.

Tenders are expected to perform a variety of tasks, including maintenance of diving equipment and machinery, operation of decompression chambers, tending the diver's air hose, painting equipment, building equipment, and, occasionally, diving. Your performance on deck and in the water will be carefully scrutinized and will be used in the final determination of whether you have earned the right to "break out" to diver status.

Almost all commercial diving today involves surface-supplied diving, i.e., diving where the diver's breathing gas is pumped down to him through a hose. The hose is bundled together into a "tether" or "umbilical", with communications wire and a depth-sensing system. The diver's tether may also include a hot water supply (for diver heating) and a video cable (to transmit pictures to topside). Less than 1% of oil field diving is performed on scuba. The reasons commercial divers use surface-supplied equipment are for extended bottom times, communications, accurate depth control, diver heating and the requirement for special breathing mixtures.

Since commercial divers work for long periods underwater, it is neither efficient nor safe for them to return to the surface to change scuba tanks. It is more productive to keep you underwater until you complete your job, within the limits of reasonable decompression times, comfort and performance. Surface-supplied diving provides this capability.

Figure 24.2 Most commercial diving is done to support offshore oil producing operations. This platform sits in 400 feet of water.

Communications are essential when divers work with hydraulic tools and other surface support, such as cranes, to handle large and bulky machinery and equipment. The diver must be able to direct topside to lower to him the tools and other items needed to get the job done. Certain tasks, such as underwater electric cutting and welding, are impossible to complete safely without communications to topside to control the electrical power source. This is another benefit of surface-supplied diving.

In colder waters, a hot water hose is usually part of the diver's tether. This hose connects to the hot water suit. A hot water suit fits like a loose-fitting wet suit. It has internal tubes which run down the diver's back and chest, as well as along each arm and leg. Hot water is pumped down through a hose, from a surface boiler and enters the hot water suit

COMMERCIAL DIVING TECHNIQUES

through a valve at the waist. The water vents from the suits at the cuffs, ankles and collar of the suit. Where the logistics of fuel for hot water burners are a problem, dry suits substitute for hot water suits.

Surface control is also imperative in deep diving where gas mixtures are changed as the diver's depth varies. As a diver, you know that as you descend the partial pressure of each gas in your breathing supply increases. At 100 feet, the partial pressure of nitrogen causes nitrogen narcosis. At 300 feet, the normal amount of oxygen in air becomes toxic. Accordingly, commercial divers usually use mixtures of helium and oxygen at depths deeper than 150 feet. Helium, an inert gas that is lighter than nitrogen, does not produce the same narcotic effect at depth. The level of oxygen is also decreased in the breathing mixture at increasing depths. For example, at 400 feet, your breathing mixture would probably be 96% helium and 4% oxygen.

The helmets and full face masks worn by commercial divers are usually made of fiberglass, steel, or brass. Modern helmets and masks incorporate some method of equalizing pressure in the ears, an oral/nasal mask for preventing a carbon dioxide (CO_2) buildup, and a microphone and earphones for communicating with topside.

For deep work, divers wear "bail-out" or "pony" bottles attached to their diving harness. The bail-out bottle is connected to the diver's helmet. If the topside air supply is interrupted, the diver uses the bail-out bottle to return to topside or to a submerged diving bell.

Diving bells are used for most work at depths greater than 250 feet. The bell functions as a dry, safe haven for divers at extreme depths. Bells are constructed of steel and are spherical or cylindrical in shape. They are equipped with thick plexiglass viewing ports and double hatches on the bottom end. The bell also carries emergency breathing gas cylinders externally along with the diver's tools. Inside the bell are valves and gauges to control the hot water and gas supplies. There is also usually an electrically powered bell heater and gas scrubber (for removal of carbon dioxide from the bell environment).

When divers are working at great depths for extended periods of time, it is impractical to decompress them after each dive. The decompression from deeper dives far exceeds the length of the dive itself. The lengthy times required for in-water decompression present tremendous risk to the diver. Under these circumstances, it is more practical to keep the divers under pressure and complete their decompression obligation at one time. This concept is called saturation diving.

The earliest saturation diving, as pioneered by Cousteau and the U.S. Navy, took place with divers living on the sea floor in underwater habitats. In commercial diving today, the divers live under pressure in very large decompression chambers on the deck of a ship, barge or drill rig.

When it is time to go to work, a diving bell is attached to the chamber by a mating flange and divers transfer into the bell under pressure. Next, the hatches on the bell and the chamber are closed and the bell is separated from the chamber. Inside the bell, the divers are at the same pressure they were under in the chamber. All of this takes place on the deck of the surface support vessel.

The bell is lowered over the side to the work site. At depth, the pressure inside the bell is equalized to the surrounding water pressure. There are usually two divers in the bell. Each takes his turn tending and diving, usually spending four hours or more in the water. At the end of their shift, the divers return to the bell, the hatches are sealed, the bell returns to the surface and a fresh team of divers changes places with the tired men in the bell. This rotation of divers will go on around the clock, 24 hours per day, seven days a week, until the job is complete.

Figure 24.3 Remotely operated vehicles, or "ROVs", like this one are now taking over a good portion of the work formerly performed by commercial divers.

The maximum length of time a diver will be committed to "sat" does not usually exceed one month. Normally, there will be three teams of saturation divers to share the work.

As a diver, you cannot return directly to the surface once your body is saturated with helium at depth. A diver cut off from the diving bell and accidentally returned to one atmosphere will suffer explosive decompression sickness and will be dead long before he hits the surface. Decompression from a saturation dive requires about one day for every 100 feet of depth, *i.e.*, a 600 foot dive requires about six days of decompression.

While the divers are saturated, there is another team of men on the deck who run all the topside machinery. This crew will be comprised of shift supervisors, other divers, life support technicians, and tenders.

There is a tremendous variety of oil field tasks which divers perform. A good diver has at least some familiarity with all of them. On exploratory drill rigs engaged in the search for oil or natural gas, divers inspect and maintain the drilling vessels and the sub-sea drilling machinery.

Once oil has been discovered in a particular area, the next step is to install a permanent platform and connect pipelines to pump the oil to shore for processing. Divers are used in all phases of this work. During platform installation, divers open valves to flood parts of the platform for sinking, check the pilings which are driven around the legs of the platform to anchor it in position, and cut away excess steel structural components used to support the platform when it was launched. Pipeline and platform installation require the diver to use massive hydraulic tools.

As offshore platforms age, divers inspect and repair them. Underwater photography, video, nondestructive testing, welding and cutting are used heavily during these activities. A written inspection report, with photographs, is expected by the customer at the completion of each platform inspection and repair job.

Finally, when platforms and pipelines are no longer producing, divers remove the aged structures. This work may involve the use of explosives and underwater cutting equipment.

The commercial diver's lifestyle is characterized by cowboy boots, Rolex watches, briefcases stuffed with calculators, chewing tobacco, passports, foreign work permits, airline tickets, magazines, paperback books, diving manuals, playing cards, letters from girlfriends, and divorce papers. It is a difficult way to live because you rarely know when, or where, you will have to go to work. You must be willing to drop everything and go to work whenever the company needs you.

As a commercial diver, you must develop certain attitudes towards your diving and work. You must be so comfortable underwater you forget entirely about your equipment, the low visibility, any discomfort involved and totally narrow your concentration to the task at hand.

Good divers develop a mind set which doesn't allow them to give up on any task. The words, "I can't...", are not a part of any successful diver's vocabulary. As a diver, you must find a way to complete every underwater task assigned. If you are unable to complete a job, there is always a line of tenders behind you waiting to break out as divers.

There are still very few female commercial divers at this time. One consideration for any female commercial diver is the hazard of decompression sickness to a fetus in a woman who is unaware she is pregnant. In commercial diving, decompression sickness is a common occurrence. Most commercial divers will suffer various types of bends many times throughout their diving career. This is due to the fact that almost all commercial dives involve decompression. This creates a much

Figure 24.4 Lauching a diving bell over the side can be complicated even under relatively good conditions.

COMMERCIAL DIVING TECHNIQUES

higher risk than sport divers are exposed to as part of their normal no-decompression profiles.

The risks involved in commercial diving extend far beyond decompression sickness. There are the usual accidents which occur around any construction job, such as mishaps with tools and electricity. Oil field work imposes special hazards such as poisonous hydrogen sulfide leaks, well "blowouts", and fires. There are the dangers of transporting men and materials between a variety of large vessels and helicopters during gale force winds and high seas. Despite all this, there are surprisingly few fatalities in the commercial diving industry. More divers are probably killed in automobile accidents on shore than in mishaps offshore during the course of an average year.

Much work formerly performed by divers during the '60s and '70s has now been taken over by remotely operated vehicles (ROVs). These "swimming robots" are driven by topside "pilots" via television monitors and controls. ROVs have displaced divers in deep water inspection and drill rig work. As the robotics industry becomes more sophisticated, the ROVs will continue to cut into the diver's work. ROVs become very economical at depths below 300 feet since their costs are fairly fixed, regardless of depth. Conversely, diving operations become more expensive with each foot of descent. While there will always be work for divers, the probable mix of offshore work in the future will be 60% ROVs (or other systems) and 40% manned, ambient-pressure diving.

The pay for commercial divers has steadily dwindled since the early '80s. The best paid divers have highly specialized abilities, such as hyperbaric pipeline welders who repair pipelines to engineering specifications in dry underwater welding habitats. Divers with this type of ability make as much as $100,000 during a good year. For a beginning diver, salaries range between $20,000 and $30,000 per year. Experienced divers generally earn between $35,000 and $50,000 per year and as much as $75,000 during a good year. If you consider the demands required by the industry, this is not a lot of money. It's possible for a competent tradesman to make this type of income in many professions on shore. To be a diver means you must place a higher value on the profession than on the amount of money you make.

Most divers in the industry rarely work offshore for more than 10 years. After that time, they either take an onshore position with the diving company or leave the industry. The stressful lifestyle and intense competition from younger, entry-level di-

Figure 24.5 Hydraulic tools, like this special underwater saw, are designed to withstand the abuse of commercial diving operations.

vers all combine to force many divers out of the business.

From this description of commercial diving, you can see that this isn't aquafarming, treasure hunting or life with Jacques Cousteau.

DIVING LEADERSHIP

By Dennis Graver NAUI #1103L

There are many, many diving activities. Some people like to sightsee, while others like to hunt or collect. Some individuals like photography or videography in shallow, calm waters, and others long to explore wrecks in deep, cold, turbulent waters. Adventure beckons some divers into caves, swift rivers and beneath the ice. The varied opportunities of diving offer something of interest to everyone who becomes qualified to scuba dive.

Some people are more interested in other people than in an underwater hobby. Others have tried nearly every activity diving has to offer and are seeking something new. Some individuals just want to be recognized as being the best there is at anything they do, diving included. And many people experience a high degree of satisfaction by turning others onto the fun and adventure of scuba diving.

For all the reasons identified in the foregoing paragraph and more, many divers become interested in diving leadership as a special interest area. Many others are searching for the activity that is right for them, but haven't found it. Perhaps that interest area is leadership. This article is an introduction to the exciting topic of diving leadership. You will learn the various leadership ratings and qualifications, what leadership training is like, and how to qualify to become a diving leader.

NAUI offers three non-instructor leadership ratings: Assistant Instructor, Divemaster, and Skin Diving Leader. Each rating fulfills a different need.

The Assistant Instructor rating is the initial leadership certification. This program is designed to test individuals in advanced waterskills and provide an introduction to the basics of diving instruction. A certified NAUI Assistant Instructor may, under the direct control and supervision of a NAUI Instructor, assist in the teaching of skin and scuba diving during sanctioned diving courses, including open water training. An Assistant Instructor is also qualified to attend a NAUI Instructor Training course, provided all prerequisites are met.

The NAUI Divemaster rating is the highest NAUI leadership-level certification other than Instructor. The course trains experienced and knowledgeable divers to organize and conduct open water dives for certified divers. Certified Divemasters may also assist NAUI Instructors with the open water training of students and may attend a NAUI Instructor Training course if all other prerequisites are met.

The NAUI Skin Diving Leader certification course trains and qualifies persons to train and issue certifications to students of skin (breath-hold) diving. Certified SDLs may independently teach NAUI-sanctioned Skin Diving courses and issue Skin Diver certifications and may, if scuba qualified, assist a NAUI Instructor with scuba courses.

An excellent introduction to a position of authority in diving is the NAUI Diving Leadership specialty course. This program introduces you to the skills and knowledge necessary for a NAUI leadership position. You are given opportunities to handle

Figure 25.1 The NAUI Divemaster program trains experienced divers to organize and conduct open water dives for certified divers.

others in open water during simple diving activities and under controlled conditions.

Training for any rating of leadership includes development of watermanship and diving skills, knowledge expansion, dive organization and control, learning communication and instruction skills, rescue, first aid and emergency procedures.

The general prerequisites for a NAUI leadership course are minimum age of 18, training and certification in the NAUI Diving Rescue Techniques Specialty course, verification of good physical condition (as indicated by a complete medical examination for diving), and diving experience of eight open-water hours for Skin Diving Leader, 10 hours underwater for Assistant Instructor, and 20 hours of bottom time for a Divemaster. You are also required to provide your own equipment. The requirements for participation in the Diving Leadership Specialty are less stringent. You need only to be 18 years of age, a certified diver and provide your own equipment.

Typical leadership training includes an orientation session with your instructor. You will handle the administrative requirements, get an overview of the training, agree on a training schedule, and become familiar with the specific requirements you need to meet to qualify for certification. You will learn where to obtain the information necessary to increase your knowledge.

Special leadership waterskill sessions are usually conducted in a pool before you begin assisting an instructor with classes or other divers. Your watermanship ability is evaluated and instruction is provided for improvement. You are shown how to perform skin and scuba skills that require a high degree of control, and practice the skills until you can perform them proficiently. Your lifesaving and

Figure 25.3 NAUI Instructors must develop strong communication skills.

rescue skills are reviewed, evaluated and enhanced. You learn how to demonstrate skills to entry-level students and some of the basics of organizing and controlling students for confined water training.

As your leadership training progresses, you learn how to brief and instruct divers, how to organize and conduct diving operations, how to recognize, prevent and cope with typical problems, how to guide and escort student divers, and how to deal with emergency situations. You work as a safety assistant for an instructor for a number of open water dives. Divemaster trainees are tasked with organizing and conducting dives under the supervision of an Instructor. The seven required excursions include shore, boat, night, deep and environmental dives.

Successful completion of your training results in a prestigious leadership certification. Additional recognition is frequently provided in the form of a special jacket, hat or other means to identify you as someone with special qualifications in your dive group. You will be proud of your achievement and will experience a new level of respect.

If you would like to help others learn to dive or to dive more safely, would like to elevate your level of knowledge and skills and increase your abilities, would like to learn leadership techniques that are useful in all aspects of life, and would like the prestige associated with higher levels of certification, consider a NAUI leadership rating. More detailed information is available from your instructor or from NAUI Headquarters. Set your goal today; make your plans and begin preparing for your leadership training. You will meet new buddies, have wonderful experiences and may even discover an exciting new career.

Figure 25.2 If you would like to help others dive more safely, NAUI leadership provides an excellent opportunity.

DIVING LEADERSHIP

LOOKING BACK TO THE FUTURE

By the time you read this, you will be close to completing your NAUI Advanced training. Congratulations on your achievement.

Your mind is probably packed with thoughts, feelings and memories due to the intensity of your course. You may well feel that you have only discovered how much you do not know about diving. That is OK, because you can never learn all there is to know about even one aspect of our incredible activity. You should, however, feel more knowledgeable and competent as a diver and should look forward to diving opportunities with more enthusiasm than ever. If this is the way you feel, then your Advanced training has been successful.

With all these thoughts and emotions in mind, think for a minute about your next step in diving. Don't let the fun of learning and increasing your diving skills stop here. The decision should already

be made to continue your education in diving. The only question is which course to take next. You have a couple of options to consider as an Advanced Diver. You can either take specialty training and pursue the goal of becoming a NAUI Master Scuba Diver, or you can enroll in one of the NAUI leadership courses and profit by sharing the wonders of diving with others. The choice is yours and you have earned the right to make it by qualifying as a NAUI Advanced Scuba Diver.

No matter which path of diving education you choose, we hope the experiences of your Advanced training have been wonderful for you. We wish you calm, clear waters and friendly, caring buddies.

We look forward to working with you in another NAUI educational publication and hope you will be studying one soon.

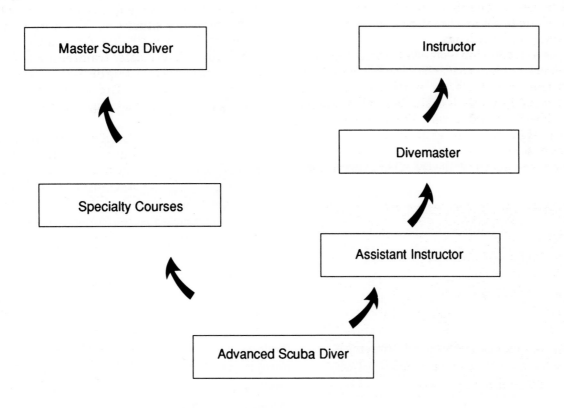

Which path will you choose?

BASIC CONVERSION TABLES

Length

1 centimeter	=	0.394 inches
1 meter	=	3.281 feet
1 meter	=	1.094 yards
1 meter	=	0.547 fathoms
1 kilometer	=	0.621 statute miles
1 kilometer	=	0.540 nautical miles
1 inch	=	2.54 centimeters
1 foot	=	0.305 meters
1 yard	=	0.914 meters
1 fathom	=	1.829 meters
1 statute mile (5280 feet)	=	1.609 kilometers
1 nautical mile (6080 feet)	=	1.853 kilometers

Capacity/Volume

1 cubic centimeter	=	0.061 cubic inches
1 cubic meter	=	35.315 cubic feet
1 cubic meter	=	1.308 cubic yards
1 liter (1000cc)	=	0.035 cubic feet
1 liter	=	0.220 gallons
1 liter	=	1.760 pints
1 cubic inch	=	16.387 cubic centimeters
1 cubic foot	=	0.028 cubic meters
1 cubic foot	=	28.316 liters
1 cubic yard	=	0.765 cubic meters
1 pint	=	0.568 liters
1 gallon	=	4.546 liters

Weight

1 kilogram	=	2.205 pounds
1 metric ton	=	0.984 long tons (2205 pounds)
1 pound	=	0.454 kilograms
1 long ton	=	1.016 metric tons (1016 kilograms)

Pressure

1 kilogram per square centimeters = 14.223 pounds per square inch

1 pound per square inch = 0.0703 kilograms per square centimeter

Depth Conversion Table

Meters	Feet	Fathoms
1	3.2808	0.5468
2	6.5616	1.0936
3	9.8424	1.6404
4	13.1	2.2
5	16.4	2.7
6	19.6	3.3
7	23.0	3.8
8	26.2	4.4
9	29.5	4.9
10	32.8	5.5
11	36.1	6.0
12	39.4	6.6
13	42.7	7.1
14	45.9	7.7
15	49.2	8.2
16	52.5	8.7
17	55.8	9.3
18	59.1	9.8
19	62.3	10.4
20	65.6	10.9
30	98.4	16.4
40	131.2	21.9
50	164.0	27.3
60	196.8	32.8
70	229.7	38.3
80	262.5	43.7
90	295.3	49.2
100	328.1	54.7
110	360.9	60.1
120	393.7	65.6
130	426.5	71.1

Water

1 litre of fresh water weighs 1 kilogram.

1 cubic foot of fresh water weighs approximately 62.5 lbs.

1 cubic foot of sea water weighs approximately 64 lbs.

Temperature

To convert degrees Centigrade to degrees Fahrenheit: multiply 9/5 and add 32.

To convert degrees Farenheit to degrees Centigrade: subtract 32 and multiply by 5/9.

Approximate Conversions

Miles to kilometers	Multiply by 8/5
Kilometers to miles	Multiply by 5/8
Statute miles to nautical miles	Deduct 1/8
Nautical miles to statute miles	Add 1/7
Pounds per square inch (psi) to atmospheres	Divide by 14.7
Atmospheres or bars to kilos per square centimeter	Nearly the same
Water depth (feet) to bars absolute	Divide by 33 and add 1 bar
Water depth (meters) to bars absolute	Divide by 10 and add 1 bar
Bars absolute to feet of water depth	Subtract 1 bar and multiply by 33
Bars absolute to meters of water depth	Subtract 1 bar and multiply by 10

GLOSSARY

As an Advanced diver, you should be familiar with the following terms as well as those on pages 52 and 53.

Absolute pressure - The total pressure, including atmospheric and hydrostatic pressures, exerted at any point.

Absolute temperature - The lowest temperature that could possibly be reached (-459 degrees F. or -273 degrees C.).

Absorption - The taking up of nitrogen in tissues.

Air embolism - A lung overexpansion injury characterized by blockage of an artery by a bubble of air.

Algae - Non-flowering aquatic plants.

Alternobaric vertigo - Vertigo produced following a sudden release of pressure in an ear during an ascent.

Alveolus - See page 52

Ambient pressure - The pressure of the fluid surrounding an object.

Amonoton's Law - "For any gas at a constant volume, the pressure of the gas will vary directly with the absolute temperature."

Analog depth gauge - An instrument with hands that point to numbers as a direct result of mechanical force.

Angle of attack - The angle between a diver's longitudinal axis and his or her trim.

Anoxia - See page 52

Anxiety - Fear or apprehension which one experiences in the face of real or imagined danger.

Apnea - See page 52

Archimede's Principle - "Any object wholly or partly immersed in a fluid is buoyed up by a force equal to the weight of the fluid displaced by the object."

Asphyxia - See page 52

Backrush - The return flow of water from waves rushing onto a shore. Sometimes mistakenly referred to as "undertow".

Balanced valve - A valve that controls pressure in such a way that the pressure does not affect the force needed to open and close the valve.

Barodontalgia - See page 52

Barotrauma - See page 52

Bearing - The angular direction to an object expressed in terms of compass degrees from north, e.g., a bearing of 270 degrees.

Benthic - Pertaining to life found in or at the bottom of the oceans.

Bends - See Decompression Sickness.

Bezel - A rotating ring on a compass or watch that can be set as a reference.

Bloom - A condition of poor visibility resulting from overpopulation of algae or plankton.

Bottom timer - A device which automatically records a diver's bottom time.

Bourdon movement gauge - An instrument that uses a curved metal tube as a pressure detector.

Boyle's Law - "For any gas at a constant temperature, the volume will vary inversely with the absolute pressure while the density will vary directly with the absolute pressure."

Bradycardia - See page 52

Bronchi - See page 52

Buoyancy - The upward force exerted on an immersed or floating body by a fluid.

Burst disc - A thin metal disc found in all valves as a safety feature and designed to rupture and relieve excessive pressure in a cylinder.

Capillaries - Tiny blood vessels that join arteries to veins in the body.

Capillary depth gauge - An instrument that indicates depth via the compression of air in a transparent tube.

Carotid arteries - The principle arteries supplying blood to the brain.

Carotid sinus - See page 52

Ceiling - A depth indicated by a dive computer above which one may not safely ascend.

Charles' Law - "For any gas at a constant pressure, the volume of the gas will vary directly with the absolute temperature."

Chart - The equivalent of a map for bodies of water and the adjacent coastlines.

Chemoreceptors - See page 52

Closed-circuit scuba - A system in which all exhaled breath is recirculated within the system and rebreathed.

Collapsing breakers - A type of surf forming from medium swells breaking over a very steep bottom. The waves break over the lower halves of themselves with very little splash or foaming.

Compass card - A magnetized disc within a compass which rotates to indicate a Northerly direction.

Conduction - The transmission of heat by direct material contact.

Conservation - Management of human usage of the waters so they may yield the greatest sustainable benefit to present and future generations. Preserving, guarding or protecting natural resources.

Console - A housing for two or more diving instruments.

Convection - The transmission of heat by the movement of heated fluids.

Coriolis effect - Deflection of winds and currents caused by the rotation of the Earth.

Cramp - A muscle spasm producing pain and temporary disability.

Cyanosis - See page 52

Cylinder pressure gauge - An instrument used to measure air pressure in a cylinder above water.

Dalton's Law - "The total pressure exerted by a mixture of gases is equal to the sum of the pressures that would be exerted by each of the gases if it alone were present and occupied the volume."

Dead reckoning - Navigation by means of estimating distance and direction.

Decompression sickness - A serious bodily afflication caused by nitrogen bubble formation in the body and caused by too rapid a reduction of pressure.

Dehydration - Abnormal loss of fluid from the body.

Density - The quantity of a substance per unit volume.

Deviation - Error induced in a compass needle reading by the effect of nearby metal or a magnetic source.

Dew point - The temperature to which air must be cooled, at a constant pressure, in order to become saturated with water, and below which condensation occurs.

Diaphragm depth gauge - An instrument that uses the movement of a metal diaphragm in conjunction with mechanical linkage to indicate depth.

Diffusion - The scattering of light. Also the movement of molecules in a liquid or gas from a region of high concentration to a region of lower concentration.

Digital depth gauge - An instrument that uses a pressure transducer, electronics, and a battery to display depth in a digital form.

Diuresis - See page 52

Diuretics - Substances that increase the output of urine by the kidneys.

Dive computer - An instrument that continuously calculates time and depth and provides a digital display of a diver's decompression status.

Dive pattern - The total course or dive path followed during a dive.

Diving reflex - Physiological changes, most notably slowing of the heart, produced by water in contact with the face.

Downstream valve - A valve that opens in the direction of gas flow.

Drag - The force of resistance to movement.

Drowning - Death due to aspiration of fluid.

Dump valve - A manually operated exhaust valve for a buoyancy compensator that allows air to be quickly expelled.

Dysbarism - See page 52

Dyspnea - See page 52

Ebb tide - An outgoing tide.

Ecology - The study of living organisms in their environments.

Edema - See page 52

Elimination - The release of nitrogen from tissues.

Embolus - See page 52

Emphysema - See page 52

Energy - The capacity to do work.

Epiglottis -A thin plate of cartilage that folds over and protects the windpipe when swallowing.

Epilimnion - The warmer layer of water above a thermocline

Equilibrium - A state of balance between opposing pressures.

Euphoria - A feeling of elation and well-being.

Eustachian Tube - See page 52

Expiratory reserve - See page 52

Feeder zone - A region in the surf zone that feeds water to a rip current.

Fetch - The time and distance over which wind blows in the process of generating waves.

Fix - The position resulting from known distances and directions to two or more land-based objects.

Flood tide - An incoming tide.

Fluid - A state of matter, either gaseous or liquid, in which matter is capable of flowing.

Food chain - The transfer of energy along a chain of animals in the marine community.

Frenzel maneuver - A method of equalizing pressure in the middle ear. See page 66.

Gas tension - The partial pressure of a gas in a liquid.

Gauge pressure - Pressure in excess of atmospheric pressure or which uses atmospheric pressure as a zero reference.

Gay-Lussac's Law - See Charles' Law.

General gas law - A combination of Boyle's and Charle's Laws used to predict the behavior of a given quantity of gas when changes may be expected in any or all of the variables.

Haldanian theory - A theory by John S. Haldane, a British physiologist. His theory of gas absorption and elimination by body tissues forms the basis for decompression tables.

Half-times - The rate of absorption or elimination of gas in tissues at an exponential rate. A "5 minute" tissue is 50% saturated in 5 minutes, 75% saturated in 10 minutes, etc., until essentially saturated after six half-times.

Halocline - The horizontal interface between waters of different densities, especially between fresh water and salt water.

Heading - A navigational course followed or to be followed.

Heat exhaustion - An illness characterized by fatigue, weakness and collapse due to inadequate fluid intake to compensate for loss of fluids from perspiration.

Hemoglobin - See page 52

Hemorrhage - See page 52

Henry's Law - "The amount of gas that will dissolve in a liquid at a given temperature is almost directly proportional to the partial pressure of that gas."

Holdfast - A rootlike structure that secures algae to the bottom.

Hookah diving - Diving with air supplied via an umbilical hose to the surface.

Hydrostatic - Non-moving water.

Humidity - The amount of water vapor in a gaseous atmosphere.

Hypercapnia - See page 52

Hyperthermia - A upward variation of body temperature.

Hypertonic - A solution saltier than blood.

Hyperventilation - See page 52

Hypocapnia - Lower than normal carbon dioxide in the blood and caused by hyperventilation.

Hypolimnion - The colder layer of water below a thermocline

Hypothermia - A downward variation in body temperature.

Hypotonic - A solution less salty than blood.

Hypoventilation - See page 52

Hypoxia - See page 52

Inert - A substance which does not normally combine with other substances.

Ingassing - The process of gas dissolving into a liquid.

Inner ear - See page 53

Inspiratory reserve - See page 53

Integrated regulator - A scuba regulator that is incorporated into an item of diving equipment such as a BC low pressure inflator.

Isotherm - A line on a chart linking areas of equal temperature.

Kelp - A giant brown algae that reaches heights of nearly 100 feet.

Kick cycle - The time from when a fin kicks downward during a flutter kick until that same fin kicks downward again.

Kinetic theory of gases - The basic explanation of the behavior of gases under all variations of temperature and pressure.

Leeway - Side-slippage in the direction of a current when moving across the current.

Littoral - Pertaining to a sea shore, such as a littoral current.

Longshore current - A current flowing parallel to the shore in the surf zone and caused by surf approaching the shore at an angle.

Low pressure inflator - A valve on a buoyancy compensator which controls low pressure air from a scuba regulator and can be manually opened to inflate the BC.

Lubber line - A fixed reference line on a compass.

Magnetic North - A point near the North Pole towards which a magnetic needle points.

Manifold - A high pressure connecting pipe between two or more air cylinders.

Mass - The quotient obtained by dividing the weight of a body by the acceleration due to gravity.

Matter - The substance of which any physical object is composed.

Maximum depth indicator - An indicator of a mechanical depth gauge that is pushed along by the needle of the gauge and which remains at the maximum reading attained by the instrument.

Mediastinal emphysema - A lung overexpansion injury characterized by air in the middle of the chest.

Mediastinum - See page 53

Middle ear - See page 53

Multi-level diving - A dive with time spent at more than one depth, especially a progression from deeper depths to shallower depths.

Neap tides - Those tides with the minimum range between high water and low water.

Near-drowning - The clinical condition that follows the aspiration of fluid into the lungs.

Necktonic - Free-swimming forms of life, including fish, which rely on speed and streamlining for their survival.

Nitrogen Narcosis - A dangerous state of stupor produced by the narcotic effect of nitrogen in the body under pressure.

Octopus - An extra second stage attached to a scuba regulator.

Open circuit demand scuba - A system in which compressed air is inhaled upon demand from a self-contained unit and exhausted into the environment.

Orifice - An opening or aperture of a tube, pipe, etc.

Outgassing - Gas dissolved in a liquid coming out of solution.

Oxygen Toxicity - A serious bodily ailment characterized by convulsions and resulting when oxygen is breathed at a partial pressure approaching two atmospheres.

Panic - The emotional and volatile human reaction which occurs in the presence of a real or imagined danger; characterized by a total loss of logic and mental control.

Parenteral toxins - Toxins delivered by means of a venom apparatus.

Paresthesia and hypesthesia - A feeling of "pins and needles" in the body.

Partial pressure - The pressure exerted by each individual gas within a mixture of gases.

Pascal's Principle - "Pressure in a fluid is transmitted uniformly in all directions."

Peer pressure - The pressure placed by peers on fellow divers.

Phytoplankton - Algae that use sunlight to produce carbohydrates. They represent the basic food source for all life in the oceans.

Pilotage - Navigation confirmed with visual check points.

Pilot-valve regulator - A regulator second stage main valve that is opened and closed using air pressure rather than mechanical leverage.

Planktonic - Drifting and floating forms of life carried passively by currents.

Pleura - See page 53

Plunging breakers - Surf that peaks quickly and breaks suddenly when large swells approach a shore with a moderately steep slope.

Pneumothorax - See page 53

Pressure gradient - The difference between the tension of a gas in a liquid and the partial pressure of the gas outside the liquid.

Propulsion - The act of driving forward.

Range - A course indicated by a set of in-line objects.

Red tide - An extremely heavy bloom of plankton or algae.

Refraction - The bending of rays of light when they pass from a medium of one density into a medium of a different density.

Residual volume - See page 53

Resuscitation - The combination of external cardiac compressions and artificial respiration.

Reverse block - A condition existing when the pressure in the middle ear exceeds the ambient pressure.

Reverse thermocline - An abrupt transition from a colder layer of water to a warmer layer of water where the colder layer is shallower than the warmer layer.

Rip current - A strong, narrow current moving away from shore and formed when water in a surf zone is funneled through a narrow gap.

Round window - An opening in the inner ear covered by a thin membrane and to which the small bones of hearing that transfer vibrations from the ear drum are attached. As the round window moves in, a corresponding inner ear window, called the oval window, moves outward.

Saturation - A state existing when the tension of a gas in a liquid reaches a value equal to the partial pressure of the gas outside the liquid.

Scrolling - A feature of a dive computer in which no-decompression limits for various depths are displayed sequentially and repeatedly.

Scuba - Self-contained underwater breathing apparatus.

Secondary drowning - Delayed death following the aspiration of fluid into the lungs.

Seiches - The oscillation of the surface of a lake or a landlocked sea and caused by wind blowing over the water.

Seismic waves - Giant waves resulting from underwater earthquakes and mistakenly referred to as "Tidal waves". Also known as "Tsunamis".

Semi-closed scuba - A system in which a portion of the exhaled breath is retained within the system and rebreathed.

Set and drift - The direction and velocity of a current.

Silent bubbles - Microscopic bubbles formed within the body as a result of decompression and theorized to contribute to the larger bubbles which cause decompression sickness.

Single-hose regulator - A regulator with a single hose joining the first and second stages.

Sinuses - See page 53

Skip breathing - The deliberate reduction of breathing.

Slack water - The period of time existing at high tide during which water movement is at a minimum.

Solid, Liquid, Gas - The three fundamental states of matter.

Specific gravity - The density of a specific substance compared with that of pure water.

Specific heat - The ratio of the amount of heat transferred to raise a unit mass of a substance one degree to that required to raise a unit mass of pure water one degree.

Spilling breakers - A form of surf where waves break far from shore on a shallowly sloping bottom and continue to break to the beach.

Spring tides - Tides with the greatest range between high water and low water.

Stage - A pressure-reduction step in a regulator or compressor.

Stipes - Strands of kelp.

Strangulation - Stoppage of breathing due to obstruction of the airway.

Stress - A physical and emotional state that evokes effort on the part of an individual to maintain or restore equilibrium.

Subcutaneous emphysema - A lung overexpansion injury characterized by air around the base of the neck.

Submersible pressure gauge - An instrument to measure cylinder pressure while submerged.

Suffocation - Stoppage of breathing for any cause and the resulting asphyxia.

Supersaturated solution - A solution holding more gas than is possible at equilibrium for a particular temperature and pressure.

Surf - Breaking waves releasing their energy in shallow water.

Surf beat - The priodic rise and fall in the height of waves and surf caused by the reinforcement or reduction of wave amplitude when two trains of waves approach an area at the same time.

Surface equivalent - The effect that the partial pressure of a gas has on the body at depth in relation to an equivalent amount of gas at sea level, e.g., breathing 1% carbon monoxide at four atmospheres is the surface equivalent of breathing 4% carbon monoxide.

Surface tension - The contractive forces at the surfaceof a liquid.

Surf zone - That area in which the water within waves is moving forward with the waves in the form of surf.

Surge - The back-and-forth sub-surface movement of water caused by waves passing overhead.

Surging breakers - Surf formed by small swells approaching a very steep bottom. These waves slide up and down the steep incline with little or no foam production.

Swash - The water on the face of a beach that washes back into the main body of water.

Swells - The low, rounded form in which wave energy is transferred through water.

Tachycardia - See page 53

Thermocline - A horizontal, abrupt transition from a warmer layer of water to a colder layer of water.

Thoracic squeeze - A lung injury resulting from compression of the lungs when the lungs are only partially filled with air.

Tidal current - Movement of water produced by tidal changes.

Tidal volume - See page 53

Tinnitus - See page 53

Toynbee maneuver - A method of equalizing pressure in the middle ear. See page 66.

Trachea - See page 53

Trapdoor effect - The inability to equalize pressure in the middle ear because the opening to the Eustachian Tube leading to the middle ear is being held closed by ambient pressure.

Trail line - A line with a float at the end extended behind a boat to assist divers in returning to the vessel if they should surface downcurrent. Also called a "current line" or "tag line".

Trim - The control of an assumed position or body attitude.

True North - A geographical location with reference to the earth's axis rather than the magnetic poles and not the same as magnetic north.

Turbidity - A reduction in underwater visibility caused by suspended sediment.

Two-hose regulator - A regulator with both stages and the exhaust valve in a single housing and with two hoses leading to a mouthpiece.

Tympanic membrane - See page 53

Unbalanced valve - A valve controlling high pressure in such a way that the pressure affects the force needed to open and close the valve.

Upstream valve - A valve that operates against the direction of gas flow.

Upwelling - The vertical movement of water in a body of water and the subsequent replacement of that water from beneath. Caused by wind blowing the surface water away from shore.

Valve snorkel - The tube extending from the bottom of a scuba cylinder valve designed to prevent foreign matter from entering the valve when the tank is inverted.

Variation - The local difference in degrees between true and magnetic north.

Vertigo - Dizziness

Vestibular system - A series of semi-circular canals within the inner ear that provide a person with orientation and a sense of balance.

Vital capacity - See page 53

Wavelength - The distance between two successive waves.

Wave period - The time required for two consecutive waves to pass a fixed point.

Waves - Forms of energy moving in water and caused by the wind.

Wave sets - See Surf Beat

Wave trough - The lowest point of a wave.

Work - The application of force through a distance.

Zooplankton - Animal plankton that generally feeds on phytoplankton.

INDEX TO TABLES

SECTION ONE

1.1	Conversion for Barometric Pressure	8
2.1	Narcotic Effects of Compressed Air Diving	33
2.2	Wind Chill Index	44
2.3	Diving Medical Terms	52
3.1	Scuba Cylinder Specifications	75
4.1	Beaufort Wind Scale	106
5.1	Haldane-Royal Navy Decompression Model Summary	132
5.2	Workman-U.S. Navy Decompression Model Summary	134
5.3	Ascent Time Table	140
5.4	Summary of Procedures for Diving at Altitude	152
5.5	Atmospheric Pressure vs. Altitude	153
5.6	Recommended Highest Repetitive Group on Ascending to Altitude Following an Ocean Dive	153
5.7	Repetitive Dive Group on Arrival at Altitude from Sea Level	153
5.8	Modified Fresh Water Ascent Rates	154
5.9	Theoretical Depth at Altitude for Given Actual Depth in Fresh Water	154
5.10	Modified Fresh Water Decompression Stops Corresponding to Standard Ocean Stop Depths	155
5.11	Corrections for Bourdon and Bellows Depth Gauges	155
5.12	Capillary Gauge Corrections	155

SECTION THREE

17.1	Ice Diving Line Signals	240
21.1	Camera Equipment Costs	258
21.2	Video System Features	263
21.4	Video Accessories	264
Basic Conversion Tables		288

INDEX

Accident management 206-207
Air compressors 101-102
Air consumption 21-22
Air embolism 42-43
Air station 101
Alternobaric vertigo 50
Altitude diving 150-156
Amonton's Law 22
Anchors 220-221
Anxiety 67
Archimede's principle 17
Area orientations 130
Artificial respiration, in-water 205
Barotrauma 37-44
Bends (See Decompression sickness)
Biology 118-130
Boat diving 209-213
Boating and seamanship 215-223
Bottom conditions 117
Bourdon movement 86-87
Boyle's Law 20-21
Breathing resistance 28
Buddy lines 185
Buddy system 167-168, 184-185, 276
Buoyancy 17
Buoyancy compensators 94-97, 240-241, 273-274
Buoyancy control 166-167
Cameras and video equipment 257-265
Carbon dioxide 6
Carbon dioxide excess 28
Carbon monoxide 6
Carbon monoxide toxicity 29
Carotid sinus reflex 36
Cave diving 243-246
Cavern diving 246
Charles' Law 22-23
Charter boats 212-213
Charts 175, 182
Commercial diving 279-283
Communications 162-164
Compass board 175-176
Compass navigation 180-182
Compasses 93-94, 173-175
Conduction 12
Cone shells 126
Conservation 121
Coriolis effect 115
Cramps 36

Currents 113-116
Cylinder pressure gauges 87
Dalton's Law 16
Dead reckoning 178
Decompression sickness 32-36, 63-64, 65-66
Decompression theories 131-137
Deep diving 197-202
Dehydration 51
Density 16-17
Dental barotrauma 40, 41
Depth gauges 88-90
Diffusion 31
Disorientation 50-51
Distance measuring 176-177
Diuresis 51
Dive computers 91-93, 142
Dive flags 219, 275
Dive lights 102, 103, 184, 188-189
Dive planning 159-162
Dive tables 137-141
Diving reflex 36
Drag 27
Drift diving 116, 253-255
Drowning 31
Drugs 56-57
Dry suit diving 233-236
Dry suits 97-101
Ear barotrauma 37-39
Emergency ascents 168-170
Energy 5, 10-11
Exposure suits 241, 274
Fish poisoning 123-124
Flying after diving 156
Food chain 120-121
Full face masks 241
Gas flow (Viscosity) 18
Gastro-intestinal barotrauma 44
General gas law 23
Haldane theory 131-132
Half-time 34, 132
Halocline 117
Hazardous animals 122-130
Heart 56
Heart attack 37
Heat 11-13
Hemoglobin 27
Henry's Law 24
Hookah diving 102

Humidity 9
Hunting and spearfishing 267-272
Hydrostatic test 76, 78
Hyperthermia 44, 48-49
Hyperventilation 30
Hypothermia 44-48
Ice diving 237-242
Infections 51
Inflatable boats 209-210
Ingassing 24, 32
Jellyfish 125
Kelp 119-120
Kick cycles 177
Kinetic theory of gases 20
Knots 220-223
Leadership 285-286
Light in water 10-11
Limited visibility diving 183-186
Longshore current 113-114
Lung barotrauma 40, 42-44
Lung volume 26
Man-made structures 118
Maneuvering board 175-176
Manifolds 80-81
Matter 5
Medical terms 52-53
Metric system 7-8
Mixed gas diving 140
Motion sickness 49-50
Multi-level diving 139-140
Natural navigation 178-179
Navigation 173-182
Near drowning 31
Night diving 187-190
Nitrogen 6
Nitrogen narcosis 31-33
Nutrition 57
Outgassing 24, 32
Overexertion 29
Oxygen 6
Oxygen toxicity 29-30
Panic 67
Parenteral toxins 122, 124-127
Partial pressure 16
Photography 257-265
Physical fitness 54-60
Pilotage 178
Plants 119-120
Pregnancy and diving 64-66
Pressure, atmospheric 14
Pressure, hydrostatic 14-15
Pressure, units of 15
Psychological fitness 66-73
Recompression chambers 142-150

Red tide 122
Refresher training 171
Regulator freeze-up 240
Regulator maintenance 164
Regulators 80-86
Rescue 203-207
Research diving 273-278
Respiration 25-30
Reverse block 38, 40
Rip currents 114-115
River currents 116, 227
River diving 227-232
Rules of the road 216-217
Saturation 32
Scuba 75
Scuba cylinders 75-78
Sea urchins 126
Search and light salvage 191-196
Search patterns 192-194
Secondary drowning 31
Seiches 113
Sharks 127-128
Silent bubbles 35
Sinuses 40, 41
Smoking 56
Snakes 127, 128-129
Sound in water 11
Spear gun safety 267-268
Stress 67
Stress 202
Submersible pressure gauges 87-88
Sudden death syndrome 36-37
Supersaturation 33
Surf 108-111
Surf beat 109
Surge 107
Temperature scales 8-9
Tether lines 185
Thermal stratification 116-117
Thermocline 116
Thoracic squeeze 40
Tides 111-113
Timers 90-91
Trim 27
Turtles 129
Upwelling 116
Valve assemblies 78-80
Valve maintenance 164
Vertigo 50-51
Videography 261-265
Visual cylinder inspection 77-78
Waves 105-109
Women and diving 60-66
Wreck diving 247-251